ARTIST'S
PAINTING
TECHNIQUES

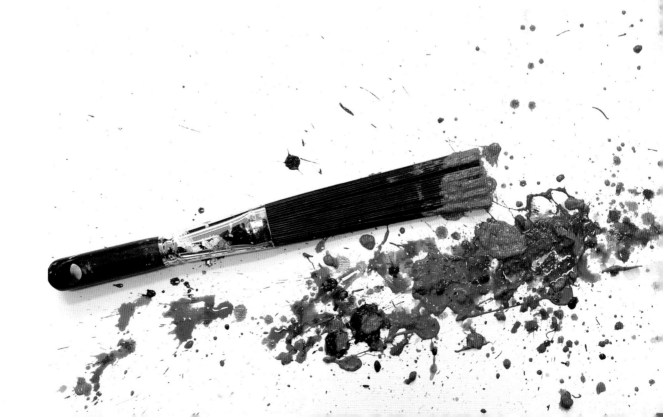

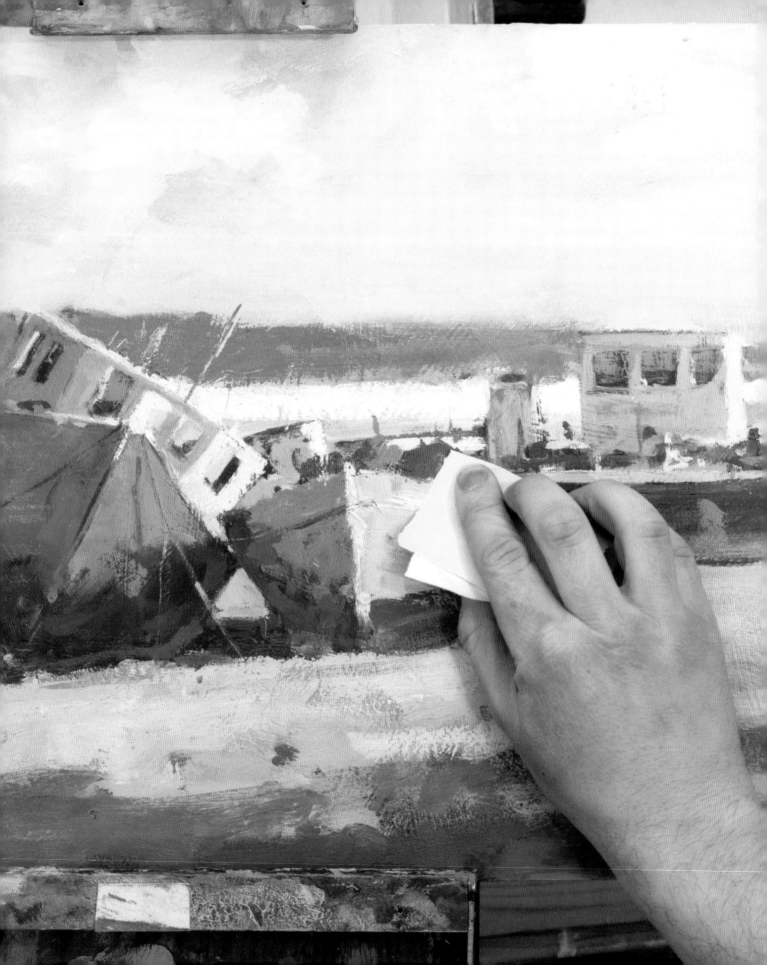

ARTIST'S
PAINTING
TECHNIQUES

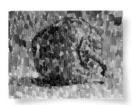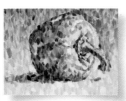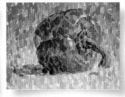

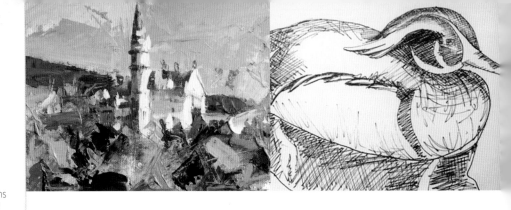

 Penguin
Random
House

Senior Editor	Bob Bridle
Senior Art Editor	Alison Gardner
Project Editors	Shashwati Tia Sarkar, Alison Sturgeon, Allie Collins
US Editors	Lori Hand, Michelle Melani
Project Designers	Simon Murrell, Helen Garvey
Senior Jacket Creative	Nicola Powling
Jackets Assistant	Libby Brown
Producer (Pre-production)	Andy Hilliard
Senior Producer	Ché Creasey
Creative Technical Support	Sonia Charbonnier
Managing Editors	Angela Wilkes, Lisa Dyer
Managing Art Editor	Marianne Markham
Art Director	Maxine Pedliham
Publishing Director	Mary-Clare Jerram
US Publisher	Mike Sanders

First American Edition, 2016
Published in the United States by DK Publishing
345 Hudson Street, New York, New York 10014

Copyright © 2016 Dorling Kindersley Limited
DK, a division of Penguin Random House LLC
16 17 18 19 20 10 9 8 7 6 5 4 3 2 1
001–286834–Aug/2016

A catalog record for this book is available from the Library of Congress.

ISBN 978-1-4654-5095-1

DK books are available at special discounts when purchased in bulk for sales promotions, premiums, fund-raising, or educational use. For details, contact: DK Publishing Special Markets, 345 Hudson Street, New York, New York 10014 SpecialSales@dk.com

Printed and bound in China

All images © Dorling Kindersley Limited
For further information see: www.dkimages.com

A WORLD OF IDEAS:
SEE ALL THERE IS TO KNOW

www.dk.com

Contents

The basics

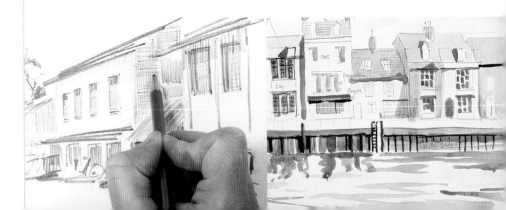

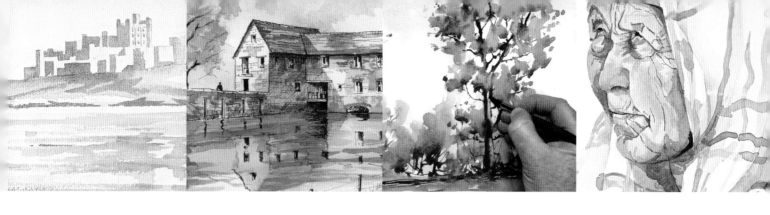

Watercolors

1 Beginner techniques

2 Intermediate techniques

3 Advanced techniques

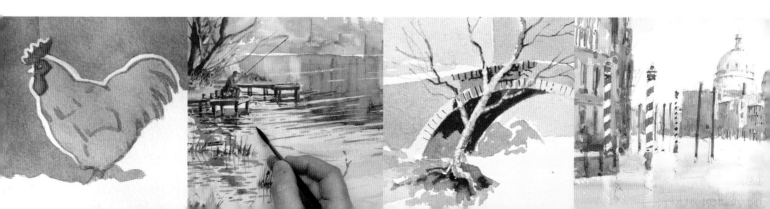

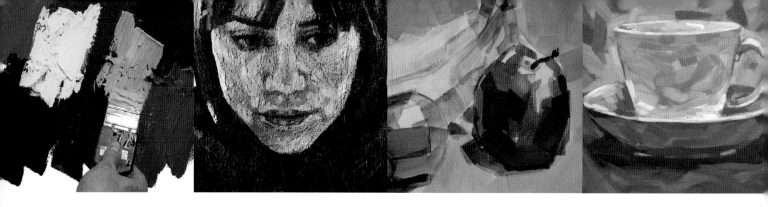

Acrylics

1 Beginner techniques

2 Intermediate techniques

3 Advanced techniques

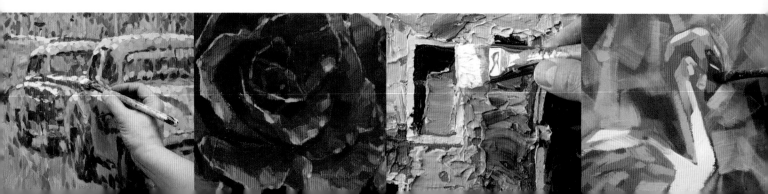

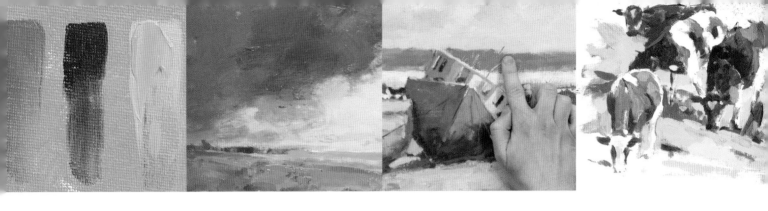

Oils

1 Beginner techniques

2 Intermediate techniques

3 Advanced techniques

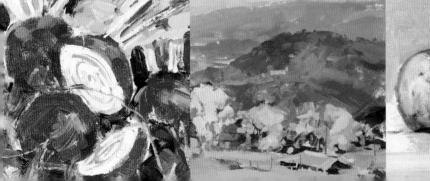
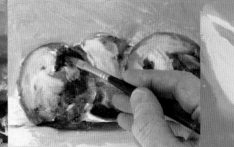
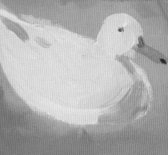

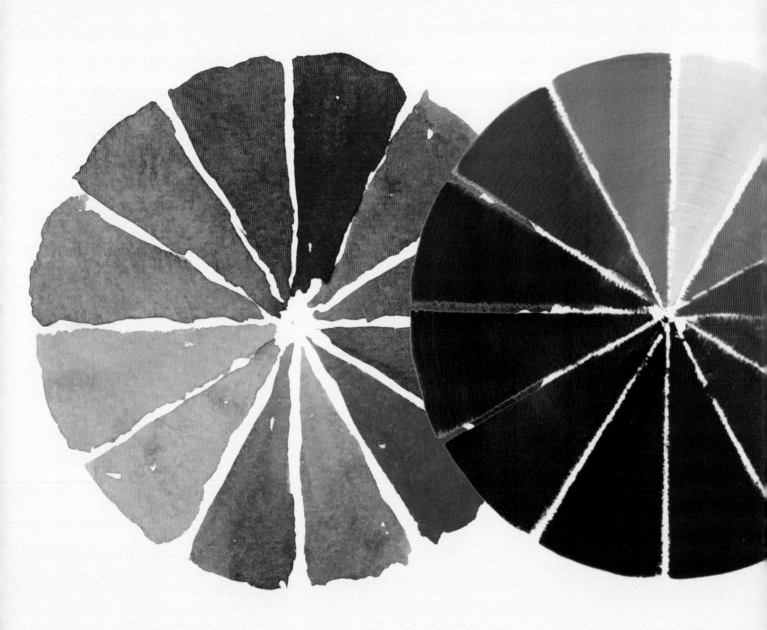

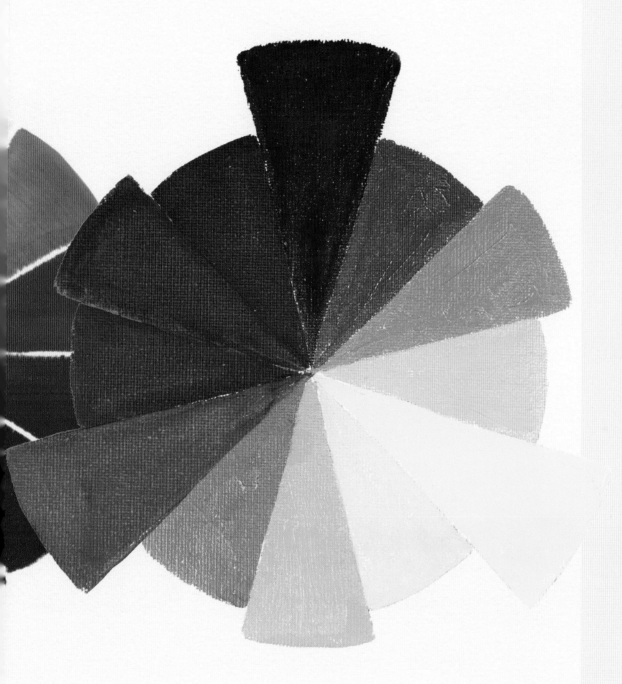

The basics

Getting started

THE ELEMENTS OF A PAINTING

If you are new to painting or haven't painted for several years, it can be difficult to know where to start. One of the best ways to overcome any hesitancy in tackling a new painting is to choose a subject that excites and inspires you. That way, you are likely to feel compelled to express yourself, and your painting will be authentic and heartfelt.

If a scene, such as a breathtaking sunset or grand building, attracts your attention, your excitement will come across in the work. Paintings that are charged with feeling and that are personal to the artist often have the most impact on the viewer.

Exploring different techniques
Apart from the emotional impact of your subject, there are also technical considerations to take into account.

Familiarize yourself with the tonal relationships between various elements in your scene, and learn how to balance color to create harmonious paintings. Considered use of shape and composition will help to structure your painting, establishing a strong base on which to add layers of color.

Choosing a medium that appeals to you (see pp. 22–23), along with the correct brushes and supports, are important factors in creating the effect

you are seeking. An understanding of the medium, a feeling for your subject, and good planning will help you to create the best work you can.

Making a connection
Paintings that have an emotional impact often need to be handled differently from those in which the subject is paramount. Emotionally charged works may rely more heavily on, for example, the texture of the paint or the types of brushstrokes used. For works that prioritize subject matter above all else, the stylistic qualities of the painting are perhaps less important than conveying the essence of the subject simply and accurately. Either way, the possibilities across the three painting media are limitless.

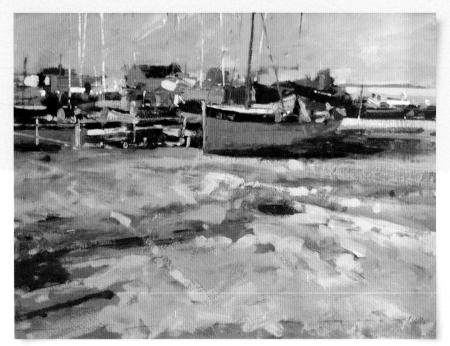

Technical considerations
This work in oils uses the lines of the track, dark tones, and bright colors to draw the eye to the blue boat, and then beyond. The masts balance the horizontal lines of the boats and fence.

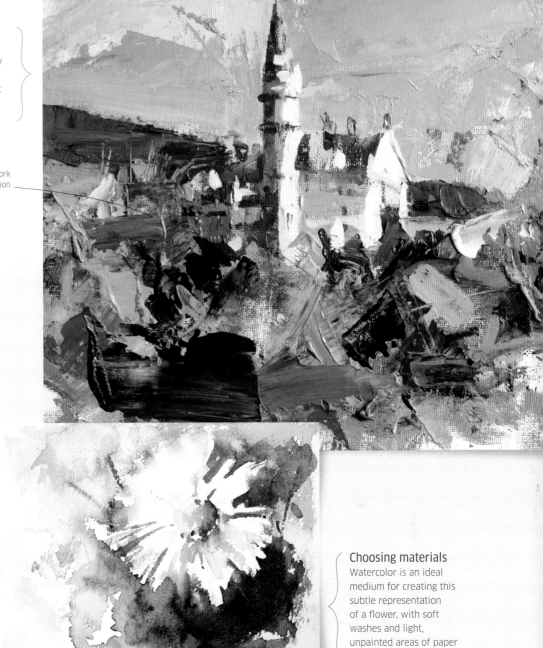

Imparting emotion
This scene, painted with acrylics, is filled with movement and feeling, conveyed by dynamic brushstrokes, the use of pure pigments, and strong contrasts. The artist imparts a sense of awe at the castle's monumental form shining in the sun.

Strong brushwork conveys emotion

A successful painting connects with viewers and holds their interest. It may provoke discussion or represent a familiar subject in a new way. If the viewer is moved to reevaluate something familiar, then you have made a positive impact with your work. However, try not to be swayed by what other people think—after all, everyone has a different idea of what makes a good painting. The most important thing is to create work that inspires you. If you can convey your own feeling in a work, then the painting will be a success.

Choosing materials
Watercolor is an ideal medium for creating this subtle representation of a flower, with soft washes and light, unpainted areas of paper suggesting its form.

"If you have been able to **convey your own feeling** in a work, then the **painting will be a success.**"

Observational skills

THE ART OF SEEING

Observation is about more than simply replicating a subject with photographic accuracy. As an artist, you have license to move, alter, emphasize, or exclude elements of your choosing. For example, you might decide to exaggerate scale or experiment with perspective to create a more dynamic arrangement. The art of seeing is not only about capturing what is in front of you, but also interpreting it in your own way.

Honing your observational skills is the first step to creating a successful painting. With a good understanding of your subject matter, you will be able to depict it more convincingly.

Take your time

Spend time with a subject before you start to paint. Try to dispel any preconceptions you may have about how you *think* something looks. Instead, learn to concentrate on what you can actually *see* in front of you.

Notice where the light falls and which areas are in shadow. Look at the edges: are they crisp and well-defined, or blurred and indistinct? What shapes can you see? (Both the positive shapes of the object itself and the negative spaces between and around it.) Make sure you are viewing the subject from the best vantage point and that you have a strong composition (see pp. 16–17). Look for a good range of tones (see p. 20) and think about where to place the main focal points.

Objects are given form by light, so producing a painting is really a matter of rendering light, with the objects taking shape as a result.

Base measurement

Where accuracy is important, take a measurement from an element in the scene, such as the width of a house or the height of a tree. Then, compare other elements to this base measure to keep the proportions true. Another tip is to squint your eyes at the subject to

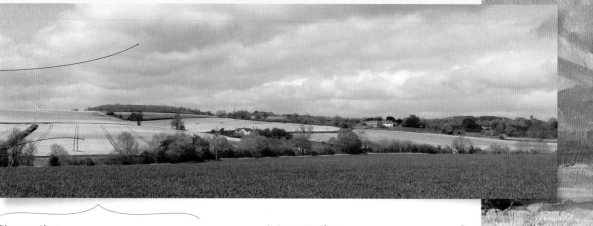

In the photograph, there is relatively little detail in the sky

The vibrant yellow looks fine in the photograph, but it would advance too much in a painting

Observation
Studying the landscape helps to identify key features and areas of interest, as well as which elements to omit or change, such as the color saturation of the background fields.

Interpretation
Artistic license was used to create a more dynamic painting. There is a greater sense of drama in the sky, and tones have been balanced across the work.

Measuring from life

Hold a pencil upright at arm's length and at eye level. Close one eye and look along your arm, lining up the top of the pencil with the top of the subject. Then use your thumb to mark off on your pencil the area measured. Transfer this measurement to your page.

Mark the measurement using your thumb

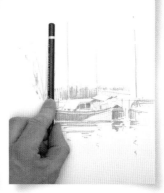

1–take measurement from life

2–check proportions on page

"Spend time with your subject. Focus on what you can see in front of you rather than what you think is there."

block out the detail. This will help you differentiate areas of light and shadow as you plan and get started on your painting.

You don't always need to copy a subject exactly or include every element. Keep sight of the final goal: conveying the scene in your own way. Remember that successful paintings are often the result of an artist's personal interpretation of a subject.

Use simple geometric shapes, like triangles

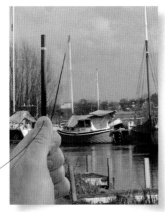

Shape and tone

Try to identify basic shapes within the subject. Use triangles, circles, and rectangles to construct form and establish proportion. This image also indicates tonal areas.

Expressive brushstrokes give the painting energy and personality

More cloud movement has been suggested in the sky, making it a key feature of the painting

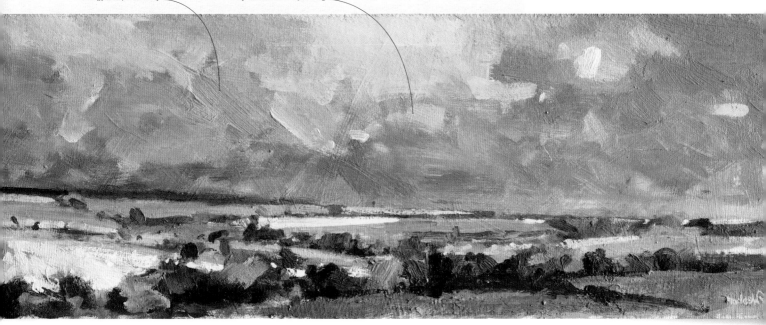

Color theory

MIXING AND COMBINING COLORS

Exploring color is one of the most exciting aspects of painting. Understanding the relationships between colors will help you to create harmony, contrast, depth, and mood in your paintings, as well as mix paints.

■ The color wheel

The color wheel shows the relationships between colors. These diagrams demonstrate how primary colors can be combined to create the whole color wheel.

Primary colors

Red, yellow, and blue are primary colors. You can't create primary colors using other paint colors, but you can combine the primaries to create a huge range of other colors.

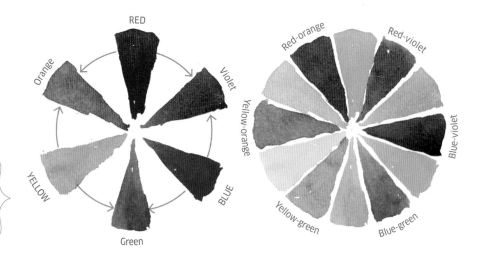

RED
Orange
Violet
YELLOW
BLUE
Green

Yellow-orange
Red-orange
Red-violet
Blue-violet
Yellow-green
Blue-green

PIGMENTS AND HUE

Paints are made from finely ground, insoluble pigments that are suspended in a base such as water or oil. Qualities such as opacity, lightfastness, and granulation vary from pigment to pigment.

Natural pigments are either organic (from animal or plant sources) or inorganic (from rocks and metals). They can be rare or expensive to process, so synthetic pigments have been developed to match them. Many popular colors, such as cobalt blue and cerulean blue, are made from synthetic mineral pigments introduced centuries ago. "Hue" usually means the same as color, but on a tube of paint, hue means that the paint color is a blend or imitation of the original pigment. Paints with "hue" in the name are usually cheaper and may "muddy" quicker than a pure pigment, but they offer other qualities, such as lightfastness.

Cerulean blue pigment

Secondary colors

Orange, green, and violet are secondary colors; they can be made by mixing two primary colors. On the color wheel, each secondary color is shown between the two primary colors that create it—for example, the wheel shows that red and yellow make orange.

Tertiary colors

You can create tertiary colors by mixing a secondary color with one of its primaries, for example adding red (a primary) to orange (a secondary) creates red-orange. The tertiary color therefore has a higher proportion of one primary, which is shown on the wheel by its position next to that primary.

■ Saturation

The intensity or strength of a color is referred to as its saturation. A color straight from the tube will be more saturated than when it is diluted or mixed.

Undiluted paint

Diluted paint

Watercolor swatches

■ Tints

Colors lightened with white are called tints (or gradations). Adding white changes the saturation of the original color, creating a pastel hue.

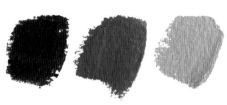

Pure cobalt blue

Cobalt blue mixed with a little white

Cobalt blue mixed with more white

Acrylic swatches

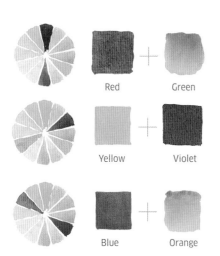

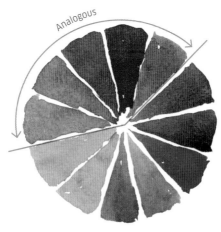

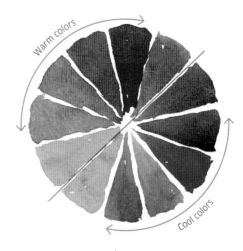

Red + Green

Yellow + Violet

Blue + Orange

Analogous

Warm colors

Cool colors

Complementary colors

Opposite colors on the color wheel, such as red and green, are complementary. They brighten each other when placed side by side but dull and darken each other when you mix them, which creates interesting neutrals.

Analogous colors

Groups of three to five colors that sit next to each other on the color wheel are known as analogous. The close relationship between analogous colors means you can use them to create harmonious color schemes.

Color temperature

Colors have qualities that we associate with temperature. In general, the yellow-orange-red half of the wheel is considered to be warm, while the violet-blue-green half is considered to be cool.

> "A little knowledge of **color theory** helps you create the effects you are aiming for in your paintings."

REDS

YELLOWS

BLUES

Alizarin crimson	Cadmium red	Lemon yellow	Cadmium yellow	Cerulean blue	French ultramarine
Cool (blue bias)	Warm (yellow bias)	Cool (blue bias)	Warm (red bias)	Cool (yellow bias)	Warm (red bias)

Color bias

There are warm and cool versions of every color because paints often have an undertone of another color—for example, you can buy a warm yellow with a red bias or a cool yellow with a blue bias. Bias affects how you use and mix a color.

▪ Shades

Colors darkened with black are called shades. Blacks with color biases can affect hue; here, yellow mixed with blue-black creates greens.

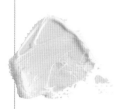

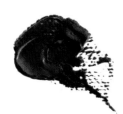

Pure lemon yellow

Lemon yellow mixed with a little black

Lemon yellow mixed with more black

Oil swatches

▪ Tonal value

The relative lightness or darkness of a color is its tonal value. Establishing value relationships in a painting is important for creating the shape and form of the subject.

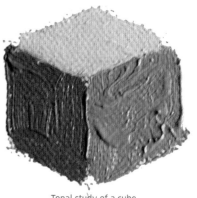

Tonal study of a cube

Perspective and composition

PORTRAYING THREE-DIMENSIONAL SPACE

Understanding linear perspective—whereby parallel lines appear to converge in the distance—is an important part of painting and drawing. It is key to portraying distance and three-dimensional space. Your distance from the ground determines your viewpoint and the position of the horizon line, which will be at your eye level. The point at which parallel lines in an artwork converge on the horizon is known as the vanishing point.

PERSPECTIVE

Some key points to remember regarding perspective are that all parallel lines appear to converge at the same vanishing point on the horizon, and that objects closer to you look larger than those farther away. An object's relationship to the horizon will depend on your location when viewing it.

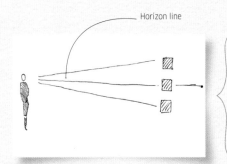

Horizon line

Viewpoint
An object you look down on appears to sit below the horizon line, while an object you look up at appears to sit above the horizon line.

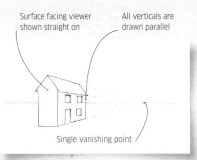

Surface facing viewer shown straight on

All verticals are drawn parallel

Single vanishing point

Second vanishing point on same horizon line as first

Object shown at an angle to the viewer

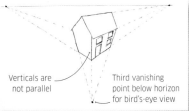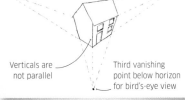

Verticals are not parallel

Third vanishing point below horizon for bird's-eye view

One-point perspective
The surface facing the viewer is seen straight on, without distortion. The object's lines should converge on one vanishing point.

Two-point perspective
Two vanishing points give a more realistic aspect. As the object is at an angle, both sides are distorted by perspective.

Three-point perspective
Use a third vanishing point for very high or low viewpoints. The closer it is to the work's center, the more dramatic the effect.

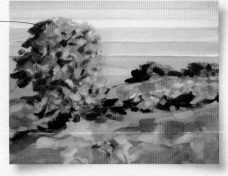

Large foreground object

Aerial perspective
Where there are few parallel lines to show perspective, such as in landscapes, use other techniques instead. For example, use scaling (making objects in the foreground larger than those in the background) and aerial perspective (see pp. 68–69, 148–49, and 242–43).

> "Linear perspective is key to depicting distance in your work."

COMPOSITION

The placement of the horizon determines your viewpoint and shapes the composition. Patterns in compositions can highlight aspects of a scene and help lead the eye to the focal point. Try sketching different compositions before deciding on one.

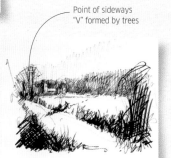

Grass and tree form the "L"

L-shaped
The image is framed on two sides by a horizontal and a vertical element. This directs the viewer's attention to the opposite side of the picture.

Main focal point

S-shaped
This composition leads the viewer from the start of the "S" in the foreground to the main focal point–the distant church. This shape is very effective in landscapes.

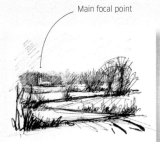

V-shaped
Exaggerating a sense of perspective and creating composition lines that lead to a single point are good ways to create a strong, dynamic image.

Point of sideways "V" formed by trees

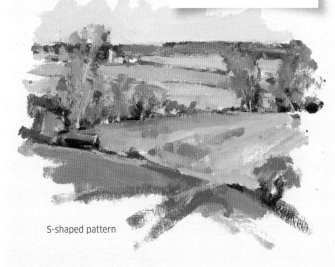

S-shaped pattern

SCALING UP
When transferring initial sketches for a composition to the final surface, you can maintain the proportions by scaling up. Make a grid on your sketch and choose a support with the same proportions. Scale up the grid to fit your final surface and copy the detail of each square onto the new grid.

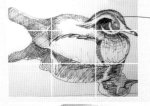

Use the proportions within each square to guide you

Horizon line is a third down from the top

Main focal point placed where lines intersect

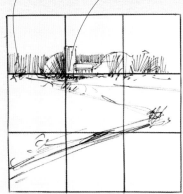

Rule of thirds
This is a popular technique for producing a balanced image. Divide the surface into thirds horizontally and vertically to create a nine-square grid. Place the horizon either a third up from the bottom or a third down from the top, and create focal points where the lines intersect.

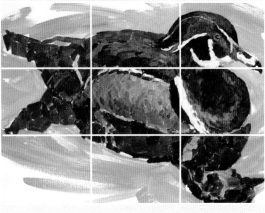

Pencil-drawing basics

TYPES OF PENCILS AND MARKS

Pencils offer a great way to create tonal images. There are different grades ranging from soft, dark pencils to hard, light ones, which can be used in many different ways. Pencils are perfect for sketching any subject matter.

TYPES OF PENCILS

Pencils are graded from hard "H" to soft "B," with "HB" and "F" between the two. Harder pencils create a lighter tone and are good for fine detail, whereas softer pencils create a darker tone and are great for shading. Although pencils from 9H to 9B are available, a 6B offers a dark enough tone, and a 5H offers a light enough tone for everyday sketching.

HARD

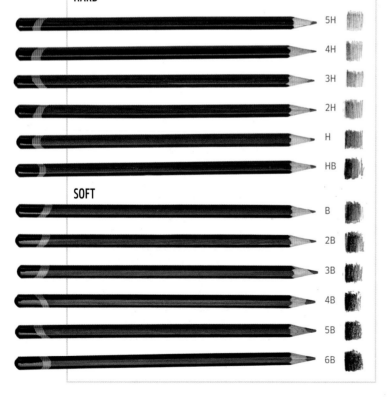

5H
4H
3H
2H
H
HB

SOFT

B
2B
3B
4B
5B
6B

BRUSHWORK

Pencils are versatile tools for working on small to mid-sized areas, but they can be difficult to use over large areas because the tip is so small. There are, however, several techniques for overcoming this problem.

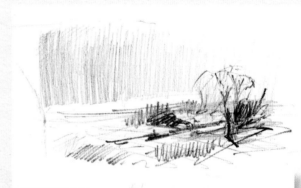

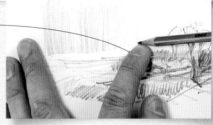

Use your finger as a stop

Broad shading

To block in large areas of tone, move the pencil back and forth without lifting it from the page. Keep the pencil tip flat against the paper to create a broader line. For accuracy, use the finger of your other hand as a stop, allowing the pencil to hit your finger as you move the pencil across the area.

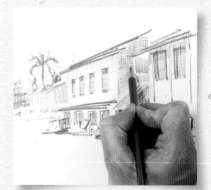

Hatching and cross-hatching

Hatching, in which many parallel lines visually blend with the white paper, is a good way to create tone. Crossing the lines (cross-hatching) creates a denser look and a darker tone.

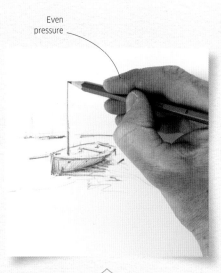

Even pressure

Fine line
To create hard lines, draw the mark in one pass, keeping the pressure even. Make sure you sharpen the pencil if it starts to become too blunt for the line you want to create.

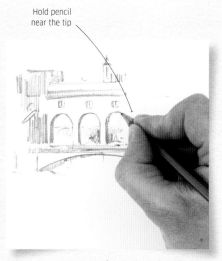

Hold pencil near the tip

Curved line–small
With your wrist resting on the paper, hold the pencil near the tip and keep it at a steep angle to the paper. Keeping your hand still, curve the line around using just your fingers.

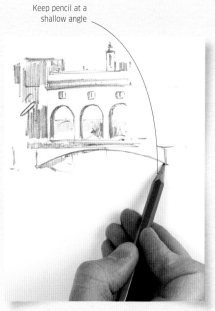

Keep pencil at a shallow angle

Curved line–large
Hold the pencil farther away from the tip and keep it at a shallow angle to the paper. With your wrist resting on the paper, swing the rest of your hand around to create a large curve.

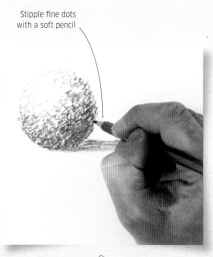

Stipple fine dots with a soft pencil

Stippling
Using the point of the pencil, stipple fine dots and marks onto the surface. The closer together they are, the darker the tone. Softer pencils are more effective for stippling.

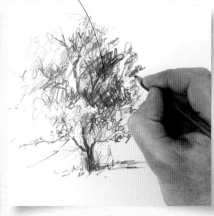

Go over areas for denser tones

Scribbling
Multidirectional scribbles create an interesting look and allow for subtle changes in tone. Use circular motions and darken the tone by going over an area several times.

ADDITIONAL EQUIPMENT

- **Pencil sharpener**–whether you're using pencils for preliminary sketches or finished pieces, you will need a pencil sharpener or knife to keep the points fine. Pencil sharpeners that collect the shavings will help keep your work area clean, while a knife will give you control over the length of graphite you wish to expose.

- **Blending stump and eraser**–use a paper blending stump or a tissue to soften pencil marks, and either a hard or soft eraser to remove unwanted areas of tone.

- **Paper**–use medium-weight cartridge paper for general work, and colored papers, watercolor paper, or tissue paper to experiment with texture and transparency in your final drawing.

- **Fixative**–a spray fixative will bond pencil marks to the paper, allowing you to work over areas without smudging.

"Painting is an **extension of drawing**, so pencils are the **best place to start**."

Using a pencil to create tone

CREATING SHADING AND HIGHLIGHTS

You can create a range of tones or values with a single pencil just by varying the amount of pressure you apply—use a light touch to cover an area with soft shading, or apply more pressure to create a harder, darker mark. You can also create a range of tonal effects using an eraser or a blade, or through blending.

◼ Tonal study

Creating a tonal sketch from a photograph or from life will help you plan your final painting. Identifying deep shadows and highlights early on in the process means you can pitch the painting in a suitable tonal key. Use a pencil to experiment with tone, making decisions about where to use strong contrast and so create focal points, and where to use tone more subtly.

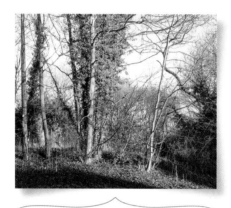

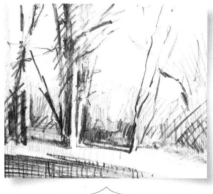

1 Reference photograph
There is a wide range of tones in this woodland scene, with the light sky providing a good backdrop for the foreground trees.

2 Pencil sketch
This initial reference sketch establishes the key tones, with areas of high contrast at the base of the tree.

3 Painted work
Using the sketch for reference, the dark area of shadow on the right of the original photograph has been lightened in order to draw attention to the main tree.

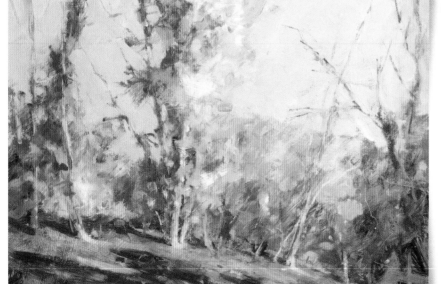

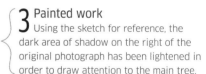

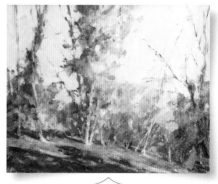

4 Black-and-white image
Looking at an image of the painting in black and white will help you to assess the tonal balance of the finished piece.

CREATING TONAL EFFECTS

With these simple techniques you can create a range of tonal effects in your drawings. Starting with a simple pencil drawing, try using erasers, blades, or paper blending stumps to adjust the tone and create highlights. This will help you get the most out of your sketches and finished drawings.

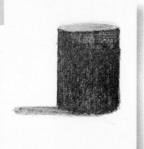

Tone too dark and flat
Use erasers to blend and lighten the tone of an area of pencil shading, particularly if the tone is too heavy.

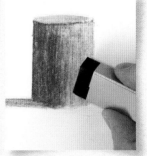

Using a hard eraser
A hard eraser will create clean lines and can be used to wipe complete sections back to paper.

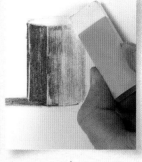

Using a soft eraser
A soft eraser will lighten tone while blending the surface. Keep the eraser clean to avoid smudging.

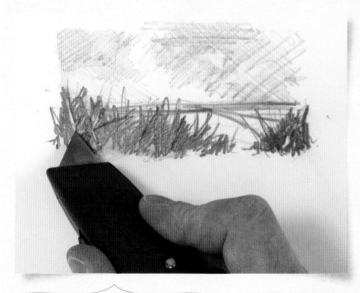

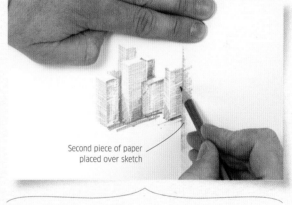

Second piece of paper placed over sketch

High-contrast paper mask
To achieve a crisp edge between tones, use a piece of paper to mask between the two areas. Shading over the paper will leave a definite line where the two tones meet.

Using a blade
Scratching the surface to create white marks in an area of pencil shading is a good way to achieve crisp lines in a dark tone. The blade will alter the smoothness of the paper, so use this technique sparingly.

Blending
You can use your finger to soften edges or blend tones. However, natural oils from your skin can affect the pencil marks, bonding them to the surface and making them harder to erase. For finer detail, use a paper blending stump or piece of tissue paper instead.

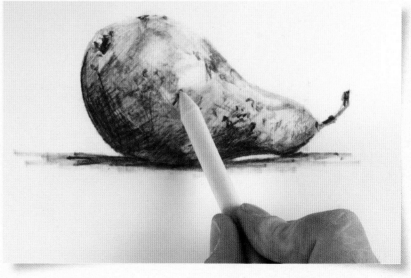

Choosing a medium

WATERCOLORS, ACRYLICS, OR OILS?

When you are choosing a medium, it can help to look at other artists' work—you may be inspired by their use of a particular type of paint. Some artists use mixed media, while others are known for their paintings in one medium. Their choice often depends on factors such as drying time, how easy the paint is to use, and scale. If you are interested in work with a certain feel, identify whether the medium has played a part in creating the image.

WATERCOLORS

Watercolor paints are diluted with water, making them easy to clean up and use. They remain dilutable even after the paint has dried, meaning fresh colors can be blended into dried color. Washes can be used to cover large areas quickly.

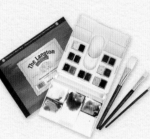

Watercolors—pros and cons

PROS	CONS
■ Relatively inexpensive to buy	■ Watercolor techniques can be difficult to master
■ Very quick to dry	■ It is harder to correct mistakes
■ Techniques such as washes, splashing, and dripping can create expressive paintings	■ Fragile—just one drop of water can damage a painting

ACRYLICS

Acrylic paints combine many of the advantages of oils and watercolors, such as a fast drying time and the fact that you can build up multiple layers quickly. They can be mixed with water, so there is no concern about paint fumes or special cleaning materials.

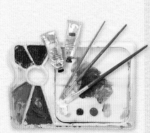

Acrylics—pros and cons

PROS	CONS
■ Can be applied in thick layers or thin washes	■ Fast drying time means you must work quickly to blend colors
■ Dries in minutes	■ Colors can change as they dry
■ Can be used on a range of materials including canvas, paper, wood, plastic, and metal	■ Can be tricky to work with over a large area

OILS

Oil paints have a long tradition and are popular due to the richness of colors available. They have a thick, sculptural quality, and techniques such as glazing, impasto, and layering can be used to produce work from dynamic abstract paintings to hyperrealistic depictions.

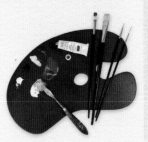

Oils—pros and cons

PROS	CONS
■ Longer drying time means oils are more flexible to work with	■ Canvases must be primed before use
■ Colors blend together smoothly	■ Special cleaning materials such as turpentine are needed
■ Can be used in thick layers to build texture	■ It can be more difficult to create clean lines because the paint stays wet for longer

"Subject matter and where you paint may influence your choice of medium. An outdoor landscape painter and an indoor portrait painter may have different requirements."

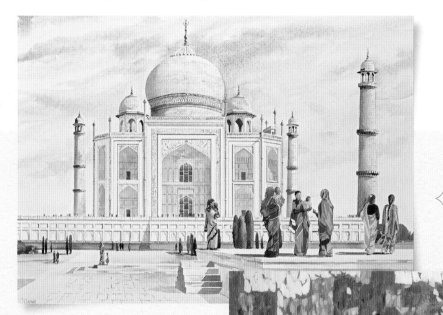

Watercolor washes
This painting shows the range of techniques that can be achieved using watercolors, from delicate washes in the sky to clean lines and white highlights in the foreground.

Bright acrylics
Acrylic paints can be used to build up vibrant layers of color, with rich tones giving depth to a painting. This striking image features small, even brushstrokes and dabs of color to build up the layers.

Oil techniques
In this painting, softly blended oil colors create the sky, while the detail on the boats showcases the richness and texture that oil paints can offer. Rougher brushstrokes and layers of color add depth and interest.

Choosing a subject

HOW TO DECIDE WHAT TO PAINT

Getting to know your subject will help enormously when trying to paint it. For example, if you know how something behaves, how heavy it is, or how fast it moves, you will have a better chance of being able to portray it accurately. The best way to get to know a subject is to spend time observing and drawing it. Then, once you have a good understanding of perspective, color, and value, you can begin to experiment with your paintings.

Different subjects can suit different styles. Large, geometric subjects may demand a bold approach, while fine, detailed paintings will suit more intricate subjects. Start by identifying what interests you in both style and subject. Try to pick appropriate subjects to match your style and medium, then get to know your subject by sketching it. This will give your work a solid foundation.

Refining your painting

To help discover how finely detailed you want your work to be, it is a good idea to develop a painting through gradual refinement. This means starting from an impressionistic, even abstract, starting point, and then adding more and more detail. The process is an easy one with acrylics and oils, because you can add layers to adjust value and color, but it is still possible with watercolors. Use opaque white paint to add light

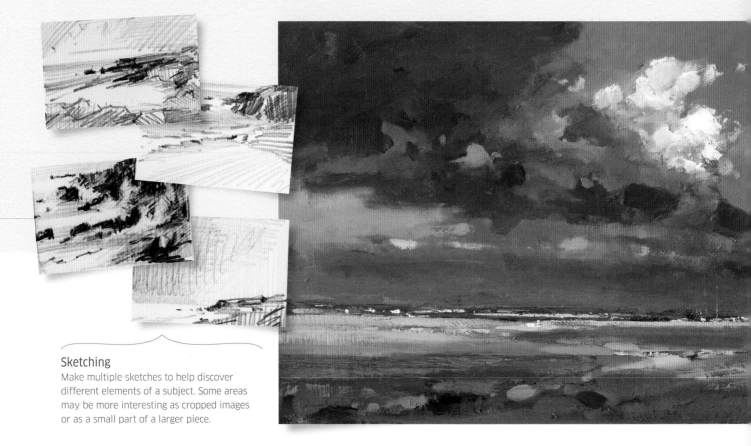

Sketching
Make multiple sketches to help discover different elements of a subject. Some areas may be more interesting as cropped images or as a small part of a larger piece.

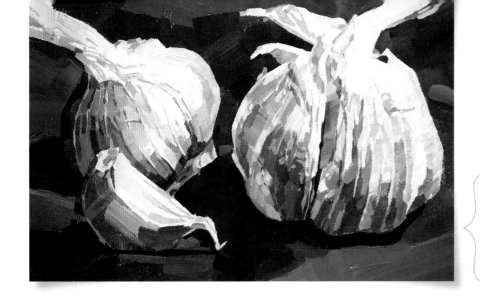

Still life

Still life paintings can be easily set up at home. You can adjust the lighting and choose a subject matter that suits the technique you want to practice. It is a great way to refine your tone and brushwork in the comfort of the studio.

areas back in, or plan ahead and use lighter initial washes so that you can achieve a layered approach.

Knowing when to stop

Working around the whole painting, rather than concentrating on one area at a time, will mean you can stop at any point and the painting can be considered "finished." Artists often find it difficult to know when to stop painting, and it can be tempting to keep on adding more to your work. It is important to take a few steps back from the painting from time to time to assess your progress. Putting too much into a painting can spoil its impact and leave it looking overworked. If you find yourself struggling to decide whether you have finished, take a break and come back to it later with fresh eyes. You could even do a little more research about your subject, perhaps with some more sketching and studies, to help you analyze the work you have already done. Then you can decide whether any areas of your painting would benefit from further refinement.

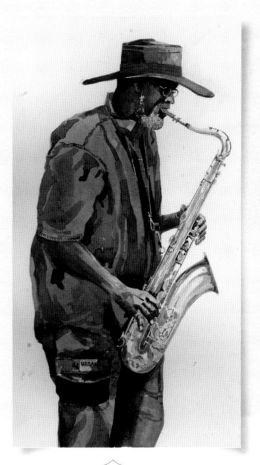

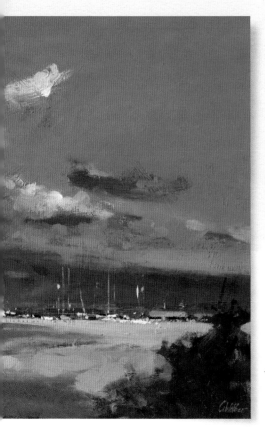

Landscape

The vastness of a dramatic landscape can lift spirits and emphasize power and scale. Landscapes offer a huge variety of subject matter, and time constraints and changing light can provide an exhilarating challenge.

People

Portraits, figures, and crowds offer a great chance for the viewer to interact with a painting. We recognize emotion in faces, and a portrait can trigger different reactions in people. Figure drawing is a useful way of developing techniques to give objects a sense of identity, weight, and balance.

Working outdoors

THE RIGHT MATERIALS FOR THE ENVIRONMENT

If your main source of inspiration is nature and the world around you, then drawing or painting from life is the best place to start. Working outdoors, also known as *plein air* painting, is particularly good for small landscapes and capturing quick impressions of a subject. Studio work, on the other hand, is better for larger paintings or those created over several sessions. There are pluses and minuses to working both outside and in the studio.

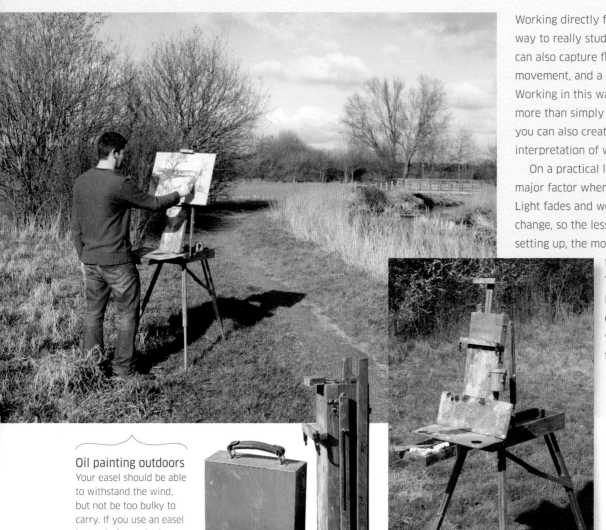

Working directly from life is the best way to really study your subject. You can also capture fleeting light effects, movement, and a sense of energy. Working in this way helps you to do more than simply replicate a subject—you can also create an emotional interpretation of what you see.

On a practical level, time is a major factor when painting outdoors. Light fades and weather conditions change, so the less time you spend setting up, the more time you have to sketch and paint. Travel light: use a limited palette of colors and restrict yourself to just a few key brushes.

Oil painting outdoors
Your easel should be able to withstand the wind, but not be too bulky to carry. If you use an easel instead of a pochade, you will also need a wet panel carrier—a box that safely holds wet paintings.

Wet panel carrier and folded box easel

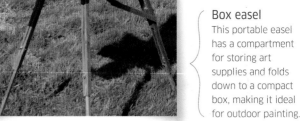

Box easel
This portable easel has a compartment for storing art supplies and folds down to a compact box, making it ideal for outdoor painting.

"Travel light when working outdoors, and consider what you can realistically achieve with the equipment and time you have available."

Camera backpack
A camera backpack is useful for stowing a tripod (see right) and other supplies. Carry half-empty paints to reduce the weight.

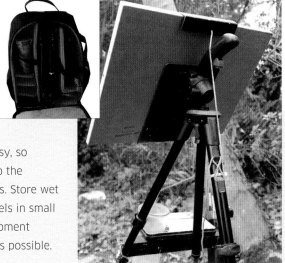

Camera tripod easel
You can convert a camera tripod into an outdoor easel by attaching a bracket to hold a board or sketch pad, and a metal shelf for the paints and water holder.

Working outside can be messy, so squeeze paint sparingly onto the palette and carry hand wipes. Store wet rags or discarded paper towels in small plastic bags, keep your equipment clean, and be as organized as possible.

Try packing your supplies into a specialist camera or fishing backpack, ideally with an attached stool. A pochade—a box with a lid hinged at an angle that acts as an easel—is also very useful. It has storage for your wet works of art and a compartment for paints and brushes. Place the pochade on your lap or attach it to a tripod. Alternatively, you can use a portable easel that includes a storage area.

WORKING IN THE STUDIO
Apart from the convenience of having heat, shelter, and your materials at hand, working in the studio has other advantages. It makes it easier to work on large paintings, you can revisit a painting over several sessions, and the lighting is consistent. Being in a studio may also allow your imagination to flow—without being restricted by what you see in front of you, your work may become more personal and exploratory. However, it is still useful to have access to multiple sources when painting in the studio, such as photographs, notes, color sketches, and preliminary drawings made on location.

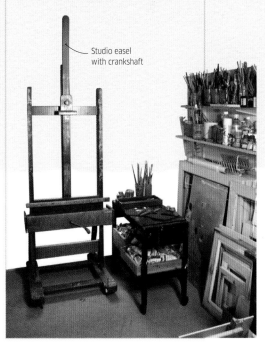

Studio easel with crankshaft

Outdoor easel for watercolor
Use a portable easel and a field palette with plenty of mixing space, a water reservoir, and pan colors (rather than tubes). Secure the pad with elastic bands.

Watercolor field palette

Mounting and displaying work

SHOWING YOUR ART

If you want to display your artworks in public, they will benefit from being properly mounted and framed. Take them to a professional framer, or create frames yourself using specialized equipment. Once your artwork is well presented, and you have some experience exhibiting in local or national shows, you might consider approaching galleries.

One approach for oil paintings and unglazed acrylic paintings is to frame smaller works in wider frames and larger works in narrower frames. Watercolor paintings are usually best presented in a mount behind glass, surrounded by a thin frame.

Inner frames and mounts

Although fashions change, it is usual to include an inner frame, or slip, of a lighter color than the frame, which will help balance and enhance the painting. Use gold with caution as it can be overbearing, although a little gold around the moulding of a frame can be effective. There is a wide range of colors available, but it is usually best to choose subtle, light colors that complement and lift your work. Avoid frames or mounts that distract from–or even conflict with–your work. You can also use more than one mount, leaving a small gap between them to lead the viewer's eye into the painting.

Framing practicalities

You can frame your work at home, although you will need to invest in some specialized equipment. For example, you will need a miter cutter to create smooth, accurate corners at 45-degree angles, V-nails to join the frame corners, and an underpinner for fixing the nails.

Alternatively, you can instruct a professional framer to make up finished frames to your specification, or ask them to create barefaced (untreated) wooden frames, which you can finish at home using a good emulsion and furniture wax, a matte or satin varnish, or even gold leaf.

Displaying your work

Look for opportunities to show your work at local art societies, and both regional and national juried shows. For more consistent exposure, consider approaching a gallery. Always do your research and prepare your artwork first (see below).

APPROACHING GALLERIES

First, assess and prepare your work. For example, does it have a recognizable style? Galleries usually want consistency and a unique selling point. List your exhibitions, juried shows, and experience, and assemble a small portfolio of original, well-presented, "ready for sale" pieces.

Choosing a gallery

- Do you have a similar experience and ability to other artists at the gallery?
- Will your work fit in without being too similar to other artists on its books?
- Are your prices in line with the paintings displayed at the gallery?
- Be consistent when setting your own prices and find out how much commission they charge.

Negotiating with a gallery

- Don't cold call–make an appointment and find out what the gallery would like you to bring.
- Listen to the staff–they know their business.
- Clarify terms before committing to work.
- Discuss their requirements and decide whether you could keep up with the work.
- Understand that the commission they take pays for running the gallery, publicity, client lists, and their reputation.

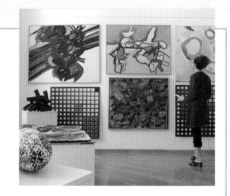

Exhibiting work
You will need to demonstrate a consistent and stylistically coherent body of work to appeal to galleries.

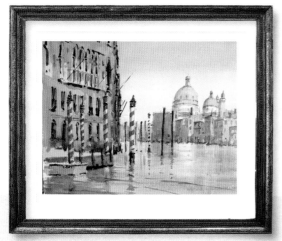

Venice in the sunshine (see pp.96–97)

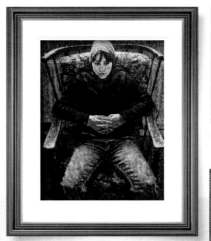

Marie, seated (see p.199)

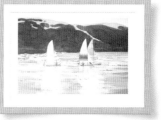

Sailing boats (see pp.72–73)

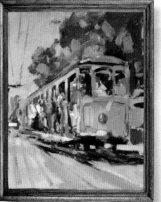

Yellow tram (see p.273)

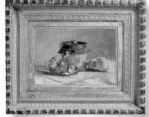

Still life with fruit (see pp.266–67)

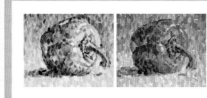

Peppers (see p.182)

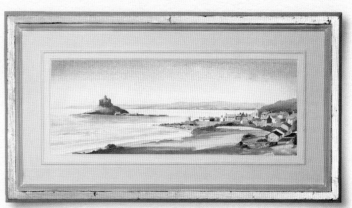

St Michael's Mount

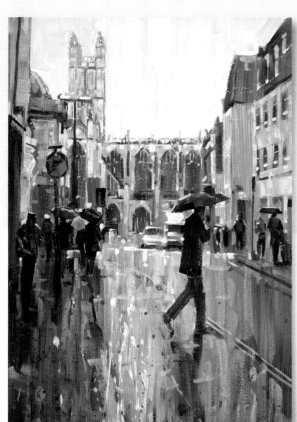

Rainy day (see pp.188–89)

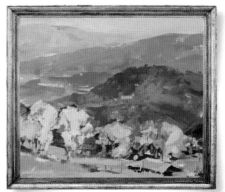

Mountain scene (see pp.242–43)

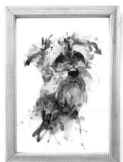

Miniature Schnauzer
(see pp.280–81)

Watercolors

Painting with **watercolors**

Watercolors are popular with artists of all abilities because they are versatile, easy to use, portable, and affordable. With a translucency that allows the white of the paper to show through, they have a luminosity that imbues paintings with a sense of light. The spontaneous, fluid nature of the paint allows you to create a range of expressive strokes and textures.

On the following pages, you can find out about the paints and materials needed to get started. Then, practice and develop your skills with more than 30 watercolor techniques, grouped into three sections of increasing sophistication—beginner, intermediate, and advanced. A showcase painting at the end of each section brings all the techniques together.

1 Beginner techniques

■ See pp. 40–61

In the first section, find out about color mixing and warm and cool colors, experiment with brushstrokes, produce a range of tonal values, paint three-dimensional objects, and learn about wet and dry applications.

2 Intermediate techniques

■ See pp. 62–89

In the second section, see how to lay flat and gradated washes—core watercolor skills—use aerial perspective to create depth, and find out how to correct minor errors or incorporate them into your painting.

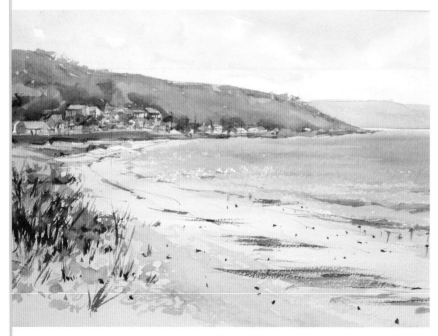

Beginner showcase painting (see pp. 60–61)

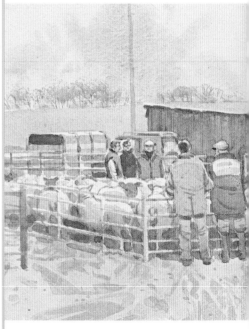

Intermediate showcase painting (see pp. 88–89)

Although water-based paints have been used for millennia, watercolors as we know them were first used during the 14th century. At the time, oils and tempera were the predominant media, but watercolors grew in popularity during the 17th century, mainly in England where the landed gentry commissioned paintings of their country estates. As a portable medium suited to outside work, watercolors came to the fore during the Romantic period of the 19th century, when there was a growing love of landscapes and the natural world.

Water-based pigments

Watercolor paints comprise pigments bound with water-soluble binders. The pigments are either dyes that dissolve, or minute particles that form a suspension in water. Paints may also include other additives to prevent them from drying out, improve color, and add body. Natural pigments are usually easier to remove from your paper with a wet brush, while dyes tend to stain.

As watercolors are transparent, the color and surface of your paper will have an effect on the final painting.

White paper is traditionally used to maximize the luminosity of the paint, although creams and other off-whites are also popular choices.

Watercolors are easy to apply, but as they are unpredictable and difficult to correct, they require practice to perfect. They are best applied quickly and boldly, with economy, to bring out their clarity. With this fluid medium, you can make subtle blends when working "wet-in-wet," or work "wet-on-dry" to create shimmering layers and precise detail.

3 Advanced techniques

■ See pp. 90–117

In the final section, find out about granulation, glazing, painting skin tones, and the value of gathering source material and trying different compositions and tonal studies before committing to a final painting.

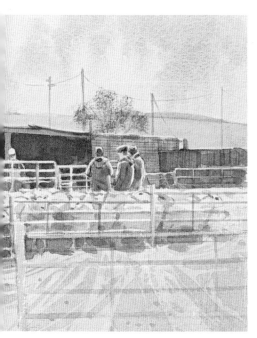

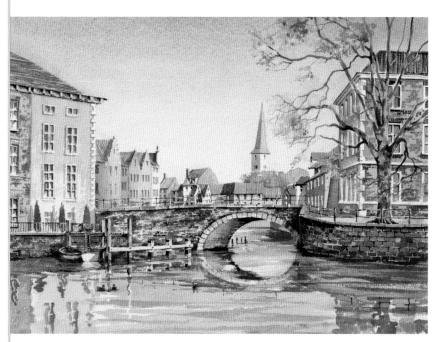

Advanced showcase painting (see pp. 116–17)

Paints

CHOOSING WATERCOLOR PAINTS

There are two main forms of watercolor: wet tube paints and dry pan paints. You can also buy watercolor "sticks," which are dry and can be used to draw and sketch as well as with a brush. These paints are available in two qualities: student quality, which is recommended for beginners, and more expensive artist-quality paints for more advanced artists.

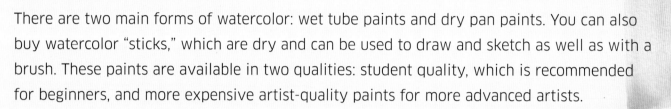

Whole pans

All paints are available individually or in sets of preselected colors. If you're new to painting, it's best to start with one of these color sets. As you progress, you can then buy individual colors to suit your own preferences and style.

Tube paints

Usually available in 5ml or 14ml tubes, these have a semi-liquid consistency and are quick and easy to mix. Since you can squeeze out as much paint as you need, tube watercolors are ideal for mixing large batches of color for washes and large-scale paintings. For the same reason, it is easy to achieve intense color saturation (see opposite) with tube paints—you can even use them undiluted for the most vibrant color. Tube watercolors will dry out if left on a palette, but can be used again if wetted. They can also be used to replenish a pan paint (see below) if left to dry.

Pan paints

Dry, cakelike pan paints are convenient and portable—perfect for working *en plein air*. Since you pick up the color a little at a time using a wet brush, they are great for small paintings and sketches. Use a damp cloth to wipe the pans clean after use to prevent contamination—pans tend to absorb colors from a dirty brush.

Pan paints are available in two sizes: half pans and whole pans. Buy whole pans for the colors you use most frequently. For example, if you specialize in landscapes, you might decide to buy whole pans for blues (skies) and earthy colors such as burnt sienna and burnt umber. Buy individual pans to customize a set.

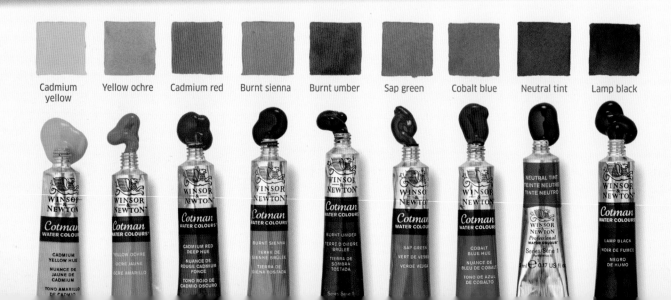

Cadmium yellow Yellow ochre Cadmium red Burnt sienna Burnt umber Sap green Cobalt blue Neutral tint Lamp black

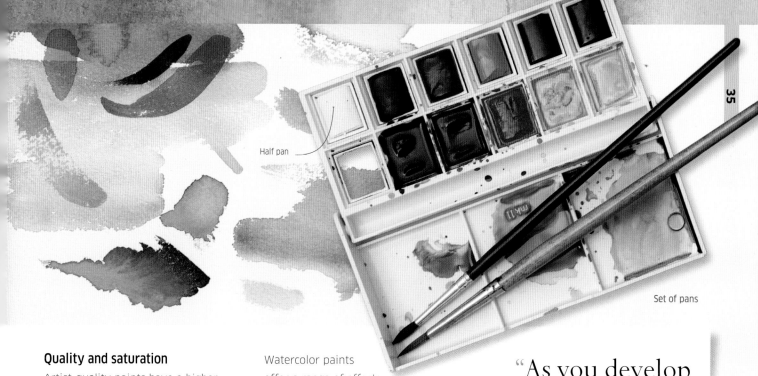

Half pan

Set of pans

Quality and saturation

Artist-quality paints have a higher proportion of pigment to filler than the more affordable student-quality versions. The pigments are more finely ground, which results in a richer paint, and they are more lightfast and consistent from tube to tube or pan to pan. However, as a beginner you should stick to student-quality paints (the same goes for other materials) until you gain confidence with the basic techniques and are sure that you want to continue with watercolors. As you progress, buy the best-quality paints you can afford.

Watercolor paints offer a range of effects in terms of saturation and transparency. Tube paints can give an intense effect because you can apply lots of pigment, whereas pan paints will create a relatively transparent effect unless they are built up in layers.

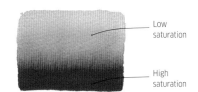

Low saturation

High saturation

Tube paint swatch

> "As you develop your skills as a watercolor artist, tailor your **palette of colors** to suit your **own style**."

Basic palette
This sample selection of colors (shown here in tube form) is a good basic palette for the beginner. Add or substitute colors as you become more familiar with the medium.

Additional colors
Explore the range of paints available as you progress. For example, all of these colors are used in the techniques in this chapter.

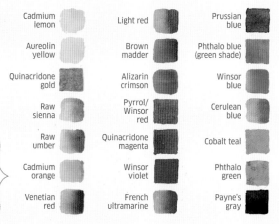

Cadmium lemon	Light red	Prussian blue
Aureolin yellow	Brown madder	Phthalo blue (green shade)
Quinacridone gold	Alizarin crimson	Winsor blue
Raw sienna	Pyrrol/Winsor red	Cerulean blue
Raw umber	Quinacridone magenta	Cobalt teal
Cadmium orange	Winsor violet	Phthalo green
Venetian red	French ultramarine	Payne's gray

Opaque white
Although it is usual to allow the white of the paper to show through, white watercolor paint is also available for a more opaque color.

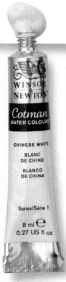

Chinese white

Brushes

HOW TO CHOOSE YOUR BRUSHES

A wide range of brushes is available, but round, soft-hair brushes are the mainstay of watercolor painting. You can create a wide range of brushstrokes with a small selection of round brushes. Other brush types, on the whole, lend themselves to specific tasks, such as washes or fine details. Add them to your collection as you need them.

Brushes are available in various materials, qualities, shapes, and sizes. High-quality brushes can be very expensive, but you don't need to spend a great deal. Whichever fiber you choose, a round brush should be supple, have a pointed shape, and be able to carry plenty of paint in its belly.

Brush fibers

Sable brushes are the traditional choice of watercolor painters, as the hairs are springy, keep their shape, and hold plenty of water and paint.

However, they are expensive (especially the larger sizes) and do wear out. The best quality are those made of kolinsky sable (a member of the weasel family); pure sable and red sable are less good, but still of high quality. When buying in a retail shop, ask for some water, wet the brush, and ensure that it comes to a perfect point before purchasing. If you buy online, you run the risk of buying an imperfect brush.

Squirrel and goat fibers are very soft and suitable for large washes, but won't give you enough control

for detailed work. Ox hair is suitable for flat brushes, and hog hair, or a synthetic equivalent, is stiff and good for scrubbing out mistakes.

There are also blends of sable and synthetic fibers, which can be a good compromise. Synthetic brushes are cheaper than sable, will last a lot longer, and are perfectly good for just about all watercolor work.

Types of brushes

Brushes are available in numerous shapes, each suited to its purpose. For most brushstrokes, a round

Round brushes

For watercolor painting, round brushes are the most frequently used type of brush. Their shape makes them versatile, suitable for detail and delicate lines, but also for applying washes and broader strokes. It is worth investing in a good-quality round brush as you will use it the most.

No. 1 round synthetic brush

No. 3 round synthetic brush

No. 5 round synthetic brush

No. 5 round sable and synthetic blend brush

No. 8 round sable and synthetic blend brush

No. 14 round sable brush

Wash brushes

Natural-bristle brushes hold and distribute paint very well, so are ideal for applying washes. The square, mop, and hake (an oriental-style wash brush) are all good for laying large areas of color, as well as absorbing excess paint. The mop is also suitable for blending.

Holding your brush

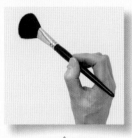

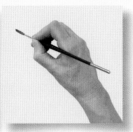

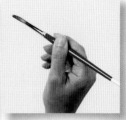

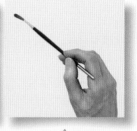

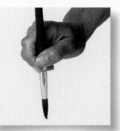

Mid-handle hold
To paint washes, hold your brush in the middle of the handle and move your entire lower arm.

Close pencil hold
To paint details, hold the brush like a pencil. Place your little finger on the paper to steady your hand.

Upright hold
Paint sweeping lines with the brush tip, keeping your wrist fixed and moving your arm from the shoulder.

Flexible pencil hold
Hold the brush like a pencil halfway down the handle to increase your range of movement for flowing lines.

End-of-handle hold
Grip the brush at the end so that you can flick your wrist—perfect for fine, delicate lines.

shape that comes to a fine point is best. Large, square brushes or large, oval mop brushes are good for applying washes to larger areas. A flat brush is suitable for strong lines and linear strokes. Wash brushes are simply larger versions of these.

Liners and riggers are long and narrow, with long hairs and pointed tips. These are ideal for painting very fine lines. Very tapered brushes, sometimes called swordliners, are also good for fine detail. For blending, fan-shaped brushes are useful.

Sizes

Brush sizes are designated by numbers from 000 (the smallest or finest) upward. If you are a beginner, start with three round brushes in sizes 03, 05, and 08. Intermediate and advanced artists can extend their collection to suit their personal style and needs.

Brushstrokes

You can use the tip, side, or edges of your brushes to make brushstrokes. Square, flat brushes produce strong, angular lines. Round brushes create loose, expressive lines when used on their side, and fine lines using their tips

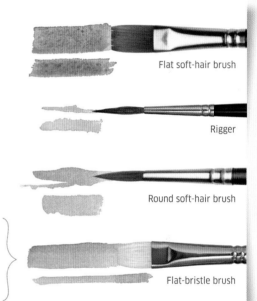

Flat soft-hair brush

Rigger

Round soft-hair brush

Flat-bristle brush

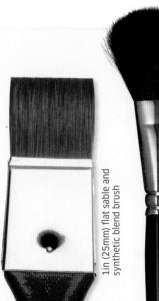

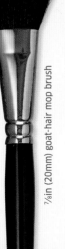
1in (25mm) flat sable and synthetic blend brush

⅞in (20mm) goat-hair mop brush

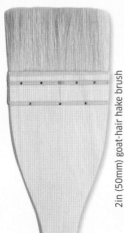
2in (50mm) goat-hair hake brush

Other brushes

Use the right brush for the job. Fan-shaped brushes are suitable for blending, while riggers are ideal for adding fine detail and outlines. Flat brushes are good for creating strong lines, and straight edges.

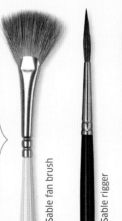
Sable fan brush

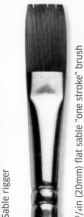
Sable rigger

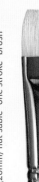
¾in (20mm) flat sable "one stroke" brush

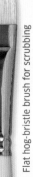
Flat hog-bristle brush for scrubbing

Supports and other materials

CHOOSING A SURFACE TO PAINT ON

The primary support, or painting surface, for watercolors is paper. It is manufactured in many different ways and has many different properties, colors, sizes, and weights (thicknesses). You can buy paper in several forms including individual sheets, rolls, bound sketchbooks, and prestretched watercolor blocks.

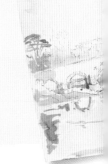

Different textures and weights of paper will create different effects in your finished paintings. It is advisable to experiment and think about the effect you want before choosing your paper. Buy single sheets of paper until you have decided which type you prefer.

Sketchbooks

Sketchbooks are essential for all artists and are bound in various ways. Spiral-bound sketchbooks are the most useful because the pages lie flat. Sizes vary. If you are using them outdoors, 11x17in is probably the largest manageable size.

The type and quality of paper in sketchbooks also varies. Choose a medium to heavyweight paper that won't buckle when wet. Lighter papers are suitable for pencil or pen work, as is rough-textured drawing paper. Sketchbooks made from watercolor paper will take washes better than drawing paper.

Watercolor papers

Watercolor papers come with different surfaces: rough, cold-pressed, and hot-pressed. Rough paper has a very textured finish, while cold-pressed paper has a relatively smooth surface.

Hot-pressed paper is run through rollers to make the surface very smooth. Although watercolor papers are generally white, the tone of the paper can vary according to the manufacturer, ranging from brilliant white to nearly cream. The whiteness will affect the luminosity of the painting. Watercolor paper has a "right" and "wrong" side. The right side has a watermark, but you can paint on both sides of most good papers. Paper is also treated with size when it is made, to control its absorbency. Manufacturers create different surface qualities in their

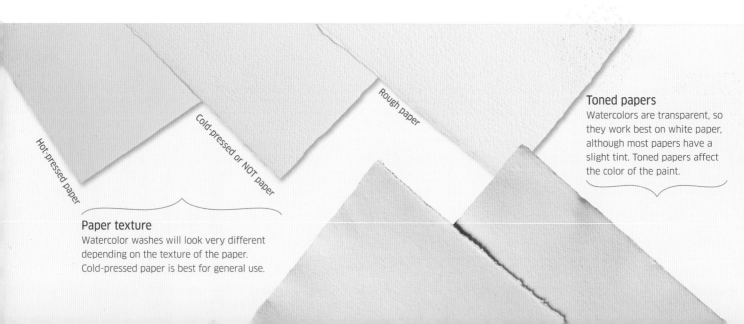

Hot-pressed paper

Cold-pressed or NOT paper

Rough paper

Toned papers
Watercolors are transparent, so they work best on white paper, although most papers have a slight tint. Toned papers affect the color of the paint.

Paper texture
Watercolor washes will look very different depending on the texture of the paper. Cold-pressed paper is best for general use.

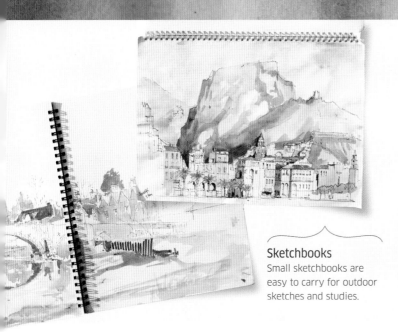

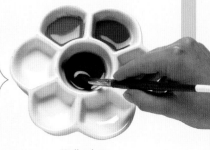

Palettes
Palettes should be white and preferably ceramic. Plastic palettes tend to stain over time. You will need at least one palette with several wells for different colors and one larger palette for mixing washes.

Well palette

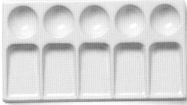

Sketchbooks
Small sketchbooks are easy to carry for outdoor sketches and studies.

Ceramic palette

sizing processes, which affect how paint behaves. Paint will not be absorbed by a highly sized paper—it will "slide" across the surface. Less sized papers will absorb paint washes quickly and the paint will sink into the surface. If paper is too highly sized for your needs, stretch it to remove some of the size (see below).

Paper sizes and weights
Individual sheets of paper come in various sizes, the largest of which is 30 x 22in (76 x 56cm). Half and quarter sheets are also available.

Should you require larger sizes of paper, you can buy paper on the roll. Weights of paper are generally 90-pound (200 grams per square meter), 140lb (300gsm), and 300lb (640gsm). You can use the heaviest-weight papers without stretching them, but they are expensive. It is also difficult to roll heavier papers, for example if you want to send a painting to be framed. It is much easier to roll 90lb and 140lb papers to store them or send them in a cardboard tube. However, you will need to stretch these weights

of paper before use or they will buckle when washes are applied.

Watercolor blocks
Watercolor blocks are made up of smaller sheets of paper that are glued down. The top layer of the block acts as the painting surface. When your painting is complete, you can simply lift it off the block, exposing the next layer. Blocks are good for use outdoors, as they provide a sturdy surface for you to work on and you don't need a separate drawing board.

Stretching paper

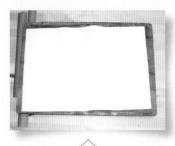

Step 1
Soak the paper thoroughly with water on both sides using a sponge. Lay right side up on a strong board.

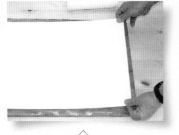

Step 2
Stick one edge of the paper down with gum strip and gently pull the paper to remove buckles.

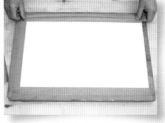

Step 3
Glue the remaining edges of the paper down with the gum strip.

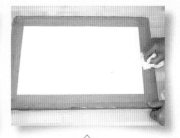

Step 4
Leave the paper to dry (this will take several hours). Keep the paper on the board while painting.

Color mixing

USING COLOR THEORY TO MIX WATERCOLOR PAINTS

Exploring color theory will help you learn how to mix your own colors and create the hues, tones, and shades that bring your work to life. However, watercolors dry noticeably lighter than the wet color you see on the paper, so you'll need to practice making your mixes stronger to compensate for this.

WET MIXING METHODS

You can mix wet paints together in a palette or combine them "wet-in-wet" directly on the paper, as shown in these examples with French ultramarine and aureolin. Don't rinse your brush between picking up colors—rinsing adds water and dilutes the mix, making it impossible to achieve strong colors.

■ Traditional versus modern color wheels

The primary colors, traditionally blue, red, and yellow, are capable of creating many other hues (see pp. 14–15). There are warm and cool variations of every color, however, so your color mixes will vary depending on which versions of blue, red, and yellow you choose. A modern approach is to use cyan, magenta, and yellow as primaries. These are cooler than the traditional primaries, and create vibrant secondary and tertiary mixes.

As the studies opposite show, neither traditional nor modern color wheels create a fully comprehensive range of colors. However, using colors from both systems will allow you to mix warm and cool primaries to create a huge range of colors, both muted and bright.

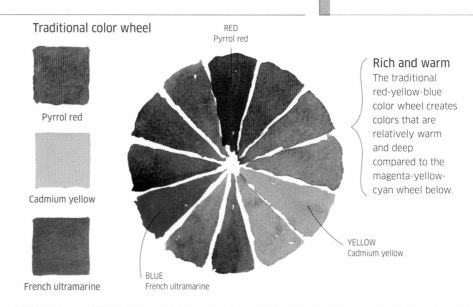

Traditional color wheel

Pyrrol red

Cadmium yellow

French ultramarine

RED
Pyrrol red

YELLOW
Cadmium yellow

BLUE
French ultramarine

Rich and warm
The traditional red-yellow-blue color wheel creates colors that are relatively warm and deep compared to the magenta-yellow-cyan wheel below.

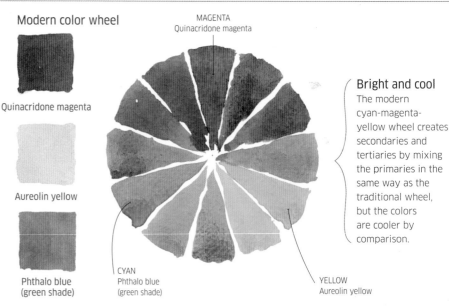

Modern color wheel

Quinacridone magenta

Aureolin yellow

Phthalo blue (green shade)

MAGENTA
Quinacridone magenta

CYAN
Phthalo blue (green shade)

YELLOW
Aureolin yellow

Bright and cool
The modern cyan-magenta-yellow wheel creates secondaries and tertiaries by mixing the primaries in the same way as the traditional wheel, but the colors are cooler by comparison.

Mixing in a palette
Using your brush, place some water in the palette, then pick up the first color and blend it with the water. Without rinsing your brush, pick up the second color and blend it with the first. This creates an evenly mixed color.

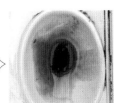
1–Blend paint with water

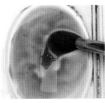
2–Add second color

3–Blend colors together

Produces even color

Mixing wet-in-wet onto the paper
Apply a wash of the first color to the paper. Add the second color while the first wash is still wet. The result will be a partially mixed color with a variegated appearance.

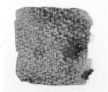
1–Apply first color

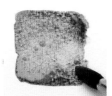
2–Add second color

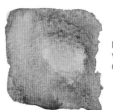
3–Blend wet colors

Produces variegated color

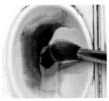

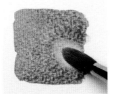

▨ Mixing traditional primaries

This study of a house was painted only with the traditional primary colors of red, yellow, and blue. The secondary color mixes made with the traditional primaries look quite earthy and muted compared to those created by the modern primaries (see below).

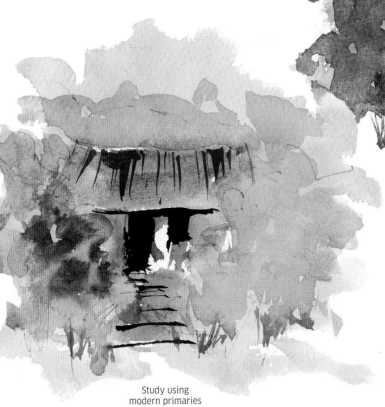

Study using
traditional primaries

Study using
modern primaries

▨ Mixing modern primaries

A trio of modern primaries was used for this study—magenta, yellow (aureolin yellow), and cyan (phthalo blue–green shade). The resulting secondary color mixes are vibrant but a little brash and unnatural compared to the secondaries created by the traditional primaries (see above).

■ Mixing three primary colors to create darks

Combining all three primaries together creates dark colors. The results are close to black, rather than pure black, and usually look less jarring in your painting than black paint. You can vary your choice of primary colors and the proportions in which you mix them to create a range of useful darks.

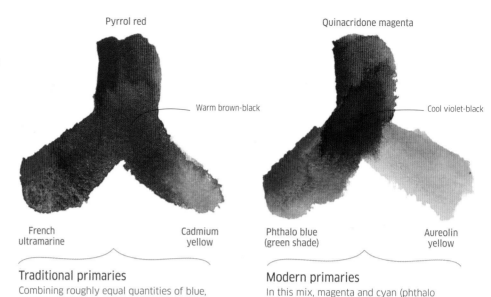

Pyrrol red

Quinacridone magenta

Warm brown-black

Cool violet-black

French ultramarine

Cadmium yellow

Phthalo blue (green shade)

Aureolin yellow

Traditional primaries
Combining roughly equal quantities of blue, red, and yellow creates a brown-black.

Modern primaries
In this mix, magenta and cyan (phthalo blue) dominate to create a violet-black.

■ Mixing complementary colors to create darks

Complementary colors sit opposite each other on the color wheel. When they are mixed together, they create a wide range of dark colors: brown, blue, gray, black. Many painters find this a better method of mixing darks than using primaries.

Combining complementaries
French ultramarine and its complementary burnt sienna (a dull orange) create a very wide range of darks. Phthalo green and magenta (substituting red) create cooler darks. The yellow and violet create a duller neutral that is less successful.

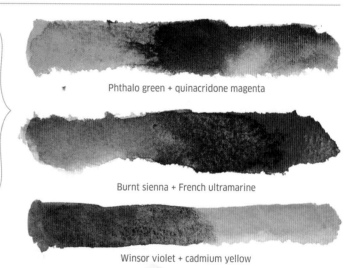

Phthalo green + quinacridone magenta

Burnt sienna + French ultramarine

Winsor violet + cadmium yellow

■ Lightening colors

In watercolor, colors are lightened by adding water to make them more transparent. Adding white paint creates pastel tones but also makes the color more opaque. Adding too much white can make colors look chalky.

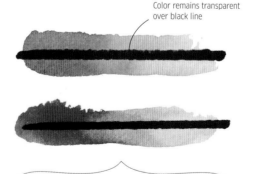

Color remains transparent over black line

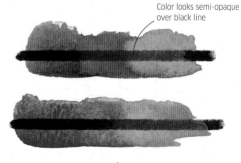

Color looks semi-opaque over black line

Lightening with water
Diluting makes the paint more transparent; this allows the paper to show through, which lightens the color optically.

Lightening with white
Adding white changes the color and makes the mix more opaque. When the paint is well diluted, the opacity is not very noticeable.

▪ Pigment staining and transparency

All pigments are staining or non-staining; and either transparent, semi-transparent, semi-opaque, or opaque. Manufacturers may classify similar pigments differently, so check when you buy. Staining pigments leave some color on the paper if you remove them. Opaque pigments become transparent when diluted, so you can mix them without fear of creating muddy colors.

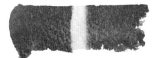

French ultramarine (non-staining)

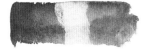

French ultramarine (non-staining)

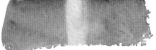

Phthalo blue (staining)

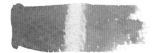

Phthalo blue (staining)

Staining – dry color
Dry paint swatches were wetted and scrubbed to lift out the paint. The staining pigment does lift out but leaves a little more color.

Staining – wet color
Wet paint was lifted from these swatches with a tissue. There is a a slight difference between the staining and non-staining results.

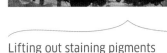

Lifting out staining pigments
Staining pigments can be removed enough to create highlights, as seen on the trunks of these trees.

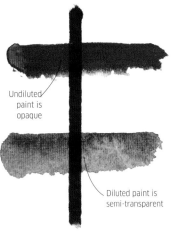

Undiluted paint is opaque

Diluted paint is semi-transparent

Cadmium red (opaque)

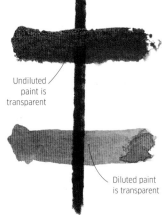

Undiluted paint is transparent

Diluted paint is transparent

Alizarin crimson (transparent)

Opaque pigment
This color is opaque enough to cover black when it is undiluted but is almost fully transparent when diluted for washes.

Transparent pigment
Some colors are transparent even when they are undiluted. Transparent pigments remain bright when they are layered.

Using opaque pigments
One of the benefits of opaque pigments is that you can apply them over a dark background, as with the undiluted cadmium yellow used here to paint daffodils.

Color charts

PRACTICING COLOR MIXES

Making color charts is a great way to practice color mixing, and you can keep them as a reference for subsequent projects. You can mix watercolors by painting washes of color over dry layers (wet-on-dry), adding one wet wash to another on the paper (wet-in-wet), or mixing paints in your palette. Try making color charts using each of these methods so that you can observe the different results.

WET-ON-DRY COLOR CHART

In this exercise, let the first layer of colors dry before adding the second. Use all the colors in your collection; the chart below uses the colors recommended in the basic palette (see pp. 34–35).

You will need

- All the colors in your collection
- Medium-size round soft-hair brush
- Jar of water for rinsing
- Cold-pressed watercolor paper

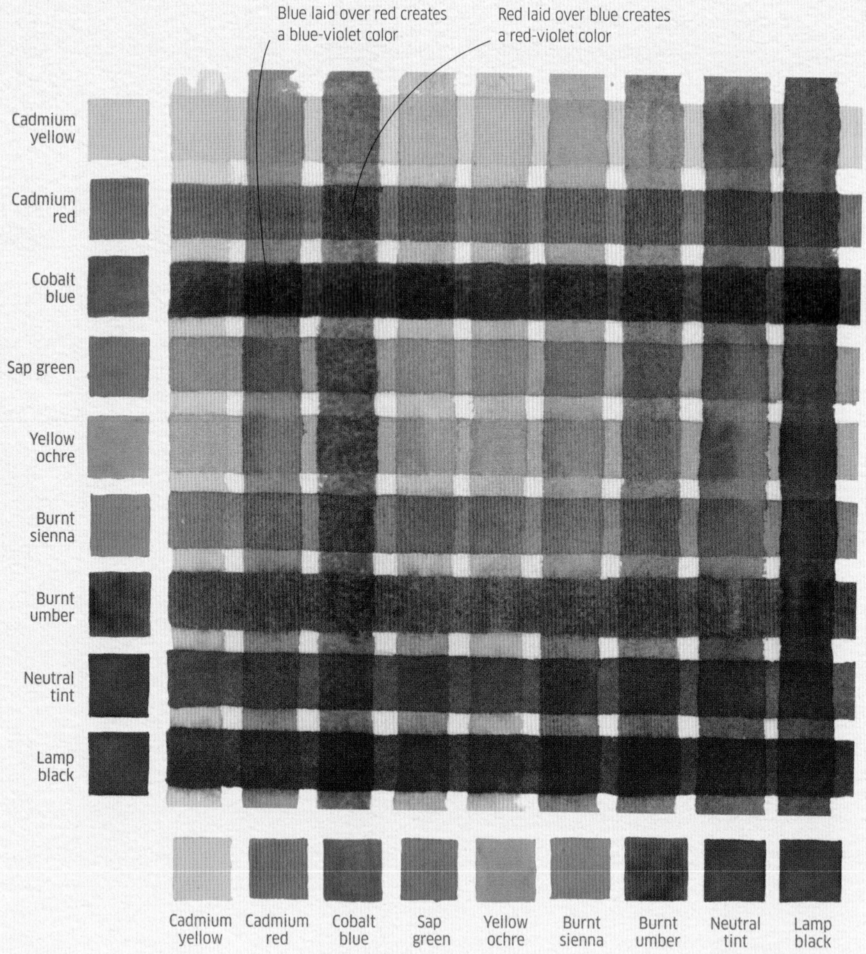

Blue laid over red creates a blue-violet color

Red laid over blue creates a red-violet color

Cadmium yellow
Cadmium red
Cobalt blue
Sap green
Yellow ochre
Burnt sienna
Burnt umber
Neutral tint
Lamp black

Cadmium yellow · Cadmium red · Cobalt blue · Sap green · Yellow ochre · Burnt sienna · Burnt umber · Neutral tint · Lamp black

1 Making a grid
Draw a grid on your paper in pencil, labeling all the columns and rows so that each of your colors is listed both horizontally and vertically.

2 Painting the lines
Paint the columns first. Once the columns are completely dry, paint the rows over the top. Aim for the same saturation level for each color.

3 Observing the effects
When the chart is dry, observe how the colors have been modified by layering. The effect depends on the hue, density of pigment, and order in which the colors were painted.

CHART OF COLORS MIXED IN YOUR PALETTE

This exercise involves mixing two wet colors together in your palette and painting them on a grid to record the result. Use all the colors in your collection. These charts show 50:50 and 70:30 ratio color mixes, respectively.

You will need

- All the colors in your collection
- Medium-size round soft-hair brush
- Jar of water for rinsing; jar of clean water for mixing
- Cold-pressed watercolor paper

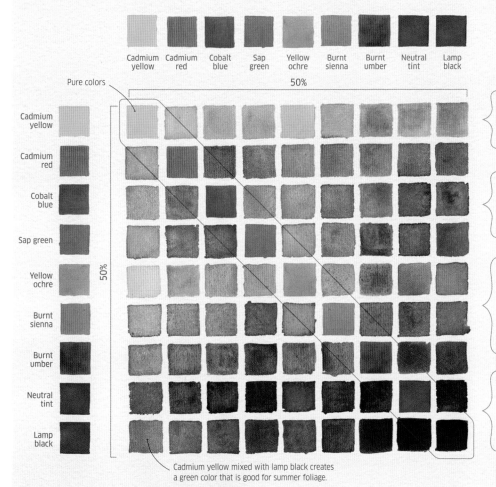

Cadmium yellow mixed with lamp black creates a green color that is good for summer foliage.

1 Making a grid
Draw a grid with spaces to list each of your colors along the top and down the side of the grid.

2 Plotting unmixed colors
Before you begin mixing, paint pure colors on the diagonal axis, where the horizontal and vertical lines for each color intersect.

3 Mixing colors 50:50
Add equal amounts of two colors to your mixing well for a 50:50 ratio. Don't rinse your brush before picking up the second color; otherwise, your mix could be too weak and diluted.

4 Plotting mixed colors
Paint the mixes in their corresponding squares on the chart. Rinse your brush before creating each new mix. Let the chart dry and keep it for reference.

5 Mixing colors 70:30
Create other charts to see how changing the ratio of one color to another extends the range of hues you can mix. The chart on the left was created with 70:30 color mixes.

30% cobalt blue mixed with 70% sap green

70% cobalt blue mixed with 30% sap green

GREENS

Green can be a difficult color to mix successfully. For this reason, you may want to include several bought greens in your palette so that you always have a suitable green on hand.

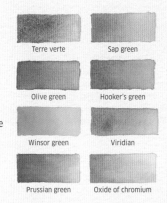

Terre verte

Sap green

Olive green

Hooker's green

Winsor green

Viridian

Prussian green

Oxide of chromium

Value exercises

CREATING ATMOSPHERE AND FORM

Value describes the lightness or darkness of a color. With watercolors, this relates to the density of paint. Paint straight from the pan or tube is as dense as it can be and the darkest value for that hue. By adding more and more water, you can create lighter and lighter values. You can use variations in value to create form (see pp. 56–57), and to suggest an overall atmosphere for your painting.

Form and mood

You can use graduations of value to convey the form of a three-dimensional object by creating shadows, highlights, and a range of values in between. You can also use value to create atmosphere, and so evoke an emotional response in the viewer. For example, paintings with a narrow value range tend to suggest a soft or subdued atmosphere, while paintings with high contrast are generally more vibrant and upbeat.

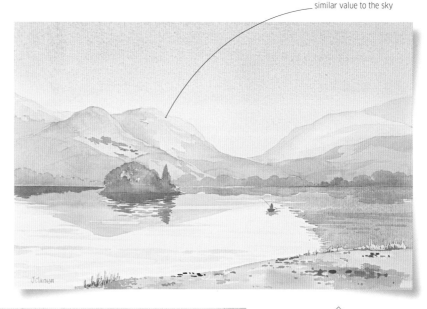

Mountains have a similar value to the sky

Narrow tonal range
In this landscape, there is very little tonal difference between the different elements. The painting aims to evoke a quiet, reflective response in the viewer, which suits the peaceful scene.

Wide tonal range
This painting of a fishing village bathed in sunshine has a wide tonal range. There are strong contrasts in value between the dark shadows and bright highlights.

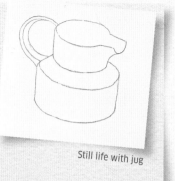
Still life with jug

PUTTING IT INTO PRACTICE

These exercises, the first in black and white and the second in color, are a great way to come to grips with value. By starting off with simple value charts, you can practice creating individual swatches of value before blending them in a simple still life.

You will need

Brown madder Lamp black

- No. 2 soft-hair and no. 4 soft-hair brushes
- 10 x 12in (25 x 30cm) rough watercolor paper

1 Black-and-white value chart
Draw a grid comprising five squares. Paint the darkest value first, using black paint straight from the tube or pan. Next, dilute the paint to create the middle box. It will then be easier to judge the value for the adjacent squares. For the final, lightest value, leave the paper white.

2 Graduated value chart
This time, draw a long bar with no segments. Load a no. 2 soft-hair brush with undiluted paint and block in one end. Apply water, a little at a time, and blend the paint from dark to light in a gradual transition.

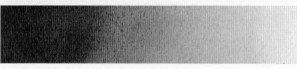

4 Color value chart
Repeat steps one to three but with a range of colors to test the density of different pigments. Here, brown madder was used.

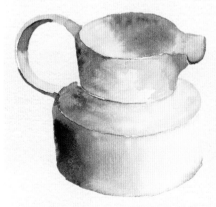

3 Black-and-white jug
Sketch a simple, curved object, such as a jug. Look at how the light falls on it, then, using a no. 4 soft-hair brush, apply values to create a three-dimensional effect. Use the darkest values for the shadows, gradually blending lighter values toward the highlights.

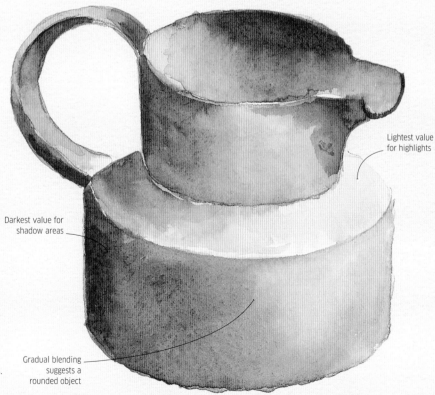

Lightest value for highlights

Darkest value for shadow areas

Gradual blending suggests a rounded object

Warm and cool colors

BALANCING COLOR TEMPERATURE

Colors have qualities that we associate with temperature—some colors, such as red, are considered to be warm, while other colors, such as blue, are cool. Using these traits can be a powerful way of conveying mood, depth, and harmony in your work.

▤ Characteristics of color temperature

Visually, warm colors appear to come forward in paintings whereas cool colors appear to recede; this illusion is very useful for creating a sense of depth. Warm and cool colors are also associated with certain emotions, which you can use to convey mood.

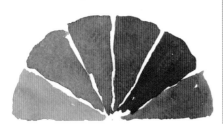

Warm colors
Reds, oranges, and yellows are generally grouped in the warm half of the color wheel (see pp. 14-15). A picture painted mostly with warm colors suggests a happy or energetic mood.

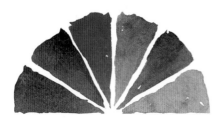

Cool colors
Violets, blues, and greens are generally grouped in the cool half of the color wheel. Including a lot of cool colors in a picture suggests a calm or subdued mood.

▤ Creating color harmony

Color harmony helps you to create visually satisfying pictures. Limiting your palette to a small range of colors, or using analogous colors, is one way to achieve a unified scheme. You can also use a common, or "atmosphere," color throughout a painting to tie elements together. Balancing colors doesn't necessarily mean using equal amounts of warm and cool—one can dominate while the other provides a pleasing contrast.

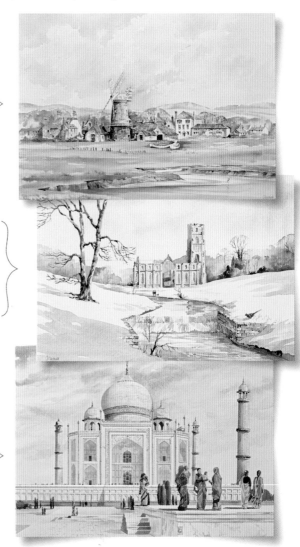

Atmosphere color
You can use one color as a unifying theme throughout a painting. In this painting, burnt sienna is used in various tones in the background, middle ground, and foreground to create a harmonized color scheme.

Balancing a cool scheme
This snowy scene calls for a cool, blue-toned palette, but the brown-gold trees and building in the background, and the bright pheasant in the foreground, provide some warmth for balance.

Balancing a warm scheme
An equal amount of warm and cool is generally unsatisfying, so in this painting the figures are mostly wearing warm yellows, oranges, and reds with only one or two cooler blues and violets.

PUTTING IT INTO PRACTICE

In this painting, the cool background colors appear to recede while the warm colors of the foreground objects seem to advance. This creates an overall sense of depth.

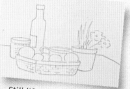

Still life with wine and fruit

You will need

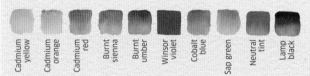

Cadmium yellow · Cadmium orange · Cadmium red · Burnt sienna · Burnt umber · Winsor violet · Cobalt blue · Sap green · Neutral tint · Lamp black

- No. 5 and no. 2 round soft-hair brushes
- 10 x 12in (25 x 30cm) rough watercolor paper

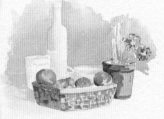

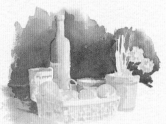

1 Background
Sketch your composition in pencil, then mix a cool, dark blue wash for the backround. Paint the wash with a no. 5 round soft-hair brush, turning the paper upside down to make it easier to paint around the bottle and other objects.

2 Warm colors
When the background is dry, paint the oranges, basket, and plant in the foreground with warm colors to help them stand out. Allow to dry.

3 Cool colors
Paint the bottle, glass tumbler, and cup with cool colors. This helps to indicate that they are behind the fruit and flowers

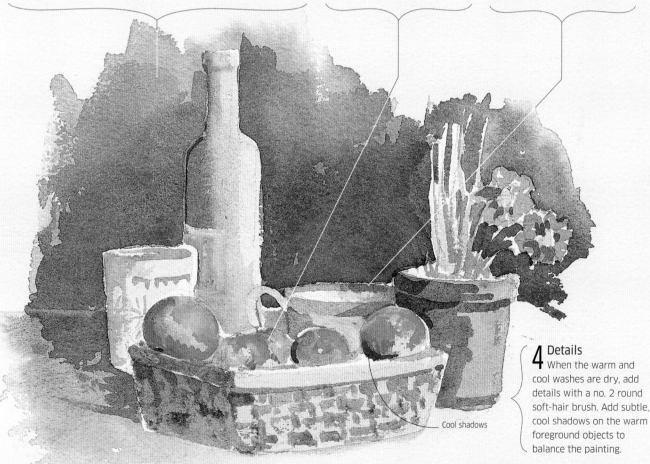

4 Details
When the warm and cool washes are dry, add details with a no. 2 round soft-hair brush. Add subtle, cool shadows on the warm foreground objects to balance the painting.

Cool shadows

Brushstrokes

TYPES OF BRUSHES AND STROKES

There are many sizes and types of brush, from tiny riggers to large mop-wash brushes. Soft-hair brushes made from sable are the best material, as they are absorbent and retain the finest point—but they are also the most expensive. There are, however, many more affordable synthetic brushes that are also of good quality.

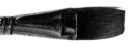
¾in (19mm)
flat brush

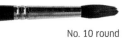
No. 10 round
soft-hair brush

No. 3 rigger brush

■ Choosing the right brush

A no. 10 round soft-hair brush is one of the most useful and versatile brushes. You can use it for both broad washes and fine, detailed line work. For larger washes, use a large, flat brush—you can also use it to create square-edged marks. The rigger, so called because it was used by painters to describe the intricate rigging on ships, is used for more delicate lines.

Square edges with flat brush

Scumbling with flat brush

Large wash with
round brush

Fine lines with
rigger brush

Scumbling with
round brush

Using tip of
round brush

Applying washes
Hold the brush close to the end of the handle when laying broad washes. This allows your hand and arm to move more easily, keeping the work loose.

Drier strokes and detail
For fine details, hold the brush as you would a pen, for greater control. Familiarize yourself with each brush by making a variety of marks, using paint at different strengths.

This landscape of winter trees was created using several brushstroke techniques. For example, a dry brush was used to suggest the tree canopies, while individual branches were picked out in fine detail.

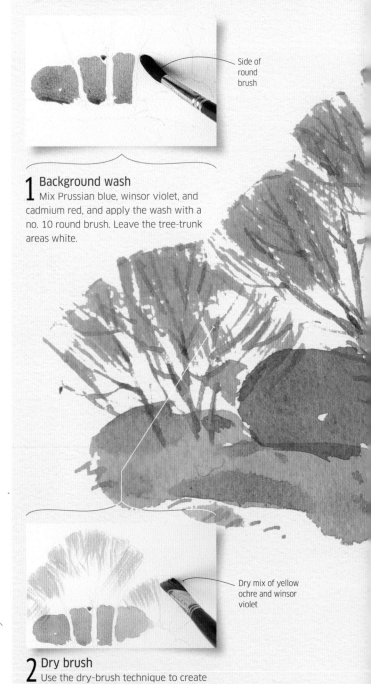

Side of
round
brush

1 Background wash
Mix Prussian blue, winsor violet, and cadmium red, and apply the wash with a no. 10 round brush. Leave the tree-trunk areas white.

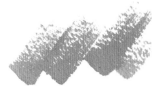
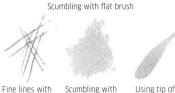

Dry mix of yellow
ochre and winsor
violet

2 Dry brush
Use the dry-brush technique to create the effect of a mass of twigs in the canopy. Drag a flat brush across the surface using downward strokes.

You will need

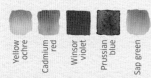

Yellow ochre · Cadmium red · Winsor violet · Prussian blue · Sap green

- No. 10 round soft-hair, ¾in (19mm) flat soft-hair, and no. 3 rigger brushes
- 11 x 15in (28 x 38cm) cold-pressed watercolor paper

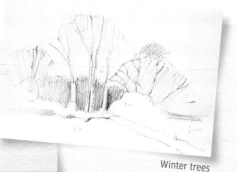

Winter trees

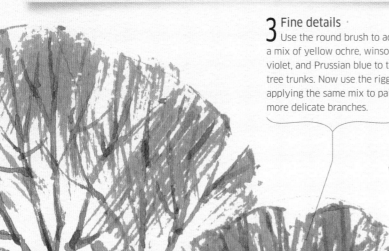

3 Fine details

Use the round brush to add a mix of yellow ochre, winsor violet, and Prussian blue to the tree trunks. Now use the rigger, applying the same mix to paint more delicate branches.

Add fine detail with a rigger brush

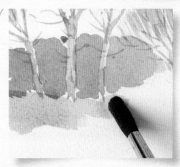

4 Foreground area

Mix sap green and yellow ochre for the foreground area. Use the side of a no. 10 round brush to add broad strokes of paint.

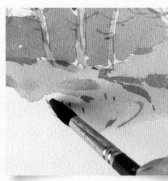

5 Foreground details

Use a darker mix of sap green and yellow ochre to add detail and texture to the grassy foreground area. Use the tip of a no. 10 round brush for these finer details.

"Familiarize yourself with brushes by making a **variety of marks,** using the paint at **different strengths and dilutions.**"

Laying paint

WET-IN-WET AND WET-ON-DRY

Applying paint on wet paper is called "wet-in-wet," and it allows the paint to spread and blend with other colors. This creates soft colors and lines, but doesn't give you much control. If you lay paint on dry paper, called "wet-on-dry," the pigment won't spread as easily, allowing you to make crisp, precise marks and apply strong color.

■ Diffusion and definition

If your paper dries out during a wet-in-wet wash, the paint won't spread easily, so prepare your mixes and water in advance. Once the paper is dry, you can re-wet it to apply further wet-in-wet washes, or apply a wet-on-dry wash for stronger color and detail.

Wash applied along top of paper ⎯

Wash applied here when paper was upside-down

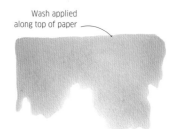
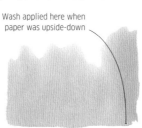

Wet-in-wet
Paint applied to wet paper will spread because the surface water disperses the pigment. Tilt the support so the paint runs down.

Upside-down wet-in-wet
To make the paint appear to spread upward in your painting, turn the paper upside-down before applying the wash.

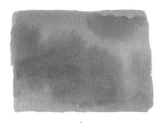

Blended wet-in-wet
Laying multiple colors on wet paper will make them blend into each other.

Wet-on-dry
Paint applied on dry paper is easier to control, which is perfect for sharp lines and details.

Try a cloud study to practice the different methods of laying paint. Before you start, prepare one jar of water to clean your brush and another jar to keep as clean water, and mix generous amounts of color.

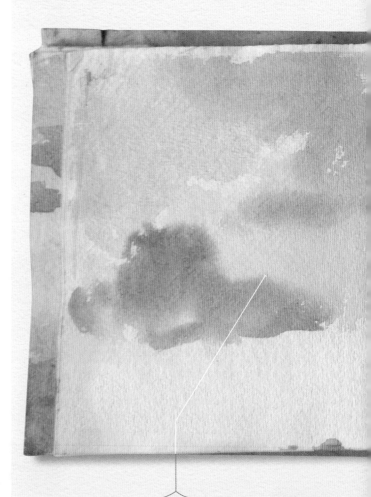

1 Wet-in-wet wash
Use a clean brush to wet the paper with clean water. Working quickly, apply a cerulean blue wash to one part of your paper. Rinse your brush immediately, then apply an ochre wash next to the blue, allowing the two colors to touch and merge at their edges.

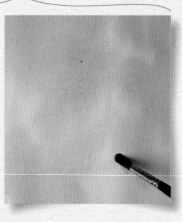

You will need

Yellow ochre

Winsor violet

Cerulean blue

- No. 10 round soft-hair brush
- Clean water

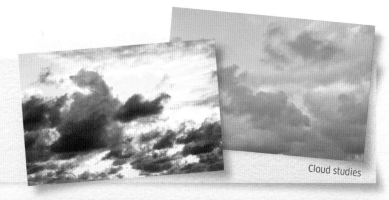

Cloud studies

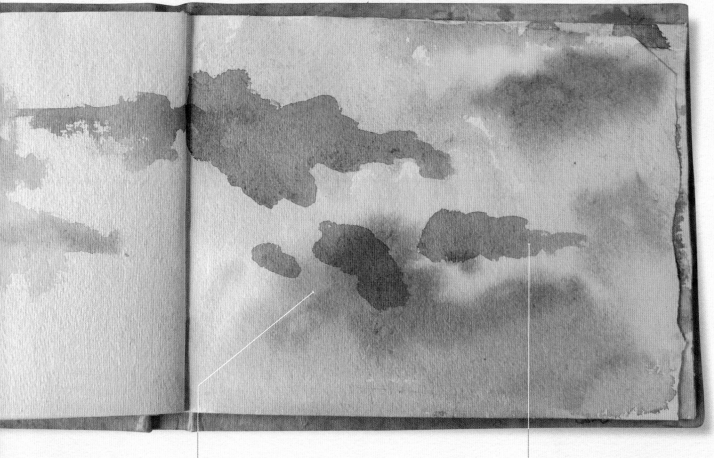

2 Rewetting the paper

Let the first washes dry completely. Rinse your brush and use clean water to re-wet the paper (using dirty water will taint the previous colors). Quickly apply a third wash to the wet paper, allowing it to blend with the previous washes. Use a stronger color (such as violet) so that the layered wash shows up.

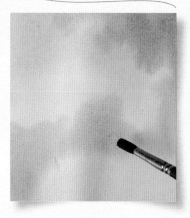

3 Wet-on-dry wash

Let the previous washes dry completely before you add more defined cloud shapes. Apply a stronger color (so that it shows up against the previous washes) on the dry paper. The wet-on-dry method will give your shapes defined edges.

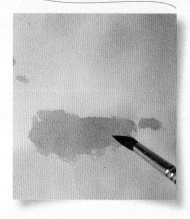

Using runs

CREATING EFFECTS WITH WATER

When used in a conventional way, watercolor has one particular quality that no other medium can match—it runs. Instead of trying to blot your work dry when this happens—or even abandoning it—why not make it a feature of your painting? Runs can create some unexpected yet beautiful effects in their own right.

■ Manipulating runs in washes

Many watercolor techniques are based on manipulating washes of diluted color. It is inevitable that at some point these washes will run together. As the outcome of a run is reasonably easy to predict, you can either exploit the results or prevent the run from happening in the first place.

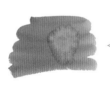

Runback, "cauliflower," or "bloom"
Be careful not to let drops of water from the brush land in a wet wash. The drip immediately spreads out, leading to this common but undesirable phenomenon.

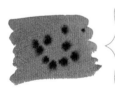

Strong into weak
To avoid runbacks, always apply strong washes into weak ones. That way, any drops will retain their shape and color and can be incorporated into your work.

Blotting
You can blot excess color from a damp wash using a paper towel or sponge. The resulting texture can create a desirable effect in its own right.

Controlling movement
Use washes of a similar strength to prevent adjacent washes from moving into one another. A weak wash will move into a strong one—the greater the disparity, the stronger the effect.

Runs can create some interesting effects. Although you can never completely control the results, with practice you will find it easier to make the best of them. The effect is useful when you want to paint a subject with a natural blend of color or tone, such as on an old stone wall.

You will need

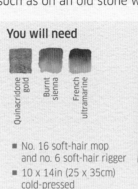

Quinacridone gold   Burnt sienna   French ultramarine

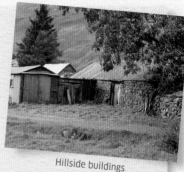

Hillside buildings

- No. 16 soft-hair mop and no. 6 soft-hair rigger
- 10 x 14in (25 x 35cm) cold-pressed watercolor paper

Washes run together

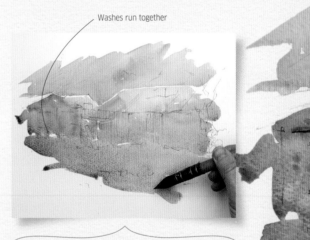

1 Background with run
Block in the hillside with a wash of ultramarine and burnt sienna using a soft-hair mop. Allow it to dry, then paint the buildings with the same mix and paint the grass with a mix of ultramarine and gold. Allow the last two washes to run together.

2 Creating mottling
Flick water onto the washes while they are still damp. Then, with your mop, apply stronger varieties of the same mixes created in the first step. This produces a mottled effect.

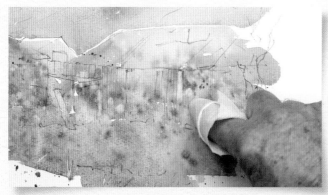

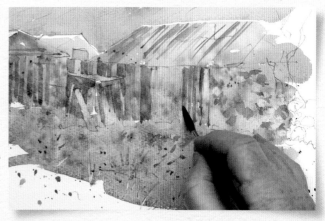

3 Blotting out
As the applications of paint from the previous step are drying, blot parts of the wash using a tissue wrapped around your finger. When the wash has just dried, paint blobs of water onto other areas, such as the planks of wood on the right-hand side of the wall, then blot after about 20 seconds.

4 Adding detail
Add details to the barn—such as the corrugated roof and wooden walls and doors—using a rigger brush. Flick paint onto the foreground and then blow on it through a straw to suggest blades of grass.

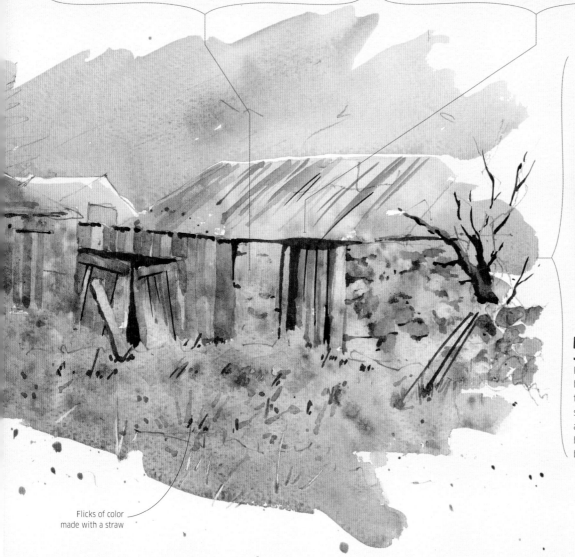

5 Final touches
Finally, apply a mix of French ultramarine and burnt sienna with a rigger to further define the structure of the buildings and to suggest the branches of a sapling behind the wall.

Flicks of color made with a straw

Modeling form

CREATING THREE-DIMENSIONAL SHAPES

A simple line drawing can convey a subject's two-dimensional shape, but it will lack a sense of solidity or form. By adding value, color, and texture, you can create the illusion of volume—that your subject is a three-dimensional object. The way in which light falls on a subject, and the shape and direction of its shadow, also reveal its shape. Using warm and cool colors can add depth, too, as cool colors appear to recede while warm colors seem to advance.

■ Turning shape into form

When creating form, it is important to show where the light is falling by varying the tone between brightly lit areas and areas of shadow. The background tone is also important, as it provides context, emphasizes the shape of the object, and helps separate the object from its surroundings.

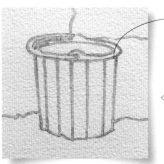

Flat shape

Two-dimensional shape
This simple line drawing shows the two-dimensional shape of the bucket, but it does not have substance or depth. The sketch reveals nothing about the nature of the background or where the light is falling.

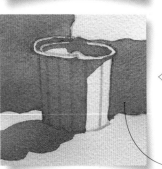

Three-dimensional object
By adding shadow, we can see that strong light is falling on the right side of the bucket, which reveals its rounded shape. The contrast between the dark background and bright foreground places the bucket firmly on the ground.

Background shadow

This sequence shows how to give form to a small group of sacks of grain. The sacks sit on hay bales, which add substance and context, while light seems to flood in from one side, as if from a nearby door.

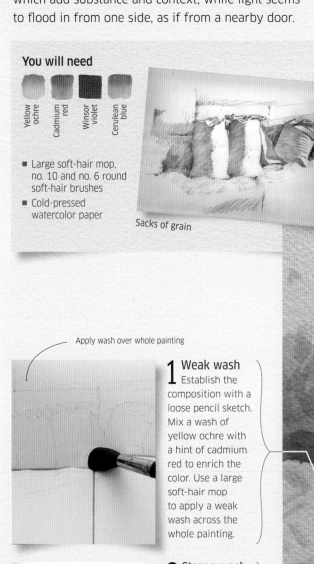

You will need

Yellow ochre

Cadmium red

Winsor violet

Cerulean blue

- Large soft-hair mop, no. 10 and no. 6 round soft-hair brushes
- Cold-pressed watercolor paper

Sacks of grain

Apply wash over whole painting

1 Weak wash
Establish the composition with a loose pencil sketch. Mix a wash of yellow ochre with a hint of cadmium red to enrich the color. Use a large soft-hair mop to apply a weak wash across the whole painting.

2 Strong wash
Using the same colors, but in a more concentrated mix, apply a second wash. This time, paint around the sacks to make them stand out from the background.

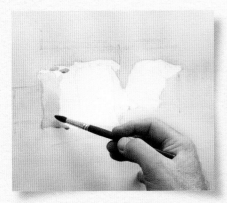

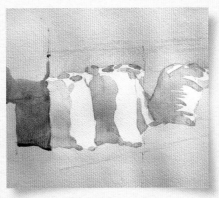

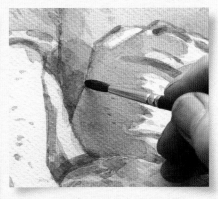

3 Shadow tone
Using a no. 6 soft-hair brush and a mix of blue and violet, add shadows to the sacks. This establishes the direction of the light and conveys the sacks' rounded shapes.

4 Background tone
Add the background tone using a mix of violet and yellow ochre. This sets the sacks in context, further reveals their shape, and emphasizes the light falling on them.

5 Final details
Refine and strengthen the shadows, warming them slightly with yellow ochre. Finally, add the details of the folds and textures of the sacks to finish the painting.

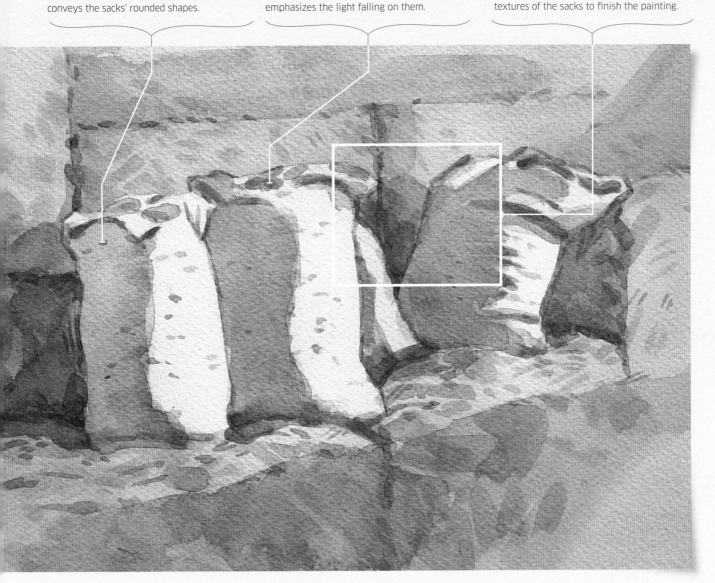

Simplifying a scene

HOW TO APPROACH A PAINTING

Always spend time planning each painting before you start. As a general rule, aim for a ratio of ten minutes' planning to one minute's painting. Use this planning time to find ways of breaking down a potentially complex subject into manageable sections. Look for one main focal point, and don't be afraid to rearrange elements of the scene if it improves the composition.

Creating a composition

A good composition consists of a few distinct shapes—some light, some dark. Link several small shapes to create a few large ones, and then create a tonal contrast between them. Don't try to paint everything you see; instead, choose one focal point and remove or subdue anything that doesn't enhance it. Keep the foreground simple to provide a restful space before the main subject.

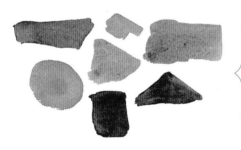

Isolated shapes
The space around these simple shapes isolates them. Several disconnected elements can be distracting, as the eye jumps from one to another.

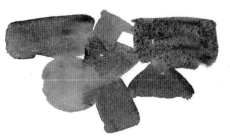

Combined shapes
Connecting the shapes promotes harmony, and we see them as a single entity. This is useful when planning the background.

PUTTING IT INTO PRACTICE

The clock tower makes a strong focal point, so simplify the scene by ignoring everything to the far right and left, making the painting portrait-shaped. The car is distracting, so that can go, too. Finally, connect the figures and shadows to make one interesting shape.

You will need

Aureolin yellow · Burnt sienna · Pyrrol red · French ultramarine

- No. 14 soft-hair mop; no. 6 and no. 10 round soft-hair brushes
- 10 x 8in (35 x 25cm) NOT watercolor paper

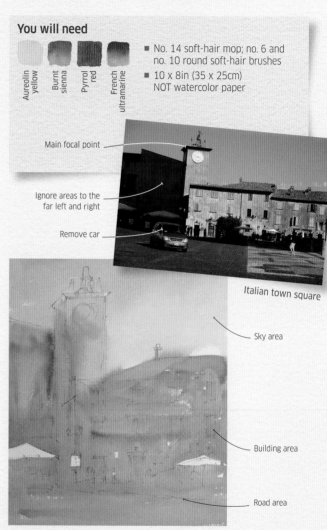

Main focal point

Ignore areas to the far left and right

Remove car

Italian town square

Sky area

Building area

Road area

1 Three main areas

Loosely sketch the scene, then paint the sky, buildings, and road as if there were no shadows. Use a no. 14 mop and apply as few strokes as possible. Start at the top and work steadily down. Begin with ultramarine, then add burnt sienna for the buildings and a little more ultramarine for the road.

"A ratio of **ten minutes of planning** for every minute of painting will give you the chance to find ways of **simplifying** the composition."

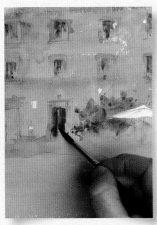

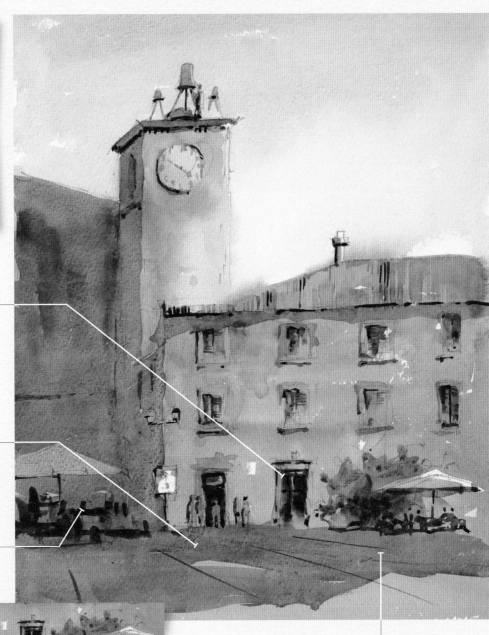

2 Initial details
When the first washes are dry, add detail to the windows and doors using a no. 6 round brush. They will look more natural if you don't paint the whole shapes. Add more detail to the tops of the objects than the bottoms.

3 Shadow areas
Paint the shadows as one shape with a wash of red and ultramarine over the buildings and road. Start at the top and work down in one pass.

4 Simple figures
Loosely indicate the shapes of the people, without painting them as separate figures.

5 Finishing off
Add finer details using a dark mix of ultramarine and burnt sienna. This will suggest an animated scene underneath the parasols.

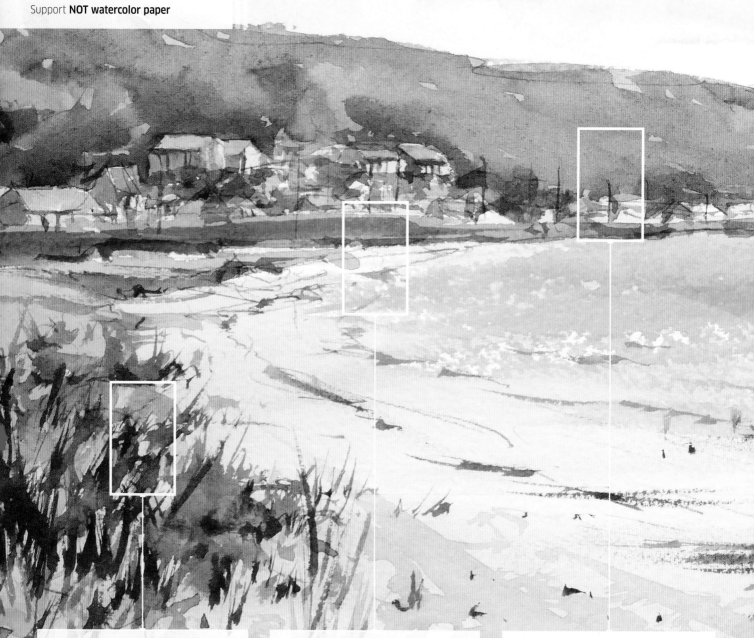

Artist **Grahame Booth**
Title **Glenarm, Antrim Coast**
Medium **Watercolor**
Support **NOT watercolor paper**

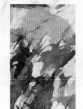

Brushstrokes
<< See pp. 50–51
A range of brushstrokes was used to paint the grass in the foreground. The tip and side of a round brush were used to suggest single blades and larger clumps.

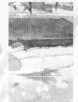

Wet-in-wet and wet-on-dry
<< See pp. 52–53
The sea and sand were painted wet-in-wet so they blend together, while the distant wall and grass were picked out using wet-on-dry.

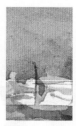

Tone
<< See pp. 46–47
A broad range of tones and hues were used to create contrast and structure throughout the painting.

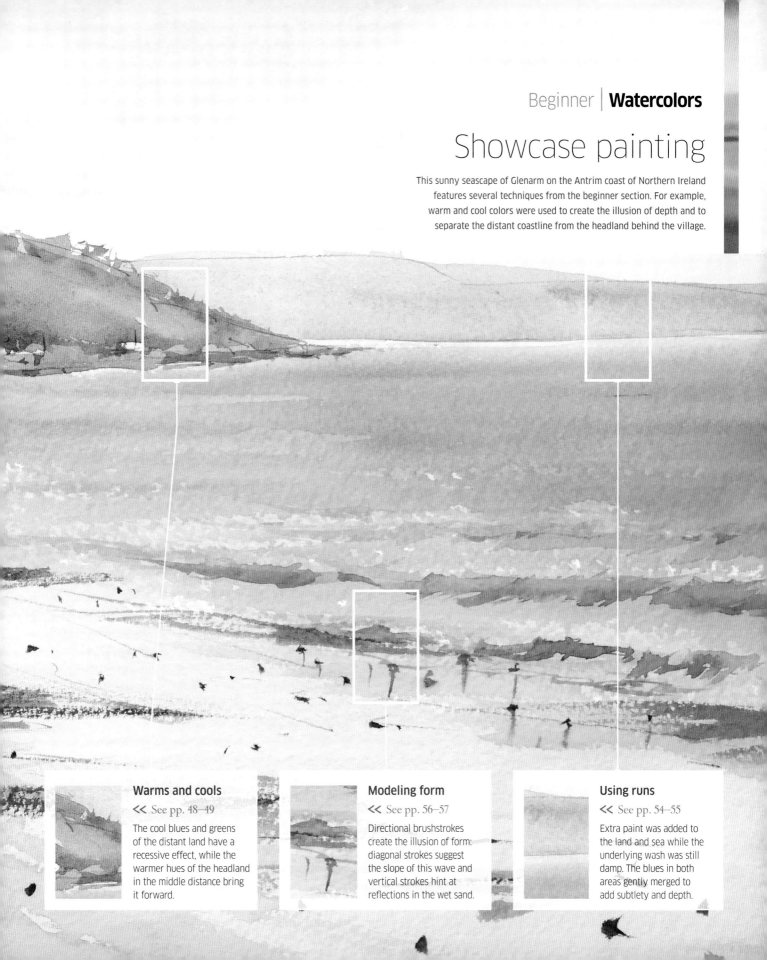

Showcase painting

This sunny seascape of Glenarm on the Antrim coast of Northern Ireland features several techniques from the beginner section. For example, warm and cool colors were used to create the illusion of depth and to separate the distant coastline from the headland behind the village.

Warms and cools

« See pp. 48–49

The cool blues and greens of the distant land have a recessive effect, while the warmer hues of the headland in the middle distance bring it forward.

Modeling form

« See pp. 56–57

Directional brushstrokes create the illusion of form: diagonal strokes suggest the slope of this wave and vertical strokes hint at reflections in the wet sand.

Using runs

« See pp. 54–55

Extra paint was added to the land and sea while the underlying wash was still damp. The blues in both areas gently merged to add subtlety and depth.

Laying a flat wash

APPLYING EVEN COLOR

Laying a flat wash is a key watercolor skill. Although the idea is a simple one—applying a wash of paint so that it dries to an even tone throughout—the technique can be surprisingly difficult to perfect. Flat washes are useful for backgrounds and skies.

■ Mix and lay a wash

Mix a darker wash than you think you'll need, because watercolor dries lighter. Mix plenty of paint so you don't run out halfway through. Set the board at a shallow angle to allow the paint to run down the paper.

Paint at a slight angle — 30°

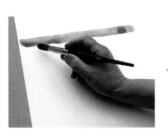

One continuous stroke
Choose a brush size commensurate with the size of the wash area. Load the brush fully, then, starting at the top, paint across the paper in one continuous stroke.

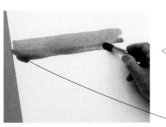

Pick up the bead
Immediately reload the brush and repeat the process, picking up the bead of color left by the previous brushstroke. This helps the strokes to blend.

Bead runs along bottom of stroke

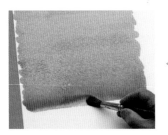

Repeat the process
Continue until you have covered the whole area. Mop up any surplus moisture at the bottom of the wash using a dry brush or piece of paper towel. Lay the board flat and allow the wash to dry thoroughly.

PUTTING IT INTO PRACTICE

In this tabletop still life with apples and a vase, a flat wash was used to create the green background. The wash was painted around the outlines of the objects with the paper turned upside down.

You will need

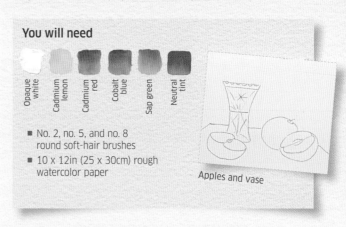

Opaque white   Cadmium lemon   Cadmium red   Cobalt blue   Sap green   Neutral tint

- No. 2, no. 5, and no. 8 round soft-hair brushes
- 10 x 12in (25 x 30cm) rough watercolor paper

Apples and vase

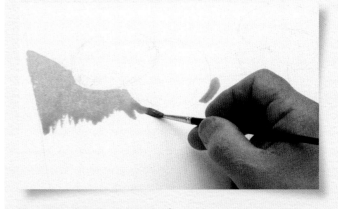

1 Turn paper upside down
Lightly sketch the scene, and then turn the paper upside down. This will allow the wash to run away from the outlines of the objects. Set the board at a slight angle and mix a wash of sap green. Using a no. 5 round brush, carefully work the wash around the edges of the apples.

"Raise the board slightly so the **wash runs down,** then work **from top to bottom** in one sitting."

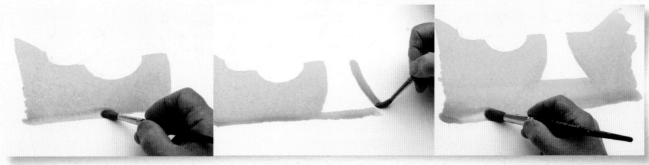

Pick up the bead

Work around the outlines

Keep the bottom edge wet across the paper

2 Work around the outlines
Continue laying the wash from top to bottom, carefully working up to and around the edges of the vase and tabletop. Once you are clear of the objects, work across the paper using continuous strokes, always keeping the bottom edge of the wash wet.

3 Tablecloth and vase
When the background wash is completely dry, repeat the process for the tablecloth using cobalt blue and neutral tint. When that's dry, add the detail on the vase using cobalt blue, neutral tint, sap green, and opaque white.

4 Apples
Apply a pale wash of cadmium lemon for the flesh of the cut apple and a darker wash of mainly cadmium red for the skins.

5 Final details
Allow the washes on the apples to dry, then add streaks of cadmium red, sap green, and opaque white to the skins. Finally, paint the seeds and stem in neutral tint.

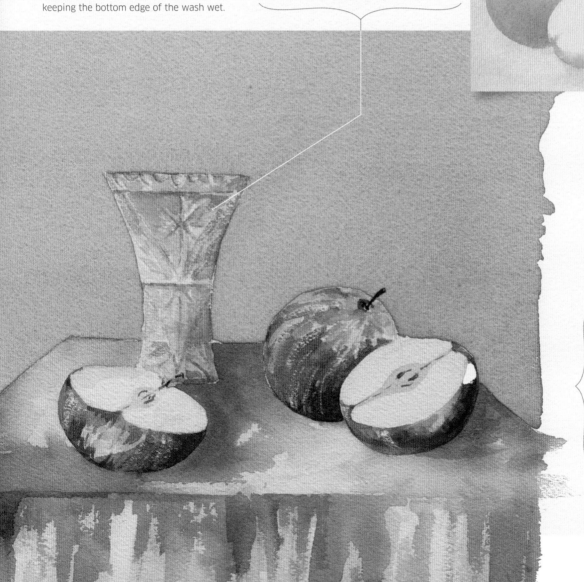

Laying a gradated wash

APPLYING GRADATED COLOR

A gradated wash fades smoothly from a strong tone to a weak tone. It is achieved by adding water to your wash little by little as you paint.

▮ Laying the wash

Set up your board at an angle of 30 degrees so that the wash will spread downward. Mix more paint for the wash than you think you'll need, and keep some clean water on hand.

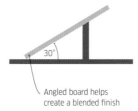

30°

Angled board helps create a blended finish

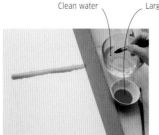

Clean water   Large quantity of paint mix

1 First line of wash
Dampen the area to be painted. Lay the first line of wash along the top. Dip the brush in the clean water, then immediately recharge it with paint.

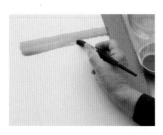

2 Subsequent lines
Pick up the bead of paint from the first line as you lay the second line of wash. Dip your brush in clean water before you pick up paint for each subsequent stroke.

3 Finishing the wash
Continue working down the paper, diluting the wash a little more with each line you paint until it fades out. Mop up excess moisture at the bottom, lay the paper flat, and allow it to dry.

A blue, gradated sky sets the mood in this atmospheric landscape. Don't pause while laying your wash—it could dry unevenly, leaving unwanted marks. Work quickly and with confidence.

You will need

Lemon yellow Yellow ochre Raw sienna Burnt sienna Burnt umber Cobalt blue Sap green Neutral tint

- No. 16 synthetic–soft-hair mix, no. 8 soft-hair, no. 5 soft-hair, and no. 2 soft-hair brushes
- Jar of clean water
- 16 x 22in (40 x 55cm) rough watercolor paper

Coastal castle

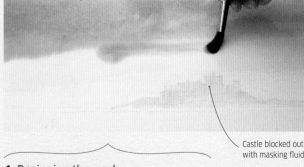

Castle blocked out with masking fluid

1 Beginning the wash
Sketch your composition and apply masking fluid over the castle using an old brush. Mix plenty of cobalt blue for the wash. Dampen the paper in the sky area, then apply the wash along the top with a large synthetic–soft-hair brush.

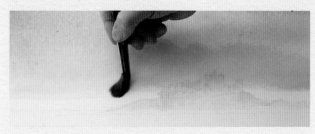

2 Completing the wash
Apply continuous strokes from one side to the other, dipping your brush in clean water before recharging it with paint for each stroke. Lay the wash down to the horizon, painting over the masked castle.

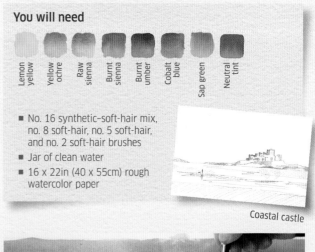

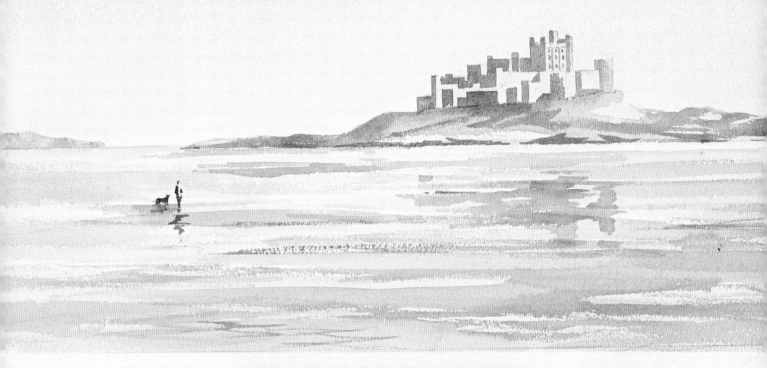

"A graduated sky that reaches down to the horizon creates a feeling of wide, open space."

5 Completing the scene
When the foreground sand colors are dry, paint in the sea. Paint the castle simply to keep the focus on the sea and sky. Finally, add the figures of the man and dog, which give the painting a sense of scale.

Textured dry brushstrokes

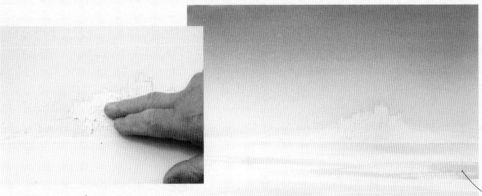

3 Removing the mask
When the wash is completely dry, rub off the masking fluid from the castle.

4 Foreground
Paint the sandbars in yellow ochre. When the ochre is dry, apply raw umber and burnt umber over the top using dry brushstrokes (see pp. 50-51 and 74-75).

Lively darks

AVOIDING FLAT, DULL COLOR

One of the most appealing qualities of watercolor is its transparency. Solid dark colors, however, do not have the same transparency as lighter colors and can sometimes look flat and dull. Applying darks quickly and simply will make them look fresh and lively.

■ Creating depth and contrast

Try not to overwork darks when you apply them, as using too many brushstrokes, or "scrubbing," can lead to a muddy look. Create tonal contrast in adjacent areas to lift flat-looking darks, and punctuate a dark wash by leaving areas of white paper or applying opaque white paint on top.

Flat wash
This swatch was applied correctly with just four brushstrokes, a loaded brush, and without scrubbing. However, you will need to add tonal contrast in adjacent areas to add interest.

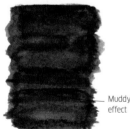

Muddy effect

Scrubbed paint
This swatch has been scrubbed on with a brush that is too dry, using too many brushstrokes. It looks flat and muddy.

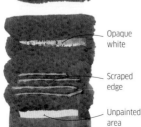

Opaque white

Scraped edge

Unpainted area

Adding white
Either leave some white areas of paper as you apply darks, or scrape off areas of paint using your fingernail or the edge of a credit card. On dry paint, you can apply opaque white or gouache.

PUTTING IT INTO PRACTICE

In this scene, the dark colors used for the grass and the light colors used for the rocks contrast well. Added points of interest were created by scraping the darkest areas to create streaks of white.

You will need

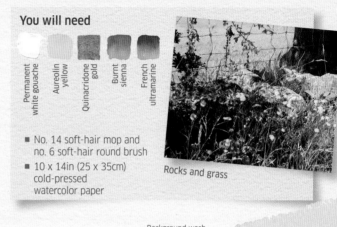

Permanent white gouache
Aureolin yellow
Quinacridone gold
Burnt sienna
French ultramarine

- No. 14 soft-hair mop and no. 6 soft-hair round brush
- 10 x 14in (25 x 35cm) cold-pressed watercolor paper

Rocks and grass

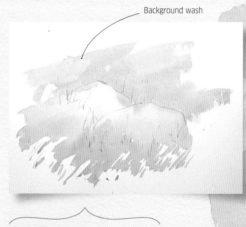

Background wash

1 Simple wash
Using a soft-hair mop, apply a simple wash of ultramarine and gold for the grassy areas, and a wash of French ultramarine and sienna for the rocks.

"Aim to **apply dark watercolor** quickly **and simply, without overworking.**"

2 Dark areas
Build up the grass behind the rocks with quick strokes of your round brush to suggest individual blades of grass. Darken the area with French ultramarine and burnt sienna to contrast with the tops of the rocks. Lift the darks by scraping areas with a credit card. This breaks up the dark tone and suggests grasslike stalks. Dampen the tops of the rocks and add a little darker wash of ultramarine and sienna to suggest their roundness.

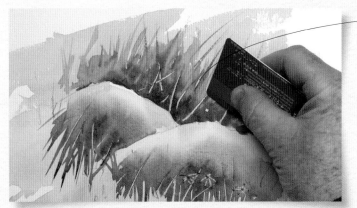

Scrape darks to create highlights

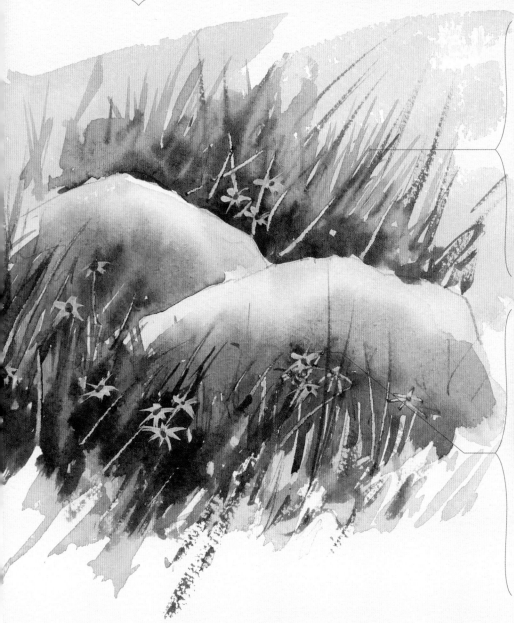

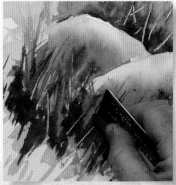

3 Foreground grasses
Repeat the technique to create the grassy area in the foreground. Again, scrape dark areas with a credit card to create white strokes.

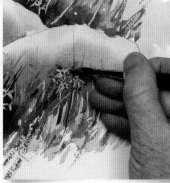

4 Flower details
Finally, still using a round brush, apply an opaque mix of aureolin yellow and permanent white to the darkest areas to suggest the flower petals. Add a darker dot of paint for the center of each flower.

Aerial perspective

EVOKING DEPTH AND DISTANCE

Aerial (or atmospheric) perspective enables you to suggest depth by simulating the effect of the atmosphere on distant objects. The farther light has to travel, the more diffused it becomes. This makes colors look softer and details less defined, the farther they are from the viewer.

■ Portraying distant objects

Atmosphere affects objects in proportion to their distance from the viewer—colors become cooler and graduate to blue-gray, light and dark tones gradually lose contrast, details diminish, and sharp edges look softer. Divide your subject into background, middle ground, and foreground to portray these effects. Apply little or no detail to the background, then add more detail and stronger color as you work toward the foreground of your painting.

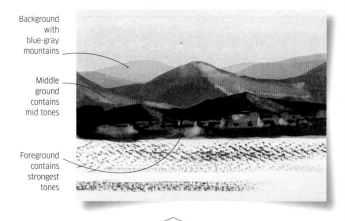

Background with blue-gray mountains

Middle ground contains mid tones

Foreground contains strongest tones

Distant mountains
You may have noticed aerial perspective when looking at a mountain range. The farthest mountains appear faint and bluish, and there are distinct changes of color with each layer of hills.

Aerial perspective can create the illusion of depth even when it might not be obvious to the naked eye in real life, as you can see in this painting of a nearby group of trees.

You will need

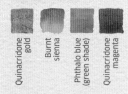

Quinacridone gold

Burnt sienna

Phthalo blue (green shade)

Quinacridone magenta

- No. 14 soft-hair mop, no. 10 and no. 8 round soft-hair brushes, and a small soft-hair sword liner
- 14 x 10in (35 x 25cm) cold-pressed watercolor paper

Group of trees

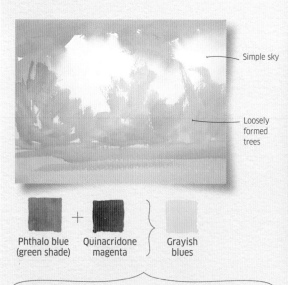

Simple sky

Loosely formed trees

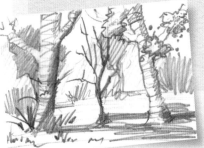

Phthalo blue (green shade) + Quinacridone magenta } Grayish blues

1 Background
Paint a simple sky and allow it to dry. Mix a pale grayish blue for the trees in the background, then paint them as a flat wash with a mop brush. Don't include details such as leaves and branches at this point—the background shapes will make sense when you add trees in front.

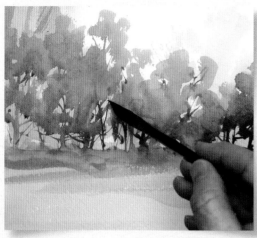

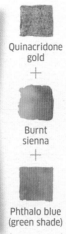

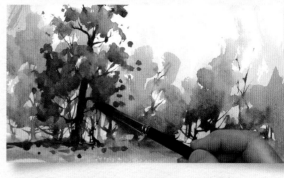

Quinacridone
gold

+

Burnt
sienna

+

Phthalo blue
(green shade)

Greens

Phthalo blue
(green shade) + Quinacridone
magenta + Burnt
sienna } Darks

2 Middle ground

Paint the trees in the middle ground with various tones of green, to distinguish them from the flat background. Use light strokes with a fine brush, such as a sword liner, to suggest trunks and branches, but don't add too much detail.

3 First foreground tree

Make the tonal differences between light and shade more obvious in the foreground. Paint the leaves with lots of tonal variety to show which areas are in sunlight and which are in shade. Add dark branches that stand out from the leaves.

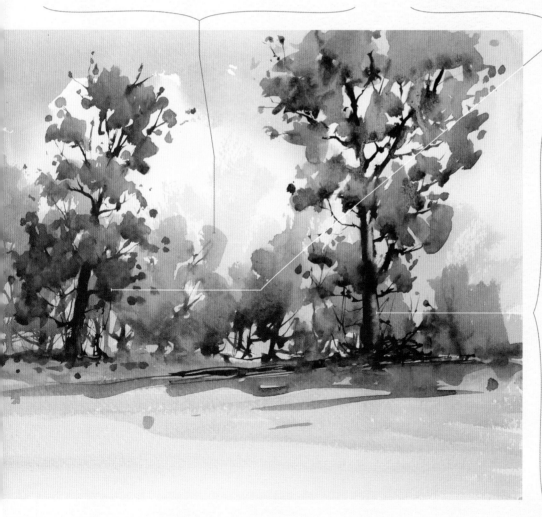

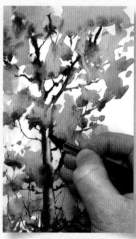

4 Closest foreground tree

The tree closest to the viewer needs the most detail, color, and tonal variety. Lift out some dark color from the right side of the trunk using a damp round, soft-hair brush to give the trunk more form.

Edges

HARD AND SOFT OUTLINES

Controlling the hardness or softness of edges is the main way to focus the eye on an object or shape. Hard edges are crisp and well defined, and draw the eye in, whereas soft edges blend into one another and seem to disappear. Being able to create hard and soft edges is one of the fundamental skills of watercolor painting.

▇ Relationships between objects

In general, use hard edges to define two objects that are *not* physically connected, such as a building against the sky. Use soft edges, on the other hand, to link two objects that *are* physically connected, such as a building and the ground on which it stands. In practice, it is best to convey objects with a variety of edges, both hard and soft. Avoid giving an object hard edges on all sides, as this separates it entirely from the rest of the painting.

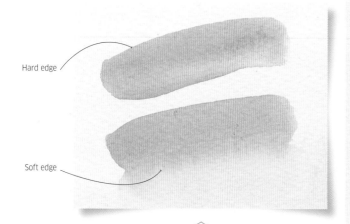

Hard edge

Soft edge

Creating hard and soft edges

Make a hard edge by simply painting wet onto dry. You can soften a wet edge with a gentle touch of a damp, but not wet, brush, or paint a second wash alongside the first, allowing the wet edges to touch.

This study of a window with shutters makes use of both hard and soft edges. It starts with softer edges that are then worked into. Hard edges have been added for definition and detail.

You will need

Quinacridone gold | Burnt sienna | Pyrrol red | Quinacridone magenta | Phthalo blue | French ultramarine | Phthalo green

- No. 14 soft-hair mop and no. 6 soft-hair round brush
- 14 x 10in (35 x25cm) cold-pressed watercolor paper

Window and shutters

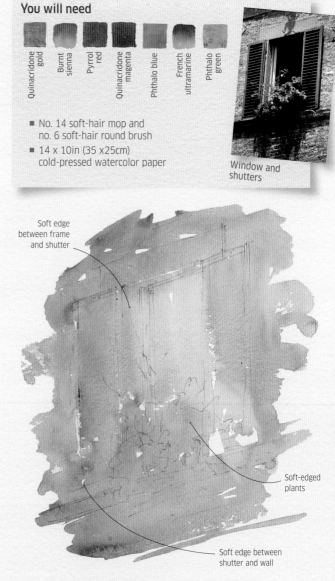

Soft edge between frame and shutter

Soft-edged plants

Soft edge between shutter and wall

1 Soft edges

Begin by creating soft edges between the frame, shutters, plants, and wall. To achieve this, apply a soft wet wash against another wet wash and then allow it to dry.

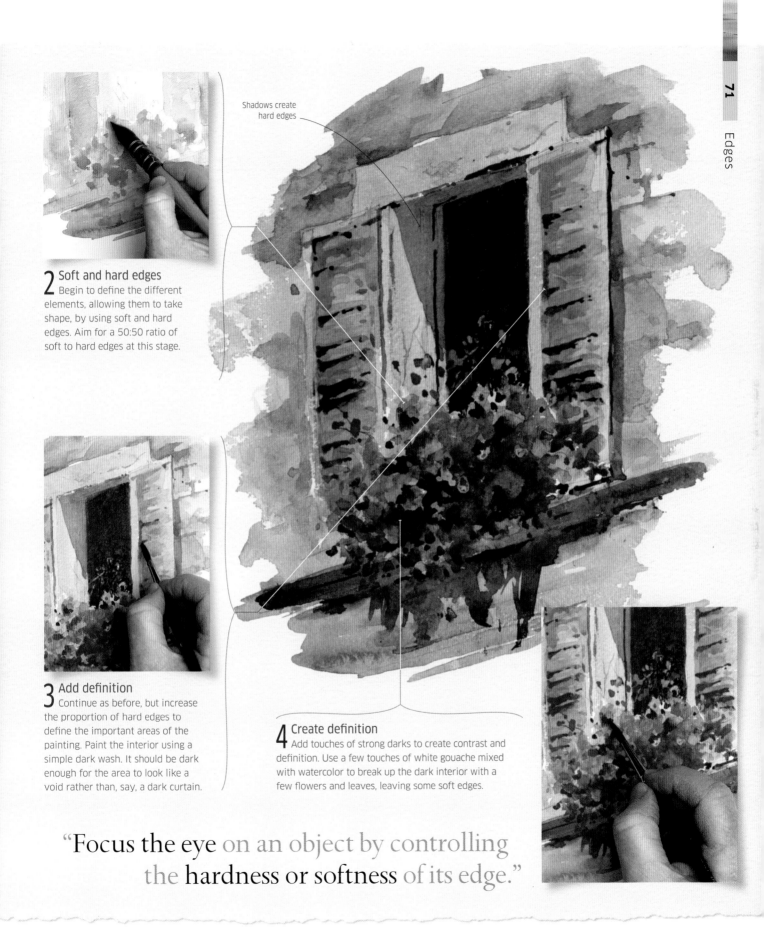

Shadows create
hard edges

2 Soft and hard edges
Begin to define the different elements, allowing them to take shape, by using soft and hard edges. Aim for a 50:50 ratio of soft to hard edges at this stage.

3 Add definition
Continue as before, but increase the proportion of hard edges to define the important areas of the painting. Paint the interior using a simple dark wash. It should be dark enough for the area to look like a void rather than, say, a dark curtain.

4 Create definition
Add touches of strong darks to create contrast and definition. Use a few touches of white gouache mixed with watercolor to break up the dark interior with a few flowers and leaves, leaving some soft edges.

"Focus the eye on an object by controlling the hardness or softness of its edge."

Highlights

SHOWING THE DIRECTION OF LIGHT

Highlights show how light falls on the illuminated or prominent forms in your composition, and are therefore the lightest tones in your painting. They are essential for creating a three-dimensional effect. In watercolor painting, the lightest tone is usually the paper, so you can create highlights by leaving some paper unpainted, or use opaque white paint to add highlights on top of painted areas.

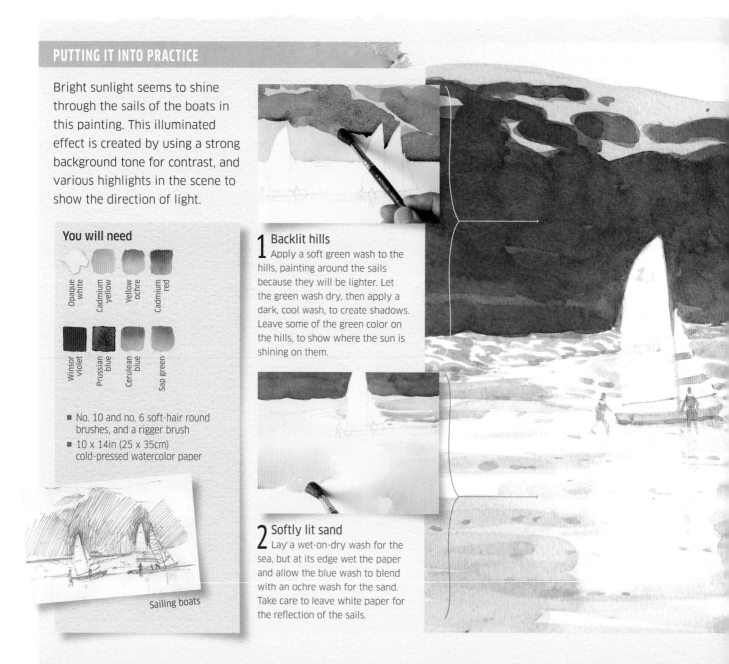

PUTTING IT INTO PRACTICE

Bright sunlight seems to shine through the sails of the boats in this painting. This illuminated effect is created by using a strong background tone for contrast, and various highlights in the scene to show the direction of light.

You will need

Opaque white   Cadmium yellow   Yellow ochre   Cadmium red

Winsor violet   Prussian blue   Cerulean blue   Sap green

- No. 10 and no. 6 soft-hair round brushes, and a rigger brush
- 10 x 14in (25 x 35cm) cold-pressed watercolor paper

Sailing boats

1 Backlit hills

Apply a soft green wash to the hills, painting around the sails because they will be lighter. Let the green wash dry, then apply a dark, cool wash, to create shadows. Leave some of the green color on the hills, to show where the sun is shining on them.

2 Softly lit sand

Lay a wet-on-dry wash for the sea, but at its edge wet the paper and allow the blue wash to blend with an ochre wash for the sand. Take care to leave white paper for the reflection of the sails.

■ Highlights and contrast

A white highlight will not show up against a pale value, so your highlights need to be contrasted with stronger tones. This will ensure that the highlights "read" as light falling on a subject. Using a good range of tones to indicate light and dark is the key to painting highlights successfully.

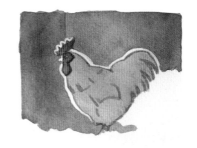

Opaque white highlights
Here, an opaque white highlight gives the chicken shape and form. The dark background suggests that the highlight is a light source behind the chicken.

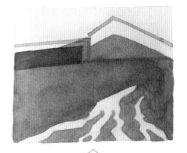

Painting around highlights
This blue wash leaves some of the pale wash below exposed, evoking light sparkling on water. Plan which areas to paint around if you use this method.

Contrast of soft green with deep blue indicates strong light behind the hills

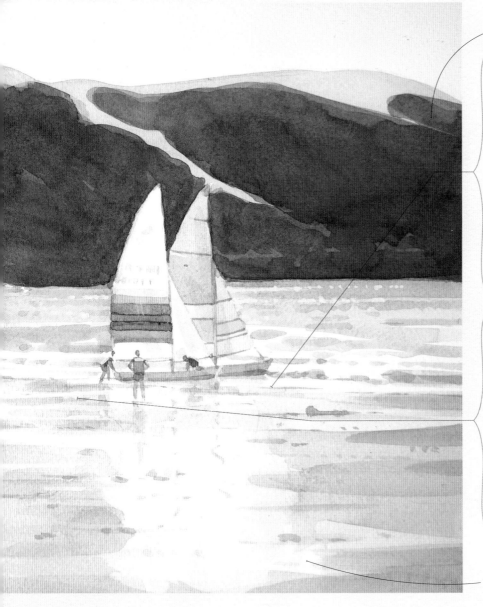

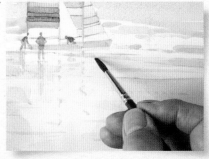

3 Strong colors
Paint in the figures and add strong color on the sails, to show that they are in full sun. Apply very light shadows to show the backlighting on the sails. Strengthen the tone of the reflections on the sand.

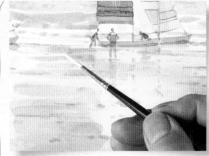

4 Final highlights
Use a rigger brush to apply final, bright highlights in opaque white paint on the sea, sails, and figures.

White paper indicates the reflection of the sails

Adding texture

USING BRUSHES AND PENS

By using different brushstrokes and pen marks, you can build up layers of texture. For example, use the side of an almost-dry brush to create a scratchy effect or the tip of the brush for fine detail. For more experimental textural effects, see pp. 86–87.

■ Smooth and rough textures

Round brushes are the most versatile for adding texture. Use the side of the brush with washes of various dilutions to build up initial layers, the side of an almost dry brush for a scratchy look, and the tip for fine lines. For precise details, use a dip pen or fiber-tip pen, and for highlights, use opaque white paint or white pastel, or gently scratch out the area with a sharp blade.

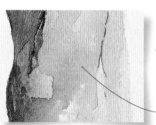

Smooth trunk
This smooth-looking section of tree trunk was created using wet washes. Various light and dark tones were used to create form.

Wet wash gives a smooth finish

Texture 1

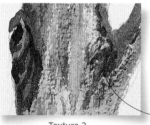

Semi-rough trunk
Once the initial washes had dried, the side of an almost-dry brush was dragged across the surface to develop the texture of the bark. Darker tones were also used.

Undiluted paint for the darkest tones

Texture 2

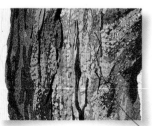

Rough trunk
Details were picked out using a dip pen with a steel nib and black paint. Excess paint was shaken off the nib to prevent blots. Highlights were added in white pastel.

Texture 3

White pastel highlights

PUTTING IT INTO PRACTICE

In this study of a country church and churchyard, the viewer's eye is drawn to the large tree in the foreground. The tree, which was painted first, includes multiple layers of texture on its trunk.

You will need

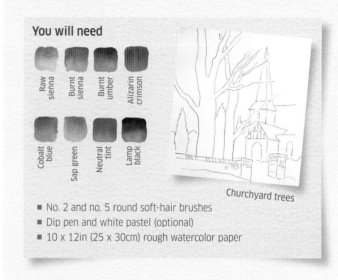

Raw sienna | Burnt sienna | Burnt umber | Alizarin crimson

Cobalt blue | Sap green | Neutral tint | Lamp black

Churchyard trees

- No. 2 and no. 5 round soft-hair brushes
- Dip pen and white pastel (optional)
- 10 x 12in (25 x 30cm) rough watercolor paper

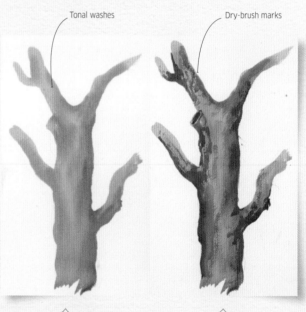

Tonal washes

Dry-brush marks

1 Initial washes
Loosely sketch the scene in pencil, paying particular attention to the foreground tree. Apply pale washes of burnt sienna, burnt umber, and neutral tint to establish the basic color and form.

2 Building texture
When the initial washes are dry, start adding texture. Load a no. 5 round brush with a darker mix than the background, and squeeze out most of the moisture. Drag the side of the almost-dry brush over parts of the trunk.

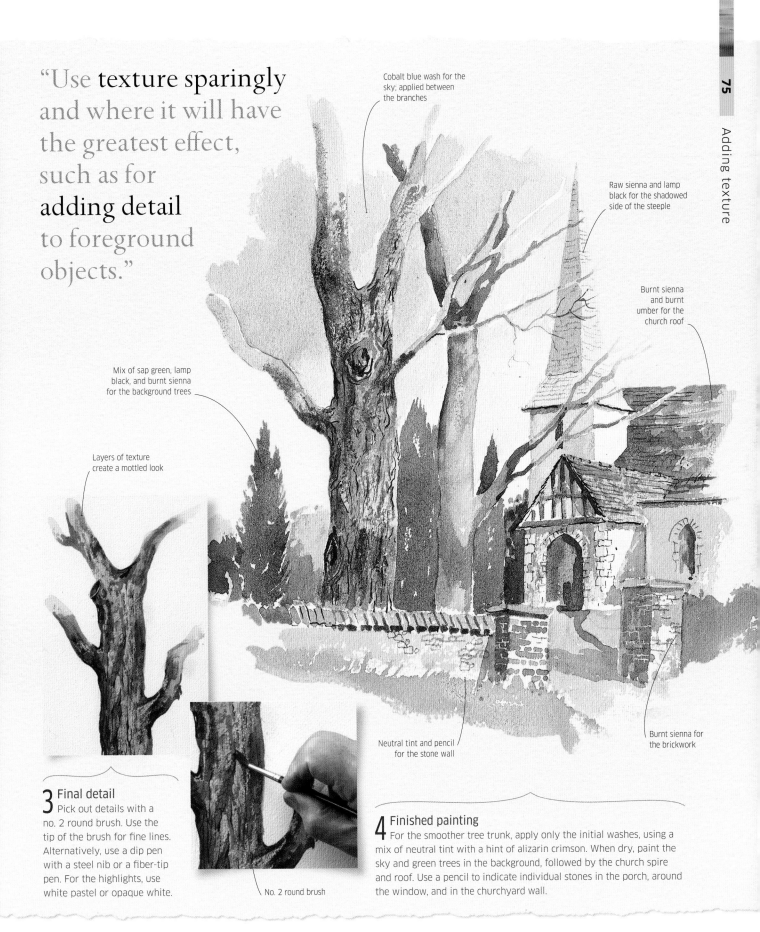

"Use **texture sparingly** and where it will have the greatest effect, such as for **adding detail** to foreground objects."

Cobalt blue wash for the sky; applied between the branches

Raw sienna and lamp black for the shadowed side of the steeple

Burnt sienna and burnt umber for the church roof

Mix of sap green, lamp black, and burnt sienna for the background trees

Layers of texture create a mottled look

Neutral tint and pencil for the stone wall

Burnt sienna for the brickwork

3 Final detail
Pick out details with a no. 2 round brush. Use the tip of the brush for fine lines. Alternatively, use a dip pen with a steel nib or a fiber-tip pen. For the highlights, use white pastel or opaque white.

No. 2 round brush

4 Finished painting
For the smoother tree trunk, apply only the initial washes, using a mix of neutral tint with a hint of alizarin crimson. When dry, paint the sky and green trees in the background, followed by the church spire and roof. Use a pencil to indicate individual stones in the porch, around the window, and in the churchyard wall.

Paper surfaces

THE EFFECT OF TEXTURE AND WETNESS

Rough paper creates a broken wash because the paint sits on the "peaks" of the paper. Cold-pressed paper is smoother, which allows you to create flatter, even washes. The wetness of your surface also has a bearing: use wet paper for soft, luminous washes and dry paper for strong color and detail.

■ Wet, damp, and dry paper

Practice working on wet and dry surfaces to help you see what effects they have. If your paint mix is too watery, when you put it on damp paper it may disturb the pigment and create watermarks. You must judge whether your paint mix is correct, or whether the paper is too wet to take the paint.

Wet paper
Prepare your color mix first. Wet the paper, then brush on the color. Avoid reworking, to prevent marks. You won't be able to fully control how the wash disperses.

Damp paper
Apply a wash when the paper has dried a little but is still damp. The wash will bleed but it won't disperse as much as on wet paper, resulting in a stronger color.

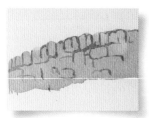

Dry paper
Lay a wash of color on dry paper. It will create a crisp, hard edge, and you'll have more control over the wash. For adding detail, the paper must be dry.

PUTTING IT INTO PRACTICE

Cold-pressed paper was ideal for laying the soft, even washes in this painting. Wet- and damp-paper washes suggest a view of distant hills through rain, while dry-paper washes sharpen the foreground for contrast.

You will need

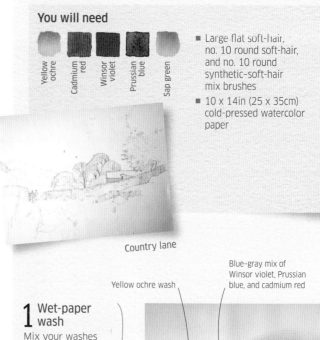

Yellow ochre

Cadmium red

Winsor violet

Prussian blue

Sap green

- Large flat soft-hair, no. 10 round soft-hair, and no. 10 round synthetic-soft-hair mix brushes
- 10 x 14in (25 x 35cm) cold-pressed watercolor paper

Country lane

Yellow ochre wash

Blue-gray mix of Winsor violet, Prussian blue, and cadmium red

1 **Wet-paper wash**
Mix your washes first. Wet the paper with clean water, then apply a blue–gray wash to the hills, working from the top downward so you can better control the line of the hills. Apply a yellow wash in the foreground.

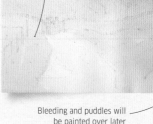

Bleeding and puddles will be painted over later

2 **Damp-paper wash**
While the paper is still damp, add a darker tone of gray to show the nearer hills and trees. The soft edges suggest aerial perspective (see pp. 70–71).

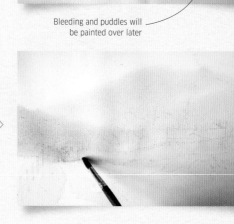

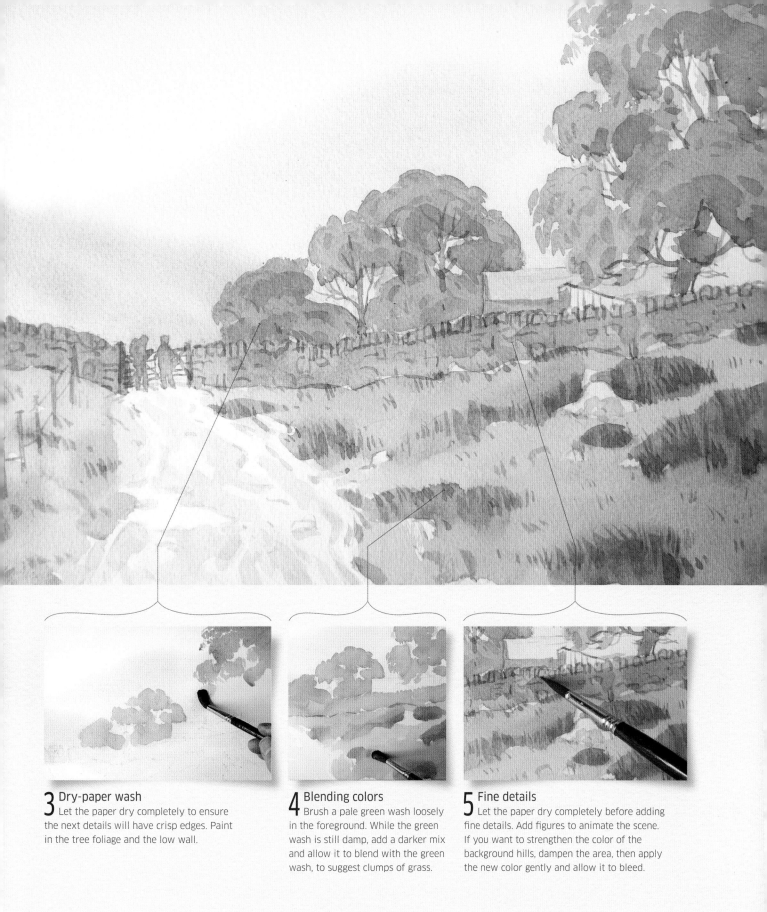

3 Dry-paper wash

Let the paper dry completely to ensure the next details will have crisp edges. Paint in the tree foliage and the low wall.

4 Blending colors

Brush a pale green wash loosely in the foreground. While the green wash is still damp, add a darker mix and allow it to blend with the green wash, to suggest clumps of grass.

5 Fine details

Let the paper dry completely before adding fine details. Add figures to animate the scene. If you want to strengthen the color of the background hills, dampen the area, then apply the new color gently and allow it to bleed.

Correcting errors

IN WET OR DRY PAINT

Despite watercolor's reputation for being difficult, you can correct small mistakes. Your options depend on the scale of the error (extensive mistakes may be too hard to rescue), the type of pigment, and the type of paper you are working with.

Five ways to correct errors

You can tackle errors by incorporating them into the painting, removing them, painting over them or, for forgotten elements, adding them in later. You will need a sponge, paper towels, a scalpel, a stiff-bristle brush, and opaque white (gouache) in your "correction kit."

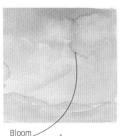
Bloom

Incorporating errors
Instead of removing errors, such as blooms, try incorporating them by changing a color, painting over it, or adding extra details around it.

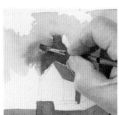

Lifting out
Mistakes in wet paint can be lifted out (blotted) right away using absorbent material, such as a damp sponge or a paper towel.

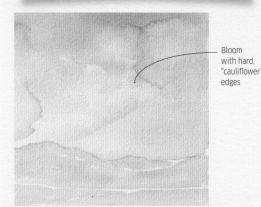

Scrubbing
Small patches of dry paint can be removed by scrubbing with a damp, stiff brush. This method is slightly abrasive, so take care with the paper.

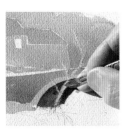

Scraping with a blade
On heavyweight paper, you can remove small details or make additions by gently scraping off dry paint with a fine blade or scalpel.

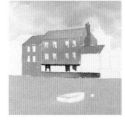

Using opaque white
You can add forgotten details with opaque white body color and then paint over it. This method is best for details rather than areas of wash.

Blooms, blobs, or bleeds don't have to be disastrous. If the error hasn't ruined your composition, consider adding an extra element–such as a tree–to disguise the area, or change the color or mood of the piece.

You will need
- Paints and brushes

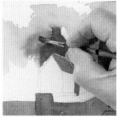
Bloom with hard, "cauliflower" edges

Problem
Blooms in the wash for the sky have dried unevenly, leaving unsightly "cauliflower" edges.

Solution
Leave the error to dry completely. Change the mood from light and sunny to cloudy and breezy to disguise the mistake in the sky.

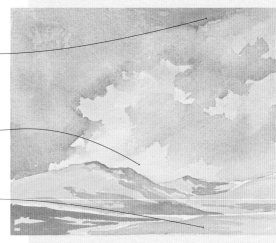
Hard-edged blooms incorporated by adding hard-edged dark clouds

Shadows of clouds added to hills and foreground

Lake added

LIFTING OUT

If you spot the error while the paint is still wet, deal with it immediately. Use a damp sponge or a paper towel to lift it out. If you apply more water to the offending area, the pigment will loosen and become easier to blot. Let the paper dry before painting over the area.

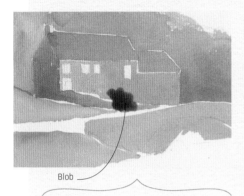

Blob

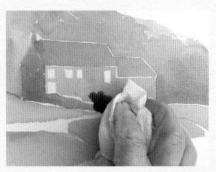

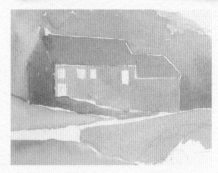

Problem
A blob of paint fell onto the painting from a wet brush. The dropped paint has not yet dried.

Solution
Wet the area immediately with water to loosen the pigment, then blot the error with a paper towel to lift it out.

Result
Once the paper is dry, repaint the whole front of the house and the wall to cover the blotted area seamlessly.

SCRUBBING

If an error dries before you can remove it, try dampening the area and gently scrubbing it with a stiff brush. Let the paper dry completely before repainting.

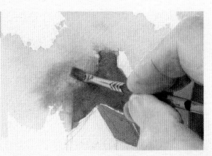

Solution–step 1

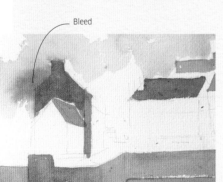

Bleed

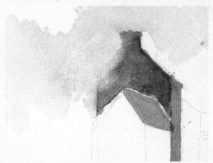

Solution–step 2

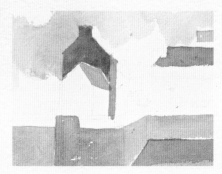

Problem
Two damp washes were placed side by side, and one bled into the other. The error wasn't dealt with before it dried.

Solution
Wet the area with water to loosen the pigment, then gently scrub off the paint with a damp bristle brush.

Result
Once the paper is dry, repaint the side of the house and the sky to cover the scrubbed areas.

SCRAPING WITH A BLADE

You can use a sharp blade or scalpel to remove dry paint when you need a more precise tool than a brush. This method is only suitable for robust, heavyweight paper—never use a blade on a delicate surface.

You will need
- Sharp blade or scalpel

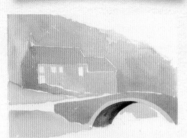

Problem
A tree is missing from the foreground because it was forgotten at an earlier stage.

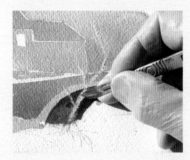

Solution
When the paper is dry, gently scrape the surface with a blade, teasing away the dry pigment to create the shape of the tree and branches.

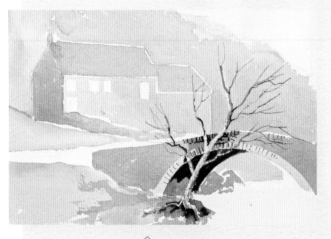

Result
Paint the tree over the scraped area using a small rigger brush. You can create highlights by leaving some of the scraped paper unpainted.

USING OPAQUE WHITE

If you need to amend or add a detail, you can cover the error with opaque white body color (gouache) or white acrylic ink, then repaint it. You may need to apply several layers of opaque white to obscure the error successfully.

You will need
- Opaque white body color (gouache) or white acrylic ink
- Round soft-hair brush

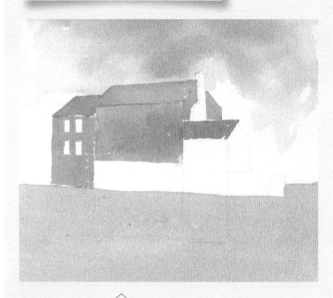

Problem
The dark flat washes on the house and water were painted without remembering to reserve white paper for the windows and boat. Now lighter colors need to be added on top.

"This method is **best for** areas where you can use **details to disguise** the edges of the **opaque paint.**"

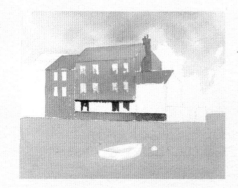

Solution – step 1
Add the windows and boat with opaque white body color. You might need to apply several layers of opaque white to cover the wash underneath effectively. Leave to dry.

Solution – step 2
Paint over the white areas with watercolor gently, to avoid pulling up the white color and mixing it with the new color. You might need to try this a few times to get it right.

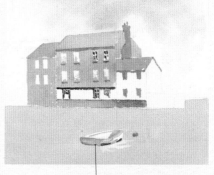

Tonal study applied first before glazing with red

Result
Once the initial tonal colors are dry, add the final colors on top. Add shadows and reflections around the boat to disguise the corrected area.

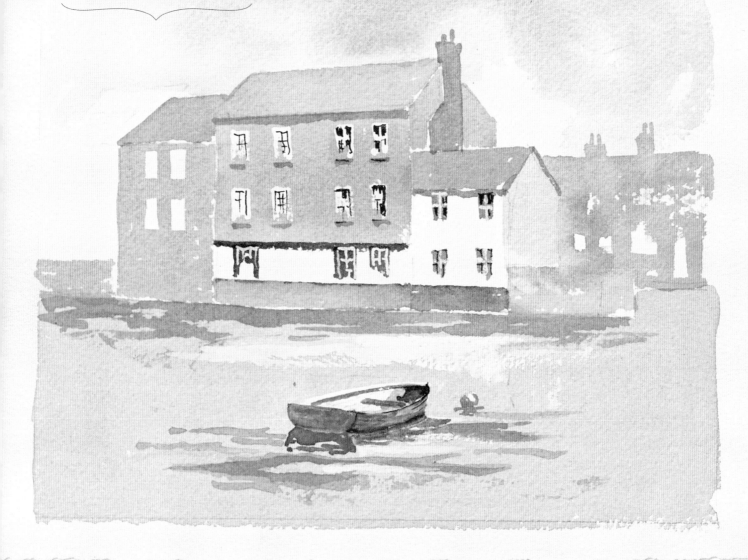

Reserving whites

CREATING LIGHT AREAS

It is not possible to apply a light watercolor tone over a dark one (unless you use opaque body color—see pp.112–13). Although you can remove paint from the paper, it is never as clean as leaving the paper untouched. The best way to create light areas is to leave "windows" of unpainted paper or a previous light wash. For tricky areas, use a resist, such as masking fluid, which you can remove later. You can then repaint the area if you wish.

PUTTING IT INTO PRACTICE

In this piece, the strong stage lighting on the pianist and piano needs to be sharp and bright—masking fluid is an ideal way of maintaining these lights. Other larger areas of white are simply left unpainted.

You will need

- Yellow ochre
- Winsor violet
- Payne's gray

- No. 10 soft-hair and rigger brushes
- Masking fluid
- 10 x 14in (25 x 35cm) cold-pressed watercolor paper

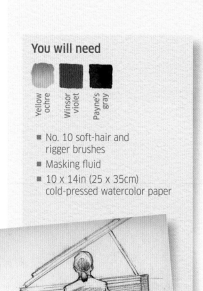

Piano recital

1 Apply masking fluid
Draw the pianist; then, with your no. 10 soft-hair brush, apply masking fluid to areas such as the keyboard, hair, piano edges, and floor. These are the areas that are illuminated by the stage lights.

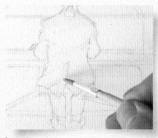

Masking fluid

Payne's gray and yellow ochre wash

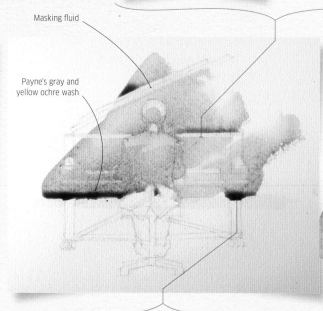

2 Dark wash
With the no. 10 brush, lay a dark wash for the background and for the shadow area underneath the piano. Use masking fluid to create a sharp edge along the bottom of the background, but paint the edges of the shadow freehand.

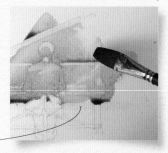

Masking fluid

Shadow painted freehand

Using masking fluid

Only apply masking fluid to dry paper or it will be very difficult to remove later. Wash brushes immediately after applying masking fluid, or they will be ruined. Avoid using your finest sable brush, even if you are careful about washing it promptly afterward. Over time, the soft hairs will become damaged.

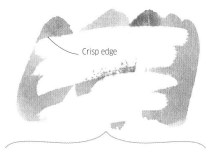

Crisp edge

Masking fluid
By applying masking fluid first, you can lay a wash freely over the top. When the wash dries, rub away the fluid to reveal white areas with crisp, clean edges.

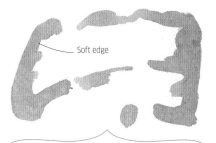

Soft edge

Leaving whites
If the edges left by masking fluid are too sharp, paint around white areas of paper for a looser feel. Keep the wet edge of the wash moving or it may dry with a visible line.

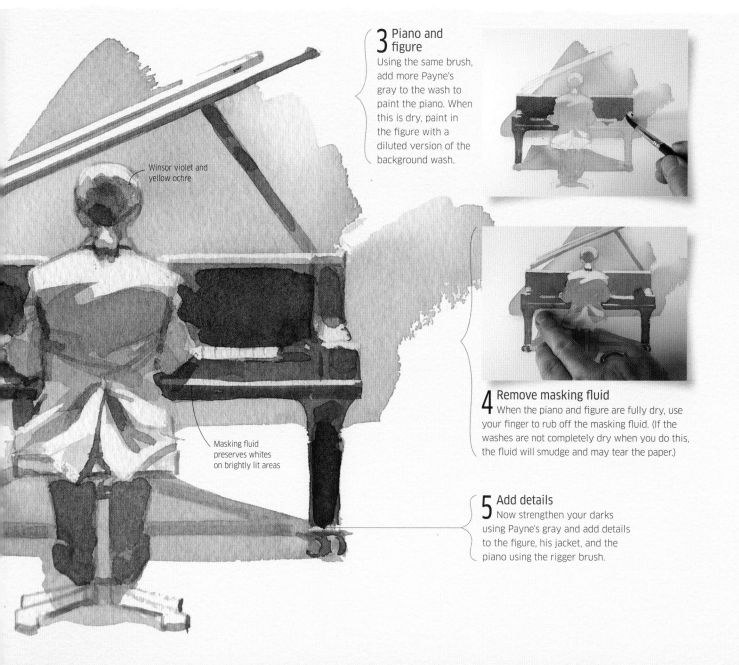

Winsor violet and yellow ochre

Masking fluid preserves whites on brightly lit areas

3 Piano and figure
Using the same brush, add more Payne's gray to the wash to paint the piano. When this is dry, paint in the figure with a diluted version of the background wash.

4 Remove masking fluid
When the piano and figure are fully dry, use your finger to rub off the masking fluid. (If the washes are not completely dry when you do this, the fluid will smudge and may tear the paper.)

5 Add details
Now strengthen your darks using Payne's gray and add details to the figure, his jacket, and the piano using the rigger brush.

Line and wash

USING PEN AND PAINTBRUSH TOGETHER

Line drawing adds structure and definition to watercolor washes. Make the lines as detailed or as minimal as you wish—altering the balance between line and wash creates different effects. You can also use this method as a way of making sketches and studies for later pictures.

▮ Balancing line and wash

You can use either line or wash to create structure, definition, tone, and form. For example, in a painting with tonal washes, you could add single lines to sharpen the edges, or dense crosshatching in place of dark tones. For line work, use a pencil, fiber-tip pen, or waterproof ink and a dip pen or brush.

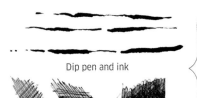

Dip pen and ink

{ **Line marks**
Pencils and fiber-tip pens create even, precise lines. Dip pens and brushes create irregular, characterful lines if you vary the pressure. You can hatch or crosshatch to add tone or texture.

Crosshatching with fiber-tip pen   Dense crosshatching with fiber-tip pen

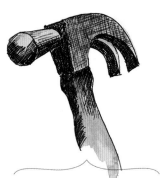 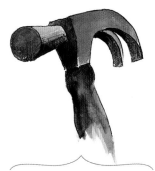

Heavy line, light wash
Here, the tonal range comes from crosshatching lines. The wash is flat and minimal. Heavy line looks prominent and is good for focal points and foreground details.

Light line, heavy wash
Here, the paint creates the tonal range, with lines playing a supporting role. Light line can help background areas recede in aerial perspective.

An intricate line drawing makes the mill the focal point in this painting. It is easiest to sketch in pencil first, so that you can correct errors, then redraw in ink.

You will need

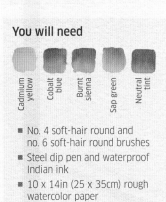

Cadmium yellow | Cobalt blue | Burnt sienna | Sap green | Neutral tint

- No. 4 soft-hair round and no. 6 soft-hair round brushes
- Steel dip pen and waterproof Indian ink
- 10 x 14in (25 x 35cm) rough watercolor paper

Watermill

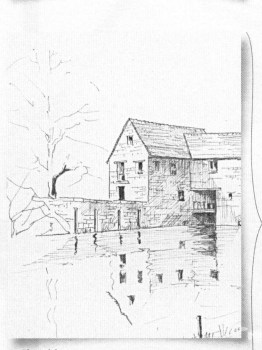

1 Sketching
Be free with your pen or pencil; you can easily ink over any mistakes. Hatch lines on the building to create shadows. Use fewer marks for the reflections and background to help them recede.

2 Light washes
Paint the sky with a wet-in-wet wash. Block in the water, hills, and and their reflections using a flat wash. Don't be too neat–keep the washes loose and fluid.

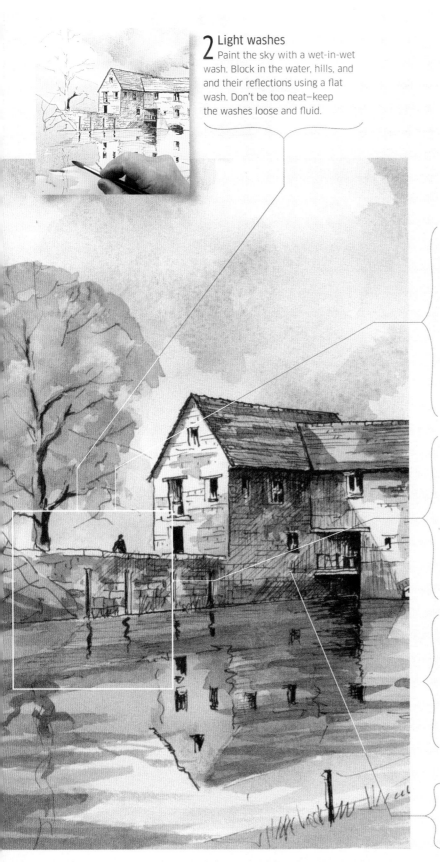

"Line and wash have different qualities that work together when combined in a painting."

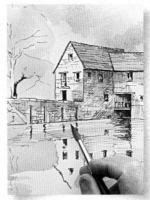

3 Building color
Apply a burnt sienna wash to the building, leaving some white paper for the lightest tones. This allows the line work to form the texture on the white walls. Dilute the sienna wash and use it for the building's reflection.

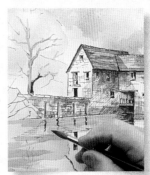

4 Adding dark tones
Paint dark tones over the hatch marks to create extra texture and shadows on the building and reflections.

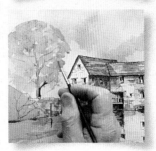

5 Heavy washes
Give the tree's light, and simple lines more shape and tone with stronger washes on the trunk and leaves.

6 Final shadows
Apply a light wash over the hatched shadows to create a blended effect of line and wash.

Experimental techniques

CREATING PATTERN AND TEXTURE

There may be times when you want to add textures and patterns to a flat wash. You can do this in several ways, using equipment as diverse as a toothbrush, candle wax, masking fluid, plastic wrap, and rock salt.

■ Highlights and textures

Apply masking fluid or rub candle wax over areas that you want to keep paint-free, and make interesting patterns with plastic wrap or bubble wrap. By sharpening a candle to a point, you can place marks accurately and precisely, whereas the impressions left by salt or plastic wrap will be more random.

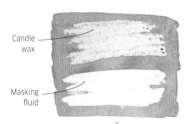

Candle wax

Masking fluid

Plastic wrap   Bubble wrap

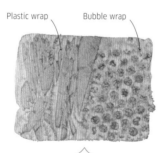

Masking fluid and wax
Apply masking fluid or candle wax to areas that you want to keep white. You can paint over masking fluid, but not wax.

Plastic and bubble wrap
Lay these onto wet paint and remove when the paint is dry. Plastic wrap creates random marks; bubble wrap regular ones.

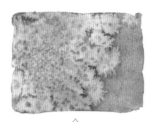

Rock salt
Apply a wash and sprinkle rock salt over it. Once the wash is dry, brush off the salt. This should leave fairly pronounced marks.

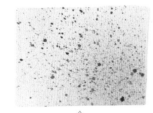

Toothbrush splatter
Load an old toothbrush with paint and flick it at the paper to create a random series of splatter marks.

An old wall and doorway make a great subject, and these experimental techniques introduce lots of texture and character.

You will need

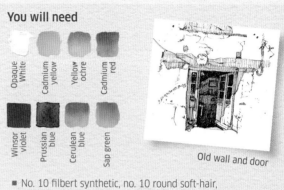

Opaque White   Cadmium yellow   Yellow ochre   Cadmium red

Winsor violet   Prussian blue   Cerulean blue   Sap green

Old wall and door

- No. 10 filbert synthetic, no. 10 round soft-hair, and no. 6 round soft-hair brushes
- Rock salt, plastic wrap, bubble wrap, and a toothbrush
- 10 x 14in (25 x 35cm) cold-pressed watercolor paper

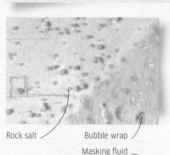

Rock salt   Bubble wrap

1 Making marks
Apply masking fluid to the door and window, then lay a wash of yellow ochre and cadmium red. Sprinkle salt over it and apply bubble wrap. When the paint is dry, remove the wrap and wipe off the salt.

Masking fluid

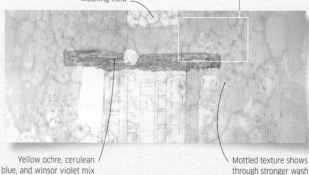

Yellow ochre, cerulean blue, and winsor violet mix

Mottled texture shows through stronger wash

2 Soften textures
Apply a second wash that is darker but that still allows texture to show through. Paint the door lintel with a no. 10 round brush, then apply plastic wrap. Remove the film once the paint is dry.

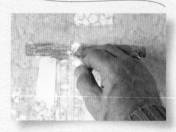

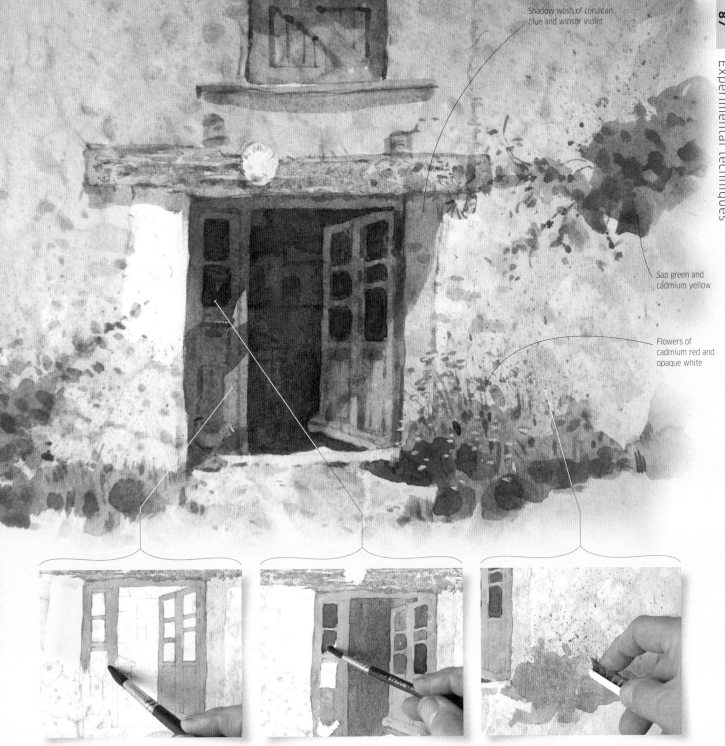

Shadow wash of cerulean
blue and winsor violet

Sap green and
cadmium yellow

Flowers of
cadmium red and
opaque white

3 Smooth area of color
With a no. 10 round brush, block in
the doors and window frame using a mix
of sap green and cerulean blue.

4 Dark tones
With a no. 6 round brush, apply a mix of
Prussian blue and cadmium red to the interior.
Add a second wash, letting areas of the first
wash show through to suggest furniture.

5 Final details
Add the shadows and greenery. Enhance
textural marks on the walls by strengthening
them with a no. 6 brush, and use a toothbrush
to add some splatter marks up the wall.

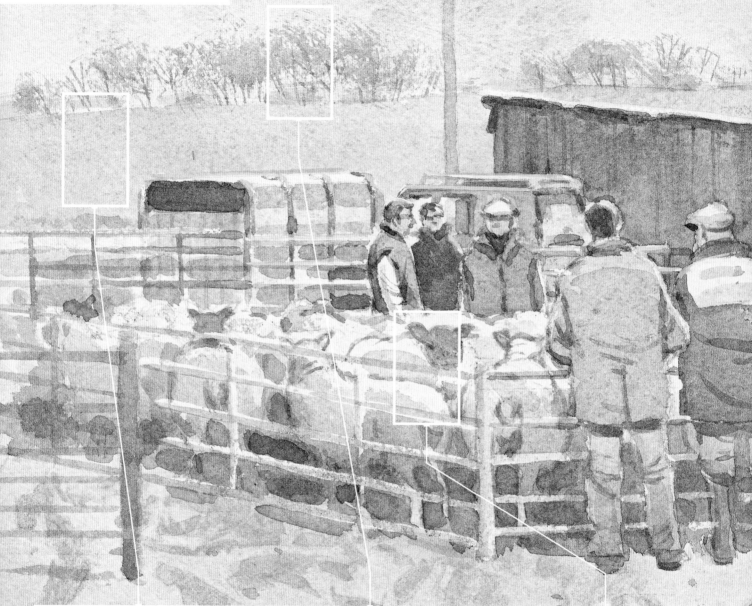

Artist **Colin Allbrook**
Title **Sheep market**
Medium **Watercolor**
Support **Handmade watercolor paper**

Aerial perspective

≪ See pp. 68–69

To give a sense of space and distance beyond the farm buildings, a cool blue-green was used for the hill, in contrast to the stronger foreground colors.

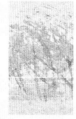

Texture

≪ See pp. 74–75

Once the sky was completed, a nearly dry brush was used to scumble a cool color on the winter trees, suggesting small twigs and branches against the skyline.

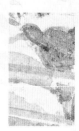

Edges

≪ See pp. 70–71

A warm wash was allowed to mix with a cooler shadow color to describe the sheep in the pen. When dry, some areas were sharpened to define the shapes.

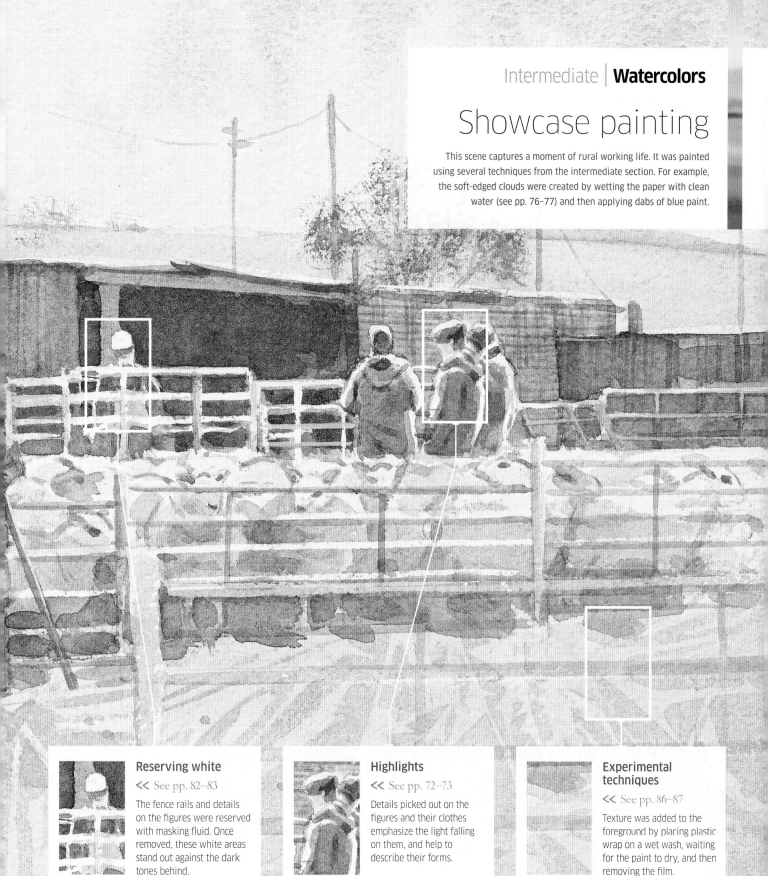

Showcase painting

This scene captures a moment of rural working life. It was painted using several techniques from the intermediate section. For example, the soft-edged clouds were created by wetting the paper with clean water (see pp. 76–77) and then applying dabs of blue paint.

Reserving white

« See pp. 82–83

The fence rails and details on the figures were reserved with masking fluid. Once removed, these white areas stand out against the dark tones behind.

Highlights

« See pp. 72–73

Details picked out on the figures and their clothes emphasize the light falling on them, and help to describe their forms.

Experimental techniques

« See pp. 86–87

Texture was added to the foreground by placing plastic wrap on a wet wash, waiting for the paint to dry, and then removing the film.

Planning a painting

GATHERING, SKETCHING, AND DEVELOPING

Regardless of the subject matter, try to plan each painting in a similar way. By working through the same stages of development before committing to a final painting, you can be satisfied that your picture is the best it can be.

PUTTING IT INTO PRACTICE

In this series of pictures of a seaside town, the artist made several sketches and took photographs on location before developing the painting and creating the final piece back in the studio.

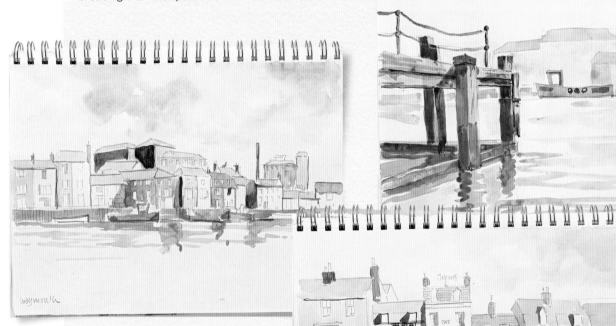

1 Location sketches
These views were all drawn and color washed on location to provide reference material for the final painting. Spend time sketching your subject from different vantage points. As well as providing useful reference material, these visual "notes" help fix the subject in your memory.

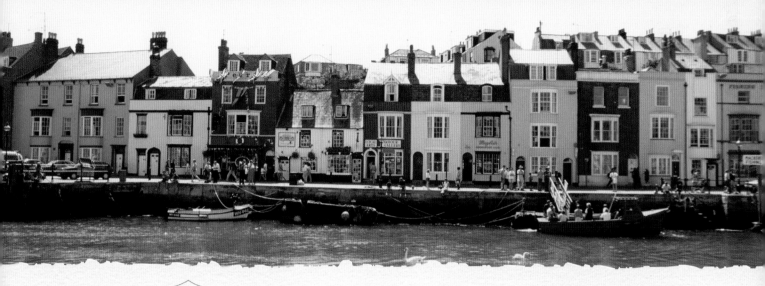

2 Reference photographs

While working from second-hand photographs alone is not always advisable, it is useful to supplement your drawings with photographs to pick up details that you have not had time to sketch on location.

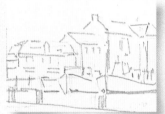

1–buildings as focal point

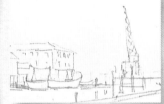

2–crane as focal point

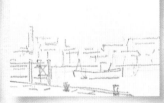

3–single boat as focal point

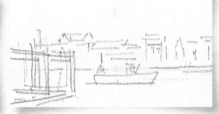

Final composition

The final composition was chosen for its pleasing progression from jetty to boat to houses.

3 Composition

Back in the studio, analyze your sketches and photographs, creating a shortlist for the final layout. Be as flexible as you can and, at this stage, try not to become wedded to one composition. Feel free to move or remove elements of the scene if it improves the arrangement. Prepare thumbnail sketches of different compositions, exploring the various views you have recorded. Look for the scene that best captures the essence of the place and will hold the viewer's attention.

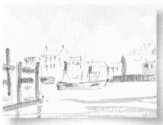

1–bright values

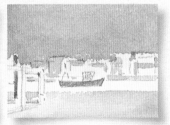

2–darker values

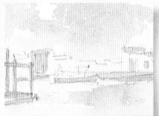

3–bright colors

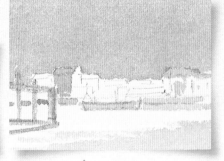

Chosen mood

The artist chose the final value and color scheme because they suggest a dark, atmospheric night scene.

4 Mood

After choosing your composition, develop tonal and color studies using various washes, to explore the mood you wish to convey. Be open minded and prepared to paint more than one version. Once you have made a decision, transfer the composition to your final paper surface at an appropriate size.

>

5 Tonal reference
This study, chosen for its mood of nocturnal calm, acts as a guide when setting out the main tonal areas in the final painting.

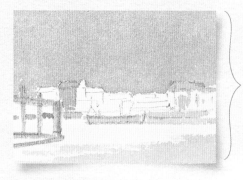

Sky sets the mood with a double granulated wash

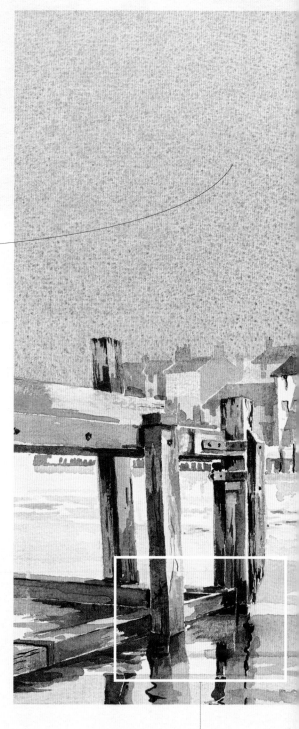

6 Reinterpretation
The final work uses artistic license to change elements of the scenes captured on location. Repositioning the jetty and changing its angle were key to the success of the composition.

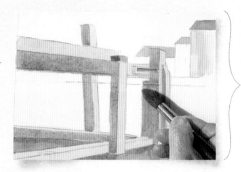

7 Recalling detail
The careful study of the jetty provides a vital reference when it comes to applying detail in the foreground. Additional photographs taken on location will also prove useful for fine-tuning.

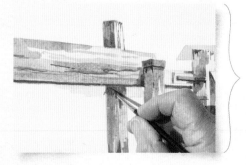

8 Final painting
During the research, planning, and completion of the work, various elements have been adapted or omitted. The final piece does not aim to faithfully record reality, but instead to best capture the spirit of the place.

"Look for the scene that **best captures the essence of the place** and will hold the viewer's attention."

Leading the eye
The detail of the jetty draws the eye. Its dynamic angle points into the center of the painting, leading the eye toward the main focal point–the solitary red boat.

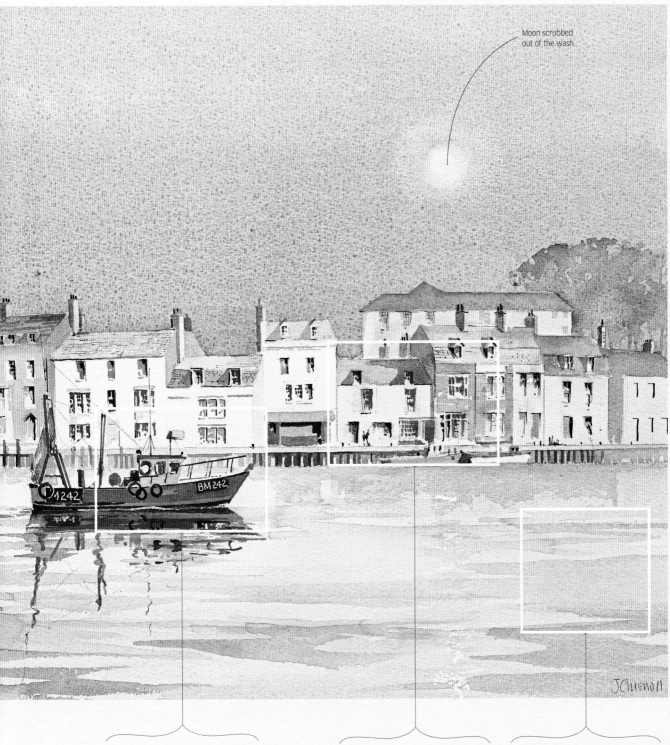

Moon scrubbed
out of the wash

JChisnall

Focal point
The boat is the focus of the work,
its bright red color and crisp
outline immediately catching
the eye.

Balance
The colorful red of the houses and
the boat balances the overall
darker, muted tone of the sky
and water.

Atmosphere
Reflections in the still water
convey a sense of peacefulness
and calm.

Mood

EVOKING ATMOSPHERE AND EMOTION

Creating a mood in your painting is partly to do with depicting environmental conditions, such as sunlight or mist, and partly about creating associations and leaving some things undefined for the viewer to interpret. If everything in a painting is perfectly defined, there is rarely a feeling of mood.

▨ Color, tone, and definition

What we perceive as mood in a painting is often due to the associations we make with colors, textures, light, and shade. All painting techniques contribute to creating mood, but the colors you use, the range of tones you include, and the areas you choose to make detailed or leave undefined are key. These factors create mood even in abstract subjects.

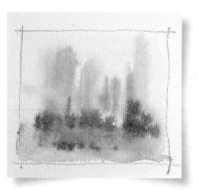

Quiet mood
The shapes in this illustration are abstract, but the muted, gray color, narrow tonal range, and softly diffused outlines convey a gentle, quiet mood.

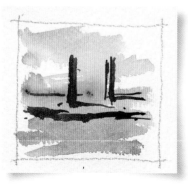

Energetic mood
We associate bright colors with liveliness. In this example, rich color combines with hard edges and a wide tonal range to suggest sunlight and heat, creating an energetic mood.

EVOKING A QUIET, SUBDUED MOOD

Simplicity is the key to depicting soft, misty subjects. Mist makes distant objects look soft and merged together, and wet-in-wet washes are best for this effect. Choose a heavy-weight paper that won't cockle (or buckle) when you apply lots of water.

You will need

Burnt sienna
Pyrrol red
French ultramarine
Phthalo green

- No. 16 soft-hair mop, no. 10 round soft-hair, and no. 6 soft-hair rigger brushes
- 10 x 14in (25 x 35cm) cold-pressed watercolor paper

Venice in the mist

Cold, gray hue mixed with French ultramarine, burnt sienna, and phthalo green

Pencil sketch

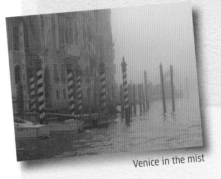

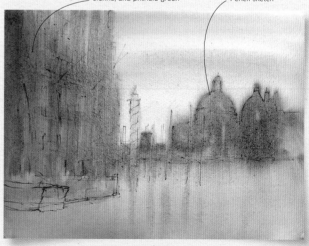

1 Soft background washes
Soak the paper with a large mop brush, then lay gray washes on the buildings. The wetter your paper, the more the paint will disperse. If your wash totally disappears, wait a minute and try again, but don't leave it so long that the paper becomes too dry—the critical time is when the shine just goes off the paper.

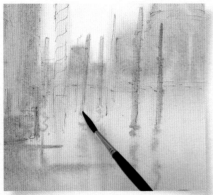

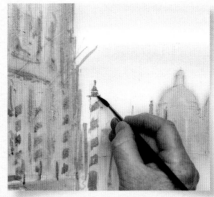

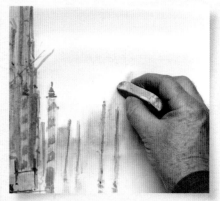

2 Suggesting detail
As the paper dries a little more, add strokes to suggest some of the architectural details, but only in the foreground. Leave the background undefined.

3 Hints of color
As the wash continues to dry, add a touch of red to the gray mix and apply it to the red-and-white striped poles, to hint at the color in the nearest foreground.

4 Finishing touches
When the paper is almost dry, add more marks to define the foreground. Once the paper is totally dry, erase your pencil lines, which will help the background to recede.

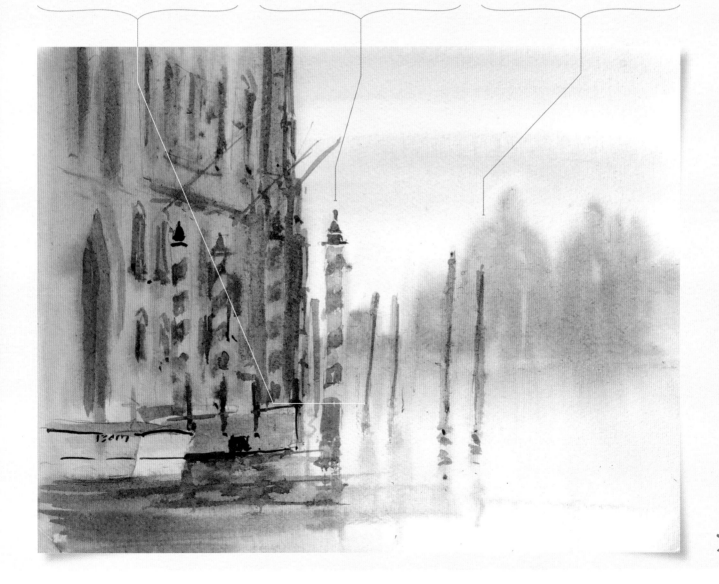

EVOKING A WARM, VIBRANT MOOD

In order to paint a bright, sunny day successfully, you need to ensure that the shadows are dark in relation to the light–the darker the shadows, the sunnier the day will seem. Rich, warm colors also enhance the feeling of a hot day.

You will need

Burnt sienna

Pyrrol red

French ultramarine

Phthalo green

- No. 16 soft-hair mop, no. 10 round soft-hair, and no. 6 soft-hair rigger brushes
- 10 x 14in (25 x 35cm) cold-pressed watercolor paper

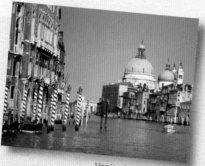

Venice in the sunshine

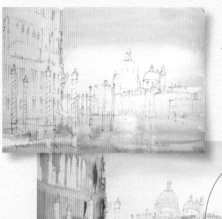

1 Bright washes
Paint the sky and water with blue washes. While the wash is still wet, lift out areas of paint with a clean, dampened brush, to create reflections in the water.

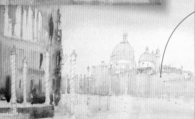

Light shadow color is burnt sienna with French ultramarine

Dark shadow color is French ultramarine with pyrrol red

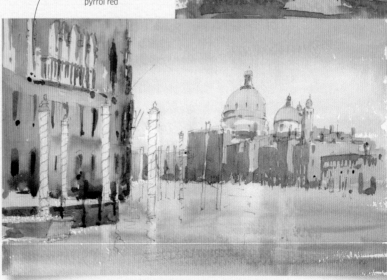

2 Blocking in the buildings
Paint the buildings with a weak wash of burnt sienna, adding French ultramarine to your mix for the distant buildings. Mix a stronger tone to paint in the windows and add texture on the walls.

3 Shadows
Add shadows to the buildings using a mix of French ultramarine and red, to create the feeling of sunshine.

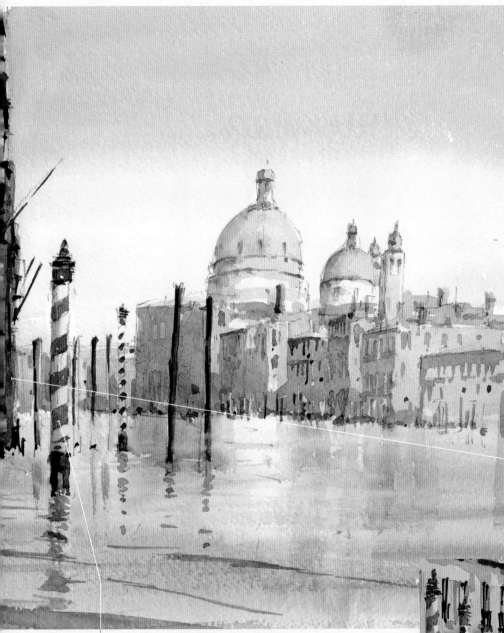

> "To create a unified look and extra contrast, try using a dark transparent glaze over the shadows at the end."

5 Final touches
Create more focus in the foreground by adding strong darks (a mix of French ultramarine and sienna), to increase the contrast between tones. Finally, create reflections in the water to enhance the sunny atmosphere.

4 Rich color
Paint the colorful poles with undiluted French ultramarine and red. Add more marks to the distant buildings to suggest their structure, but try not to overdo the details.

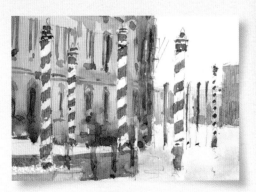

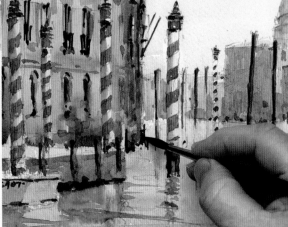

Laying a double gradated wash

BLENDING TWO GRADATED COLORS

You can create beautiful, complex backgrounds and skies with washes that transition from one color to another. This technique involves laying two gradated washes (see pp. 64-65) on top of each other in opposite directions so that they meet in the middle and blend. It takes some practice, so persevere if you aren't happy with your first attempts.

■ Laying the wash

Tilt your support to lay the wash—gravity will help the paint to spread downward, smoothing out marks while the wash is wet. For this reason, lay the wash at the top of the board, turning your paper around if necessary. Apply the lighter color first.

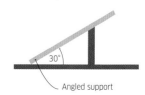

Angled support

PUTTING IT INTO PRACTICE

A double gradated background can be a striking feature in its own right if you keep the rest of the composition pared back.

You will need

Opaque white
Cadmium yellow
Light red
Cobalt blue

French ultramarine
Phthalo blue (green shade)
Neutral tint

- No. 8 and no. 5 soft-hair brushes
- Jar of clean water
- 14 x 22in (35 x 55cm) rough watercolor paper

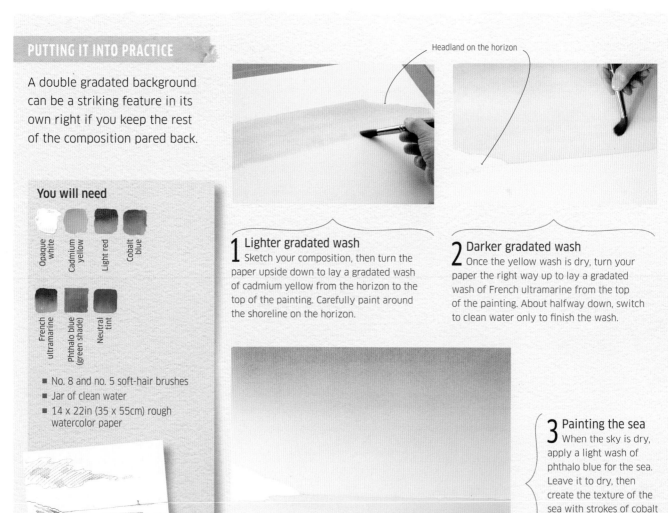

Headland on the horizon

1 Lighter gradated wash
Sketch your composition, then turn the paper upside down to lay a gradated wash of cadmium yellow from the horizon to the top of the painting. Carefully paint around the shoreline on the horizon.

2 Darker gradated wash
Once the yellow wash is dry, turn your paper the right way up to lay a gradated wash of French ultramarine from the top of the painting. About halfway down, switch to clean water only to finish the wash.

3 Painting the sea
When the sky is dry, apply a light wash of phthalo blue for the sea. Leave it to dry, then create the texture of the sea with strokes of cobalt blue and a mix of neutral tint and cobalt blue for the shadows.

Calm sea

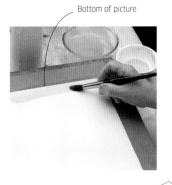
Bottom of picture

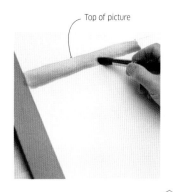
Top of picture

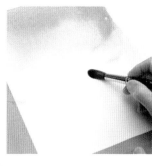

First wash—yellow

Turn the paper around to lay a wash at the bottom of the picture. Wet the paper, charge a large brush with paint, and lay the wash in horizontal strokes. After every stroke, dip the brush in clean water and then in paint to gradually dilute the wash, which should fade to nothing at the bottom.

Second wash—blue

Allow the first wash to dry, then turn the paper around so you are working from the top of the picture. Begin laying the second wash, gradually diluting it as before. About halfway down, use clean water only, to keep the color of the first wash intact.

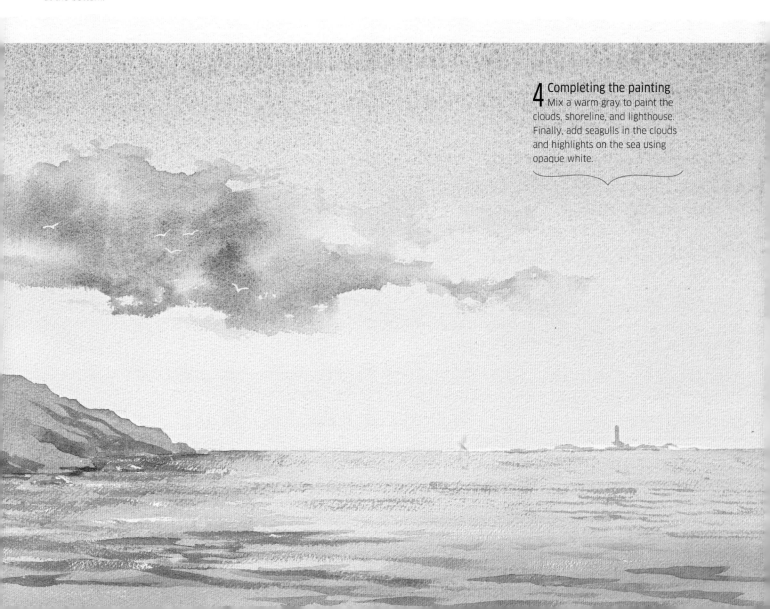

4 Completing the painting
Mix a warm gray to paint the clouds, shoreline, and lighthouse. Finally, add seagulls in the clouds and highlights on the sea using opaque white.

Laying a granulated wash

CREATING GRAINY EFFECTS

Some colors naturally granulate, creating a grainy effect when dry. This happens when pigments separate from the binder and wash, and settle in the hollows of the paper. Some pigments granulate more than others. For example, French ultramarine granulates well, while phthalo blue, which has very fine particles of color, does not granulate at all.

■ Encouraging granulation

Pigments that granulate well include cobalt blue, terre verte, cerulean blue, cadmium red, light red, and French ultramarine. You can encourage these pigments to granulate more effectively by tipping the board back and forth, and from side to side, while the wash is still wet. This will shake the pigment from the mix, and help distribute the grains of pigment evenly across the surface. The effect will be more pronounced on rough paper.

Cobalt blue

Terre verte

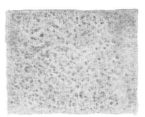
Cerulean blue

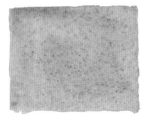
Cadmium red

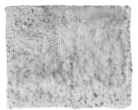
Light red

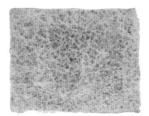
French ultramarine

Mixing colors

Mixing certain pigments together—such as French ultramarine and light red—also encourages granulation and can enhance the effect.

Light red

French ultramarine

Mix of light red and French ultramarine

In this landscape, naturally granulating pigments were used to enhance the sky and dark clouds behind the poppy seed heads.

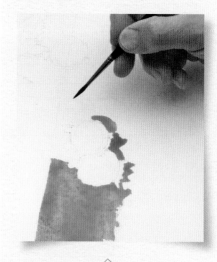

1 Turn board upside down
Sketch the scene, then place the board upside down and at a slight angle so the wash runs away from the poppies. Work a wash of cerulean blue around the poppy outlines using a no. 2 round brush.

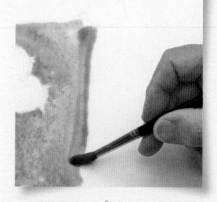

2 Continue wash
Switch to a no. 5 round brush for less intricate areas of the wash. Use continuous brushstrokes across the paper, working your way from top to bottom. Keep the wash fairly wet at all times.

You will need

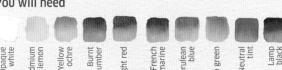

Opaque white	Cadmium lemon	Yellow ochre	Burnt umber	Light red	French ultramarine	Cerulean blue	Sap green	Neutral tint	Lamp black

- No. 2, no. 5, and no. 8 round soft-hair brushes
- 10 x 12in (25 x 30cm) hot-pressed watercolor paper

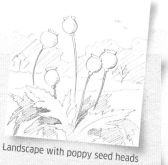

Landscape with poppy seed heads

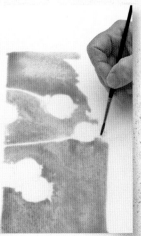

3 Tip the board

Switch back to a no. 2 round brush to apply the wash around the edges of the taller poppies. Tip the board from side to side and backward and forward to evenly distribute the color, and then shake the board to encourage granulation.

4 Final painting

When the first wash is completely dry, paint the field using burnt umber, working carefully around the poppies again. Then, paint the poppy heads, stems, and leaves using mixes of sap green and cadmium lemon. Once these washes are dry, use opaque white for the highlights and lamp black for the shadows. Add the clouds, using French ultramarine, light red, and a hint of yellow ochre.

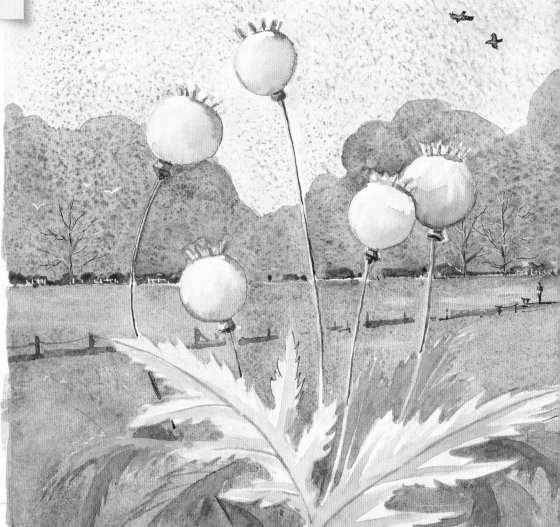

Monochrome

UNDERSTANDING TONE

For a painting to succeed, it should usually exhibit a full range of tones, from extremely light to extremely dark. Painting in a single color will help you to look carefully at tone without being distracted by the colors you see before you.

■ Using tone to distinguish objects

To distinguish one object from another and prevent them from appearing to merge together, you must vary their tones. A common mistake is to differentiate objects by color alone, which can make paintings bland. Convert a photograph of your painting into black and white. If the painting is reduced to a variety of dull grays, you need to think more about tone. Painting in monochrome will help you to do this.

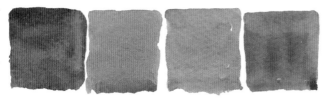

Colors created in similar strengths

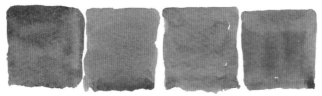

Similar shades of gray

Color versus value

The first swatch appears to be full of contrast, but this is a contrast of colors only. After converting the first swatch to grayscale, it's apparent that there are no distinguishing values present.

Choose a dark color for your monochrome painting. Neutral tint was used for this painting of a flower stall, but sepia, paynes gray, and indigo would be good alternatives.

You will need

Neutral tint

- No. 14 and no. 6 soft-hair mops; no. 6 soft-hair round brush
- 10 x 14in (25 x 35cm) cold-pressed watercolor paper

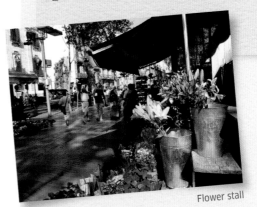

Flower stall

Don't paint the areas of brightest tone

Initial pencil sketch

1 Background wash

Although it would be easier to use a black and white photo as reference, the value of this exercise lies in translating colors to tones. Using a no. 14 soft-hair mop, cover most of the paper with a pale wash, leaving only the brightest highlights unpainted.

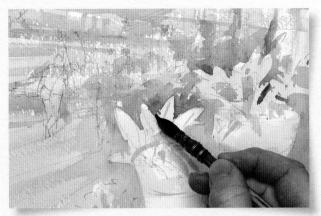

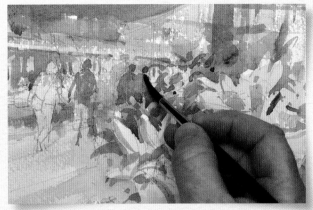

2 Second wash

Add a darker, second wash with a no. 6 soft-hair mop. A smaller brush helps you to start adding more detailed tonal differences between the different areas of the painting.

3 Build up tone

Using a no. 6 soft-hair round brush, gradually build up tone to create the different shapes. Forget about color and avoid being too literal in your interpretation: merely hint at elements that might seem quite definite in the photograph.

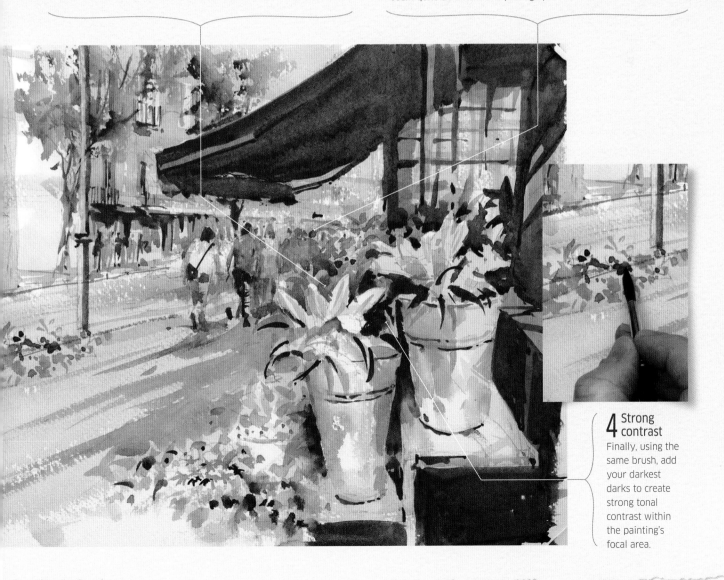

4 Strong contrast

Finally, using the same brush, add your darkest darks to create strong tonal contrast within the painting's focal area.

Glazing

ADDING TINTS TO AN UNDERPAINTING

A glaze is a thin wash applied on top of an area of dry paint. Glazing over an underpainting can change the mood of a painting, help connect separate areas, and create depth. Being transparent, watercolors are the ideal medium for achieving glazing effects.

◼ Color and warmth

You can use glazes to subtly adjust colors, alter the warmth and coolness of an area, or add color to a monochrome underpainting. You can overpaint subjects and darken the true color in shadow areas. Glazes can also create or enhance aerial perspective. For example, you can use cool glazes to make background areas recede, and warm glazes to make the foreground advance. A glaze can also gently soften and unite areas that may look disconnected.

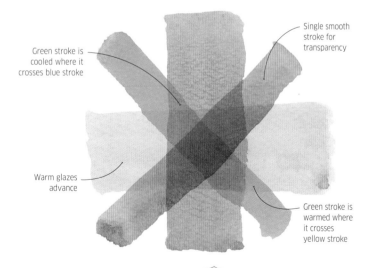

Green stroke is cooled where it crosses blue stroke

Single smooth stroke for transparency

Warm glazes advance

Green stroke is warmed where it crosses yellow stroke

Transparent glazes
Where the different glazes of transparent color cross, optical mixing creates the illusion of purple from the red and blue, green from the blue and yellow, and orange from the yellow and red.

In this depiction of a town square, warm and cool glazes were applied where appropriate to add shadows and enhance the depth of an otherwise flat-looking scene.

You will need

Raw sienna

Cobalt blue

- No. 10 soft-hair round brush
- 10 x 14in (25 x 35cm) cold-pressed watercolor paper

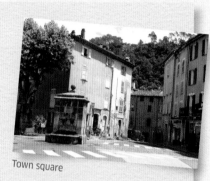

Town square

"Glazes subtly change color, and alter warmth and coolness."

Deliberate lack of depth

Similar color mix to the foreground tree

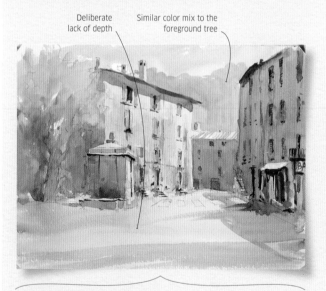

1 Apply the underpainting
In this initial underpainting, similar color mixes were deliberately applied for both the background and foreground, inevitably leading to a lack of depth. A no. 10 soft-hair round brush was used throughout.

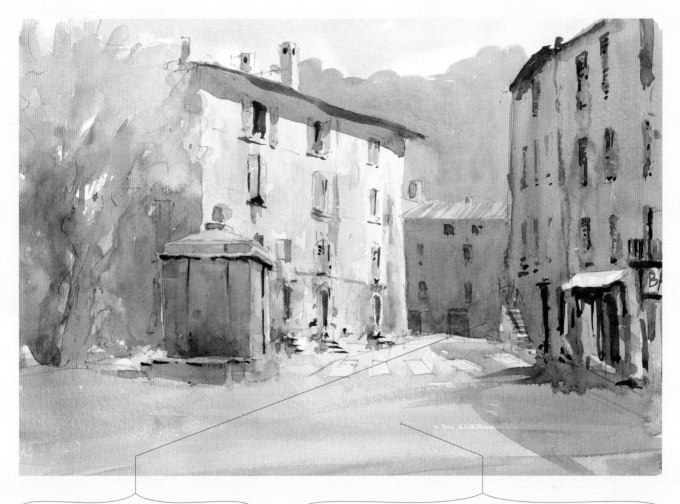

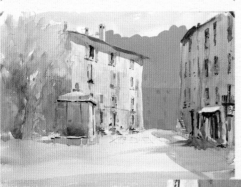

3 Foreground glaze
Glaze the foreground with raw sienna to warm and advance this area. Again, use a wash just strong enough to create a subtle effect that alters the warmth of the underlying colors without changing them entirely.

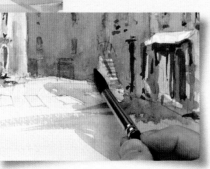

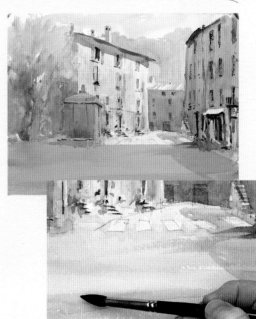

2 Background glaze
Gently, and with as few strokes as possible, glaze the background area of trees and buildings with a cobalt blue wash. Make it strong enough to give a cool and slightly softening effect, but without coloring everything bright blue. The area will seem to recede.

Building layers

OVERLAPPING WASHES

The transparent quality of watercolors makes them ideal for layering. Successive washes of color will give your painting a sense of luminosity and depth. As long as the previous wash is totally dry, you can lay a new wash without disturbing the pigment underneath and creating unwanted marks.

■ Working from light to dark

Build up layers gradually, working from light tones to dark tones. That way, you can easily darken a tone by adding an extra wash. Layering over dry paint will create hard lines, which you can use to your advantage by painting negative shapes to let lighter tones show through. Be aware that new layers will modify the color or tone of the previous layer, in a similar way to glazing (see pp. 104–05).

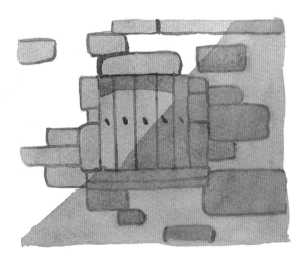

Transparent layers
A blue wash has been applied to half of this picture over a dry layer of paint. The details of the bottom layer are still clear underneath the blue wash, but the tones are deeper.

(see pp. 104–05).

PUTTING IT INTO PRACTICE

In this stable scene, layered washes create a sense of depth with a clever interplay of light and dark. Use a large mop brush to apply the initial layers, to give the painting a loose, organic feel.

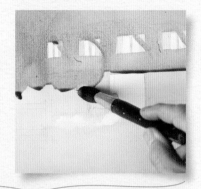

1 Lightest layers
Create a warm tone with a light wash of ochre mixed with violet. Leave white paper where the windows and door will be. Layer a deeper tone on top, using ochre mixed with violet and Prussian blue.

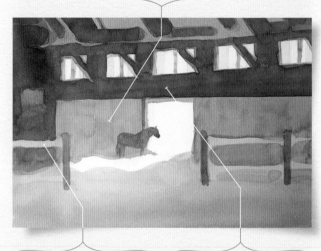

Negative shape of fence rail

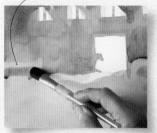

2 Negative shapes
Paint around the fence rails in the foreground as you apply a mid tone to the walls. This creates light-colored negative shapes that emerge from the darker background.

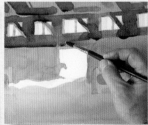

3 Darkest layers
Apply the darkest tones to the shadows around the roof and window frames, but leave some of the previous layer showing to suggest sunlight striking the beams.

You will need

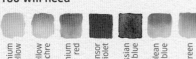

- Cadmium yellow
- Yellow ochre
- Cadmium red
- Winsor violet
- Prussian blue
- Cerulean blue
- Sap green

- Large soft-hair mop, no. 10 filbert synthetic, no. 10 round soft-hair, and no. 10 round synthetic brushes
- 10 x 14in (25 x 35cm) cold-pressed watercolor paper

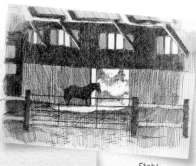

Stable scene

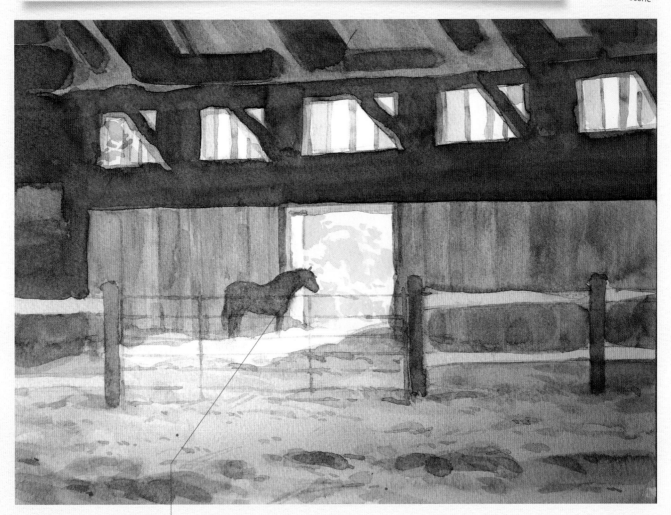

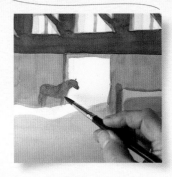

4 Horse silhouette

Pick out the figure of the horse with a mix of red, ochre, and violet. The warm color will bring the horse forward from the background, but make sure its tone is darker than that of the wall behind it.

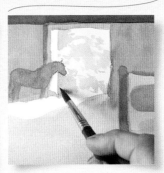

5 Finishing touches

Apply a pale green wash for the foliage and, once dry, model it further with darker tones. Review your painting and decide whether to add details—such as the straw and floor—or perhaps adjust the tonal contrast to help everything come together.

Adding details

CREATING FEATURES AND FOCAL POINTS

Think about the overall balance of your painting when you decide where to add details—they should enhance the scene rather than overwhelm it. Details help objects to stand out, so are best used on focal points or on foreground elements in aerial perspective (see pp. 68–69). Build up details slowly as you add layers.

▓ Ways to add detail

Details can encompass a range of effects, from textures, to fine lines, to highlights. Using paint and various brushstrokes to add details works very well, but you can also introduce other media to great effect.

PUTTING IT INTO PRACTICE

Delicately drawn details make the artichokes the focal point in this painting, while the oranges in the background are painted more simply.

You will need

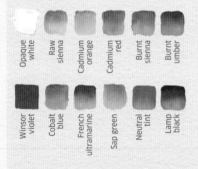

Opaque white | Raw sienna | Cadmium orange | Cadmium red | Burnt sienna | Burnt umber

Winsor violet | Cobalt blue | French ultramarine | Sap green | Neutral tint | Lamp black

- No. 5 and no. 2 round soft-hair brushes
- Dip pen with steel nib and waterproof Indian ink
- 12 x 14in (30 x 35cm) hot-pressed watercolor paper

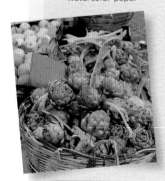

Basket of artichokes

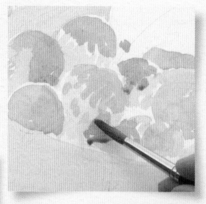

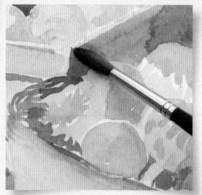

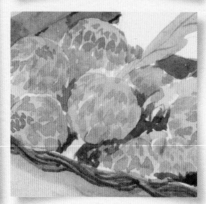

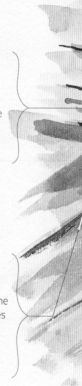

1 Initial washes
Apply light washes with a no. 5 round soft-hair brush to establish the basic shapes and colors. Allow to dry, then add shadows to give the objects form.

2 First details
Using the side of your brush, apply darker tones on the box of oranges and the table. Switch to the tip of your brush to paint the wood grain.

3 Developing the shapes
Continue using the tip of your brush to add the petals on the artichokes and the weave on the basket. Add further details to develop the table and box.

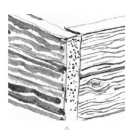

Brush tip and side
Make thick marks with the side of your brush or thin marks with the tip for fine details.

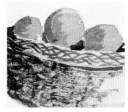

Dry brush
Squeeze excess moisture from your brush before dragging it over the paper to create texture.

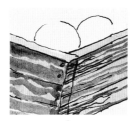

Pen and ink
Use a dip pen and ink or a fiber-tip pen to add dark, fine lines for crisp detail.

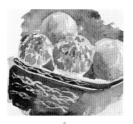

White gouache
Gouache is opaque, which allows you to add highlights and details over dry paint.

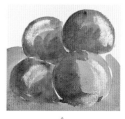

White pastel
You can add textured, expressive details on top of dry paint with white pastel.

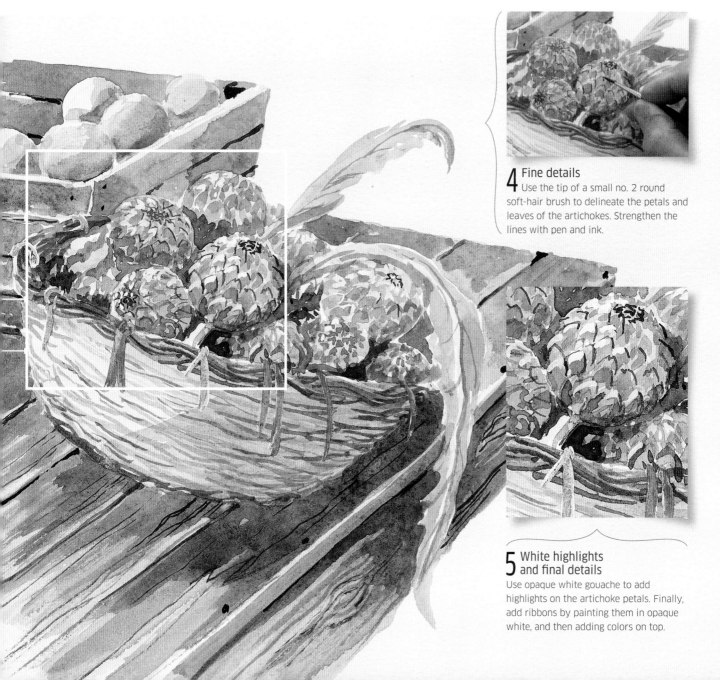

4 Fine details
Use the tip of a small no. 2 round soft-hair brush to delineate the petals and leaves of the artichokes. Strengthen the lines with pen and ink.

5 White highlights and final details
Use opaque white gouache to add highlights on the artichoke petals. Finally, add ribbons by painting them in opaque white, and then adding colors on top.

Reflections

PAINTING MIRROR IMAGES ON WATER

Depending on the direction of the light and clarity of the water, the colors of a reflection can vary from slightly less intense than the object being reflected to completely muted. Disturbances on the surface of the water will also affect a reflection's quality.

▨ Surfaces and reflections

You can create the effect of a rippled surface by painting bands of softened color. With rougher water, colors will become more subdued, and the horizontal bands will become increasingly fragmented.

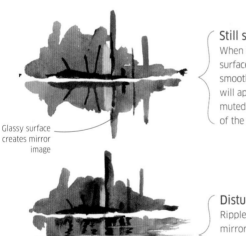

Glassy surface creates mirror image

Still surface
When the water's surface is completely smooth, a reflection will appear as a slightly muted, mirror image of the shore.

Horizontal bands of merging color

Disturbed surface
Ripples act like curved mirrors, distorting reflections and making them longer, while softening details.

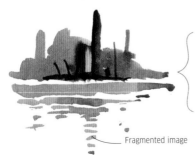

Fragmented image

Broken surface
As the water's surface becomes more uneven, reflections will break up and can even disappear completely.

In this river scene, bands of muted colors and subdued tones were used to recreate the softer reflections on the river's surface and to suggest movement.

You will need

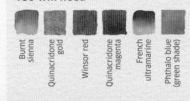

Burnt sienna · Quinacridone gold · Winsor red · Quinacridone magenta · French ultramarine · Phthalo blue (green shade)

- No. 14 soft-hair mop, no. 10 soft-hair round, no. 6 soft-hair round, no. 6 soft-hair rigger, and small swordliner brushes
- 10 x 13in (25 x 35cm) cold-pressed watercolor paper

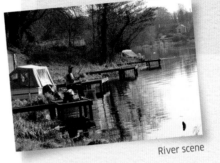

River scene

French ultramarine and quinacridone gold

Varied mix of French ultramarine and burnt sienna

Phthalo blue, quinacridone magenta, and quinacridone gold

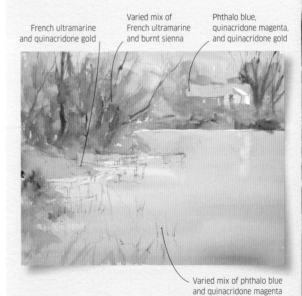

Varied mix of phthalo blue and quinacridone magenta

1 Underlying wash

Lay a merging wash across the whole paper with a no. 14 soft-hair mop and using various mixes. Paint in a suggestion of the house and vegetation. Leave simple, light shapes to hint at the structure of the house.

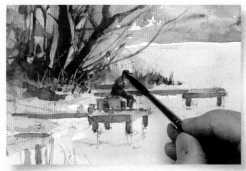

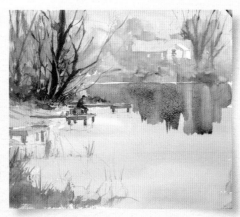

2 Foreground elements

With your no. 10 round, no. 6 round, and swordline brushes, indicate the trees, vegetation, fisherman, and fishing stands with mixes of the below colors.

 + +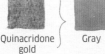

French ultramarine | Burnt sienna | Quinacridone gold | Gray

3 Reflections

Use the no. 10 soft-hair round brush to suggest reflections with horizontal bands of color and tone. Make these deliberately subdued compared to the reflected objects, with lights less light, darks less dark, and colors more muted.

"Watercolor is an **ideal medium** to show the **subtlety and beauty** of reflections in water."

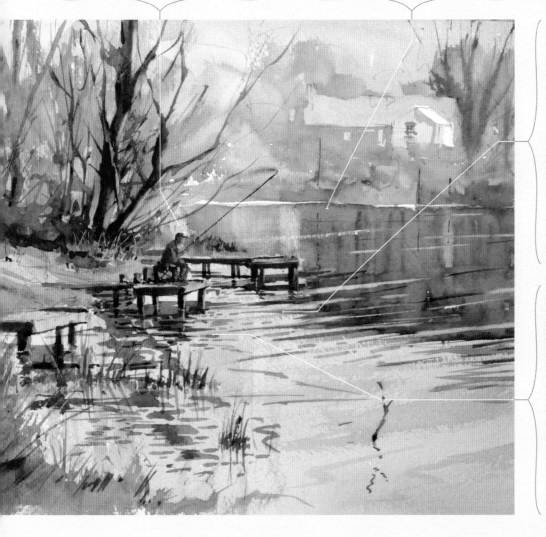

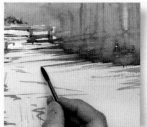

4 Ripples

While the reflections are wet, use a dry no. 6 rigger to create horizontal ripples, breaking up the edges of the vertical bands. Apply extra ripple reflections under the trees and fishing stands.

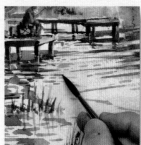

5 Darks

Using a no. 6 round brush and no. 6 rigger, add detailed darks to the trees, fisherman, and ripples under the stands to draw the viewer's eye.

Opaque whites

USING SOLID WHITE COLOR

Opaque whites are useful in watercolor for adding areas of solid color, or correcting and altering your artwork. White gouache is perfect for this purpose. While Chinese white can also be used, it is thinner and does not cover as well. When mixed with watercolor, the gouache turns the paint into an opaque body color which, when diluted, will become a semi-opaque, chalky glaze.

■ Lights and opaque whites

For the cleanest end result, apply opaque white to areas of paper that you have left unpainted (see pp.82–83). A tinted watercolor paper will show off the technique at its best. Use gouache to create effects such as shimmering reflections on water, or to make adjustments.

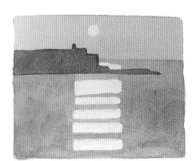

Add shimmer
Here, opaque white paint has been used to enhance the effect of evening sunlight shimmering on water. A touch of yellow ochre in the white will make it a warmer color, whereas a little blue will cool it.

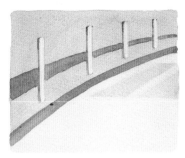

Alterations
These fence posts were painted in opaque white on top of a background wash. The shaded edges of the posts were added using a layer of opaque body color.

This French café scene is flooded with morning light, conveyed by the brightness of the leaves, tabletops, and awning. This piece was painted on cream paper to emphasize the highlights added in opaque white and body color.

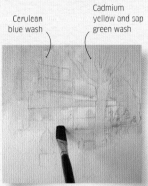

Cerulean blue wash

Cadmium yellow and sap green wash

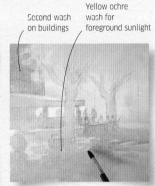

Second wash on buildings

Yellow ochre wash for foreground sunlight

1 Establish forms
Using your large flat brush, lay blues and greens wet-in-wet to loosely establish the forms of the buildings and trees, leaving light areas clean.

2 Second wash
With your no. 10 round brush, lay a second, cooler wash over the buildings. Paint carefully, allowing the leaves of the trees to stand out.

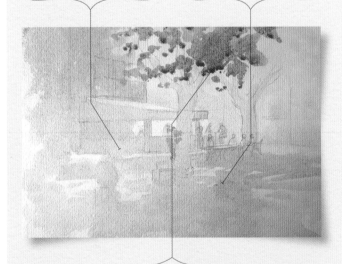

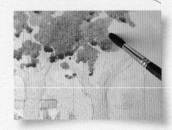

3 Add depth
When modeling the leaves, use a darker wash of cadmium yellow, sap green, yellow ochre, and winsor violet. This will give them depth and shadow. Use your no. 10 soft-hair brush.

You will need

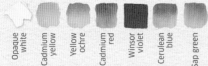

Opaque white · Cadmium yellow · Yellow ochre · Cadmium red · Winsor violet · Cerulean blue · Sap green

- Large flat soft-hair, no. 10 round soft-hair, and no. 6 round soft-hair brushes
- 10 x 14in (25 x 35cm) cream, cold-pressed watercolor paper

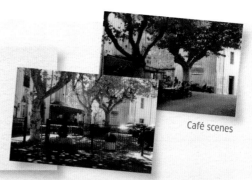

Café scenes

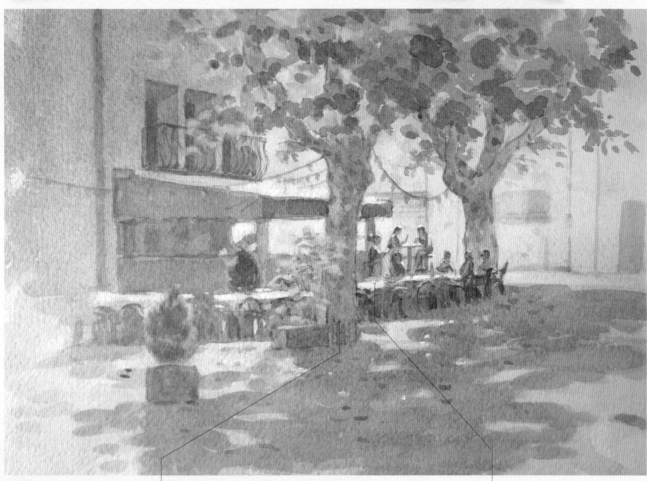

4 Add color
Using the same brush, paint the sap green awning and use yellow ochre and cerulean blue for the tree trunks. Freely indicate the chairs with a mix of winsor violet and cadmium red, then place the figures and show the window detail.

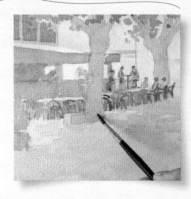

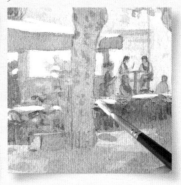

5 Add opaques
With a no. 6 soft-hair brush, strengthen the shadow in the foreground and under the tables, as well as the tree trunks. Also apply white to the tabletops. Using a no. 10 round brush, add body color to the figures and foliage, strengthening detail. Finally, adjust any tone or color that requires attention.

Skin tones

PAINTING FLESH COLORS

Painting faces and figures from life will give you a great understanding of form, tone, and color, which you can apply to everything you paint. When depicting facial features, it's best to tone down the whites of the eyes and the whiteness of teeth, which can otherwise seem too stark. Also, show mouths either closed or with lips only slightly apart, as wide open, laughing mouths can sometimes look awkward.

◼ Basic palette

Skin tones vary widely depending on age, ethnic background, and even lifestyle. For example, someone who spends a lot of time outdoors is likely to have rugged, weathered features. Rather than using a standard color, such as "flesh tone," use a basic palette of colors (see below) to recreate the many varied tones seen in life.

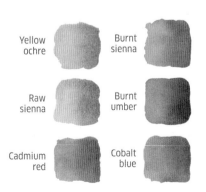

Yellow ochre

Raw sienna

Cadmium red

Burnt sienna

Burnt umber

Cobalt blue

◼ Dark skin tones

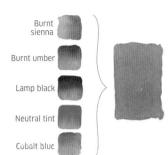

Burnt sienna

Burnt umber

Lamp black

Neutral tint

Cobalt blue

Dark skin palette
Use burnt umber and lamp black for very dark skin, or burnt sienna and burnt umber for medium-dark tones. Shadows and highlights often need hints of blue.

Eyeglasses painted with opaque white and lamp black using a dip pen

Painting dark skin
The overall hue of the saxophone player was established with a wash of burnt sienna and burnt umber. Once dry, burnt umber and lamp black were added to show the shadows created by the muscles and veins of the arms. Highlights of opaque white were used to indicate the nose and cheek.

Ring helps describe round form of finger

Detail of hand
Once the basic wash was dry, shadows were added to create form. Paler tones were used for the fingernails and to suggest movement of the fingers.

Olive skin tones

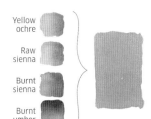

Yellow ochre

Raw sienna

Burnt sienna

Burnt umber

Olive skin tone palette
Establish overall hue and tone, adding darker tones of the basic mix for shadows. Use only subtle variations of color and tone for olive skin.

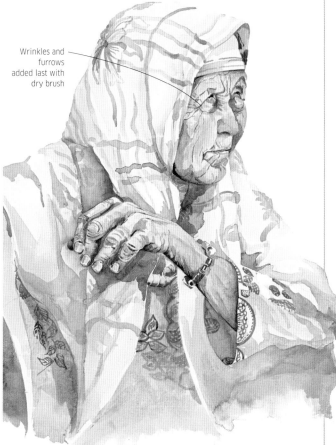

Wrinkles and furrows added last with dry brush

Painting olive skin
A basic wash of raw sienna and a touch of burnt sienna was used for the face and arm. Once dry, a darker mix was used to enhance form. The structure of the face was then added, using a dry brush to delineate the eyes, nose, mouth, and chin.

Detail of hand
Detail on the hand was added using dark tones of the basic wash. The wrinkles, knuckles, and nails were painted with a dry brush to add texture.

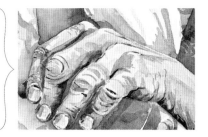

Light skin tones

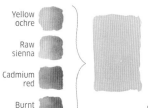

Yellow ochre

Raw sienna

Cadmium red

Burnt sienna

Pale skin palette
Use the basic palette for pale skin, using darker tones of the mix for shadow areas.

Painting light skin
The head and neck were built up using basic washes of yellow ochre, burnt sienna, and a touch of cadmium red. The wash was strengthed for the shadows, with burnt umber and neutral tint used for the darkest areas. Cadmium red and opaque white were used for the lips, and burnt umber and lamp black for the eyes, with the highlights added in opaque white.

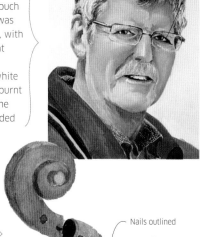

Hair is lamp black and opaque white

Hint of gray in whites of eyes

Cellist's hand
An initial pale wash of yellow ochre and cadmium red was applied first, with a darker wash used to create form but still keeping the fresh, pink colors.

Nails outlined

Darker shadows

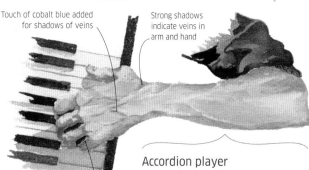

Touch of cobalt blue added for shadows of veins

Strong shadows indicate veins in arm and hand

Burnt umber and cobalt blue for dark shadows

Accordion player
A preliminary wash of yellow ochre, burnt sienna, and a little cadmium red was applied for the whole arm, to show tanned skin.

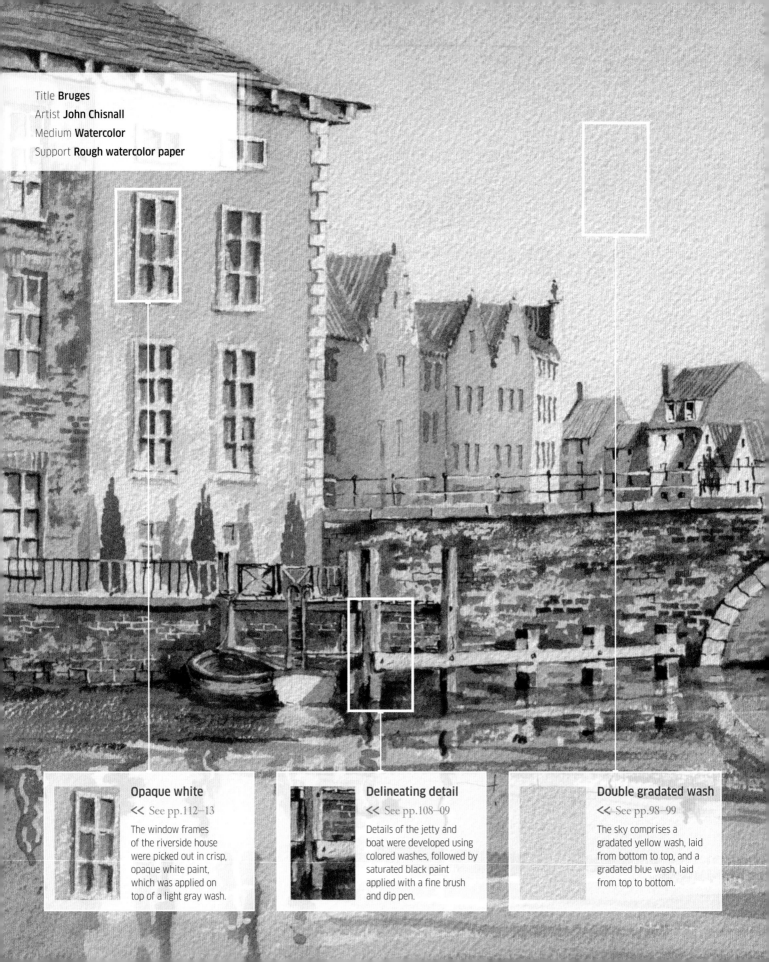

Title **Bruges**
Artist **John Chisnall**
Medium **Watercolor**
Support **Rough watercolor paper**

Opaque white

« See pp.112–13

The window frames of the riverside house were picked out in crisp, opaque white paint, which was applied on top of a light gray wash.

Delineating detail

« See pp.108–09

Details of the jetty and boat were developed using colored washes, followed by saturated black paint applied with a fine brush and dip pen.

Double gradated wash

« See pp.98–99

The sky comprises a gradated yellow wash, laid from bottom to top, and a gradated blue wash, laid from top to bottom.

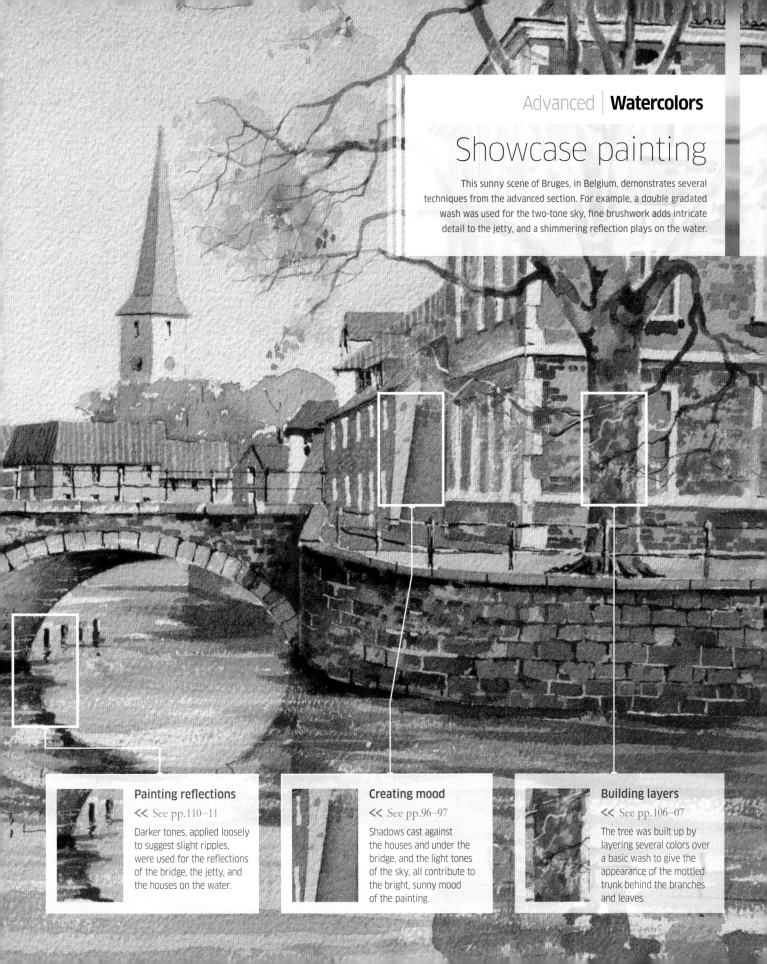

Showcase painting

This sunny scene of Bruges, in Belgium, demonstrates several techniques from the advanced section. For example, a double gradated wash was used for the two-tone sky, fine brushwork adds intricate detail to the jetty, and a shimmering reflection plays on the water.

Painting reflections

≪ See pp.110–11

Darker tones, applied loosely to suggest slight ripples, were used for the reflections of the bridge, the jetty, and the houses on the water.

Creating mood

≪ See pp.96–97

Shadows cast against the houses and under the bridge, and the light tones of the sky, all contribute to the bright, sunny mood of the painting.

Building layers

≪ See pp.106–07

The tree was built up by layering several colors over a basic wash to give the appearance of the mottled trunk behind the branches and leaves.

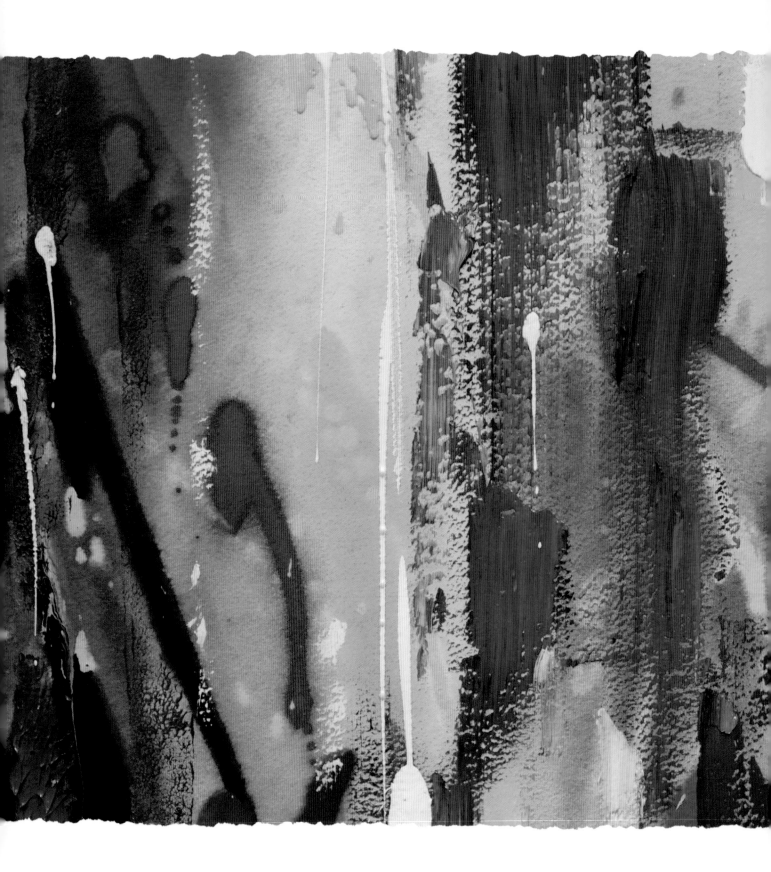

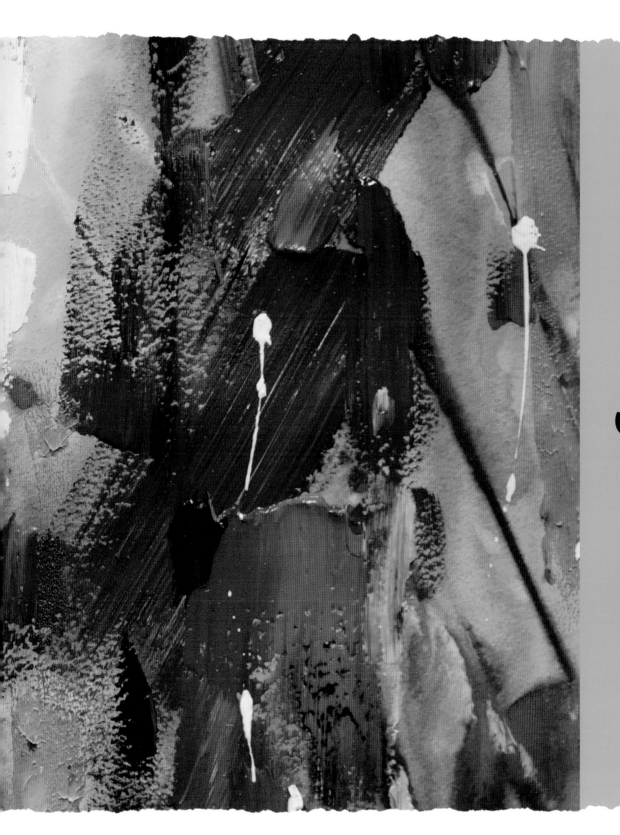

Acrylics

Painting with **acrylics**

A quick-drying, water-based medium that becomes water resistant when dry, acrylic paints are quick and easy to use. They are renowned for their brilliant color, convenience, and versatility. Acrylic paints can be diluted with water to create watercolor effects or used undiluted to reproduce the thick, impasto layers used in oil painting.

On the following pages, you can find out about the paints and materials you will need to get started. Then, practice and develop your skills with more than 25 acrylic techniques, grouped into three sections of increasing sophistication—beginner, intermediate, and advanced. A showcase painting at the end of each section brings all the techniques together.

1 Beginner techniques

■ See pp. 128–51

In the first section you can find out about color mixing, and using a limited palette. You'll also learn about aerial perspective and how to paint with both diluted washes and thick applications of acrylic paint.

2 Intermediate techniques

■ See pp. 152–79

In the second section, discover how modeling paste can add texture, see the effects produced from using a colored ground, and learn how to blend, glaze, and use warm and cool colors.

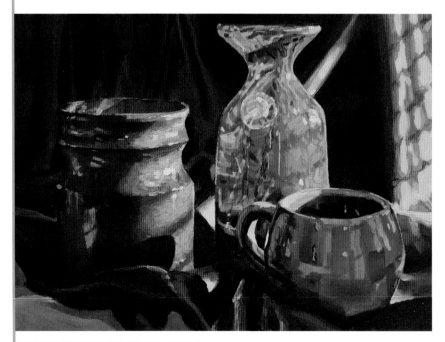

Beginner showcase painting (see pp. 150–51)

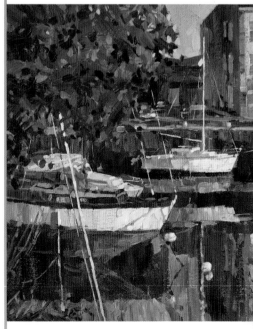

Intermediate showcase painting (see pp. 178–79)

Acrylic paints have a relatively short history—certainly in comparison to watercolors or oils (see pp. 32-33 and pp. 208-09). Developed as interior wall paints in the early 1950s, the first artist-grade paints were introduced in the mid '50s. By the middle of the following decade, manufacturers had vastly improved the quality of their paints by using richer pigments. The popularity of acrylics soon grew among artists, thanks to their quick drying time, lack of toxic ingredients, and their versatility.

Quick and easy

One of the major benefits of the quick drying time of acrylics is that you can easily complete a painting—which might consist of several layers—in one sitting. However, as thin applications will be touch dry in 20-30 minutes, it can be difficult to create subtle blends or soft graduations of color.

Brilliant color

Acrylic paints have a great brilliance of color straight from the tube, although they do have a tendency to dry slightly darker. It is best not to overwork them, either—whether in the palette or on the canvas—because they can become slightly dull with a matte finish.

There is a vast range of pigments to choose from, including metallic and iridescent colors, and acrylics will adhere to most unvarnished surfaces.

Since you can use acrylics to produce precise, detailed paintings or large, abstract pieces, they are undoubtedly an exciting and versatile medium—whether you are a professional artist or are picking up a brush for the first time.

3 Advanced techniques

■ See pp. 180-205

In the final section, further develop your skills by creating dramatic focal points, using optical color mixing, and painting people, skin tones, animal fur, movement, skies, and rainy weather.

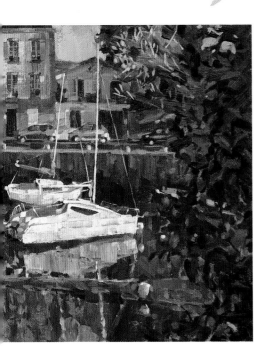

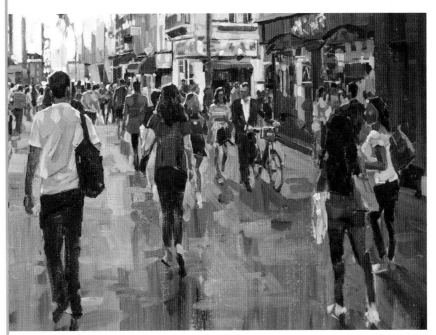

Advanced showcase painting (see pp. 204-05)

Acrylic paints

THE PROPERTIES OF ACRYLICS

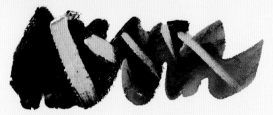

Carbon black with titanium white

Acrylics are easier to manipulate than oils, as they are water soluble and have a faster drying time. They are available in a huge range of colors and consistencies. Whatever your preference, choosing a good-quality acrylic paint of pure pigment is best to ensure lasting color on your paintings.

Acrylics are available in many forms—as spray paint, ink, markers, and tubes and tubs of paint. The consistency of acrylic paint also varies widely. Soft-body paint has a smooth, creamy quality, while heavy-body and super-heavy-body paints are exceptionally thick and buttery. Acrylics can also be obtained in liquid form.

The style you work in will determine the type of paint you choose. A thicker paint is ideal for very expressive and textural work, where you would like brushmarks to remain visible in the paint. A smoother consistency is preferable for detailed work or where you are aiming for a flat finish, particularly on large surfaces.

Paint quality ranges from basic—to student— to artist-quality. Prices reflect the level of pure pigment balanced with binder: the purer the pigment, the costlier the paint. A purer pigment will have less color shift—the difference in color between wet and dry paint. It will also have greater permanence or "lightfastness," meaning it is more resistant to fading when exposed to sunlight. Acrylic paintings are generally more durable than oil artworks.

There is a huge range of acrylic colors available from different manufacturers, and different brands of acrylic paints can be mixed together if the binder is the same. As well as the long-standing traditional colors, new additions are occasionally introduced.

Black and white

There are a few variations to choose from when selecting black or white acrylic paint. Differences can range from very subtle distinctions, such as being slightly more transparent or opaque, to very stark contrasts.

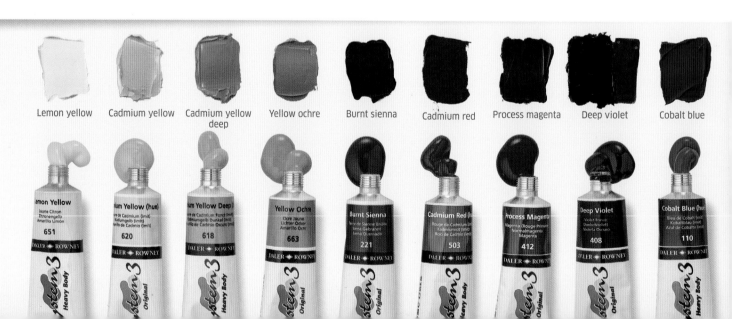

| Lemon yellow | Cadmium yellow | Cadmium yellow deep | Yellow ochre | Burnt sienna | Cadmium red | Process magenta | Deep violet | Cobalt blue |

Lemon Yellow
Jaune Citron
Zitronengelb
Amarillo Limón
651

um Yellow (hue)
de Cadmium Fonce (imit)
Kadmiumgelb (imit)
rillo de Cadmio (imit)
620

um Yellow Deep
re de Cadmium Fonce (imit)
Kadmiumgelb Dunkel (imit)
rillo de Cadmio Oscuro (imit)
618

Yellow Ochre
Ocre Jaune
Lichter Ocker
Amarillo Ocre
663

Burnt Sienna
Terre de Sienne Brûlée
Siena Gebrannt
Siena Quemada
221

Cadmium Red (hue)
Rouge de Cadmium (imit)
Kadmiumrot (imit)
Rojo de Cadmio (imit)
503

Process Magenta
Magenta (Rouge Primaire)
Normalmagenta
Magenta
412

Deep Violet
Violet Foncé
Dunkelviolett
Violeta Oscuro
408

Cobalt Blue (hue)
Bleu de Cobalt (imit)
Kobaltblau (imit)
Azul de Cobalto (imit)
110

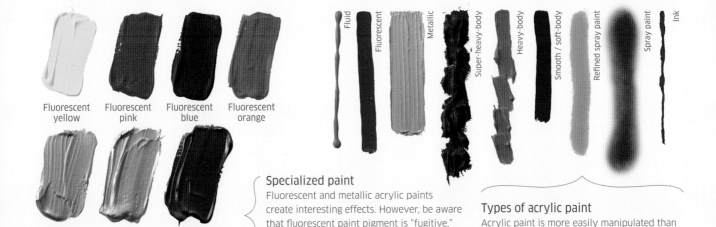

Fluorescent yellow · Fluorescent pink · Fluorescent blue · Fluorescent orange

Pale gold · Silver · Copper

Fluid · Fluorescent · Metallic · Super-heavy-body · Heavy-body · Smooth / soft-body · Refined spray paint · Spray paint · Ink

Specialized paint

Fluorescent and metallic acrylic paints create interesting effects. However, be aware that fluorescent paint pigment is "fugitive," meaning that it fades away in direct sunlight and can disappear completely over time.

Types of acrylic paint

Acrylic paint is more easily manipulated than oil paint and can be applied using a number of methods, from aerosol cans to pens.

Among the different blacks available are bone, mars, ivory, and carbon. Carbon is the darkest black available. When choosing white, the options are zinc, mixing, and titanium, titanium being the most opaque. Your choice will depend on your subject matter and style: a portrait might call for a softer color mix, while a painting of strong colors may require a more dominant version.

Care of paint

Keep acrylic paint away from heat sources and from direct sunlight, because the paint may dry inside

the container. Paint that has been frozen will also be adversely affected. Keep paint containers well sealed and free of contaminants. Acrylics should last several years, but have a much shorter shelf life than oils, which can last decades. Once opened, the intensity of the color may diminish with time. Look out for mold or a sour smell, which may indicate that your acrylics have passed their expiry date.

To prevent colors you have already mixed from drying out overnight, use a palette with deep wells and an airtight lid. Keep it covered and in a

cool place when not in use. If a film forms on the paint's surface, simply pierce it with a palette knife to keep the paint workable.

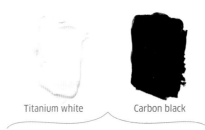

Titanium white · Carbon black

White and black paint

Titanium white is the most opaque of the whites, which means you need less paint to give good coverage. Carbon black has a natural sheen and is the darkest black.

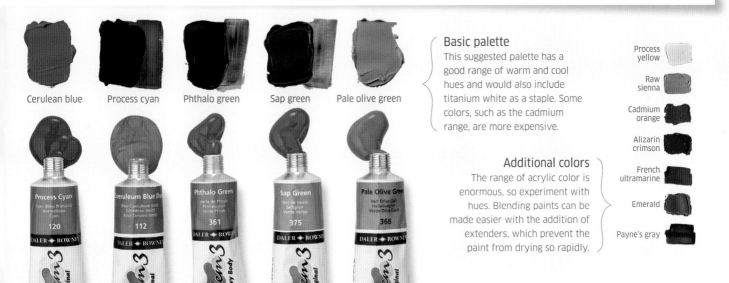

Cerulean blue · Process cyan · Phthalo green · Sap green · Pale olive green

Process Cyan — Cyan (Bleu Primaire) Normalblau Cyan — 120 — DALER·ROWNEY

Coeruleum Blue (hue) — Bleu Caeruleum (imit) Coelinblau (imit) Azul Cerúleo (imit) — 112 — DALER·ROWNEY

Phthalo Green — Verte de Phtalo Phthalogrün Verde Phtalo — 361 — DALER·ROWNEY

Sap Green — Vert de Vessie Saftgrün Verde Vejiga — 375 — DALER·ROWNEY

Pale Olive Green — Vert Olive Clair Helllolivgrün Verde Oliva Claro — 368 — DALER·ROWNEY

Basic palette

This suggested palette has a good range of warm and cool hues and would also include titanium white as a staple. Some colors, such as the cadmium range, are more expensive.

Process yellow · Raw sienna · Cadmium orange · Alizarin crimson · French ultramarine · Emerald · Payne's gray

Additional colors

The range of acrylic color is enormous, so experiment with hues. Blending paints can be made easier with the addition of extenders, which prevent the paint from drying so rapidly.

Brushes and palette knives

HOW TO CHOOSE YOUR BRUSHES

The choice of brushes for acrylics is huge. Brushes come in many shapes and sizes, and your selection depends partly on whether you are diluting the paint or using it thick and neat. The bristles can be either made from animal hair, which is costlier, or synthetic fibre, which works very well for this medium, especially when using thick paint.

Stiff, bristle brushes can manipulate thick paint, while soft-hair brushes can carry lots of fluid, diluted paint. Synthetic brushes come in both bristle and soft-hair types, and are robust enough for acrylic paint. Hog hair brushes (popular in oil painting) are stiff and suitable for acrylics, but soft, sable hair brushes may be too delicate.

Types of brush
The main types of brush to look for are flat, round, and filbert brushes. Flat brushes have a square edge, which is good for broad, loose strokes and bold lines. Round brushes hold lots of paint and have a pointed tip, which makes them ideal for painting details and using with diluted paint. Filbert brushes have a flat shape but a round edge, which makes them versatile. Other types of brush include liners, for fine line work, and fans, for blending. As a beginner, start with two large brushes, two medium, and two small, in a mixture of flat and round shapes. If you prefer to create finely detailed paintings, choose more round brushes, but if you prefer to paint loosely and expressively, large flat brushes may suit you better.

Practise holding your brush in different ways to create different effects (see opposite) – for example, painting fluffy clouds will need gentle skimming brushstrokes but depicting rocks requires firmer strokes.

Caring for your brushes
Since acrylic paint is a water-based medium, you can clean your brushes with soap and water. Special cleaning solutions are also available to buy if you wish. If you have a brush made from animal hair, you should rinse it occasionally with shampoo and water.

Brushes
Brushes come in different shapes and sizes. They can be round, flat, filbert, or rigger and are numbered: the higher the number, the larger the brush. Using a variety of brushes, you can create everything from fine lines to broad washes.

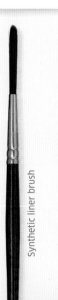
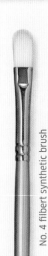
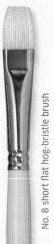
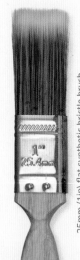

Synthetic liner brush

No. 6 round synthetic brush

No. 4 filbert synthetic brush

No. 8 short flat hog-bristle brush

25mm (1in) flat synthetic bristle brush

Hog-bristle fan brush

Holding a brush

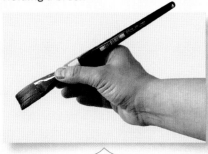

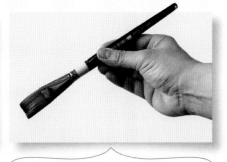

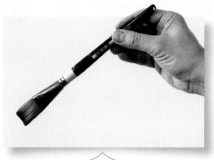

Pencil hold
To paint fine details, hold the brush as if you were holding a pen, with your fingers close to the brush head. This gives you greater control.

Flexible hold
For flowing marks, hold the brush farther up the handle, which allows you to move your wrist and arm freely over the painting.

Maximum-range hold
Hold the brush toward the end of the handle to create very bold, free strokes. This hold helps you to cover large areas quickly.

Never allow acrylic paint to dry on your brushes because this can ruin them permanently.

Palette knives and other tools

There are numerous other ways to apply acrylics for exciting effects. Palette knives come in a range of shapes and sizes, and create very sculptural, textured marks. You can also use palette knives to mix paints quickly and cleanly. To create textural effects, try using sponges, spray bottles, toothbrushes, splatter brushes, or foam rollers.

Other ways to apply acrylics

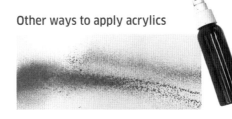

Spray
Try mixing acrylic paint and water in a small spray bottle. You will need to experiment with the amount of water—too much will weaken the color, but too little will clog the bottle.

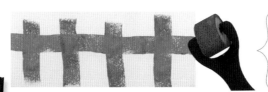

Sponge
Sponges can create bold effects. Use them to give the impression of trees, or try mixing colors on a sponge for interesting, uneven passages of paint.

Roller
Acrylic paints work well with paint rollers. These come in different sizes and textures, and you can use them to cover large areas or to create lines and other marks.

Brushes for special effects
You can make interesting splatter marks using a toothbrush or splatter brush. Paddle brushes are great for spreading thick color and making broad marks over large areas.

Toothbrush

Splatter brush

Paddle brush

Palette knives
You can apply paint using the flat, edge, or tip of a palette knife to create a variety of effects. As with brushes, painting knives come in a variety of sizes and shapes. To hold a palette knife, grip it with a closed fist as you would a trowel.

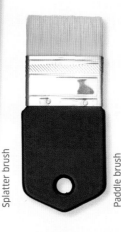

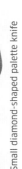

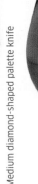

Small diamond-shaped palette knife

Medium diamond-shaped palette knife

Large trowel-shaped palette knife

Supports and other materials

CHOOSING A SURFACE FOR ACRYLICS

Acrylics can be used on most surfaces, or supports, that have not been varnished. These surfaces may include wood, stone, ceramics, fabric, paper, canvas, and board. Certain supports will require priming with acrylic primer or gesso to help the acrylic paint to adhere.

It is important to think carefully about your choice of support, since the type of surface you paint on will affect the way the paint is absorbed and how the finished painting will look.

Watercolor paper

Paper surfaces may require a base layer of white acrylic paint so that subsequent applications of paint will glide over the surface rather than sink into the paper. This is not necessary if you are using a diluted watercolor technique with acrylics.

Stretched canvas

This is one of the best supports to work on because it is sturdy and lightweight. It generally comes ready primed and there is less need for a frame (and the associated costs) since you can simply run a cord behind the canvas to hang it. Canvas comes in many forms, including rolls—either primed or unprimed—canvas boards, and pads. These vary in cost from cheaper cotton canvases to more expensive linen ones. There are also subtle differences in the grain of the canvas, from highly textured to extra fine. It is important that the canvas you buy is taut, because this

Canvas board

MDF

Hardboard

Acrylic paper

Watercolor paper

Keeping your canvas taut
Stretched canvas usually comes with a pack of wooden wedges. If the canvas starts to sag, place them in the grooves in the corners of the wooden stretcher.

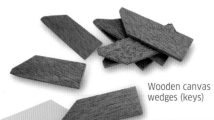
Wooden canvas wedges (keys)

Canvas, board, and paper
Experiment with different supports—you can even leave some areas unpainted so that the background color of the support adds to the painting.

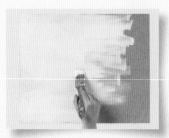

Priming supports
Use horizontal and vertical brushstrokes to apply primer to ensure even coverage. Leave to dry for 30 minutes to an hour before painting over the top.

Stretched canvas

Canvas grain

Grain
Canvas comes in different grains, or textures. Using different grains will produce different effects in your finished paintings.

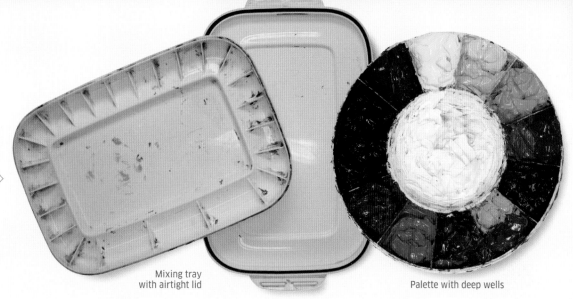

Palettes
Palettes with deep wells conserve acrylic paint for longer. Large, plastic mixing trays allow you to experiment with colors before using them on the canvas. Use warm water to rinse off excess paint afterward.

Mixing tray with airtight lid

Palette with deep wells

will provide a good surface to paint on. Artist-quality canvases are usually more taut and cheaper versions less so. Be careful not to place canvas in direct sunlight or next to a heat source because this can warp the wooden stretchers.

Choosing an easel
Free-standing and table easels are ideal to work on because they allow you to paint standing upright, reducing the stress on your back. You are more likely to create expressive brushmarks if you're standing up. Using a free-

standing easel means you can take a few steps back from time to time to consider the overall painting.

Using palettes
Acrylic paints dry fast. The advantage of this is that it means you can rework areas of your painting almost immediately. But beware—the paints on your palette will also dry out exceptionally quickly. It is advisable to use a palette with an airtight lid, because this will help prevent the paints from drying out. Alternatively, you can use a stay-wet palette. This has a damp layer under the

mixing surface to keep the paints moist. You can either buy a stay-wet palette or make your own (see below).

Additional materials
Because acrylic paints are water based, you do not need any special cleaning products. Just make sure you have a couple of large jars of water nearby while you are painting, to clean unwanted paint off brushes or to dilute thick paint. Paper towels or old rags are useful for wiping excess paint off brushes or skimming paint off the canvas if you make a mistake.

Making a stay-wet palette

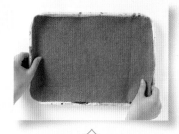 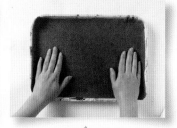 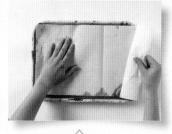 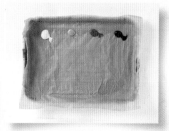

Step 1
Cut a capillary mat (available from a florist or nursery) to fit the bottom of a shallow plastic tray.

Step 2
Tuck the mat into the tray. Pour on water and press the mat down until the water is fully absorbed.

Step 3
Cover the mat with three layers of paper towel, followed by a layer of baking parchment or waxed paper.

Step 4
Now you can mix paints on the parchment. When you take a break, cover the palette with plastic wrap.

Color mixing

USING COLOR THEORY TO MIX ACRYLIC PAINTS

Many of the colors you may need for a painting won't be possible (or practical) to buy in a tube—a landscape, for example, contains many subtle variations of green. Understanding color theory helps you to mix your own colors and create the range of hues and values you need to give your work added dimension.

◼ Mixing primary colors

Practice mixing colors by creating color wheels using a limited palette of three primaries. There are different versions of each color, so your choice of primaries will determine the resulting hue of your secondaries and tertiaries.

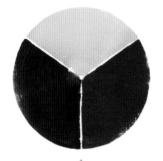

Primary color wheel
Begin with the primary colors yellow, red, and blue. You can create all the other colors from these three.

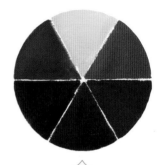

Adding secondary colors
Mix two primaries to create each secondary color: yellow and red for orange, red and blue for violet, and blue and yellow to mix green.

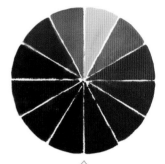

Adding tertiary colors
Mix a secondary color with one of its primaries to make tertiary colors. This creates colors that are closer to one primary, such as yellow-green or blue-green.

◼ Optical color mixing

Optical color mixing involves placing dabs of color next to each other to create the illusion of a mixed color, instead of physically mixing them. Acrylic paint can sometimes look dull when it is overmixed, so optical color mixing is an alternative method that keeps the individual colors vibrant.

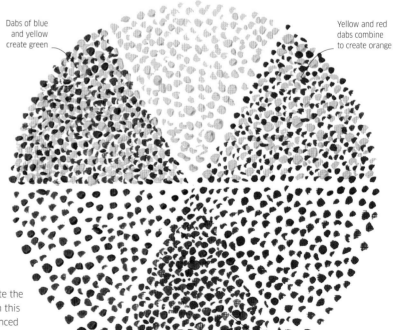

Dabs of blue and yellow create green

Yellow and red dabs combine to create orange

Red and blue dabs create violet

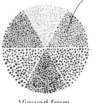

Impression of orange is more intense

Viewed from a distance

Optical mixing and scale
Dabs of pure primary colors create the impression of secondary colors in this wheel. The effect is more pronounced the farther away the viewer is from the painting because the dabs look more dense.

MIXING METHODS

For beginners, it is easier to mix the color you want on a palette first before applying it to your support. This method is best if you want to create a flat, even color because premixing will help to achieve this. If you are using undiluted paint, you can create an interesting, variegated finish by mixing colors directly on the support using either a palette knife or a brush. In these examples, red and yellow are used to create orange.

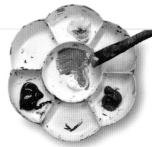

Mixing on a palette
Use either a palette knife or a brush to mix the paint before applying it to your support. This method usually creates a flat, even color.

Flat orange color

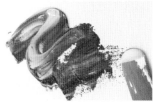

Mixing with a palette knife
Pick up two colors and apply them with a thick "impasto" application using a palette knife. Stir them together loosely for a marbled effect.

Impasto application

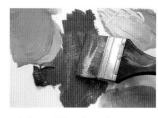

Mixing with a brush
Pick up two colors on your brush at the same time. Move the brush in different directions to loosely mix the colors.

Loosely mixed color

Tints, tones, and shades

Adding white, gray, or black allows you to create tonal ranges. These examples show how to create tints, tones, and shades in primary and secondary colors.

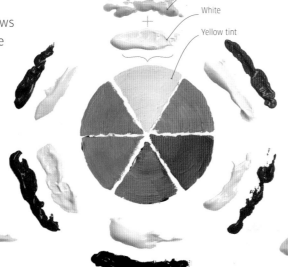

Yellow

White

Yellow tint

Tints—adding white
Tints are colors that have been lightened with white. Adding white creates pastel shades and highlights, but too much can make your colors look chalky.

Shades—adding black
Shades are colors that have been darkened with black. They are useful for shadow areas. Black is very strong, so use it sparingly.

Tones—adding gray
Tones are colors that have been adjusted by adding gray. Different grays create a wide variety of tones, from light to dark.

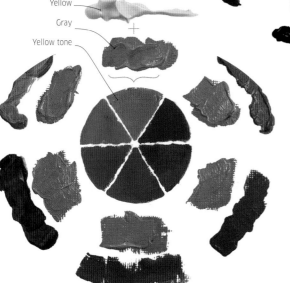

Yellow

Gray

Yellow tone

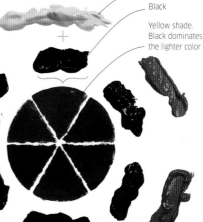

Yellow

Black

Yellow shade.
Black dominates the lighter color

Mixing complementary colors

Complementary colors sit opposite each other on the color wheel. Every primary has a complementary secondary color, and vice versa. Mixing a color with its opposite dulls it, creating a range of useful neutral hues.

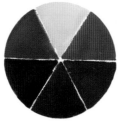

Wheel of primary and secondary colors

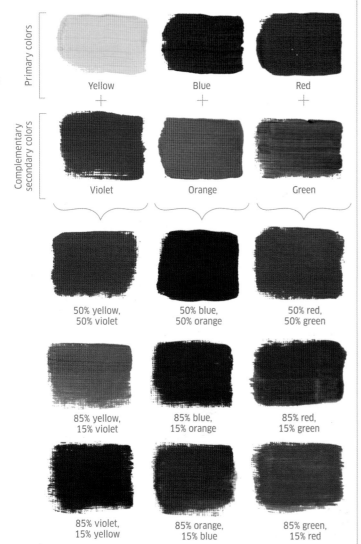

Primary colors

Yellow +

Blue +

Red +

Complementary secondary colors

Violet

Orange

Green

50% yellow, 50% violet

50% blue, 50% orange

50% red, 50% green

85% yellow, 15% violet

85% blue, 15% orange

85% red, 15% green

85% violet, 15% yellow

85% orange, 15% blue

85% green, 15% red

Yellow + violet

Yellow is a light color, so violet dominates it in a 50:50 mix. A dab of violet with yellow creates golden brown.

Blue + orange

An equal mix of blue and orange creates a rich, dark color that can be used instead of black.

Red + green

Mixing red and green equally creates a warm gray. Altering the ratio creates dark greens and purples.

Vibrant color

A limited palette of primary colors and white was used in this painting. The primary colors were combined to create the bright secondary colors that convey the sunny atmosphere in the upper half of the painting.

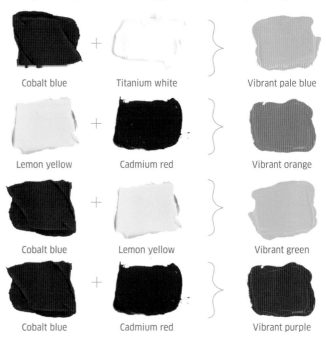

Cobalt blue + Titanium white } Vibrant pale blue

Lemon yellow + Cadmium red } Vibrant orange

Cobalt blue + Lemon yellow } Vibrant green

Cobalt blue + Cadmium red } Vibrant purple

Muted color

To paint the shadows and reflections in the lower half of the painting, the original color mixes were muted by adding complementary colors. Darkening with complementaries, or opposites of warm and cool, can be more subtle than mixing with black.

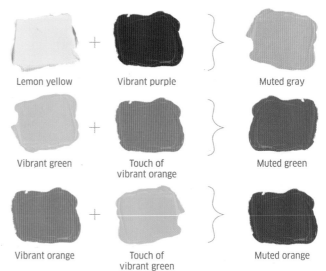

Lemon yellow + Vibrant purple } Muted gray

Vibrant green + Touch of vibrant orange } Muted green

Vibrant orange + Touch of vibrant green } Muted orange

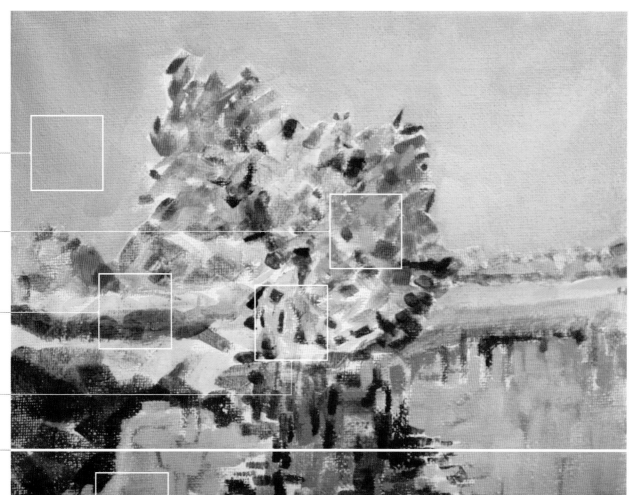

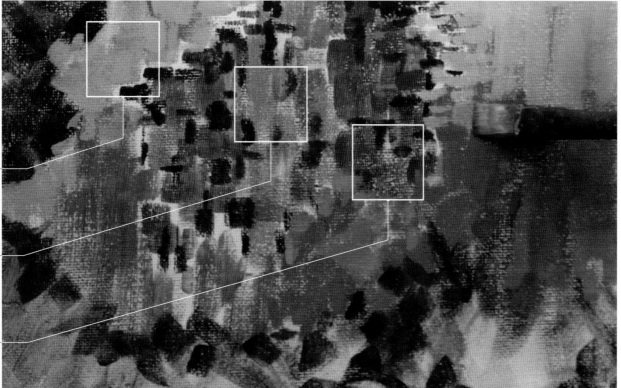

Using a limited palette

PAINTING WITH PRIMARY COLORS

The best way to come to grips with color mixing is to limit yourself to the three primary colors. From this simple starting point you can create a wide range of secondary and tertiary colors. With the addition of white, you can introduce pastel tints, too. Choose a simple subject, which features bold colors and has two or three elements of varying shape and scale.

◼ Choosing primary colors

You can buy many different versions of each color. When used in a mix, light and dark versions of the same primary can produce very different results. Lighter, more passive hues tend to be easier to balance than darker, more dominant ones. However, passive primaries can lead to earthy, somewhat dull mixes.

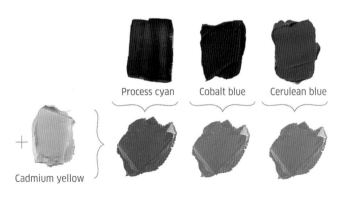

Process cyan   Cobalt blue   Cerulean blue

+

Cadmium yellow

Mixing green with different blues
Process cyan (dark) creates vibrant secondaries; cobalt blue (mid) creates earthy secondaries; and cerulean blue (light) creates soft secondaries.

This simple still life is a great showcase for the primary colors. The palette includes a mid red and yellow, and a dominant blue (cyan) to create a strong green for the lime. Each color mix is echoed throughout the painting to create a sense of balance.

You will need

Titanium white · Cadmium yellow · Cadmium red · Process cyan

- 1½in (38mm) and 1in (25mm) flat synthetic-bristle brushes
- 14 x 19in (37 x 49cm) NOT watercolor paper (apply a base coat of white acrylic first)

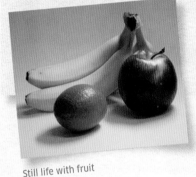

Still life with fruit

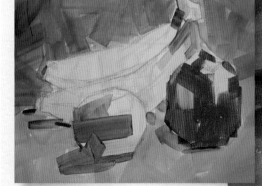

Large multidirectional strokes add interest

1 Primary colors
First, draw a pencil outline of the fruit to establish composition. Then, using the largest flat brush, apply blocks of pure yellow, red, and blue. Dilute the blue to create lighter areas in the foreground.

Cadmium yellow

Process cyan

Mixed green

Process cyan

Cadmium red

Mixed violet

Cadmium yellow

Cadmium red

Mixed orange

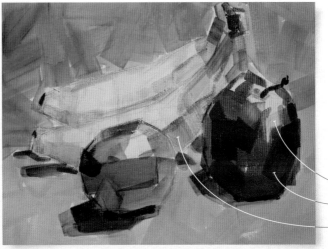

2 Secondary colors

Once the first layer is dry, add the secondary colors. Mix a strong green for the lime and parts of the banana and apple. Mix a deep violet for the dark flecks on the fruit. Mix orange to dab the apple and for areas of the bananas that reflect the apple.

— Mixed green

— Mixed violet

— Mixed orange

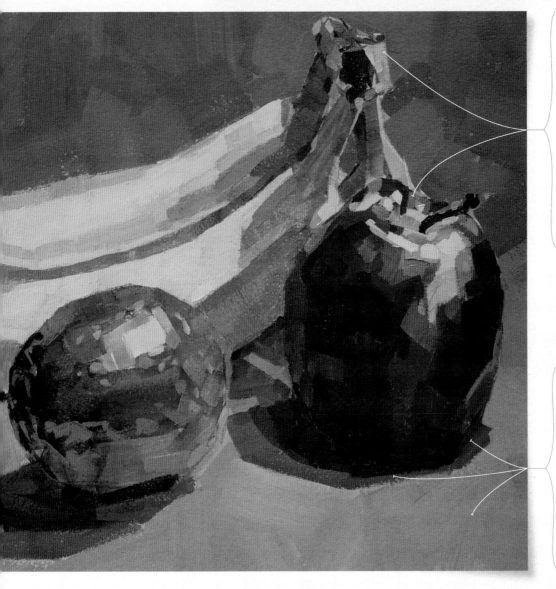

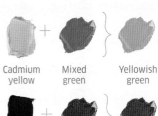

Cadmium yellow

Mixed green

Yellowish green

Cadmium red

Mixed orange

Orangey red

3 Tertiary green and orange

Mix a yellowish green to add subtlety to the bananas and lime. Mix an orangey red to add subtlety to the apple.

4 Tertiary violets

Add white to violet to create a pastel tint for the background, then divide the mix into three. Add blue for a cool, receding effect at the top and for the darker areas of shadow; add red for the middle section and lighter areas of shadow; and add yellow and more white to give the foreground warmth. Finally, use a 1in (25mm) flat brush to add highlights and fine details.

Drawing with a brush

CREATING INITIAL OUTLINES WITH PAINT

Developing good drawing skills is an important part of learning to paint. However, devoting too much time and energy to creating the perfect preliminary sketch can hamper your creativity when it comes to the painting itself. Instead, try using paint and a brush to map out the initial shapes. This will keep the process fluid and encourage you to capture only the key elements of your subject during the early stages.

■ Establishing basic shapes

Whether you're planning a simple still life or a detailed portrait, an initial drawing will help you create basic shapes and establish composition. Detail is not necessary at this stage—using a brush will help keep your sketch simple and impressionistic.

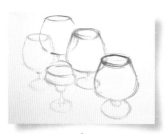

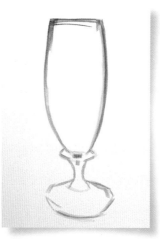

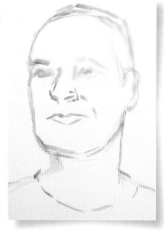

Lines and ellipses
Start off with a few simple, easily recognizable shapes and objects, such as a group of similar-shaped glasses. Practice drawing the lines and ellipses.

Group of objects
Focus on shapes and outlines, using a large group of glasses of different shapes and sizes. Resist the urge to block in any areas of color.

No. 8 round synthetic brush

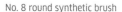

½in (13mm) flat synthetic brush

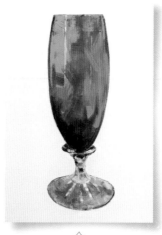

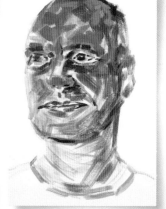

Brushes for sketching
Round and flat brushes are the most versatile for drawing, allowing you to vary the thickness of the line and add shape and tone. You will need just two brushes for the exercises here: a no. 8 round for the simple sketches opposite, and a ½in (13mm) flat for blocking in the color on the exercise on pp. 136-37.

Single object
Once you have established the overall shape of an object with simple line work, you can switch your attention to the colors and details.

Portrait
The drawing stage of a portrait helps you place the features correctly and establish the form of the face before you block in shapes with dark and light tones.

LINES AND ELLIPSES

This simple still life of a small group of similar-shaped glasses is a good subject for practicing lines and ellipses. Experiment drawing with two or three brushes.

You will need

- ½in (13mm) flat synthetic brush
- 16 x 20in (40 x 50cm) medium-grain canvas

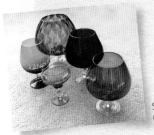

Small group of glasses

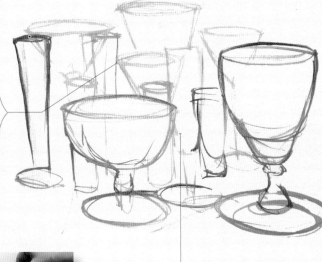

1 Free-flowing lines
Establish the basic shapes and forms of all the glasses using one brush and color. This keeps the drawing process free-flowing.

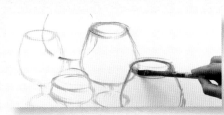

2 Add definition
Introduce darker tones to differentiate the shapes. Experiment with different marks and brushstrokes.

GROUP OF OBJECTS

In this large group of glasses, there are several different shapes and sizes to contend with. As well as accurately describing their shapes, focus on their relative positions, too.

You will need

- No. 8 round synthetic brush
- 16 x 20in (40 x 50cm) medium-grain canvas

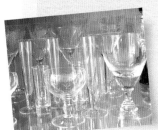

Large group of glasses

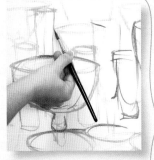

1 Shapes and positions
Draw the various shapes and carefully position each glass. Use the negative spaces between the glasses for guidance.

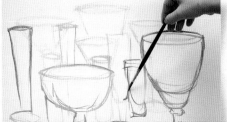

2 Bolder lines
Develop two or three glasses in the foreground with stronger color and bolder line work. This will create a sense of depth.

SINGLE OBJECT

A single-object still life, such as this ornate, colored glass, is a great follow-up exercise. By focusing on one subject without the distraction of surrounding objects, you can work up an initial brush drawing into a more finished painting.

You will need

Titanium white

Burnt sienna

Cerulean blue

Phthalo green

- ½in (13mm) and 1in (25mm) flat synthetic brushes
- 16 x 20in (40 x 50cm) medium-grain canvas

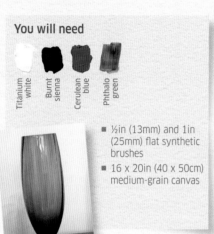

Ornate glass

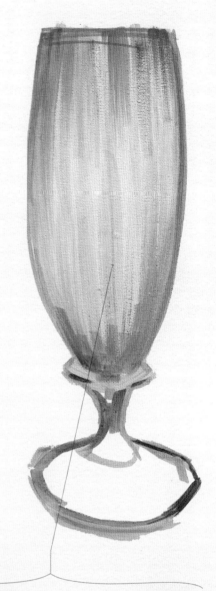

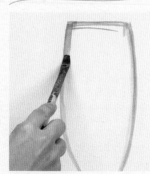

1 Initial outline
Establish the basic shape of the glass, sketching its contours with a ½in (13mm) flat brush. Use cerulean blue to match the hue of the subject.

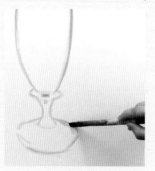

2 Consistent line work
Keep the thickness of the outlines consistent throughout, and use the same mix and concentration of color. This helps create cohesion.

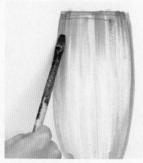

3 Block in color
Using the same brush and starting from the top, fill in the center of the glass with color. Make sure all the brushstrokes are in the same direction.

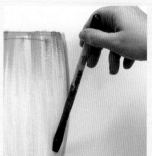

4 Darker tones
Add darker, heavier tones of cerulean blue near the edges of the outline and lighter tones toward the center. This creates depth and form.

"Establish the shape and form of the subject using one color and one brush. This will help you draw quickly and freely, without having to stop and start as you change brushes and mix new colors."

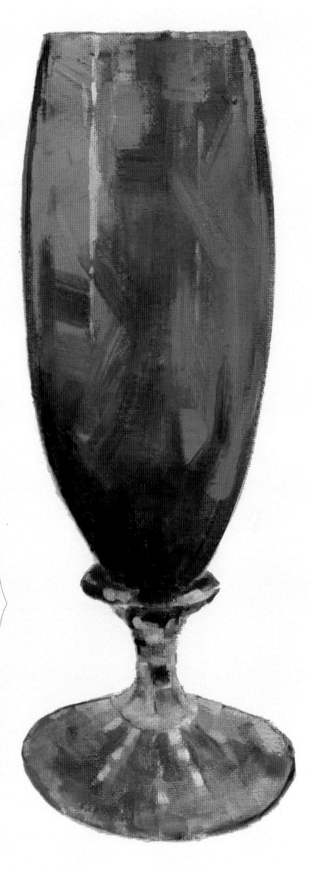

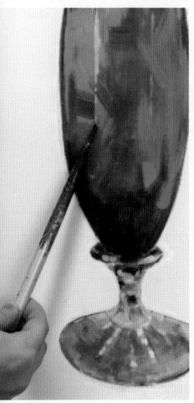

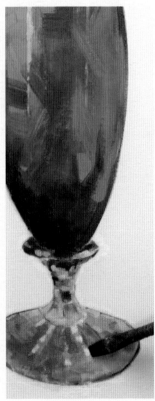

5 Light tints
Use a mix of cerulean blue and phthalo green for the darkest tones. Add white to create a range of light tints, which suggest reflections in the glass.

6 Finishing touches
Apply dabs of color to the base of the glass for a sparkly effect. Include subtle hints of burnt sienna to pick out the reflections of the surroundings.

Tints, tones, and shades

EXPLORING TONAL RANGE

Every color has a tonal range of tints, tones, and shades—a scale of brightness from light to dark. You can use tonal color for everything, from your strongest highlights to your deepest shadows. By doing this you can emulate the way in which light behaves on an object or scene and create a three-dimensional effect.

■ Tints

Adding white to colors creates tints. White softens the brightness of colors and creates a range of pastel hues, depending on how much of it you use.

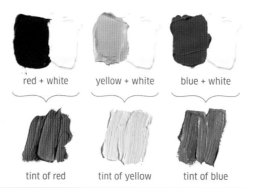

red + white   yellow + white   blue + white

tint of red   tint of yellow   tint of blue

■ Tones

Adding gray, or a mix of black and white, to colors creates tones. You can achieve many complex variations by adjusting the quantities of black and white in the mix.

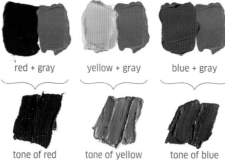

red + gray   yellow + gray   blue + gray

tone of red   tone of yellow   tone of blue

■ Shades

Adding black to colors creates shades. Use black sparingly—it can be very dominant and too much will make the color of the shade barely visible.

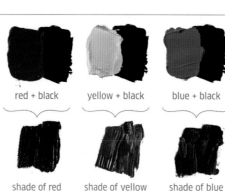

red + black   yellow + black   blue + black

shade of red   shade of yellow   shade of blue

PUTTING IT INTO PRACTICE

Each color in this painting is mixed with white, gray, or black to create tonal effects of light and shade. A strongly lit photograph, such as the one of garlic bulbs below, provides lots of contrast with which to experiment. Whatever subject you choose, you can test your success by photographing your finished color painting in black and white. Doing this will make it easier to see if your use of tonal range is correct.

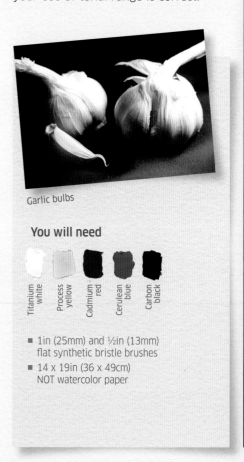

Garlic bulbs

You will need

Titanium white   Process yellow   Cadmium red   Cerulean blue   Carbon black

■ 1in (25mm) and ½in (13mm) flat synthetic bristle brushes
■ 14 x 19in (36 x 49cm) NOT watercolor paper

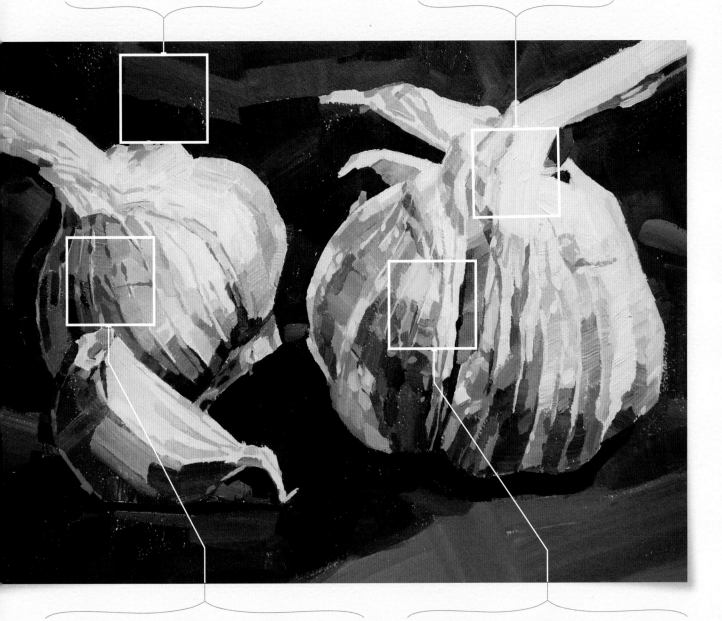

Shades

Apply deep shades of blue to the background and shadows—the striking contrast of darks against the light garlic helps define the shapes. Where the shadows meet the foreground, introduce softer tones with blue–and–gray mixes.

Tints

Add plenty of pale yellow tints to evoke a sense of light striking the garlic. Use tints of red and blue among the yellow to add interest. The tonal difference between tints and shades provides satisfying contrasts, and creates dramatic lighting effects.

Tones

Suggest the curving sides of the garlic with subtly graded tones of blue, yellow, and red. Use darker tones near the shadows and lighter tones to blend into the tints at the top. Experiment first on a palette, adjusting the ratio of black to white in your gray mixes to make multiple tones.

Secondary color mixes

Link the primary colors in your painting by mixing tints, tones, or shades of secondary colors. Extend the range of red tints by adding blue to red to make pastel purples; or add a hint of yellow to your blue-gray mixes for a greenish tone.

Acrylic washes

USING DILUTED PAINT

When you dilute acrylics with water, they gain a transparency similar to that of watercolors. The colors don't fade when they dry, you can apply multiple washes with no interference from dry base layers, and you can paint over any mistakes using thicker paint. Acrylic washes don't spread or blend as easily as watercolor, however, so they can look streaky.

Wet-in-wet and wet-on-dry

Applying diluted paint to a wet surface is called "wet-in-wet" and it will give you a soft, diffused wash of color. Applying diluted paint to a dry surface is called "wet-on-dry" and creates a clean, translucent color.

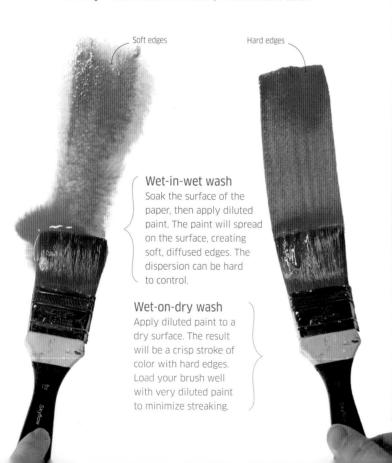

Soft edges

Hard edges

Wet-in-wet wash
Soak the surface of the paper, then apply diluted paint. The paint will spread on the surface, creating soft, diffused edges. The dispersion can be hard to control.

Wet-on-dry wash
Apply diluted paint to a dry surface. The result will be a crisp stroke of color with hard edges. Load your brush well with very diluted paint to minimize streaking.

This painting combines both wet-in-wet and wet-on-dry washes to create luminous layers of color. The details are finished with undiluted paint to create interesting contrasts.

You will need

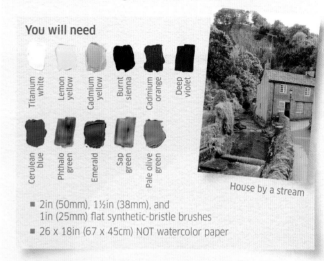

Titanium white | Lemon yellow | Cadmium yellow | Burnt sienna | Cadmium orange | Deep violet

Cerulean blue | Phthalo green | Emerald | Sap green | Pale olive green

House by a stream

- 2in (50mm), 1½in (38mm), and 1in (25mm) flat synthetic-bristle brushes
- 26 x 18in (67 x 45cm) NOT watercolor paper

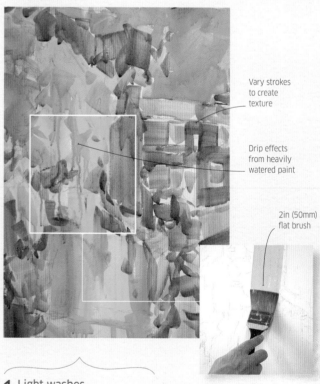

Vary strokes to create texture

Drip effects from heavily watered paint

2in (50mm) flat brush

1 Light washes
Use very diluted washes initially. Lay wet-on-dry washes for the trees. Wet the paper in the stream area and apply green wet-in-wet washes for a watery effect. Apply grays mixed from cerulean, violet, and sienna as wet-on-dry washes for the stone house and cliff.

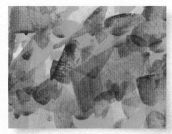

2 Dark washes
When the initial washes are dry, use a 1½in (38mm) flat brush to add darker tones for the shadows. Use less water in the paint to give you greater definition and more control over the washes.

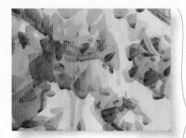

3 Adjusting the contrast
Add a third layer of mid tones to bridge the gap between the lights and darks, and to create texture and detail. This won't disrupt the layers of colors underneath.

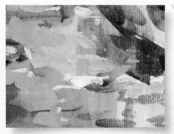

4 Highlights
Use a moist 1in (25mm) brush and barely diluted paint to give definition to the last details. Mix pale green tints to add as highlights to the trees and stream.

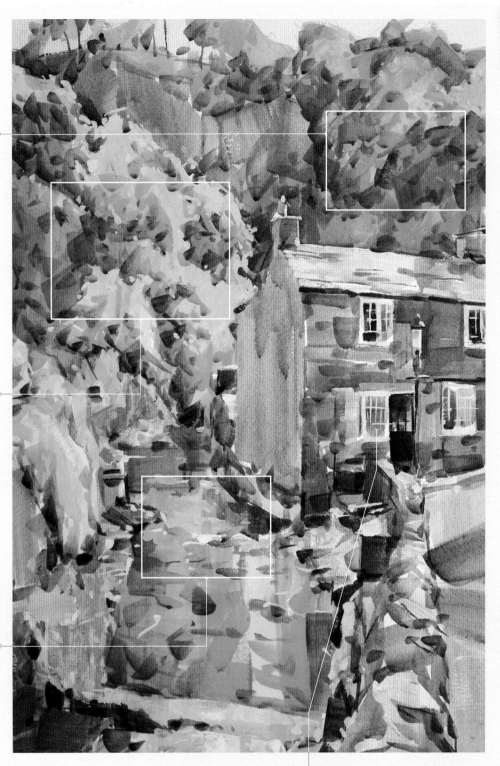

5 Finishing touches
Pick out the window frames in white with hints of lemon and cerulean blue. Don't overdo the finishing touches, though—allow the glowing, translucent quality of the washes to take center stage.

Thick acrylics

USING PAINT STRAIGHT FROM THE TUBE

Undiluted acrylic paint is punchy and vibrant. You can create textured, sculptural impasto effects using artist-quality, heavy body acrylics, as these thick paints hold brushmarks well. They also have a luster and sheen that is comparable to oil paint. Undiluted paints are expensive to use in large quantities, however, so use them on a small scale to begin with.

■ Layering undiluted acrylics

You can apply thick layers of acrylic in quick succession because they dry so rapidly. Too many heavy layers, though, will reduce the "tooth" of the surface and prevent upper layers from sticking; they may also look dull and overworked.

Acrylic opacity

Undiluted acrylics are vibrant and opaque because no pigment is lost through dilution. You can layer light colors on top of dark ones with no show-through.

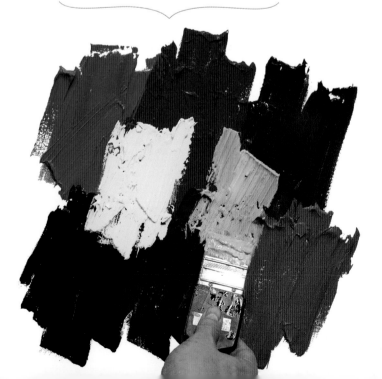

The saturated color of undiluted acrylics gives this painting of a rose drama. Large, flat brushes were used to create expressive impasto marks, keeping the botanical subject from looking too scientific.

You will need

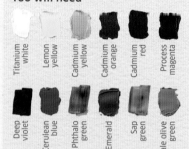

Titanium white | Lemon yellow | Cadmium yellow | Cadmium orange | Cadmium red | Process magenta

Deep violet | Cerulean blue | Phthalo green | Emerald | Sap green | Pale olive green

- 2in (50mm), 1½in (38mm), and 1in (25mm) flat, synthetic-bristle brushes
- 20 x 28in (50 x 70cm) stretched, medium-grain canvas

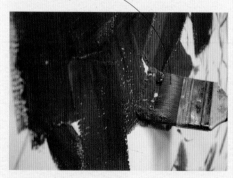

Red rose

Crisscrossing brushstrokes

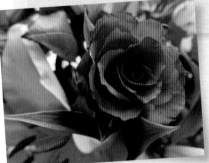

1 Blocking in the rose

Draw a simple sketch on your canvas. Using a 2in (50mm) flat brush, block in the rose with a mix of red, magenta, violet, and orange to give it a dynamic color. Block in the rose with crisscrossing strokes to create texture. Introduce a soft red tint at the edges of the petals.

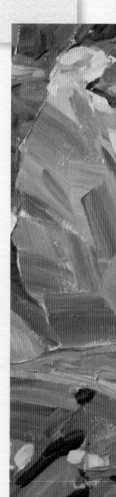

2 The background

Try to establish the right combination of colors at this stage to avoid having to build up too many thick background layers later. Experiment with different mixes: mix loosely to keep the colors vital; add violet to mix dark greens; let colors from other mixes bleed into the pastel color for the lily. Using a clean 2in (50mm) flat brush, fill in the leaves, lily, and areas of background light using crisscrossing brushstrokes.

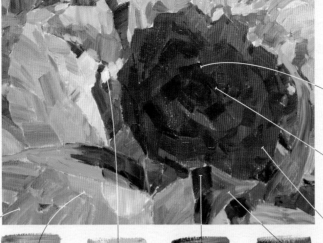

3 Rose shades

Mix red with violet to create darker shades of red and use these to define individual petals.

Dark red mix

Mid red mix

Pink lily mix

Light green mix

Blue background light mix

Dark green mix

Mid green mix

Bright red mix

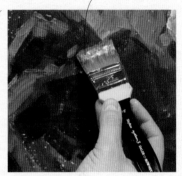

1½in (38mm) flat brush

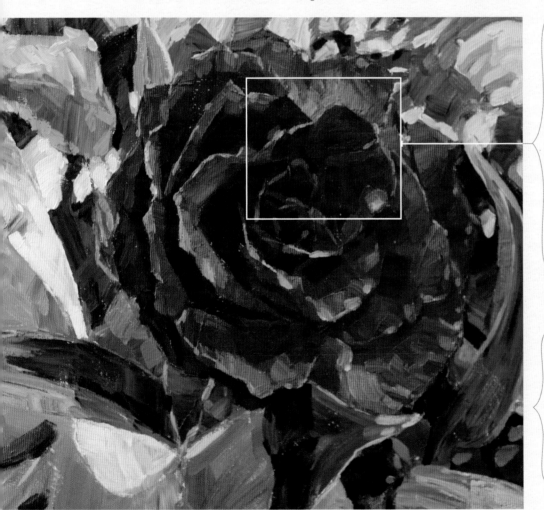

4 Rose tints

Once the dark reds have dried, add light tints to the outer parts of the petals. The multiple layers of paint create a three-dimensional quality.

5 Finishing touches

Develop the background, but don't overwork it as it may lose its vibrancy and compete with the rose. Use a 1in (25mm) flat brush to add strong darks and white–lemon highlights. Try to keep the vigor of the impasto marks as you continue to refine the rose.

Painting shapes

SIMPLIFYING COMPOSITION

If some subjects seem too daunting, try breaking them down into basic shapes. For example, the clothes and face of a walking man are less important than the fact that he is walking—a stick figure would work to convey this action initially. Once you start relating basic shapes to more complex ones, you'll find it easier to block in a preliminary composition.

▩ Identifying basic shapes

Look for the basic geometric shapes in any object or scene and use these to compose your painting. You might draw a mountain range as several triangles sitting side by side, for example, or convey an archway as a rectangle with a circle on top. You can practice this technique with almost any subject.

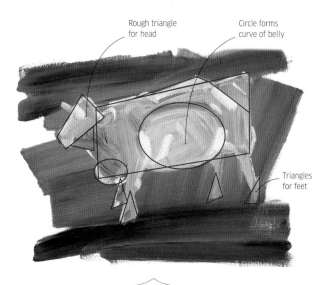

Rough triangle for head

Circle forms curve of belly

Triangles for feet

Dissecting into shapes
You can find geometric shapes even in organic subjects. This quick study of a cow was composed from a variety of simple circles, triangles, and rectangles.

This painting shows how starting with some basic shapes to represent elements of a picture establishes the structure of a complex street scene.

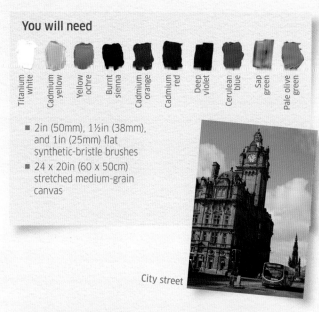

You will need

Titanium white · Cadmium yellow · Yellow ochre · Burnt sienna · Cadmium orange · Cadmium red · Deep violet · Cerulean blue · Sap green · Pale olive green

- 2in (50mm), 1½in (38mm), and 1in (25mm) flat synthetic-bristle brushes
- 24 x 20in (60 x 50cm) stretched medium-grain canvas

City street

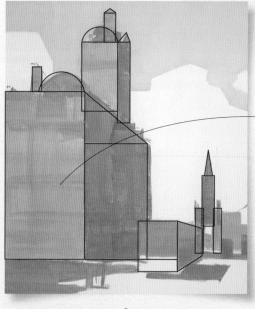

Floors of the building are lightly marked out

1 Preliminary shapes
Draw the scene using basic shapes (highlighted above). For tricky shapes, such as the dark side of the building, try using a rectangle with a right-angled triangle on top. Paint in the shapes with slightly diluted acrylics, using tonal colors for light and shade.

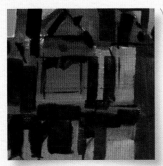

2 Dark tones

Use simple dark shapes and lines to suggest the windows. Mix a gray from cerulean blue, sienna, and white for the clouds and road. Don't worry if your strokes look blocky—you can soften them later.

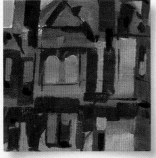

3 Light tones

Add blue tints to the windows and the circular clock face. Apply gray tints to create a softer effect for the clouds—they will bridge the gap between the white canvas and dark grays.

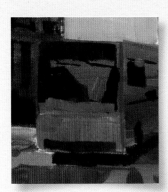

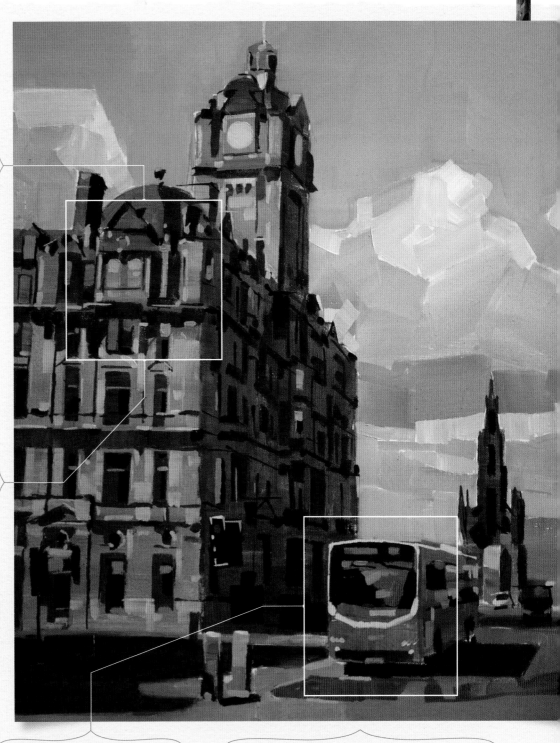

4 Developing details

The bus makes a good focal point. Add dark tones to suggest shadows in the glass, then apply shots of color. Finally, add tints to pick out the lights and reflections in the bus windows.

5 Finishing touches

Strengthen the shadows and apply ochre tints to the building; this increases the contrasts and separates elements from each other. Add an expressive splash of red in the road, to provide a counterpoint to the rigid geometric forms in the rest of the painting.

White subjects

PAINTING WHITE USING COLOR

White objects can be challenging to paint—too much white can appear lifeless, chalky, or washed out. White shows up best when it is juxtaposed or mixed with colors. To paint a white subject, such as a cup or a snow scene, you'll need to look carefully at how it relates to the colors around it—you may see only white at first, but you'll quickly find that you can identify more color within the white than you imagined.

▮ Identifying colors in white

White objects reflect the colors around them. These reflected colors can be subtle or intense, and you can depict them using white tints (see pp.138–39). A strong background color presents a counterpoint to the white object and provides a good tonal range for you to create form, a three-dimensional effect.

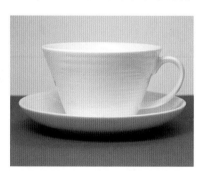

Photograph of a cup and saucer
Colored paper gives the white shapes definition. The blue color reflects strongly where the saucer sits on the paper, but casts a fainter hue at the rim of the cup.

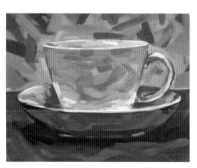

Painting the cup and saucer
Background and foreground color helps the pale tints stand out. Stronger tones were applied first, with white tints introduced gradually, and highlights added at the end.

In this painting, the swan's surroundings provide the colors reflected in its feathers, and help to define its shape. Bright sunlight makes the contrast between the light and dark colors very pronounced.

You will need

Titanium white | Lemon yellow | Cadmium yellow | Yellow ochre | Cadmium orange | Cadmium red | Alizarin crimson | Cerulean blue | Process cyan

- 1in (25mm) and ½in (13mm) flat synthetic brushes
- 20 x 16in (50 x 40cm) medium-grain canvas

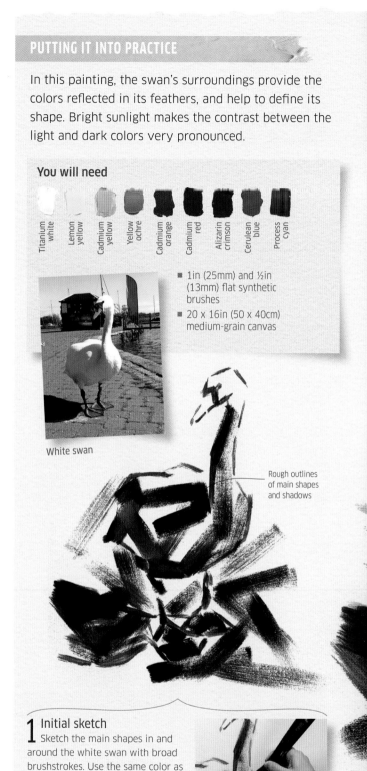

White swan

Rough outlines of main shapes and shadows

1 Initial sketch
Sketch the main shapes in and around the white swan with broad brushstrokes. Use the same color as your background to unify the painting. A strong color will help future white mixes stand out.

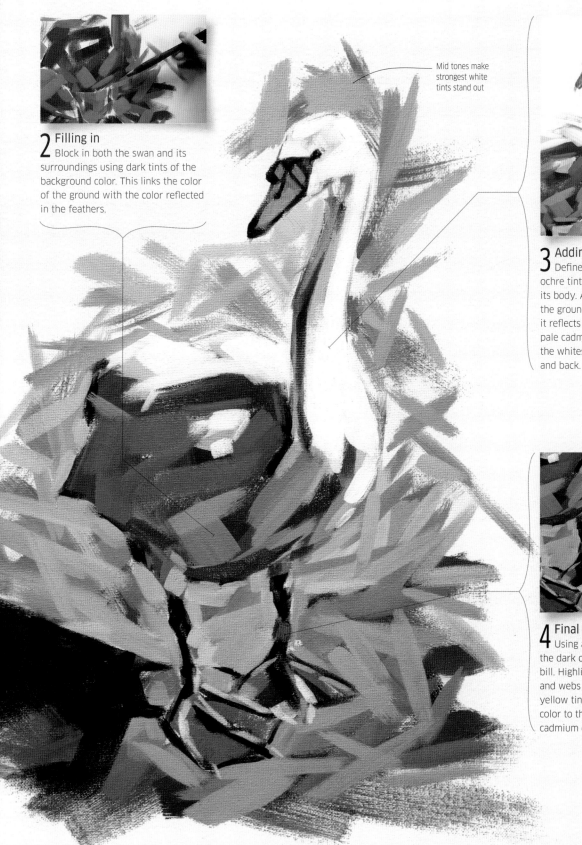

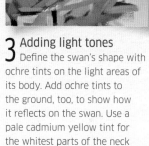

Mid tones make
strongest white
tints stand out

2 Filling in
Block in both the swan and its
surroundings using dark tints of the
background color. This links the color
of the ground with the color reflected
in the feathers.

3 Adding light tones
Define the swan's shape with
ochre tints on the light areas of
its body. Add ochre tints to
the ground, too, to show how
it reflects on the swan. Use a
pale cadmium yellow tint for
the whitest parts of the neck
and back.

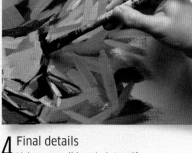

4 Final details
Using a small brush, intensify
the dark colors of the feet and
bill. Highlight the neck, head,
and webs of the feet with a light
yellow tint. Finally, add pops of
color to the beak and leg with
cadmium orange and yellow.

Aerial perspective

DEPICTING DISTANCE

Aerial, or atmospheric, perspective describes the way in which atmospheric conditions affect the appearance of distant objects. This effect can be recreated in art by applying the most vibrant colors and tones in the foreground, then tinting them with softer, often bluer, hues as they recede.

■ Color and distance

By gradually lightening the shade of a color, you can create a sense of depth. The darker, purer shades look strong and close; as you gradually add white, these lighter tints appear to be farther away.

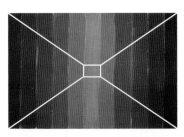

Orange gradation
A shade of pure cadmium orange on both the left and right fades toward the center as white is gradually added, creating a corridor of receding color.

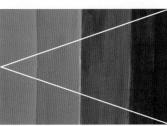

Green gradation
Here, using phthalo green, the perspective recedes from right to left, and fewer tonal gradation lines have been used.

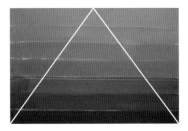

Blue gradation
The first band is a pure cobalt blue, with incrementally paler tones leading the eye to the horizon, creating the appearance of sea giving way to sky.

This piece uses color gradation as an exercise; the background gradations have deliberately been left exposed. The blue bands of color suggest the sea fading into the distance where it meets a yellow sky.

You will need

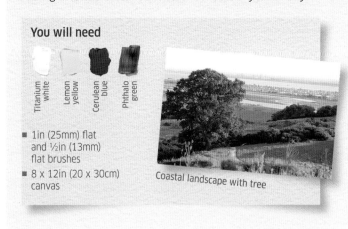

Titanium white
Lemon yellow
Cerulean blue
Phthalo green

- 1in (25mm) flat and ½in (13mm) flat brushes
- 8 x 12in (20 x 30cm) canvas

Coastal landscape with tree

In this landscape overlooking the sea, the foreground is still quite far away, so shapes, colors, and tonal variations are emphasized without overstating small details. This allows you to be creative without trying to replicate the photograph. The blue in the distance indicates land but its haziness suggests distance.

You will need

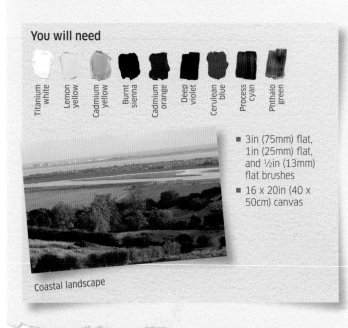

Titanium white
Lemon yellow
Cadmium yellow
Burnt sienna
Cadmium orange
Deep violet
Cerulean blue
Process cyan
Phthalo green

- 3in (75mm) flat, 1in (25mm) flat, and ½in (13mm) flat brushes
- 16 x 20in (40 x 50cm) canvas

Coastal landscape

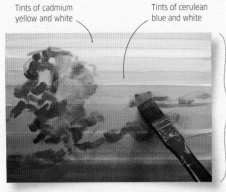

Tints of cadmium yellow and white

Tints of cerulean blue and white

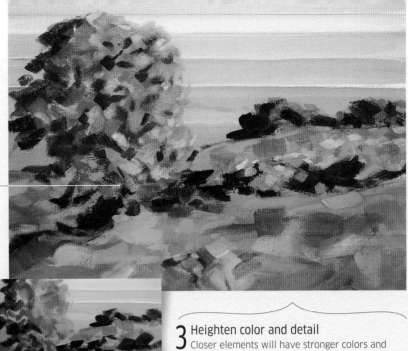

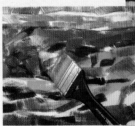

1 Establish forms
Paint the background bands with your 1in (25mm) brush, then sketch in the foreground trees and land using phthalo green.

2 Lighten areas
Still using the 1in (25mm) brush, apply lighter tints of cerulean blue and lemon yellow to the green areas.

3 Heighten color and detail
Closer elements will have stronger colors and greater clarity, so intensify color and definition in the foreground. Use your ½in (13mm) brush for the detail on the tree.

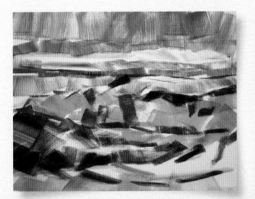

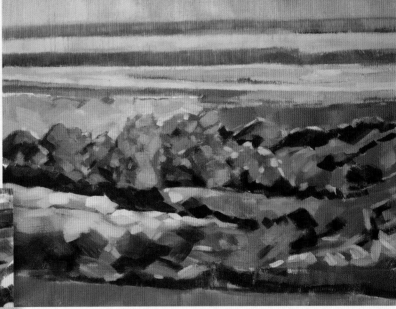

1 Sketch forms
Use your 3in (75mm) brush to loosely establish different elements. Use pure process cyan for the sky and phthalo green with cadmium yellow to create tonal differences in the greens. Create some horizontal lines using phthalo green, and use burnt sienna to divide parts of the landscape.

2 Intensify colors
Continue with the same brush, adding cadmium yellow and cadmium orange over the green to indicate trees. Use deep violet with burnt sienna between the green masses.

3 Solidify the scene
Use the 1in (25mm) brush to form strong shapes by varying color and tone. Lighten the ground between the green areas with a mix of white, violet, and sienna. Also vary the green tones.

4 Finishing touches
With your 3in (75mm) brush, add more process cyan and plenty of white for the sky. Then gently skim the distant, blue landmass with downward directional marks to give it a hazy edge. Use the ½in (13mm) brush to lighten areas on the trees.

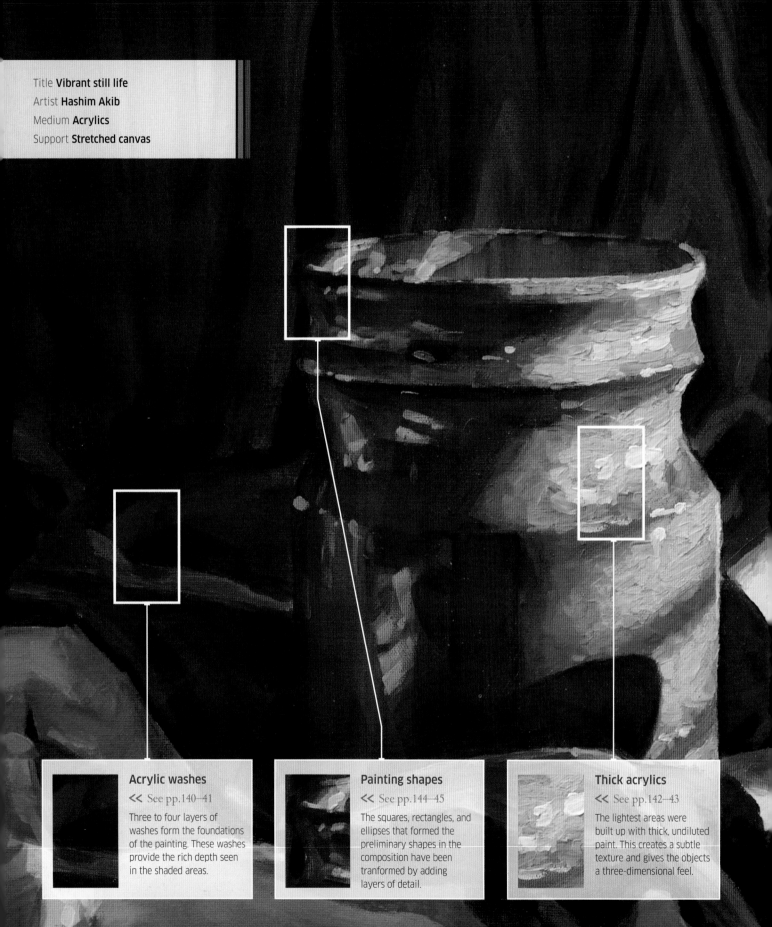

Title **Vibrant still life**
Artist **Hashim Akib**
Medium **Acrylics**
Support **Stretched canvas**

Acrylic washes

<< See pp.140–41

Three to four layers of washes form the foundations of the painting. These washes provide the rich depth seen in the shaded areas.

Painting shapes

<< See pp.144–45

The squares, rectangles, and ellipses that formed the preliminary shapes in the composition have been tranformed by adding layers of detail.

Thick acrylics

<< See pp.142–43

The lightest areas were built up with thick, undiluted paint. This creates a subtle texture and gives the objects a three-dimensional feel.

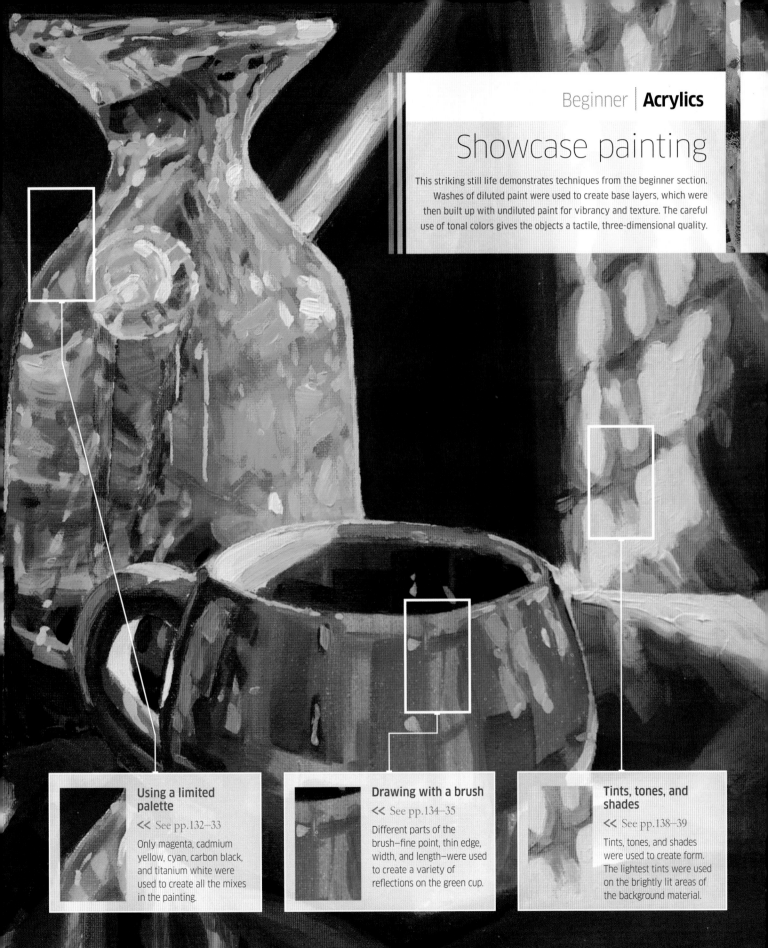

Showcase painting

This striking still life demonstrates techniques from the beginner section. Washes of diluted paint were used to create base layers, which were then built up with undiluted paint for vibrancy and texture. The careful use of tonal colors gives the objects a tactile, three-dimensional quality.

Using a limited palette

≪ See pp.132–33

Only magenta, cadmium yellow, cyan, carbon black, and titanium white were used to create all the mixes in the painting.

Drawing with a brush

≪ See pp.134–35

Different parts of the brush—fine point, thin edge, width, and length—were used to create a variety of reflections on the green cup.

Tints, tones, and shades

≪ See pp.138–39

Tints, tones, and shades were used to create form. The lightest tints were used on the brightly lit areas of the background material.

Adding texture

USING MEDIUMS FOR TEXTURAL EFFECTS

You can use mediums such as texture gels and pastes to create a range of impasto and textural effects. Heavy structure gel will allow you to create the most dramatic effects. White in color and with a buttery consistency, it dries to a hard, clear, satin finish. Lay the gel directly on the canvas to create a more tactile surface, or mix it with acrylics for a thicker, smoother paint for sculpting layers of color.

▪ Textural effects

Apply heavy structure gel with a palette knife, sponge, or brush. You can also introduce additional elements while it is wet, such as sand, twigs, or paper for collage. There are several other mediums you can use in conjunction with acrylic paint to create a range of dramatic textural effects.

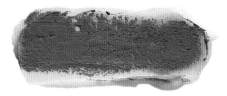

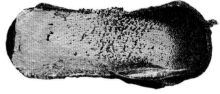

Sand texture gel
A gel containing small particles of natural sand. It retains its texture when mixed with paint and produces a fine, sandy effect.

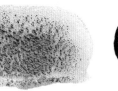

Glass beads texture gel
A colorless, medium-body gel containing fine, spherical beads of glass, which create a bubbly effect.

Black lava texture gel
A granular gel containing fine particles of black flint. Gray when wet, it dries to a speckled black when mixed with color.

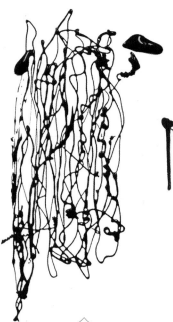

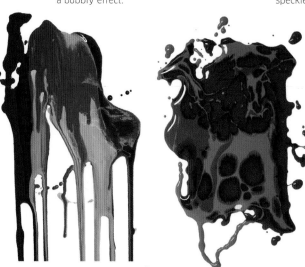

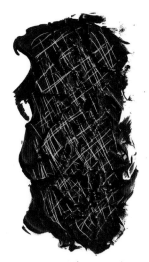

String gel
Mix string gel with acrylic paint to produce a stringlike web of color with increased transparency and flow.

Pouring mediums
Add liquid pouring mediums to acrylic paint to produce a range of effects, such as long, thin drips of paint, intricate marbling patterns, and slick, glassy pools of color. It's great for multicolored compositions working wet-in-wet.

Modeling paste
This paste is similar to heavy structure gel but not as smooth. When dry, it can be carved or sanded into dramatic shapes.

This striking still life was created using a base layer of heavy structure gel. Natural sand was then added to introduce more texture and capture the essence of the seashell.

You will need

Titanium white • Yellow ochre • Process cyan • Phthalo green

- 1½in (38mm) flat bristle brush
- Palette knife
- Heavy structure gel; natural sand
- 16 x 20in (40 x 50cm) stretched canvas

Seashell

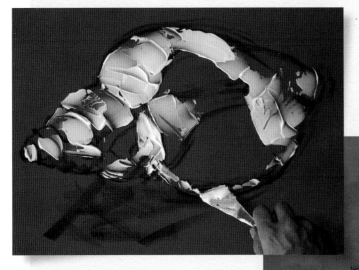

1 Base layer of gel
On a cyan and white ground, sketch the outline of the shell. Apply heavy structure gel with a palette knife, varying the thickness to emphasize the contours of the shell.

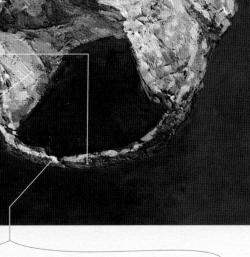

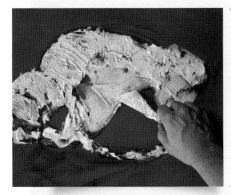

2 Add sand
When the first layer is dry, apply more gel, this time mixed with a little natural sand. Before the gel dries, chisel a series of lines into the shell with the palette knife.

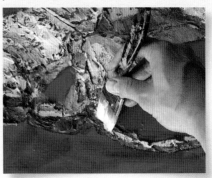

3 Apply paint
Once the gel has dried to a clear finish, you can apply the paint. Using a 1½in (38mm) flat-bristle brush, apply layers of acrylic mixed with heavy structure gel, which gives the paint body. The thick, smooth consistency of the paint on top of the heavy structure gel and sand will give the painting a distinctive, three-dimensional quality. Finally, create more detail and depth by adding highlights and darks.

PUTTING IT INTO PRACTICE

The distressed wall on this canal-side building in Venice, Italy, is a perfect subject for exploring a range of textural effects.

You will need

Titanium white | Lemon yellow | Cadmium yellow deep | Yellow ochre | Burnt sienna | Cadmium red | Deep violet | Cobalt Blue

Cerulean blue | Process cyan | Sap green | Pale olive green

- ¾in (18mm) and ½in (13mm) flat-bristle brushes
- Large- and medium-sized palette knives
- Heavy structure gel
- 20 x 24in (50 x 60cm) medium-grain stretched canvas

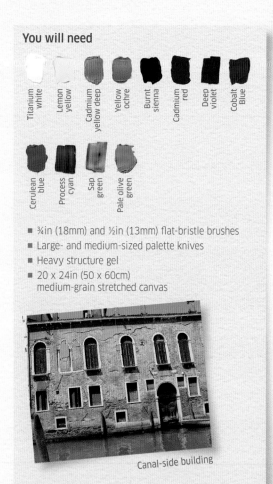

Canal-side building

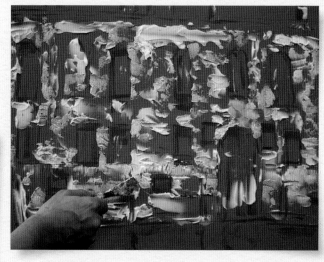

1 Heavy structure gel and sand
On a violet and white ground, sketch the scene. Mix a little sand into the gel and apply the mixture with a palette knife. Focus on the most distressed areas of wall, avoiding the windows, door, sky, and water.

2 Paint and gel mix
Wait for the initial layers to dry, and then skim the wall area with a mix of gel and heavy-body acrylic paint. Use different-sized palette knives and both long and short strokes to vary the marks. Use delicate touches around the windows, but don't worry about being too precise.

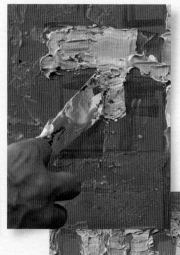

"Heavy structure gel **thickens and smoothes** acrylic paint, allowing you to **sculpt thick layers** with a palette knife, sponge, or brush."

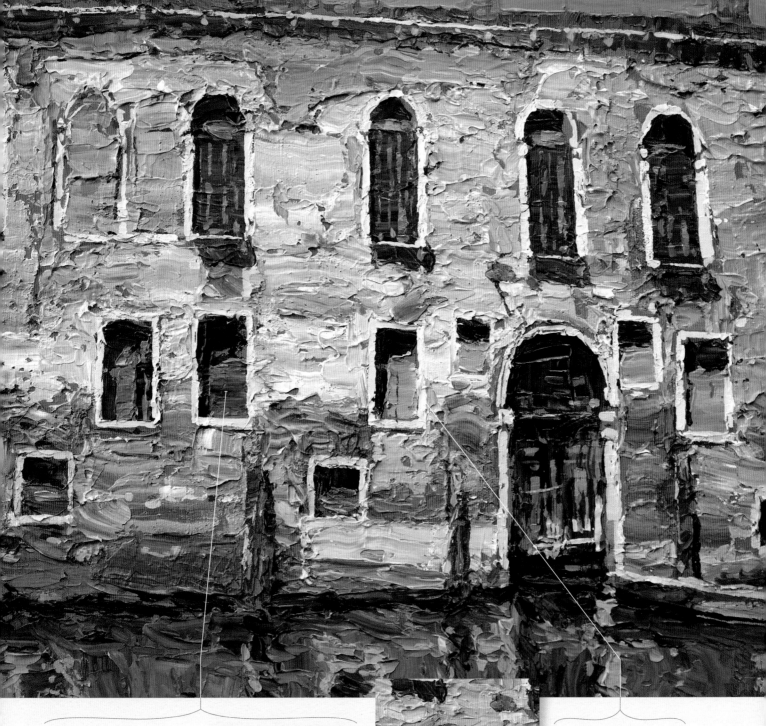

3 Darker shadows

Add dark shadows to the windows, doorway, and the top of the roof using a large palette knife. Apply rich greens to the windows with a smaller palette knife. Add the sky with a cyan and white mix, but no gel. Paint the canal with greens and blues, again with no gel in the mix.

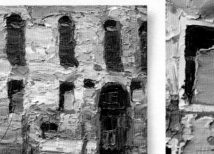

Rich green mix

4 Fine details

Add final details using a ¾in (18mm) flat-bristle brush. This sharpens the image and contrasts with the thicker paint. Plan where to make these marks first, as it will be hard to make successive fine layers adhere to the heavy, textural layers of paint.

Using ground colors

ADDING A BASE LAYER TO THE CANVAS

Applying a base color to your canvas can help to tie elements together and unify your scene. You can also make the most of exposed areas of base color by letting them substitute for the dark or light tones in your painting. Laying down a base color can also make a large, white canvas feel less daunting. Your acrylic ground can range from a light, watered-down stain to a thicker, solid application of color.

PUTTING IT INTO PRACTICE

In this sequence, the vibrant green ground remains visible in the finished painting. A range of purples was used to create harmony, light areas were enhanced to bring the cat forward, and warmer tones were used for the cat's markings to form a contrast with the background.

Materials used

Titanium white · Cadmium yellow · Yellow ochre · Burnt sienna · Deep violet · Cerulean blue · Phthalo green

- 2in (50mm), 1in (25mm), and ½in (13mm) flat-bristle brushes
- 15 x 20in (40 x 50cm) stretched canvas

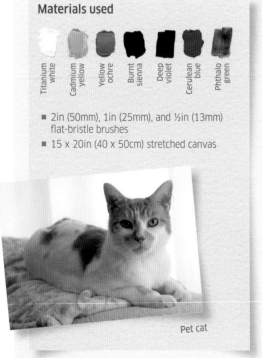

Pet cat

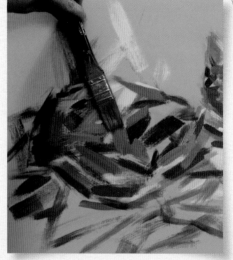

1 Getting started
With a 2in (50mm) brush, apply a ground color of phthalo green, cadmium yellow, and titanium white. Use deep violet and white to establish the side of the cat in shadow, and yellow ochre and whites to fill the cat's lighter areas. Indicate the cat's markings with phthalo green and burnt sienna. Apply some of these mixes in the areas around the cat to anchor it in the scene.

"Art should be **experimental**, so try **different** **ground colors.**"

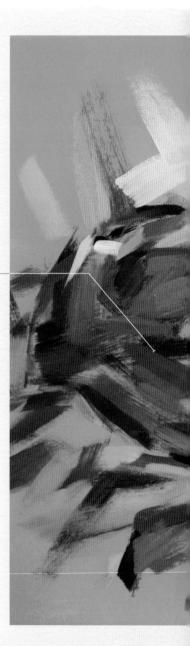

Neutrality, mood, or contrast

Traditional ground colors include raw or burnt sienna, yellow ochre, burnt umber, and neutral grays. These are good mid tones, which make it easier to work light and dark areas into the painting. Your choice of ground, whether bright or muted, can help determine the overall atmosphere. You might prefer a warm ground if you are using cool hues to create impact for your main subject, or the reverse. Try out different grounds with your subject to review the effects.

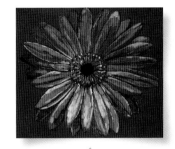

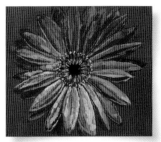

Contrasting ground
The complementary colors blue and orange create vibrancy and impact when juxtaposed in this study of a flower.

Harmonious ground
Using orange for the ground and subject here creates harmony. The darks and lights have been emphasized so they stand out.

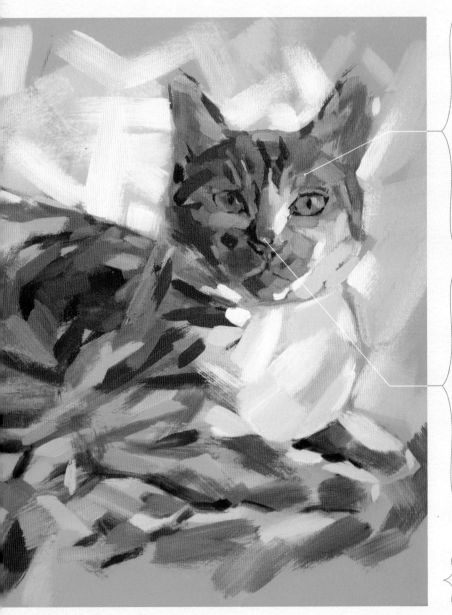

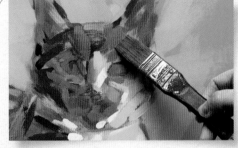

2 Build up areas
Using the same color mixes but with a 1in (25mm) brush, build up areas of the cat. On the left-hand side of its body, apply deep violet with extra white added. In other strokes, include a touch of burnt sienna, to create tonal variations.

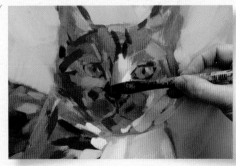

3 Finishing touches
With a ½in (13mm) brush, work on the facial features, creating a more finished look to contrast with looser areas in the body. Add extra highlights in the background to bring the subject forward.

4 The overall effect
With large areas left exposed, the ground color plays an important role in the finished painting, creating a unique interpretation of the subject.

Blending

PAINTING TRANSITIONS OF COLOR

Acrylic paints dry so quickly that they can be difficult to blend evenly. To overcome this problem, you can use mediums to improve the paint flow (mimicking watercolor), or inhibit the paint's drying time, keeping the pigment "open" or "active," so that you can work into it for longer (like oil paints). You can also use certain brushstrokes to create the graduated appearance of blending.

◾ Mediums and enhancers

"Open" or "interactive" acrylic paints are available, but they are suitable for thin layers only. If you want to blend thicker paint, use a fluid retarder to prolong drying time. Diluting with water improves paint flow, but too much affects vibrancy and the paint's ability to adhere. This is where mediums can help.

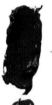

Heavy body paint
This formulation is great for textural effects but needs diluting with water or mediums to create smooth blends.

Soft body paint
This type of acrylic paint has a smoother consistency and is easier to spread than the heavy body version.

Soft body paint with gloss medium added
A gloss medium increases transparency but retains color strength. It is not as runny as flow improver.

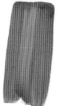

Soft body paint with flow improver added
Flow improver creates a very fluid, transparent mix. Add it undiluted to paint, for vibrancy, or with water.

◾ Blending techniques

Blending involves mixing colors into each other, but if acrylic paint is mixed too much, it can look dull and lifeless when it dries. To avoid this, you can add a medium, or use short brushstrokes to build up a blended effect gradually. There are various ways to do this.

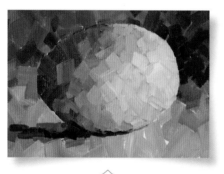

Crosshatching
These diagonal marks weave a semi-smooth impression of the image. Smaller marks and more layers simulate a smoother blend.

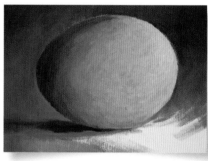

Feathering
These light strokes fade at the edges. You need to make lots of marks rapidly for a seamless effect, so it's better for small areas.

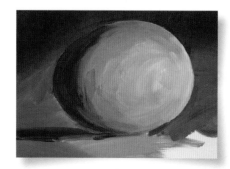

Retarder
This liquid or gel extends the paint's drying time, allowing you to blend colors together. Use no more than 1:1 retarder to paint.

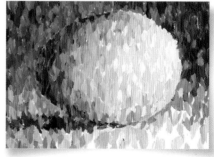

Dabbing
Similar to crosshatching, these impressionistic dabs of color build up to create the illusion of a blended image. (See also pp.182–85.)

This colorful duck presents a good challenge for the acrylic painter. Added mediums and crosshatching brushstrokes were used to blend the graduated colors of the feathers.

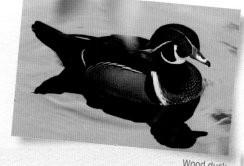

Wood duck

You will need

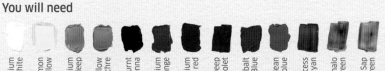

Titanium white · Lemon yellow · Cadmium yellow deep · Yellow ochre · Burnt sienna · Cadmium orange · Cadmium red · Deep violet · Cobalt Blue · Cerulean blue · Process cyan · Phthalo green · Sap green

- 1½in (38mm), ¾in (19mm), and ½in (13mm) flat synthetic brushes
- Flow improver and fluid retarder
- 20 x 28in (50 x 70cm) stretched, medium-grain canvas

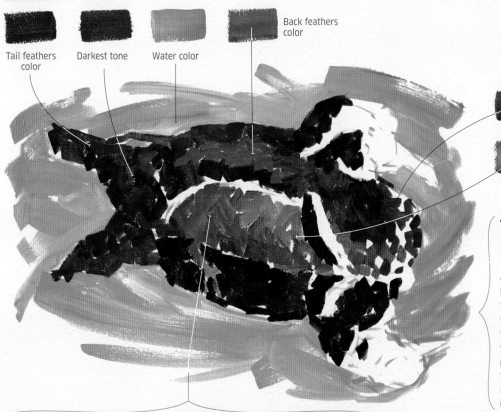

Tail feathers color

Darkest tone

Water color

Back feathers color

Breast feathers color

Wing feathers color

1 Base colors
Mix a light blue with flow improver, then apply it to the water area with a 1½in (38mm) flat brush. Use long, loose brushstrokes to suggest the fluidity of water. Allow to dry. Mix the main colors for the duck with fluid retarder to prolong the paint's drying time. This will allow the layers you apply later to merge and blend.

2 Crosshatching
Fill in the main colors of the duck with a 1½in (38mm) flat brush, using short, crosshatching brushstrokes. Keep the marks similar in size to create an even finish. If you use dark color mixes that are similar in tone, they will create subtle transitions of color.

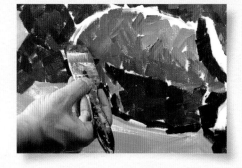

"Use a retarder to to keep the paint active, giving you more time to blend."

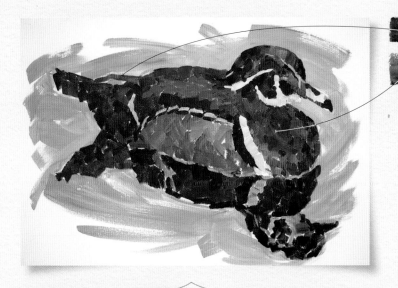

Head color

Reflection of
head color

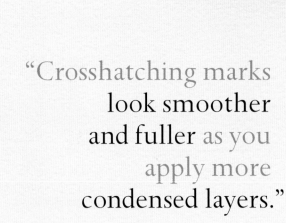

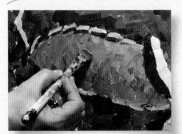

3 Developing the form
Switch to a smaller ¾in (19mm) flat
brush for the next layer, in which you
will refine the form of the duck. Follow
the contours of the head and body,
such as the rounded chest and sleek
line of feathers on the back, as you
make more crosshatching marks.

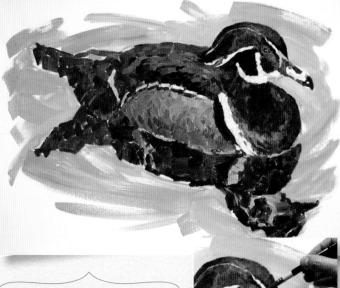

4 Refining the blends
The next layer "polishes" the color
blends. Use a ½in (13mm) flat brush to
paint even smaller crosshatching marks.
Develop the colors on the eyes and bill,
too. You will need less fluid retarder in
the latter stages.

"Crosshatching marks
look smoother
and fuller as you
apply more
condensed layers."

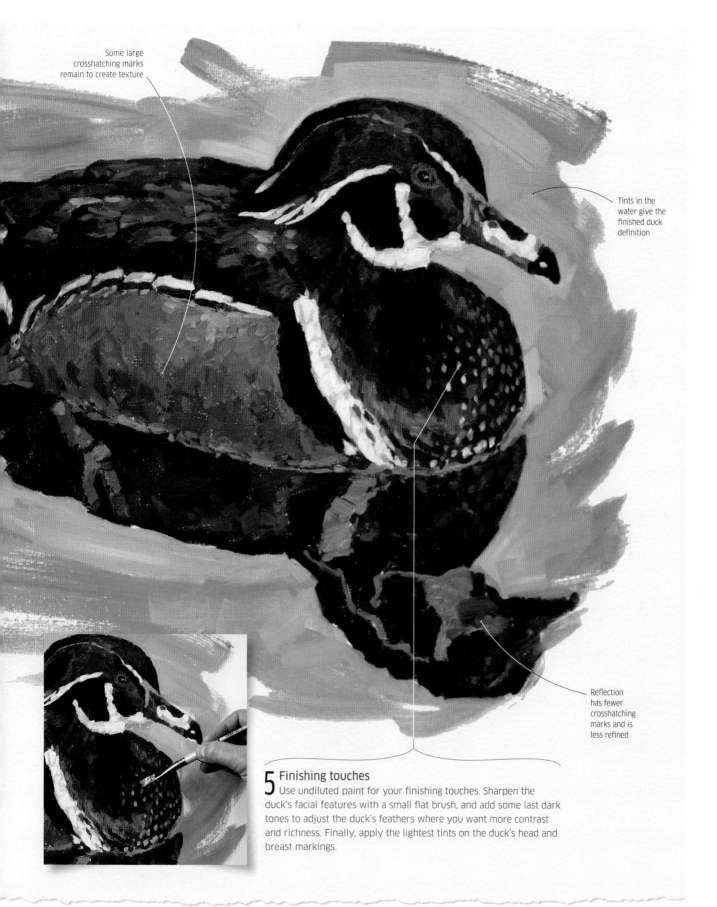

Some large crosshatching marks remain to create texture

Tints in the water give the finished duck definition

Reflection has fewer crosshatching marks and is less refined

5 Finishing touches

Use undiluted paint for your finishing touches. Sharpen the duck's facial features with a small flat brush, and add some last dark tones to adjust the duck's feathers where you want more contrast and richness. Finally, apply the lightest tints on the duck's head and breast markings.

Glazing

BLENDING THIN WASHES OF COLOR

Glazes are thin, transparent washes that modify colors when you layer them. This allows you to create transparent mixes of color, which give your painting luminosity and depth. It is important to let each glaze dry completely before you add a new one.

Layering glazes

Mix glazes with a diluting medium, rather than water alone, to avoid reducing the binder in your paint too much. In general, dark colors dominate light colors when you layer them, but color theory (see pp. 14–15 and pp. 128–31) helps you to gauge the outcomes. Too many glazes will create muddy shades.

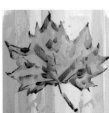

Harmonious glazes
Colors that sit side by side in the color wheel enhance each other. Harmonious colors are reliable and create pleasing mixes, but too many layers can look flat.

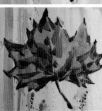

Cool glazes
Blue, green, and violet glazes create a calming effect. Here, a cerulean blue glaze makes cadmium red look purple. Cool hues can dominate—the red looks darker where the blue is deeper.

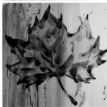

Warm glazes
Yellow, orange, and red glazes create warmth. Here, a yellow glaze makes cerulean blue look bright green; an orange glaze (complementary to blue) creates an earthier green.

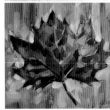

Milky glazes
White gives your glazes opacity. This creates diverse results depending on how much you add, but too much white can look chalky.

Warm glazes create the translucent glow of the sunset in this painting. The washes were diluted with flow improver, and the glazes with flow improver and water.

1 Mid tones and shadows
Sketch your scene (shown in magenta), then apply washes in cool colors to the mid tone and shadow areas. The cool colors will look dark under the warm glazes to follow.

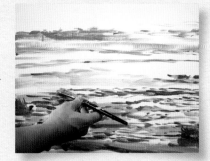

2 Adding intensity
Let the initial layers dry. Apply a magenta wash to the sky and foreground—this warm color will look intense beneath the warm glazes to follow.

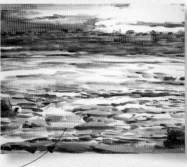

Magenta wash

3 First glaze
Let the magenta layer dry. Use a wide brush to spread a thin orange glaze over the entire scene, with long, even brushstrokes.

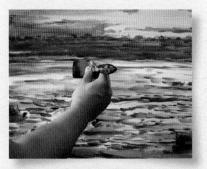

4 Lifting out
Use a damp tissue to lift out the orange glaze where you want the next glaze to look bright, and from shadow areas, where you want to retain the blue color.

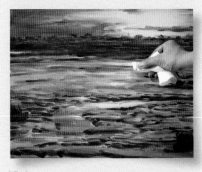

You will need

Titanium white

Cadmium yellow

Yellow ochre

Cadmium orange

Process magenta

Cobalt blue

Cerulean blue

Phthalo green

- 1½in (38mm) and ¾in (19mm) flat synthetic brushes
- 16 x 20in (40 x 50cm) stretched, medium-grain canvas

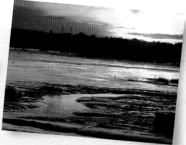

Estuary at sunset

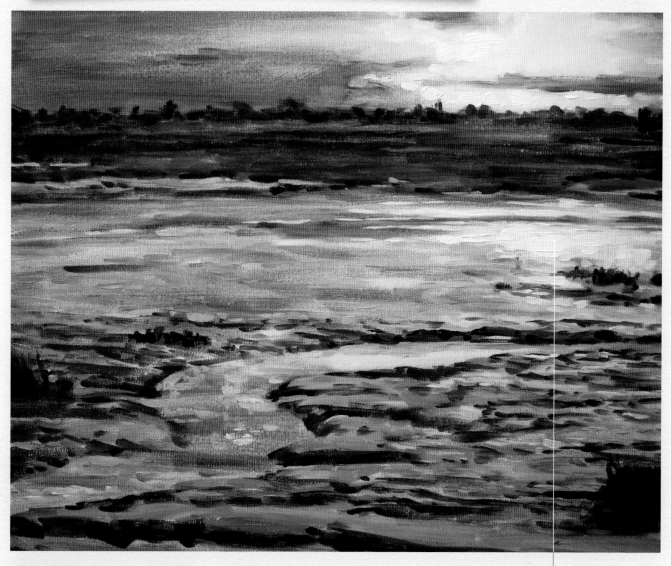

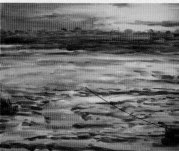

Yellow glaze

5 Second glaze
Let the orange glaze dry. Apply a harmonizing yellow glaze over the whole scene to unify it. This also creates the sunset's glow.

6 Finishing touches
Use a damp tissue to lift out the yellow glaze from the lightest sky areas, and from the blue foreground areas. Finally, apply highlights with thicker paint for definition.

Warm colors

TEMPERATURE AND ATMOSPHERE

We often ascribe hot or cold qualities to colors, for example associating reds, yellows, and oranges with heat, warmth, and fire. You can exploit this sense of association in your work to give your paintings atmosphere. This can be physical—such as a cold, snowy landscape or warm, balmy scene—or emotional You can also use strong warm or cool tones to create focal points.

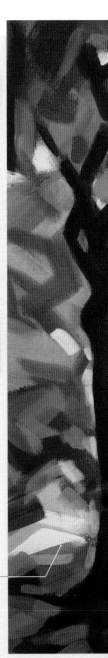

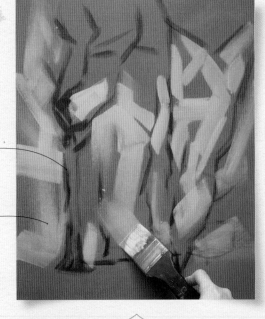

PUTTING IT INTO PRACTICE

Use a black and white photograph of your subject. Instead of being distracted by actual color variations, you can focus on creating a sense of atmosphere by using powerful warm tones.

Materials used

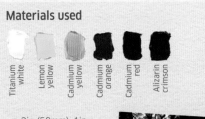

Titanium white · Lemon yellow · Cadmium yellow · Cadmium orange · Cadmium red · Alizarin crimson

- 2in (50mm), 1in (25mm), and ½in (12mm) flat-bristle brushes
- 16 x 20in (40 x 50cm) stretched, medium-grain canvas

Darkest red for darkest tones

Yellow with some whites for highlights

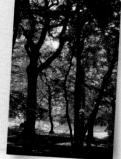

Woodland scene

1 Background fill
With your 2in (50mm) brush, apply a base of cadmium orange, then loosely sketch out the scene using alizarin crimson. Block in lighter tones with mixes of cadmium yellow and orange. Lighter mixes include cadmium orange with lemon yellow.

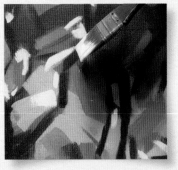

2 Highlights
Once you have established the forms of the trees, pick out some of the strongest highlights in the scene, using lemon yellow and titanium white with a 1in (25mm) brush.

"Use color to **evoke emotions** and create a **sense of atmosphere**."

Mood and harmony

You can use color to help evoke emotion and create a mood. Limit your palette to warm colors to create a disciplined, harmonious piece, bearing in mind that warm colors tend to come forward in a scene. Even when you use them sparingly, warm colors will still dominate.

Warm and cool

Two color approaches (far right) show how warm colors convey the heat of a candle, and how you can alter the atmosphere by repainting it with cool hues.

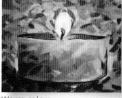

WARM COLORS

COOL COLORS

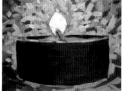
Warm colors

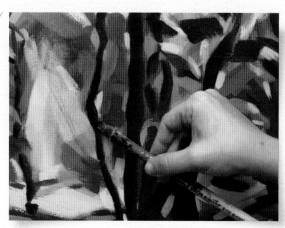
Cool colors

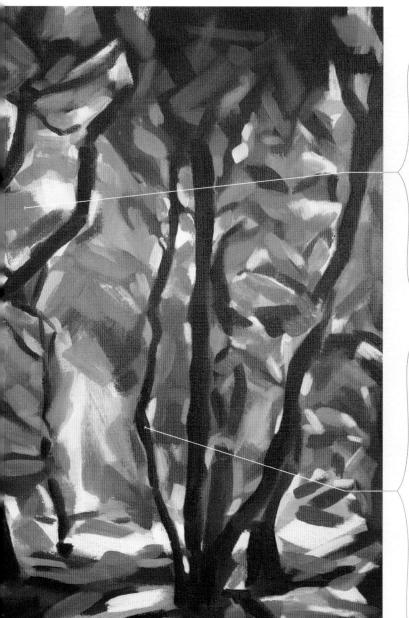

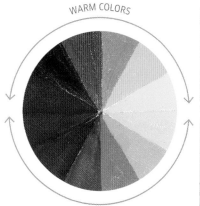

3 Create movement

With your 1in (25mm) brush, use multidirectional brushstrokes, allowing the brush marks to show through to create a sense of dynamism. Dab excess water from your brush after cleaning it to keep the colors strong.

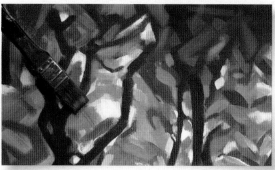

4 Finishing touches

Create some mid-tone variations in and around the trees using cadmium yellow and red with your 1in (25mm) brush. Make some softer transitions of color in light areas. Finally, apply alizarin crimson with your ½in (12mm) brush to define the structure of the trees.

Cool colors

TONE, TEMPERATURE, AND MOOD

On the color spectrum, cool colors tend to be made up of blues, purples, and greens. Just as we associate reds with heat (see pp.164–65), we link blues with the cooler elements, such as water, ice, and sky. Like warm colors, cool hues in a painting can be used to influence the viewer, evoking a sense of coolness and peace.

PUTTING IT INTO PRACTICE

Paint from a black and white photograph to remove all references to color. This will allow you to be more adventurous when it comes to depicting the scene in cool colors, to create a calm, tranquil atmosphere.

Materials

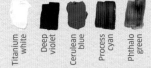

- Titanium white
- Deep violet
- Cerulean blue
- Process cyan
- Phthalo green

- 2in (50mm), 1in (25mm), and ½in (13mm) flat-bristle brushes
- 16 x 20in (40 x 50cm) stretched, medium-grain canvas

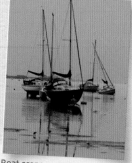

Boat scene

> "You can use cool colors to **influence the viewer** and evoke a **sense of peace.**"

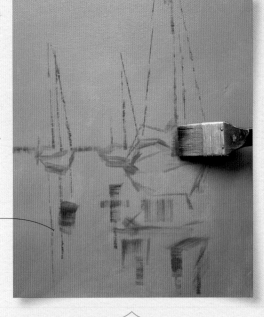

Cerulean blue provides a good mid-tone base

1 Laying the groundwork
With your 2in (50mm) brush, lay a ground color of cerulean blue before loosely sketching the scene with a pure mix of process cyan. Fill in lighter areas, adding plenty of white to the process cyan.

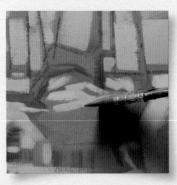

2 Establish forms
With the same brush, establish the shapes of the boats and their reflections. Mix ceruleun blue, phthalo green, and white, adjusting the mix to help the boats stand out from the background.

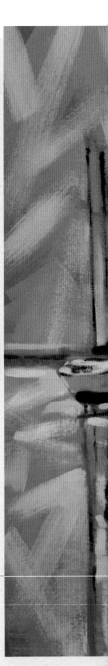

Tone and depth

As cool colors recede, you will need to introduce dark hues—which advance—to make cool tones stand out against one another. This will enable you to create a painting with depth and atmosphere without the distraction of other colors. Cool tones work well for shadow, sky, or water, and to create more tranquil moods.

Cool and warm

In the blue painting (far right), darker blues at the base of the candle advance, while the paler background recedes. Dark reds in the warm version achieve a similar effect

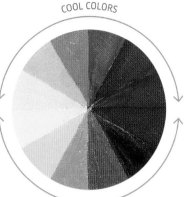
COOL COLORS

WARM COLORS

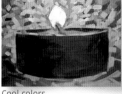
Cool colors

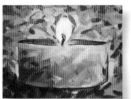
Warm colors

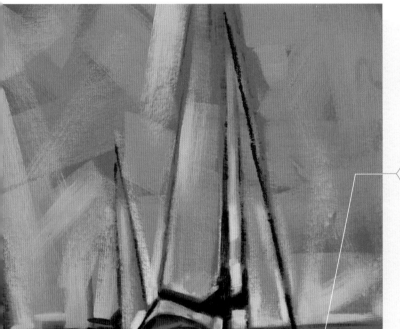

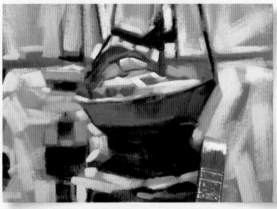

3 Lighten the background
Scale down to a 1in (25mm) brush and lighten the background using a hint of process cyan in a predominantly white mix.

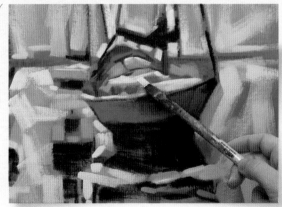

4 Dark and light details
Using a ½in (13mm) brush, apply finishing touches to the dark and light areas of the boats. For the darkest points, use a mix of deep violet and phthalo green, reserving pure white for the lightest areas.

Painting with warm and cool colors

BALANCING COLOR TEMPERATURE

Some colors, such as red, are considered warm (see pp. 164–65), while others, such as blue, are considered cool (see pp. 166–67). There are also warm and cool versions of each color. For example, cadmium yellow is warm because it contains some red, while lemon yellow is cool because it contains some blue. This is called color temperature. By combining warm and cool colors, you can create paintings with vibrancy and impact.

■ Warm and cool palette

These swatches include all the colors used in the step-by-step technique (opposite) grouped by temperature. With experience, you can combine several warm and cool versions to find increasingly more complex mixes.

Warm colors

| Process yellow | Cadmium yellow | Burnt sienna | Cadmium orange | Cadmium red | Process magenta | Cobalt blue | Emerald | Pale olive green |

Cool colors

Lemon yellow

Emphasis on warms
More warms than cools were used in the painting, opposite, because the main focal points are in the sunlit background area.

| Deep violet | Cerulean blue | Process cyan | Phthalo green |

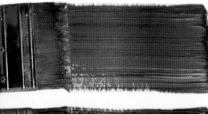

Mainly warm colors mixed with subtle additions of cools

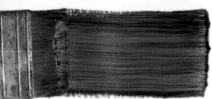

Mainly cool colors mixed with subtle additions of warms

■ Mixing warm and cool colors together

When mixing warm and cool colors, make sure that one hue always dominates. By loading your brush with a large amount of orange, along with small dabs of cool blues or greens, you will always create appealing variations of orange. Using equal quantities of each color, on the other hand, often results in a flat, muddy mix. Overmixing on a palette beforehand can also lead to muddy colors.

PUTTING IT INTO PRACTICE

This painting of a city square includes areas of bright sunshine and dark shadow. A warm and vibrant atmosphere has been conveyed by emphasizing and combining warm and cool colors.

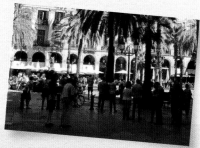

City square in sun and shade

You will need

Titanium white · Lemon yellow · Process yellow · Cadmium yellow · Burnt sienna · Cadmium orange · Cadmium red · Process magenta · Deep violet · Cobalt blue · Cerulean blue · Process cyan · Phthalo green · Emerald · Pale olive green

- 1½in (38mm), 1in (25mm), and ¾in (19mm) flat synthetic-bristle brushes
- 20 x 28in (50 x 70cm) stretched, medium-grain canvas

1 Block in warm colors

Apply a cool ground color of light phthalo green, which will contrast well with the first blocks of warm color. Sketch the scene with magenta, then apply blocky strokes of warm yellow and white, using the two largest brushes. Add subtle variations of other warm colors to vary the mixes. For example, use a warm brown mix of magenta, sienna, violet, orange with less yellow, and white to create the mid tones in the arches, around the windows, and for the trees.

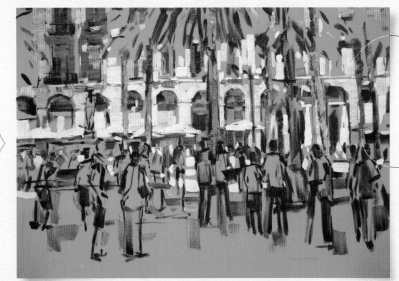

Warm yellow mix

Warm brown mix

2 Block in cool colors

With clean brushes, apply cool mixes to the foreground and figures. At this stage, simply place warms and cools side by side. Mix cobalt and cerulean, with touches of violet, phthalo green, sienna, and white. Use large blocks of color in the near foreground and smaller blocks to provide definition on the figures. For the figures and palm trees in deepest shade, use a strong, dark mix of cyan, violet, sienna, cobalt, cerulean, and phthalo green, again with a hint of white.

Cool blue mix

Cool blue mix with white

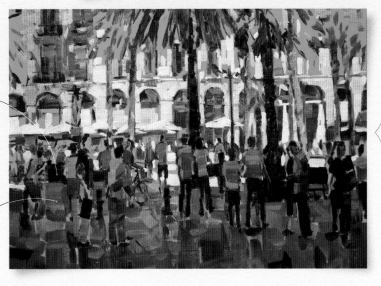

>

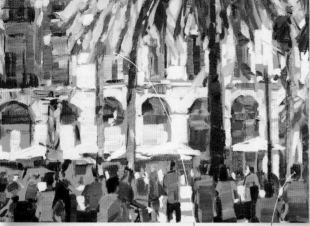

3 Greens and skin tones
Apply a warm green for the leaves of the palm trees, using a mix of pale olive and emerald, lemon and process yellow, burnt sienna, and white. Add further darks in the archways and apply flesh colors to the figures using a mix of white, violet, blue, and sienna.

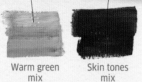

Warm green mix

Skin tones mix

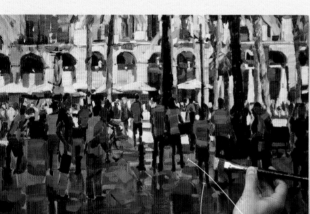

4 Integrate warms and cools
Blend warms and cools in the foreground, where sunlight filters through the trees. To avoid muddy mixes, make sure either a cool or a warm color dominates. So, for the earthy warm color of the paving stones, mix cadmium yellow, sienna, orange, and white, with just a hint of violet and cerulean blue.

Cool green mixed with earthy warm

Earthy warm mixed with cool green

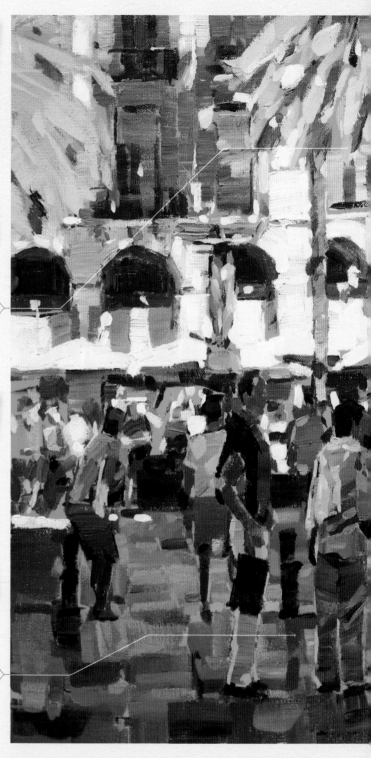

"In this vibrant, **brightly colored scene**, the **main focal points** are in the background, where **flecks of warm colors** draw the eye."

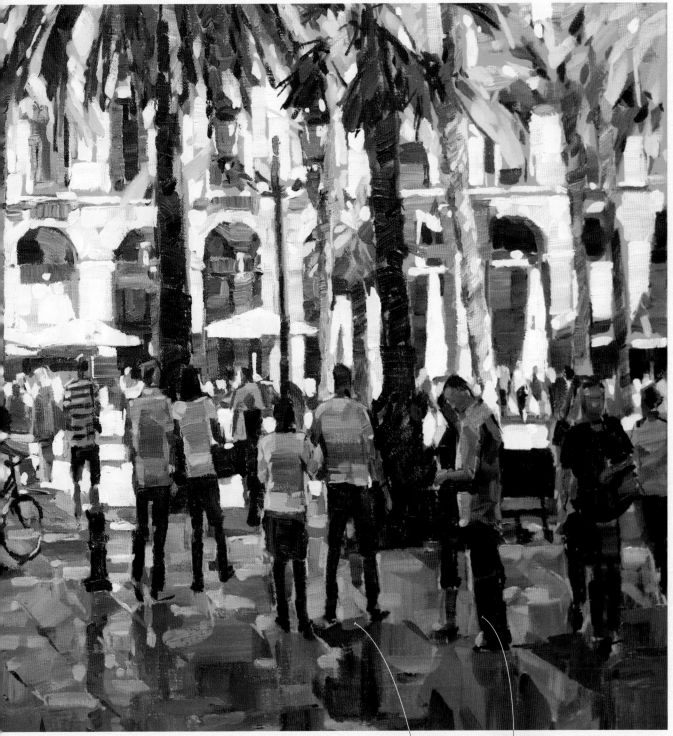

5 **Final touches to increase contrast**
For the final touches, switch to a ¾in (19mm) flat brush.
Apply small details to the figures and lampposts, and add strong
highlights to the buildings in the background. Use the darkest
darks and lightest lights in these areas, to draw the viewer in.

Blue highlight
mix

Darkest blue
mix

Negative space

EXPLORING THE SHAPES AROUND A SUBJECT

Negative spaces are the areas that fall between and around the primary subjects, or "positive" spaces, in a painting. The way in which you treat them is an important element of composition. For example, you might choose a particular subject because of its interesting shape, so it follows that all shapes—whether positive or negative—have artistic value. You may even decide to make negative space the main area of interest.

■ Ways with negative space

Exploring negative space encourages you to look at subjects in a new way as you assess areas you might otherwise neglect. For a more abstract approach, you could use negative space as the main subject. In practical terms, negative spaces help divide a scene into manageable shapes and sections.

In these four studies, although the positive shapes of the birds, tiger, and tree are the main focus of interest, negative space is an important consideration.

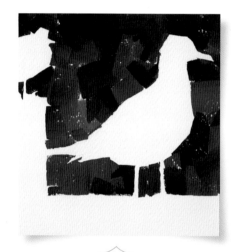

Canvas background
This bird was formed from the white of the canvas using applications of blue paint in the background. This emphasizes the abstract shape of the bird and its L-shaped platform.

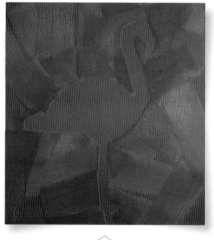

Painted background
In this example (see also opposite), the painting consists of an initial wash of violet, to add interest, with the subject created by painting the negative spaces in green.

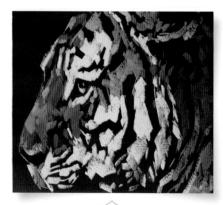

Negative spaces integrated
Here, the tiger's dark stripes were formed from negative spaces, making them feel less contrived and helping to unify the painting.

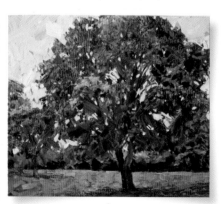

Negative spaces enhanced
In this example (see also pp. 174-75), the positive shape of the tree was painted first, with the negative spaces enhanced later.

> "Negative space is an **important part of composition.** All shapes—whether positive or negative—**have artistic value.**"

A flamingo was chosen to demonstrate the use of negative space because of its distinctive shape. The initial stages of painting involved working on the negative space around the bird, rather than on the subject itself. The painted negative space then formed a silhouette of the subject, which was developed for the finished painting.

You will need

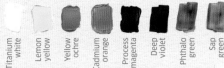

Titanium white | Lemon yellow | Yellow ochre | Cadmium orange | Process magenta | Deep violet | Phthalo green | Sap green

- 3in (75mm) and ½in (13mm) flat-bristle brushes
- 20 x 16in (50 x 40cm) medium-grain canvas

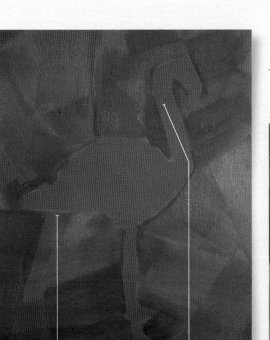

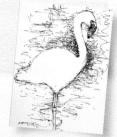

1 Negative spaces
Prime the canvas with a mix of deep violet and titanium white using a 3in (75mm) flat-bristle brush. Apply a mix of sap green and lemon yellow to the negative spaces around where you want the subject to appear.

Flamingo

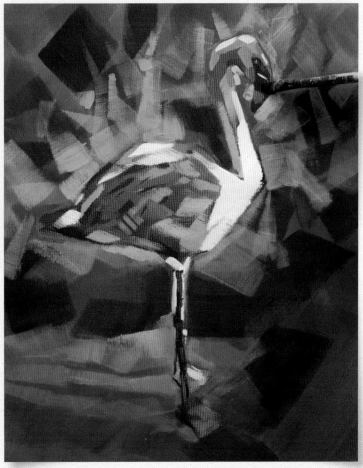

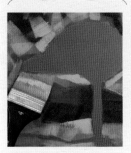

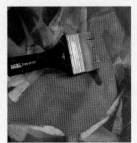

2 Tonal range
To keep the negative space from simply becoming a flat area of color, add more lemon to create lighter tones. Use sap green and a little deep violet for dark areas.

3 Add pink
Once you have filled the negative space, a silhouette of the subject will remain. Now fill the positive image, using a mix of violet, process magenta, and white.

4 Final details
Introduce cadmium orange and process magenta to create different tones of pink, adding white for the lightest areas. Using a ½in (13mm) brush, work up details on the bird's head, using orange and violet for the dark areas of the beak.

In this painting, the positive image of the tree was created first, and then light tints were added to the negative spaces between and around the branches to create a striking, backlit effect.

Negative space   Small "holes" of negative space   Negative space

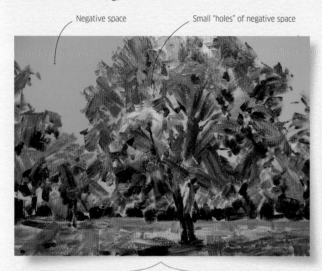

1 Paint positive subject
On a blue base, create an impression of the tree—the positive shape. Apply blues, greens, and yellows with a 2in (50mm) flat brush. Add reds and oranges for contrast.

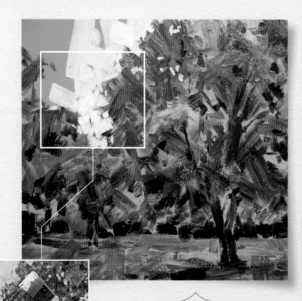

Light tint for negative spaces

2 First negative space marks
Introduce light tints of white with a little lemon and blue to fill the sky and refine the outside edge of the tree.

You will need

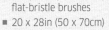

- Titanium white
- Cadmium yellow deep
- Yellow ochre
- Burnt sienna
- Cadmium red
- Deep violet
- Cerulean blue
- Process cyan
- Phthalo green
- Sap green

- 2in (50mm) and ½in (13mm) flat-bristle brushes
- 20 x 28in (50 x 70cm) canvas

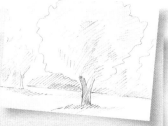

Fall tree

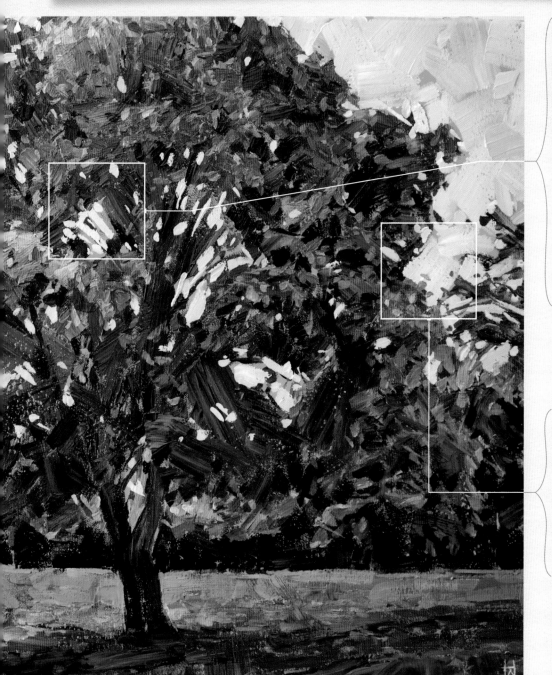

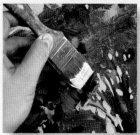

3 Smaller marks
Use the tip of the 2in (50mm) flat brush to create the more refined "sky holes" in the center of the tree. The branches will take shape from the lines and edges of these negative spaces. Apply the marks loosely to retain the natural feel of the subject.

4 Final painting
Add more light tint to the background to refine the shape of the tree. Once you have filled in the sky, use a ½in (13mm) flat brush to go back and develop the positive shapes at the center of the tree, especially the cluster of multicolored leaves. Place more emphasis on the positive shapes in these areas.

Reflections

DEPICTING WATER AND SHINY SURFACES

A constant surface, such as a mirror or still water, creates a solid reflection, whereas a moving or curved surface creates a distorted reflection. The relative position of the reflective surface also has an effect. For example, if the surface is in front of the subject, the image is mirrored, but if the surface is underneath the subject, it will reflect the underside of the subject instead—an area that might not normally be visible.

PUTTING IT INTO PRACTICE

This painting shows how to treat reflections in moving water, both in the foreground and in the distance. Take advantage of quick-drying acrylics by building the image in layers.

You will need

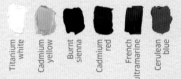

Titanium white · Cadmium yellow · Burnt sienna · Cadmium red · French ultramarine · Cerulean blue

- No. 6 flat synthetic, no. 1 round synthetic, and synthetic rigger brushes
- 12 x 14in (30 x 35cm) medium-grain canvas board

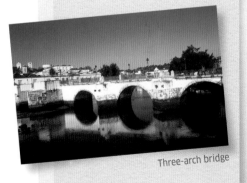

Three-arch bridge

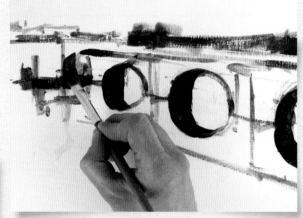

1 Drawing in the subject
Apply the darkest tones first, using a diluted mix of burnt sienna and French ultramarine. Block in the main shapes with a flat brush, including where the reflections appear.

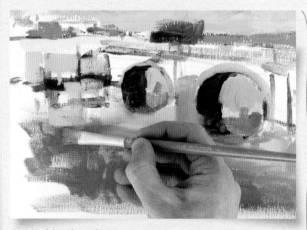

2 Blocking in color
Apply a pale blue mix for the background water and a stronger blue in the foreground. Block in the reflections with darker, more muted colors than on the bridge itself. Work quickly to blend the colors together.

▪ Mirror images

Painting reflections generally involves creating a mirror image of the subject, but rippled surfaces can distort shapes and spread color. Usually, reflections have a smaller tonal range, with darker highlights and lighter shadows.

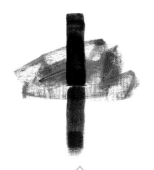

Static reflection
Use crisp lines to show reflections in still water. Note that the tone of the reflection is slightly muted.

Wavering reflection
Reflections in moving water are broken, so use wiggly lines to suggest ripples in the surface.

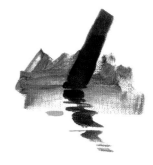

Leaning object
If an object is at an angle, its reflection should lean in the same direction.

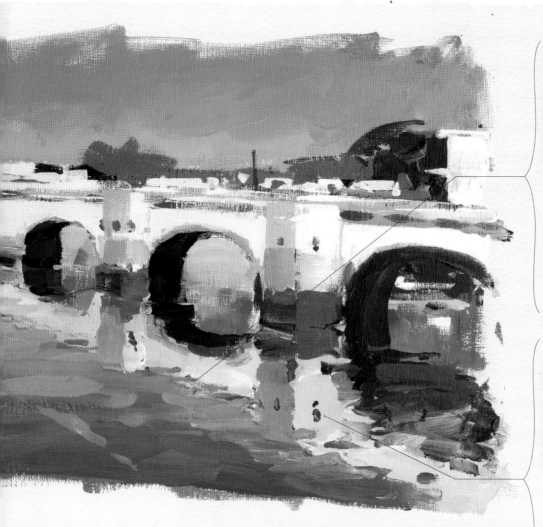

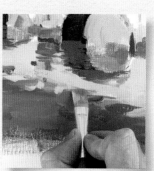

3 Adding movement
Suggest moving water by breaking up the edge of the bridge's reflection. Paint larger wiggly lines in the foreground, and finer wiggles the farther back the reflection is.

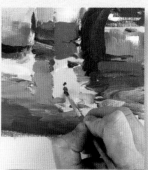

4 Final details
Add more highlights and details with free, loose strokes using small round and rigger brushes. Sharpen the nearest foreground areas with thicker mixes of gray, white, and brown for the base of the bridge.

"Create a **sense of depth** by treating foreground and background reflections in different ways."

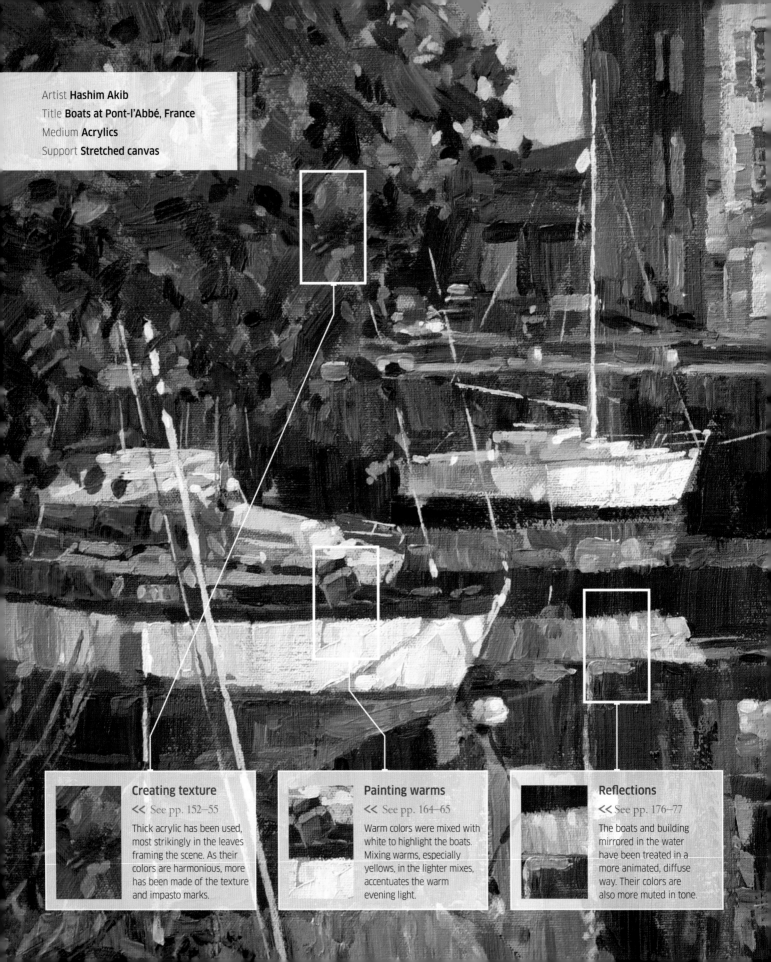

Artist **Hashim Akib**
Title **Boats at Pont-l'Abbé, France**
Medium **Acrylics**
Support **Stretched canvas**

Creating texture

≪ See pp. 152–55

Thick acrylic has been used, most strikingly in the leaves framing the scene. As their colors are harmonious, more has been made of the texture and impasto marks.

Painting warms

≪ See pp. 164–65

Warm colors were mixed with white to highlight the boats. Mixing warms, especially yellows, in the lighter mixes, accentuates the warm evening light.

Reflections

≪ See pp. 176–77

The boats and building mirrored in the water have been treated in a more animated, diffuse way. Their colors are also more muted in tone.

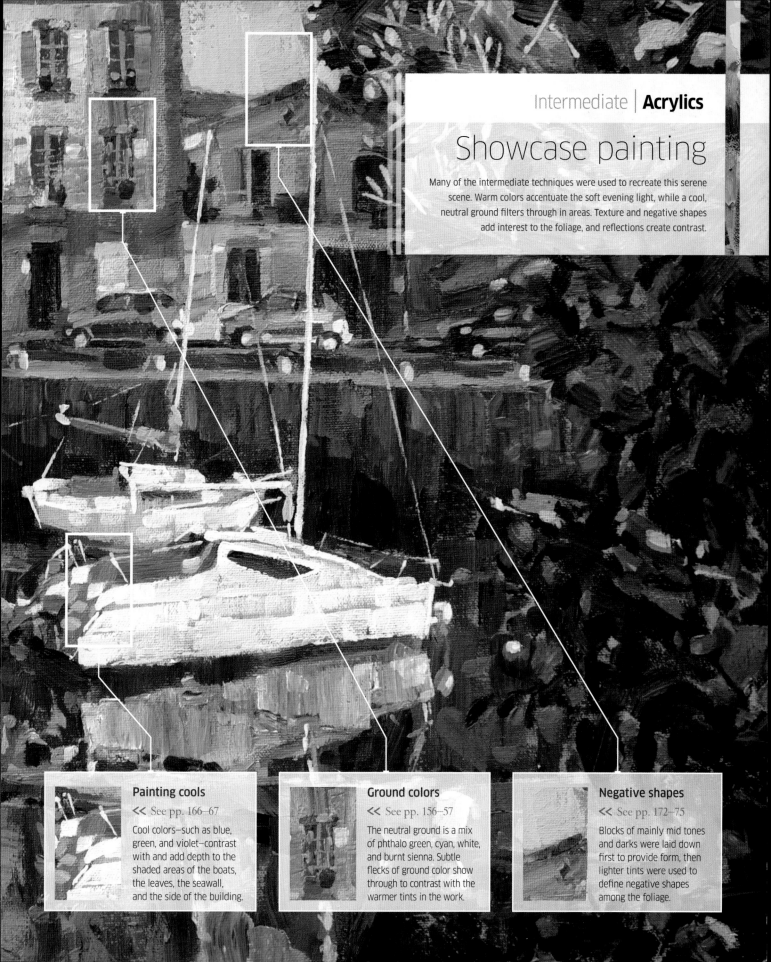

Showcase painting

Many of the intermediate techniques were used to recreate this serene scene. Warm colors accentuate the soft evening light, while a cool, neutral ground filters through in areas. Texture and negative shapes add interest to the foliage, and reflections create contrast.

Painting cools

≪ See pp. 166–67

Cool colors—such as blue, green, and violet—contrast with and add depth to the shaded areas of the boats, the leaves, the seawall, and the side of the building.

Ground colors

≪ See pp. 156–57

The neutral ground is a mix of phthalo green, cyan, white, and burnt sienna. Subtle flecks of ground color show through to contrast with the warmer tints in the work.

Negative shapes

≪ See pp. 172–75

Blocks of mainly mid tones and darks were laid down first to provide form, then lighter tints were used to define negative shapes among the foliage.

Creating focal points

LEADING THE EYE

Combining loose, broad areas of brushwork with areas of focused detail will help balance the composition and flow of a painting. Use more detailed brushstrokes to anchor the point of interest, and catch the viewer's eye with a streak of color or area of contrast.

▀ Emphasizing areas of interest

Increasing contrast, using more intense colors and more detail are good ways of emphasizing an area of a painting. By ensuring that the surrounding areas remain secondary to the focal point, you can create a dramatic, punchy image.

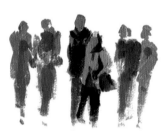

Contrast
Increasing the contrast of the figures in the center makes them stand out from the rest of the crowd. They are the clear point of interest.

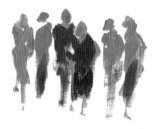

Color
A flash of red, emphasized by the subtle colors of the surrounding figures, identifies this figure as the subject of the painting.

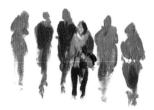

Detail
Developing a figure with finely detailed brushstrokes leads the eye toward it. Again, the central figure is the focal point.

This brightly colored figure makes a dramatic focal point. The use of high contrast, saturation, and detail help to give the monk presence.

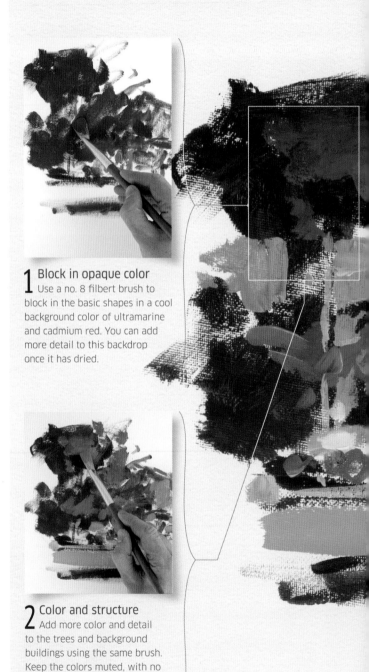

1 Block in opaque color
Use a no. 8 filbert brush to block in the basic shapes in a cool background color of ultramarine and cadmium red. You can add more detail to this backdrop once it has dried.

2 Color and structure
Add more color and detail to the trees and background buildings using the same brush. Keep the colors muted, with no significant changes in tone, to prevent them from conflicting with the main figure.

You will need

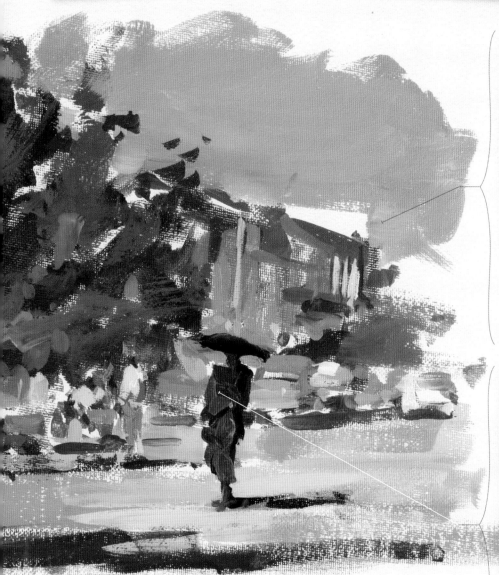

Titanium white

Lemon yellow

Cadmium yellow

Burnt sienna

Cadmium red

French ultramarine

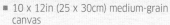
Cerulean blue

- No. 8 filbert synthetic, no. 6 flat synthetic, and no. 1 round synthetic brushes
- 10 x 12in (25 x 30cm) medium-grain canvas

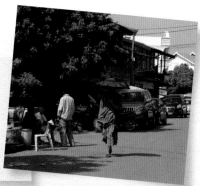

Walking figure

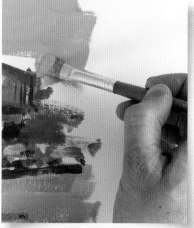

3 Finish the backdrop
Use a no. 6 flat brush to add the sky and include more detail in the background buildings. Balance the mid tones, adjusting and adding brushstrokes to provide a subtle background for the figure.

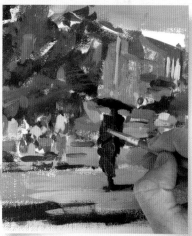

4 Add the focal point
Mix a bright orange from cadmium red and cadmium yellow and use a no. 1 round brush to paint in the figure. Use a darker mix for shadow areas around the figure to separate it from the background.

"Increase **contrast**, use more intense colors, and include extra detail to emphasize an area."

Optical color mixing

PAINTING WITH DOTS AND DABS TO MAKE COLOR SPARKLE

When you place dabs of color side by side, mosaic-fashion, they create the illusion of a new color. This allows you to "blend" colors without physically mixing them, with the bonus that the original colors remain intense. This technique is especially useful for complementary colors, which can look muddy when you mix them but make each other look brighter if you place them side by side.

Using complementary colors

Complementary colors sit opposite each other on the color wheel, with the primary pairings being red and green, blue and orange, and yellow and violet. They can make your painting very dynamic because they appear more vivid when they are used together. Balance complementaries carefully, however, to keep them from jarring.

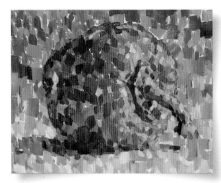

Creating brightness
Orange highlights and blue shadows create a dramatic brightening effect in this illustration. Flecks of each color were placed around the painting to prevent the colors from clashing, and to unify the picture.

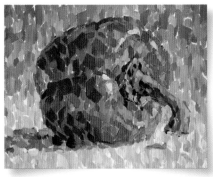

Creating grays and neutrals
In this painting, orange and blue were mixed together to create grays and neutrals. Warmer mixes contained more orange, and more blue was added to the cooler mixes. These muted hues provide subtlety and balance.

Using analogous colors

Analogous colors sit next to each other on the color wheel (see pp. 14–15). If you work within a small color range, your painting will look harmonious, but possibly uninteresting if the range is too narrow. You can substitute analogous colors for tones; when you place them next to each other they will emulate a scale of light and dark.

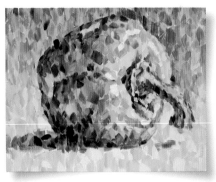

Creating tonal blends
This pepper was painted using yellow, yellow-green, green, and blue-green. The adjacent dabs blend as though they are tones and give the object form.

Size and spacing of dabs

When dabs (which don't have to be round) are all the same size, they create a uniform finish. If you vary the relative sizes, smaller dabs will appear to recede and draw the eye in. Closely spaced dabs make colors look brighter than dabs that are spaced farther apart, which enables you to create focal areas.

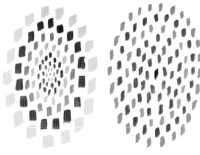

Progressively
smaller dabs

Evenly sized dabs

Effects of size
Small dabs placed next to larger ones seem to recede and create depth. Uniform, evenly sized dabs can balance a complex composition.

Red and green cars make a great study for complementary colors. Optical color mixing was used to both balance and enhance the strong colors, creating a sparkling effect.

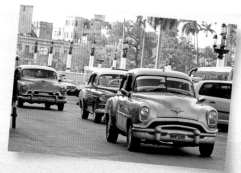

Vintage cars

You will need

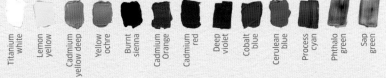

Titanium white · Lemon yellow · Cadmium yellow deep · Yellow ochre · Burnt sienna · Cadmium Orange · Cadmium red · Deep violet · Cobalt blue · Cerulean blue · Process cyan · Phthalo green · Sap green

- 1in (25mm) and ¾in (19mm) flat synthetic brushes
- 20 x 28in (50 x 70cm) stretched, medium-grain canvas

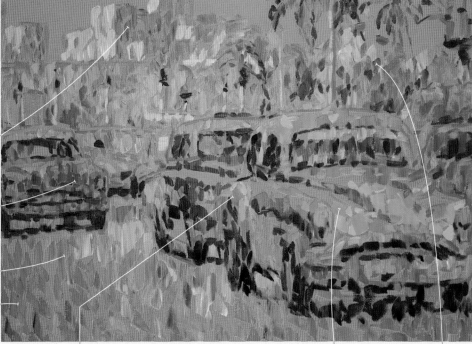

1 Main colors
Apply a complementary base color. Here, magenta brightens the main colors in the painting–green and blue. Mix bright tones for the foreground, dark shades for shadows, and earthy tones to temper the vibrant colors.

Earthy blue–sienna mix

Dark-blue mix

Light-blue mix

Light-blue variation

Bright-green mix

Earthy green mix

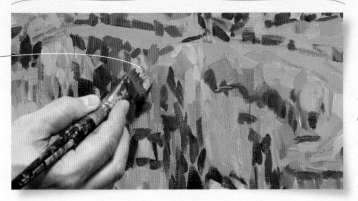

Dabs are fairly evenly sized in the foreground

2 Initial layer
Lay down the main colors before developing details. Use a ¾in (19mm) flat brush to paint dabs on the cars and background, and a 1in (25mm) flat brush for larger dabs to cover the foreground. Keep the size of the marks fairly consistent if the composition is already intricate.

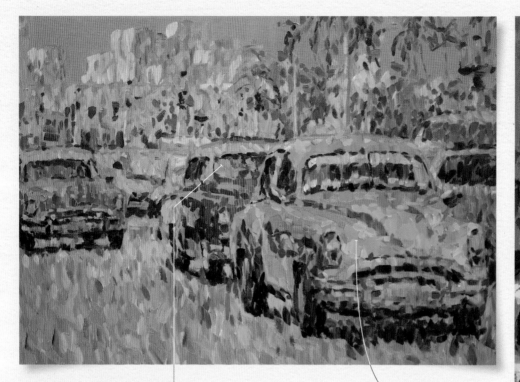

Close dabs make focal
areas more intense
and stand out

Flecks of the
magenta base color
show through,
unifying the whole

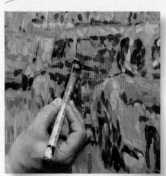

3 Balance and form

Develop the forms of the cars,
trees, and buildings with tints of
the main colors. Tone down some
of the colors by mixing them
with their complementary colors;
apply the resulting neutrals to
balance the painting. Place dabs
of pure complementary colors to
brighten areas such as the
shadows inside the cars.

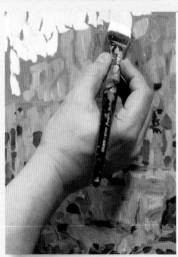

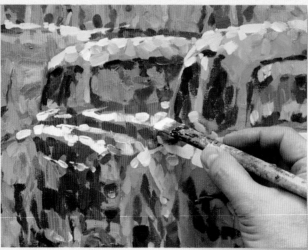

4 Final details

Apply the darkest shadows
and lightest tints last with a
smaller brush. Use the light sky
color for highlights on the cars to
create a unified look.

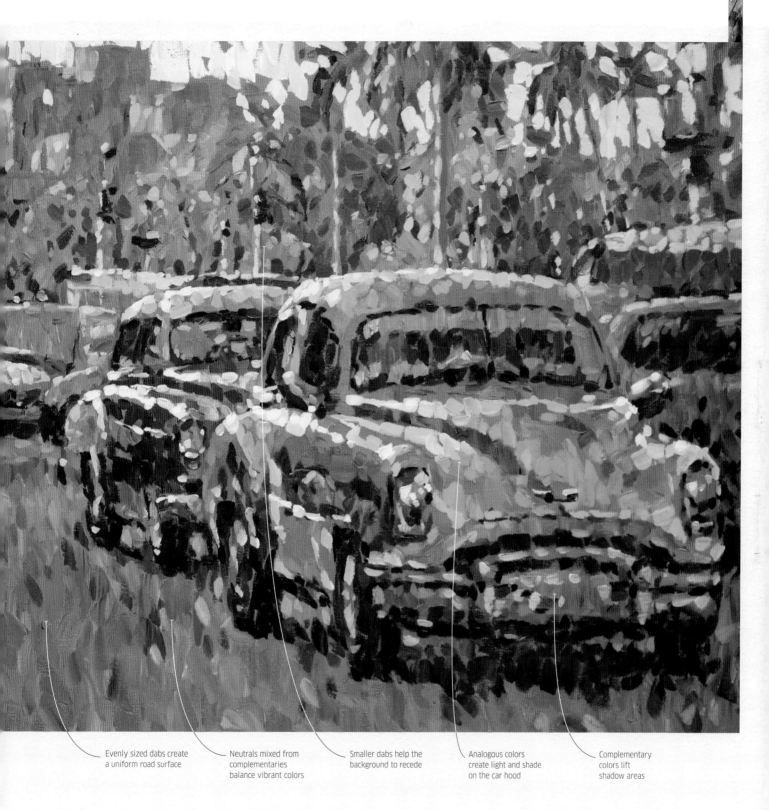

Evenly sized dabs create a uniform road surface

Neutrals mixed from complementaries balance vibrant colors

Smaller dabs help the background to recede

Analogous colors create light and shade on the car hood

Complementary colors lift shadow areas

"Optical color mixing exploits the full potential of color theory to scintillating effect."

Painting rain

USING STREAKS AND SPLATTER

Misty or rainy scenes can be challenging to paint because you need to create soft, diffused edges and mix earthy tints without them looking dull. Loosely mixed streaks of color create a wet look that is great for portraying rain, as do splatters of paint. Both techniques require practice to master.

■ Brushes for special effects

For streaks, load a wide paddle brush with several colors and drag it down the canvas in a single motion. For splatter effects, flick a splatter brush from the wrist to create an erratic spray that makes a range of random marks. A toothbrush creates a more even spray, which is useful for small areas.

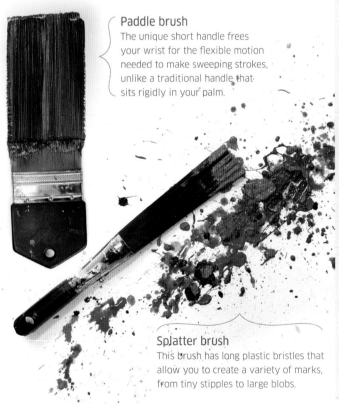

Paddle brush
The unique short handle frees your wrist for the flexible motion needed to make sweeping strokes, unlike a traditional handle that sits rigidly in your palm.

Splatter brush
This brush has long plastic bristles that allow you to create a variety of marks, from tiny stipples to large blobs.

PUTTING IT INTO PRACTICE

In this painting, streaks of color evoke wind and rain with exciting energy. Brightly colored raincoats, umbrellas, reflections, and darting figures make sure the scene is rainy but not dull.

You will need

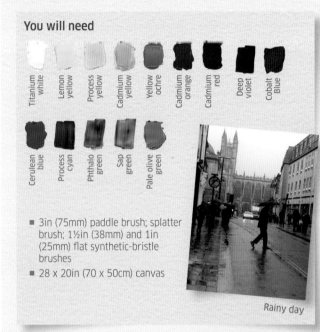

Titanium white · Lemon yellow · Process yellow · Cadmium yellow · Yellow ochre · Cadmium orange · Cadmium red · Deep violet · Cobalt Blue

Cerulean blue · Process cyan · Phthalo green · Sap green · Pale olive green

- 3in (75mm) paddle brush; splatter brush; 1½in (38mm) and 1in (25mm) flat synthetic-bristle brushes
- 28 x 20in (70 x 50cm) canvas

Rainy day

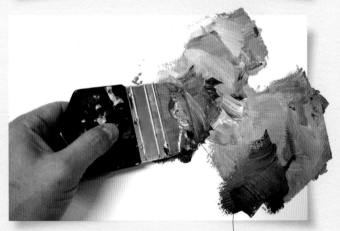

1 Mixing streaks
Squeeze more paint than usual onto your palette, to make it easy to pick up multiple colors on a damp 3in (75mm) paddle brush. Dab at the paint, rather than scoop or swirl, to avoid too much mixing. If you have white in the mix, you'll need to blend slightly more—otherwise strong highlights will show in the streaks.

Practice your mixes on a scrap of paper

2 Painting streaks

Apply a violet base to counterbalance the warm ochres and blues in the main mixes. Draw a loose composition, then use the paddle brush to apply multiple streaks using single downward strokes. Apply light colors first, and use the same brush (without cleaning) to allow the colors to bleed together. The running color evokes the effects of rain.

Building color

Ochre, sienna, and white, and small amounts of orange, olive, greens, and blues

Building color variation

Cerulean, cobalt, phthalo green, ochre, sienna, violet, and a small amount of white

Road color 1

Ochre and sienna, small amounts of orange, olive, greens, and violet

"Inject some color. Rainy days may be gray, but your painting doesn't have to be."

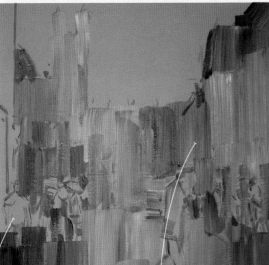

Work around any sketched figures

Add blue and green to the color used for the buildings for the lightest part of the road

Mixes don't need to match each other; apply darker tones to shadowed areas

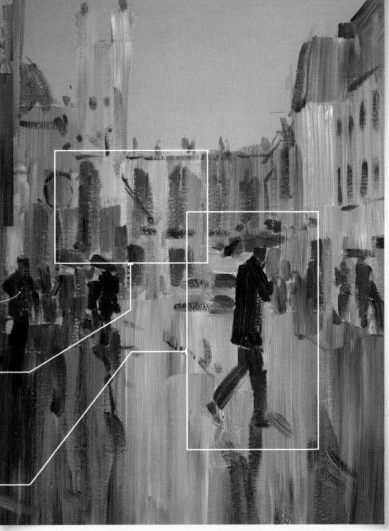

Colorful red raincoat

3 Blocking in details

Once the large areas are filled, use a 1½in (38mm) flat brush to block in initial details for the buildings, street signs, and cars. Keep the brushstrokes loose—you can add more detail later.

4 Adding people

Block in shapes for the figures using loosely mixed dark colors to create a sense of depth. The red raincoat introduces a shot of color. Match the spontaneity of the streaks by painting the people with loose brushstrokes at this stage.

5 Sky and highlights
Using a clean paddle brush, mix a strong, light color for the sky. Apply streaks with the same dragging action as before. Use the same color for the vehicles. Add sienna, phthalo green, cerulean, and violet to the sky color for streaks to highlight the center of the road. Use a 1½in (38mm) flat brush to apply details to the buildings in a soft ochre tint, and to add shadows to the people.

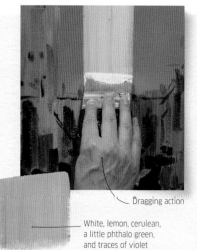

Dragging action

White, lemon, cerulean, a little phthalo green, and traces of violet

Sky color

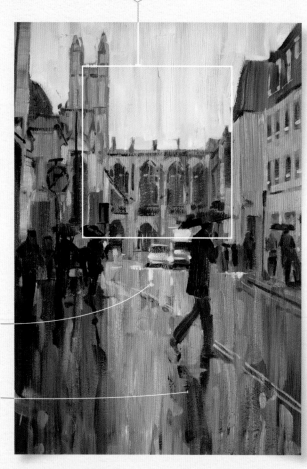

Add highlights to suggest wet reflections

Add shadows for the figures

"Paint around the buildings carefully but not too neatly to keep a sense of spontaneity."

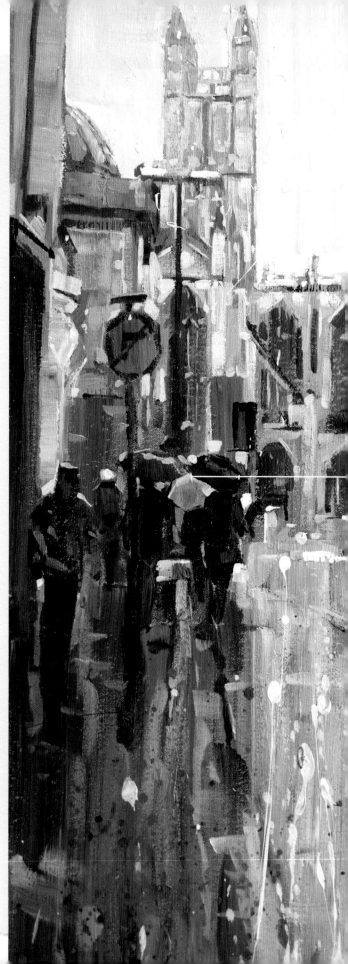

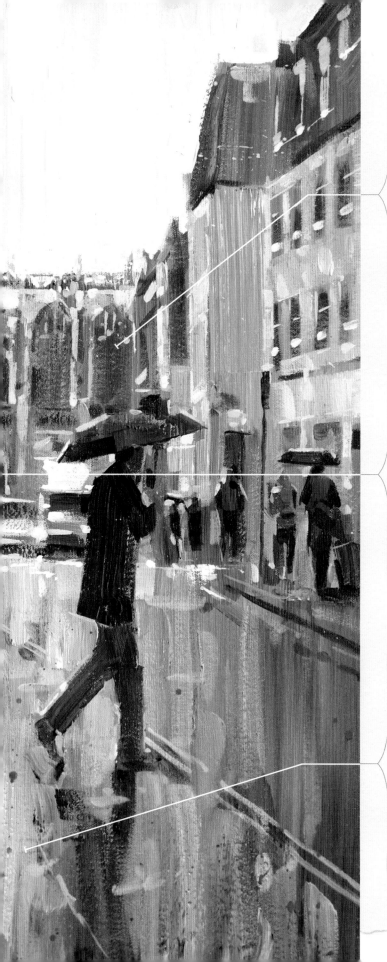

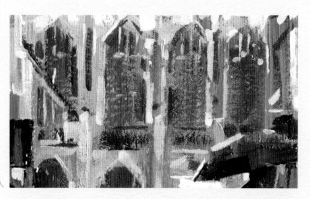

6 Finishing the buildings

Sharpen the details with a 1in (25mm) flat brush. Apply strong, definitive darks and light tints of ochre to pick out details in the buildings, such as on windows and roofs.

7 Finer details

Pick out details in the street scene using the 1in (25mm) flat brush. Add highlights and flecks of rich color to areas such as the green umbrella and red raincoat.

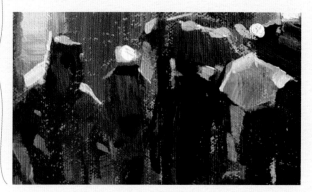

8 Splatter marks

Finally, add splatter marks with diluted paint. Experiment first on paper and be careful not to overdo them on your painting. Use a mixture of runny and thick mixes to get a variety of marks. Load the splatter brush fully with paint for heavier streaks or pick up a small amount for a sprinkling of dots.

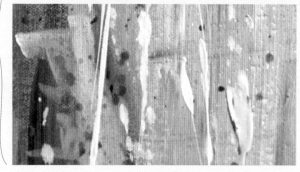

Painting fur

INTERPRETING INTRICATE DETAILS

The eye perceives the general characteristics of fur—patterns, color, markings, textures—more than individual hairs, so focus your efforts on creating an impression of these traits. You can also convey the wild nature of your subject with your color mixes and brushstrokes.

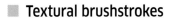

Textural brushstrokes

Consider the attributes of the fur you are painting (is it fluffy, smooth, spotted, rough?) and match your brushstrokes to them. For example, use loose strokes for soft fur, and broad, smooth strokes for sleek coats.

Fluffy fur
Hold the brush lightly and make short, flicking movements to create feathery strokes in different directions. Add dark tones to create depth.

Fur markings
Use different parts of a flat brush head, such as the corner or the tip, to make individual marks. Mix faded and stronger spots for a natural effect.

Sleek, shiny fur
Apply long, fluid strokes in one direction, following the animal's contours. Add lighter tones on top of dark ones to create the impression of wet or shiny fur.

Spiky coat
Gently dab the corner edge of a flat brush to create lots of tiny dots. Vary the size by altering the pressure. Add light dots on top to suggest sharp points.

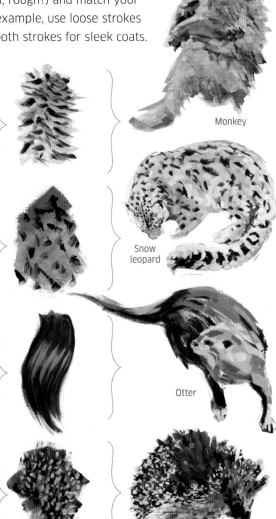

Monkey

Snow leopard

Otter

Hedgehog

This meerkat's fluffy body was painted with expressive brushstrokes. By contrast, controlled brushstrokes define its delicate facial features.

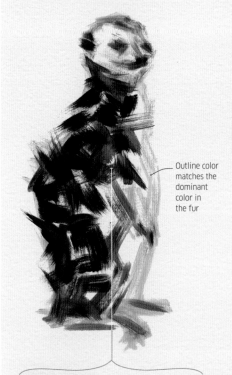

Outline color matches the dominant color in the fur

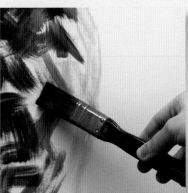

1 Establishing the shapes
Draw the outline of the meerkat in raw sienna with a 1in (25mm) flat brush. Apply an undiluted mix of burnt sienna and violet with short, crisscrossing flicks of the brush, to establish the texture of the fluffy fur.

You will need

Titanium white
Yellow ochre
Raw sienna
Burnt sienna
Deep violet

- 1in (25mm) and ½in (13mm) flat synthetic brushes
- 20 x 16in (50 x 40cm) medium-grain canvas

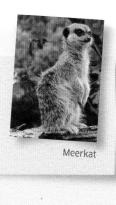

Meerkat

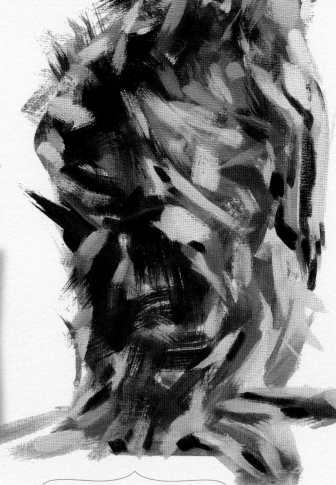

Controlled brushstrokes

Crisscrossing brushstrokes

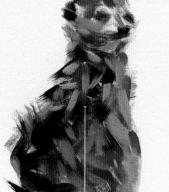

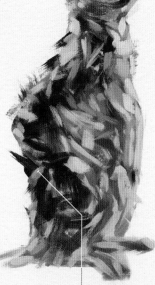

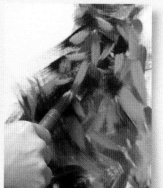

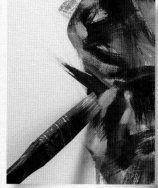

2 Developing form

Apply a mix of yellow ochre and raw sienna on one side of the body with crisscrossing strokes, as before. This lighter color shows where the light is falling on the meerkat and creates its rounded shape.

3 Enhancing the fur

Add white to the lighter brown mix to create a highlight color. Apply this with feathery strokes to enhance the fluffy texture.

4 Completing the face

Use a ½in (13mm) flat brush to finish the face with fine strokes. Add strong dark and light tones to create extra definition.

Dramatic skies

PAINTING SKY AND CLOUDS

It is important to pitch the tonal range correctly to achieve a dramatic sky. In order to create a sense of depth, start painting at the horizon, moving forward with thicker layers of paint until you reach the nearest clouds. Dramatic skies often have a lot of color, and darkening hues with blues or browns will help give your painting life and energy.

■ Creating characterful skies

You can use a range of techniques to create dramatic skies. Use simple strokes for dark, heavy clouds, blends for varied skies, or a dry brush for detail.

Single brushstroke

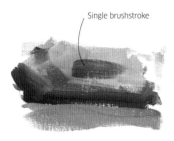

Strong strokes
Use bold, defined brushstrokes to depict a threatening cloud. A single brushstroke can give the impression of a dominant cloud.

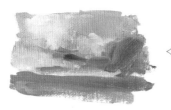

Blending
Balance heavy cloud with gently blended passages. A good mixture of blended and definite marks will add interest and character to skies.

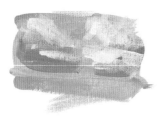

Dry brush
Use a dry-brush technique to add detail. Exploit the texture of the canvas by dragging paint along the surface to suggest light catching the clouds.

This landscape, with strong directional clouds, shows how blending, dry brushwork, and dominant brushstrokes can all create the impression of a dramatic summer sky.

You will need

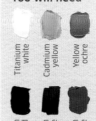

Titanium white Cadmium yellow Yellow ochre

Cadmium red French ultramarine Cerulean blue

- No. 8 filbert synthetic and no. 6 flat synthetic brushes
- 8 x 12in (20 x 30cm) medium-grain canvas

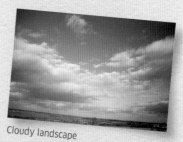

Cloudy landscape

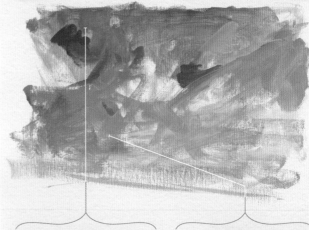

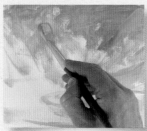

1 Establish main colors
Using a no. 8 filbert, paint an ultramarine blue and white mix, keeping the brushstrokes loose. Add more white and a touch of cerulean blue to suggest distance as you near the horizon.

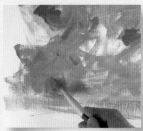

2 Cloud shadows
Use a darker mix of ultramarine and cadmium red to block in the darker areas. Apply strokes in the direction in which the clouds are drifting, to suggest movement.

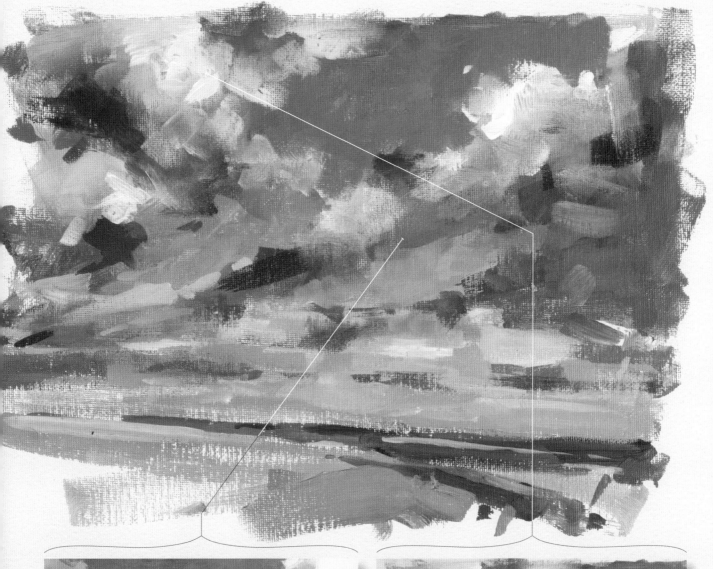

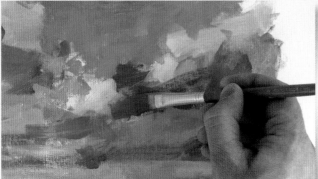

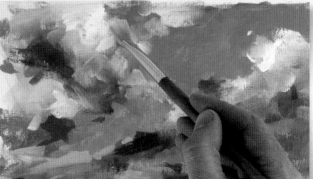

3 Add depth

Once the first two layers have dried, add another dark mix of blue. Using a no. 6 flat brush, blend lighter and darker mixes together to create depth. Lighten the color with white for the tops of the clouds, but avoid making the color too bright.

4 Create highlights

With the same brush, use a whiter mix to add highlights to the clouds while the previous layer is still wet. When dry, use the lightest mix to drag highlights over the clouds using a dry-brush technique. Add more detail to the nearest clouds, using less white in the distance.

Painting people simply

CAPTURING THE ESSENCE OF FIGURES

Including people in your work can bring it to life, but you don't need to paint individual portraits. If you focus on the overall activity and spacial relationships between people rather than their facial features and details, your figures will become successful, integrated elements of your painting.

■ The principle at work

Proportion and scale are the most important factors when you paint figures, and the most noticeable if they are wrong. There are a few basic rules that can make painting figures easier.

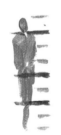

Proportion
Although the proportions of individuals vary, the average adult's height is roughly equal to eight head lengths. Children's body lengths are made up of fewer head lengths the younger they are.

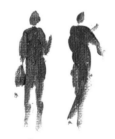

Scale
Heads, hands, and feet can be challenging to depict on middle-distance figures, so it's best to avoid painting them in any detail. Start by making the head smaller than you think; you can adjust it later if necessary.

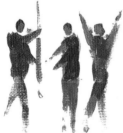

Space
Include slivers of space around the head, arms, and legs of your figures. This stops them from looking too solid, and creates a sense of movement, detail, and structure.

In this painting, the soccer players' shapes have been simplified to create an impression of movement. Nothing is painted in too much detail, to keep the focus on the activity rather than individuals.

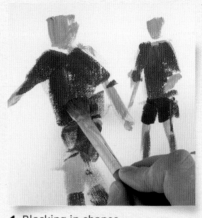

1 Blocking in shapes
Use a no. 6 flat brush to roughly block in the three players. Focus on getting the proportions and positions of the figures right, using approximate colors at this stage. You can refine the details later.

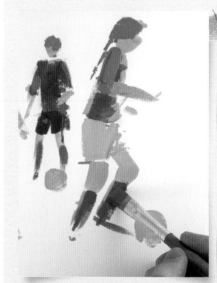

2 Adding structure
Refine your drawing by painting shadows onto the figures and adjusting the color and value of their clothing. This gives them more solidity and form.

You will need

Titanium white

Cadmium yellow

Yellow ochre

Cadmium red

French ultramarine

Cerulean blue

- No. 6 flat synthetic and no. 1 round synthetic brushes
- 10 x 10in (25 x 25cm) medium-grain canvas board

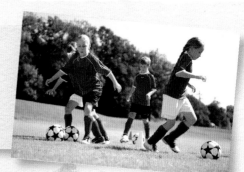

Soccer practice

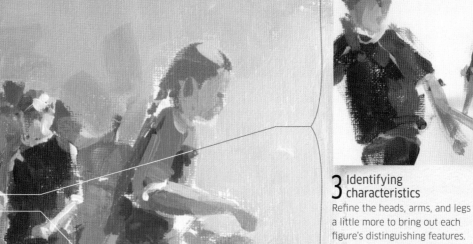

3 Identifying characteristics

Refine the heads, arms, and legs a little more to bring out each figure's distinguishing features. Use a no. 1 round brush for these details, and paint freely to maintain a sense of movement.

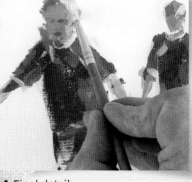

4 Final details

Add small details and highlights to create definition, but don't go into too much detail. To finish, cut in around the figures to fill in the background, and add shadows on the ground to anchor the figures.

Skin tones

PAINTING FLESH COLORS

Painting different skin tones or showing subtle variations in pigmentation can seem challenging. Amateur painters sometimes just opt for "flesh tint," or use pink for light complexions and brown for darker ones, but these choices fail to capture the luminosity of skin. Instead you need a palette of colors, including red, yellow, green, blue, and violet—with white to soften tones. The proportions of the mixes will vary according to skin tone.

Basic palette for skin tones

This range of colors provides the building blocks to create various skin tones. Begin by mixing all colors together in very small amounts with one or two dominant colors. Add varying amounts of white to create lighter tints and highlights.

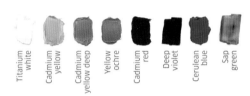

Titanium white · Cadmium yellow · Cadmium yellow deep · Yellow ochre · Cadmium red · Deep violet · Cerulean blue · Sap green

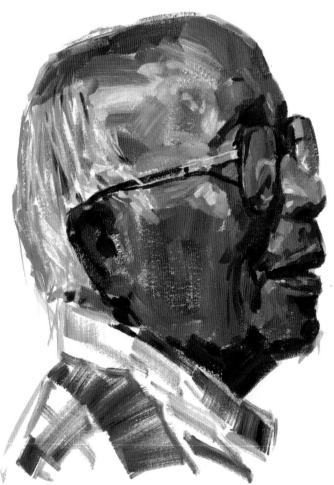

Brown skin tones

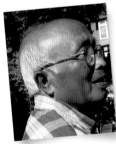

Color sketch
Create an initial color sketch to experiment with warm colors and dark tones. You can expand on these in the final work.

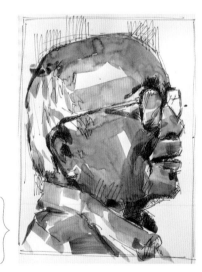

Ochre hues
This face's glowing brown color is achieved by a greater proportion of cadmium red and cadmium yellow in the basic mix. Add more deep violet for darker tones. For lighter tints add white, with a hint of sap green and cerulean blue to temper the vibrancy of the warm hue.

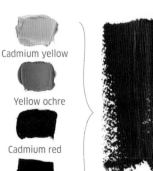

Cadmium yellow

Yellow ochre

Cadmium red

Deep violet

Basic mix for brown skin tones

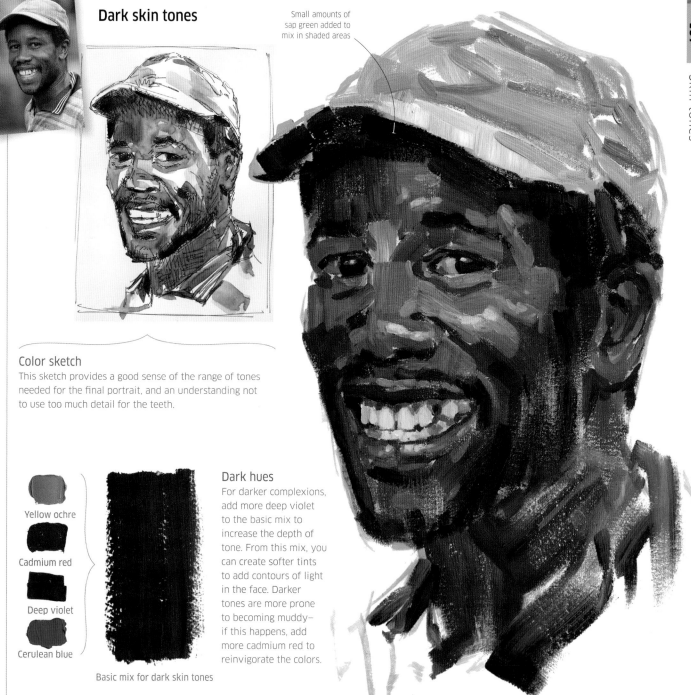

Dark skin tones

Small amounts of sap green added to mix in shaded areas

Color sketch
This sketch provides a good sense of the range of tones needed for the final portrait, and an understanding not to use too much detail for the teeth.

Yellow ochre

Cadmium red

Deep violet

Cerulean blue

Basic mix for dark skin tones

Dark hues
For darker complexions, add more deep violet to the basic mix to increase the depth of tone. From this mix, you can create softer tints to add contours of light in the face. Darker tones are more prone to becoming muddy—if this happens, add more cadmium red to reinvigorate the colors.

"Painting from life provides **valuable information** about the **subtlety of skin tones,** and gives insight into your **sitter's character.**"

Light skin tones– older face

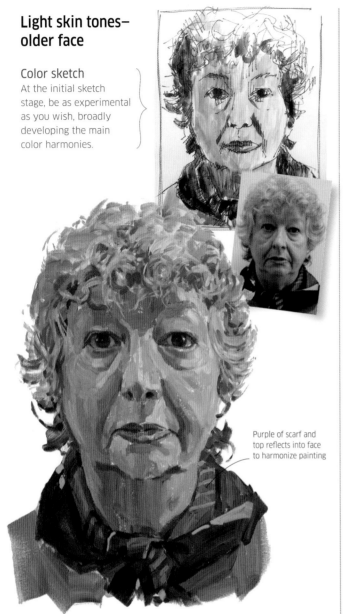

Color sketch
At the initial sketch stage, be as experimental as you wish, broadly developing the main color harmonies.

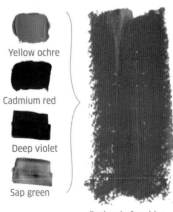

Purple of scarf and top reflects into face to harmonize painting

Light skin tones– younger face

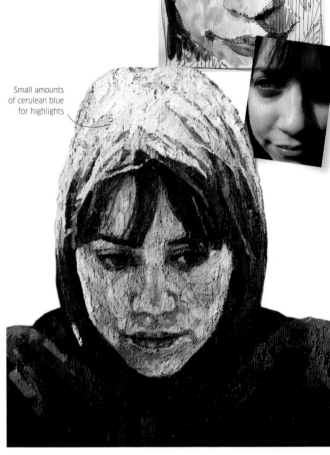

Color sketch
A quick color sketch emphasizes the complementary colors of yellow and purple in the light and shadow areas.

Small amounts of cerulean blue for highlights

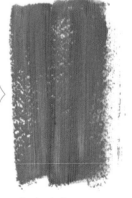

Light hues
In an older complexion, the skin is deeply textured and there are more shadows. Here, subtle changes of light from left to right leave half the face in soft shadow. For the deepest darks, use more deep violet and sap green in the basic mix. For the lightest areas of the face and for the hair, add small amounts of cerulean blue and white to the mix.

Yellow ochre

Cadmium red

Deep violet

Sap green

Basic mix for older, light skin tones

Light, even hues
In a young complexion, the tones are generally even, with subtle combinations of color. Use plenty of white with mainly cadmium red, cadmium yellow, and deep violet. (Using too much white, however, can result in flat, chalky color–if this happens, re-energize the mix with cadmium yellow.) For the lightest tints, use more sap green and add cerulean blue to temper the warm colors and create a natural look.

Cadmium yellow

Cadmium red

Deep violet

Sap green

Basic mix for younger, light skin tones

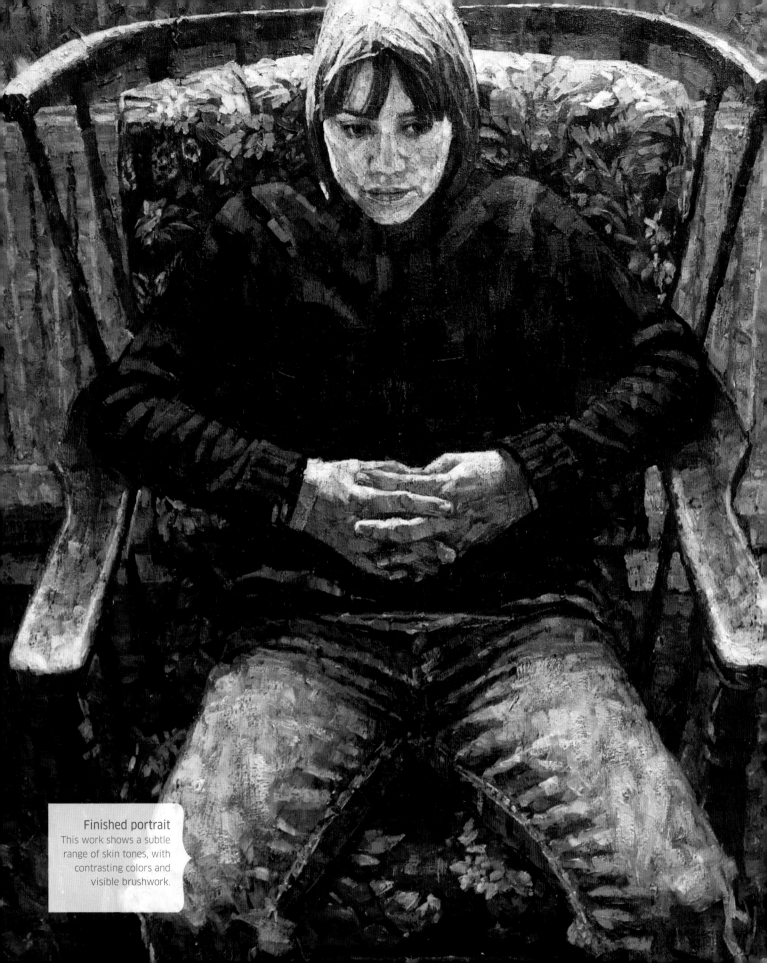

Finished portrait
This work shows a subtle range of skin tones, with contrasting colors and visible brushwork.

Painting movement

CREATING THE IMPRESSION OF MOTION

Conveying a sense of movement in a scene can be the ingredient that brings a painting to life. Movement can be present in a street scene or even in a still life. By using directional brushstrokes, breaking the outline of forms, and avoiding detail, you can create an impression of dynamism. The fast drying time of acrylics allows you to overlap marks, while exploring vibrant colors will give your painting a more contemporary feel.

PUTTING IT INTO PRACTICE

In this image, the brushstrokes in the background match the direction in which the subject is walking. Movement away from the viewer is further emphasized by brushstrokes breaking the outline of the figure.

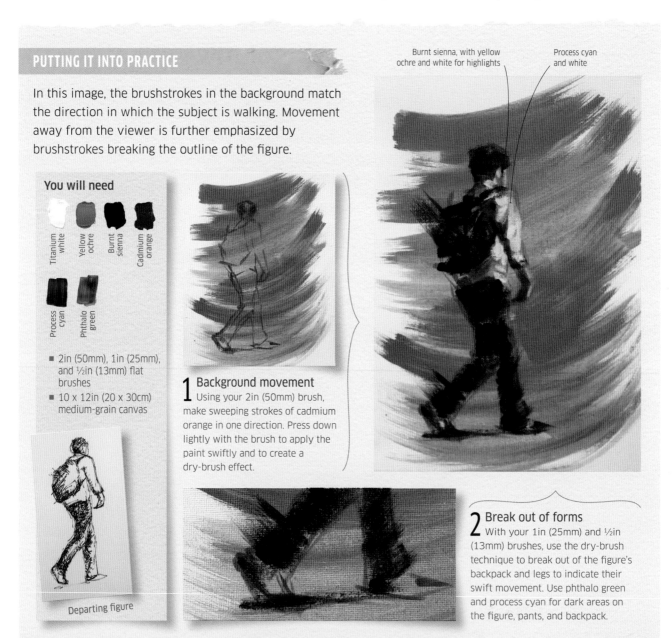

Burnt sienna, with yellow ochre and white for highlights

Process cyan and white

You will need

Titanium white

Yellow ochre

Burnt sienna

Cadmium orange

Process cyan

Phthalo green

- 2in (50mm), 1in (25mm), and ½in (13mm) flat brushes
- 10 x 12in (20 x 30cm) medium-grain canvas

Departing figure

1 Background movement
Using your 2in (50mm) brush, make sweeping strokes of cadmium orange in one direction. Press down lightly with the brush to apply the paint swiftly and to create a dry-brush effect.

2 Break out of forms
With your 1in (25mm) and ½in (13mm) brushes, use the dry-brush technique to break out of the figure's backpack and legs to indicate their swift movement. Use phthalo green and process cyan for dark areas on the figure, pants, and backpack.

Conveying motion

Leaving areas exposed, breaking out of shapes, and avoiding overworking a scene can all help to create the illusion of movement. Make a bold statement by using vibrant colors and use prominent, visible brushstrokes to give the viewer a sense of the fluidity and action behind every mark.

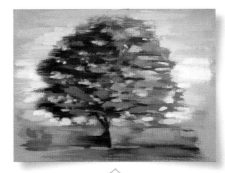

Movement past a static object
By using sweeping brushstrokes in a single direction, and by omitting detail, you can create the impression of moving at speed past a stationary object—in this case, a tree.

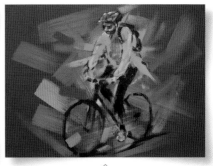

Moving subject
Applying brushstrokes in multiple directions to the background and subject suggests movement. Avoiding too much detail helps suggest a cyclist speeding past the viewer.

PUTTING IT INTO PRACTICE

In this image, directional brushstrokes and indistinct forms work together to suggest the windswept couple's forward movement, as well as the gusts of wind around them. Bold color gives the everyday scene energy.

You will need

- Titanium white
- Yellow ochre
- Burnt sienna
- Process magenta
- Deep violet
- Process cyan

- 2in (50mm) and ½in (13mm) flat brushes
- 9 x 12in (20 x 30cm) medium-grain canvas

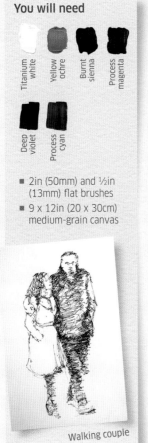

Walking couple

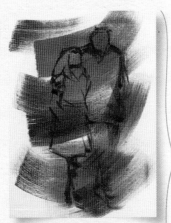

1 Dynamic background
Make directional brushstrokes with your 2in (50mm) brush to create movement and suggest windy conditions. Sketch figures with the ½in (13mm) brush.

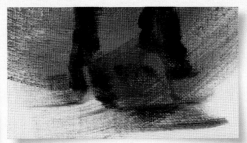

2 Energy through color
Use your ½in (13mm) brush to imply features in the face and feet, keeping them indistinct to create a sense of movement. Use brushstrokes with soft edges and enliven the image by using bold color in pure mixes.

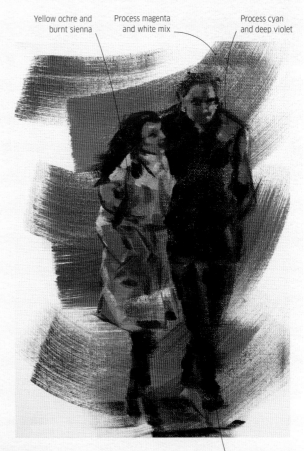

Yellow ochre and burnt sienna

Process magenta and white mix

Process cyan and deep violet

Deep violet, burnt sienna, and process cyan

PUTTING IT INTO PRACTICE

This artwork shows how you can first apply energized marks before introducing the main subject (the cyclist). When adding to the figure, be careful not to overwork it and lose the sense of movement already established by the initial dynamic strokes.

You will need

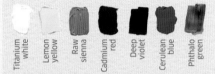

Titanium white · Lemon yellow · Raw sienna · Cadmium red · Deep violet · Cerulean blue · Phthalo green

- 2in (50mm), 1in (25mm), and ½in (13mm) flat brushes
- 16 x 20in (50 x 40cm) medium-grain canvas

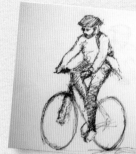

Cyclist in motion

1 Background motion
On a ground color of deep violet and titanium white, begin by applying a few random directional brushstrokes with a 2in (50mm) brush. Use a mix of cerulean blue, deep violet, and titanium white.

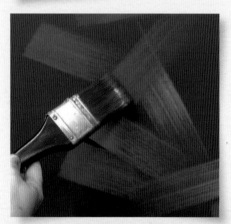

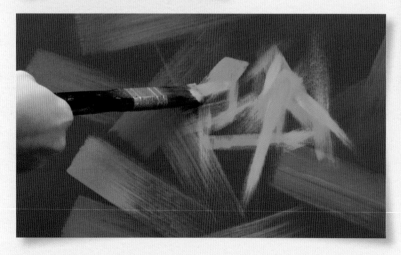

2 Dynamic sketch
Using a ½in (13mm) brush, add a few more directional brushstrokes—using phthalo green and lemon yellow—to roughly indicate the position of the cyclist's jacket.

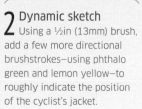

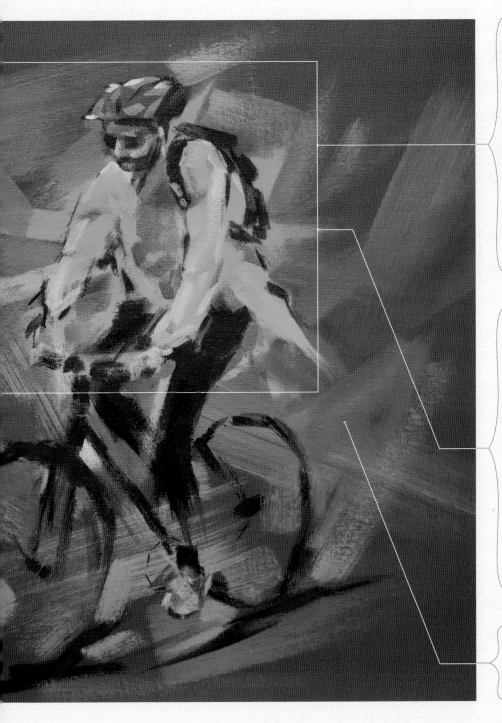

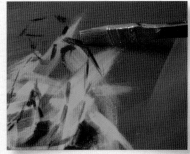

3 Outline the subject
Now begin to plot the figure and bike on top of the marks created in the previous step, using a 1in (25mm) brush with deep violet to indicate dark areas. Then apply a mix of cadmium red and raw sienna for the flesh tones of the figure.

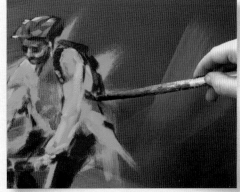

4 Work up figure
Use a ½in (13mm) brush to pull out dark areas of color. Establish the figure using cadmium orange and process cyan. Avoid overworking the image or sharpening it too much.

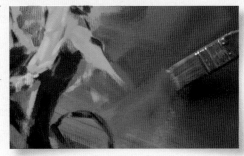

5 Finishing touches
Use a 1in (25mm) brush for your final additions to the background, emphasizing the directional brushstrokes.

"Leaving areas exposed, breaking out of shapes, and avoiding detail all help to create the illusion of movement."

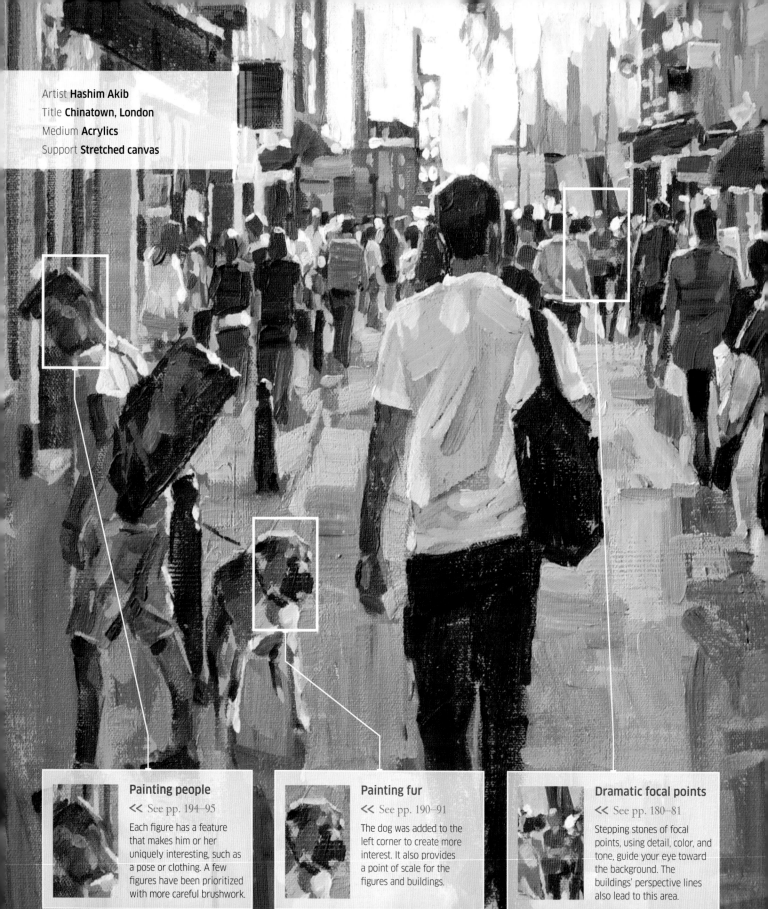

Artist **Hashim Akib**
Title **Chinatown, London**
Medium **Acrylics**
Support **Stretched canvas**

Painting people

« See pp. 194–95

Each figure has a feature that makes him or her uniquely interesting, such as a pose or clothing. A few figures have been prioritized with more careful brushwork.

Painting fur

« See pp. 190–91

The dog was added to the left corner to create more interest. It also provides a point of scale for the figures and buildings.

Dramatic focal points

« See pp. 180–81

Stepping stones of focal points, using detail, color, and tone, guide your eye toward the background. The buildings' perspective lines also lead to this area.

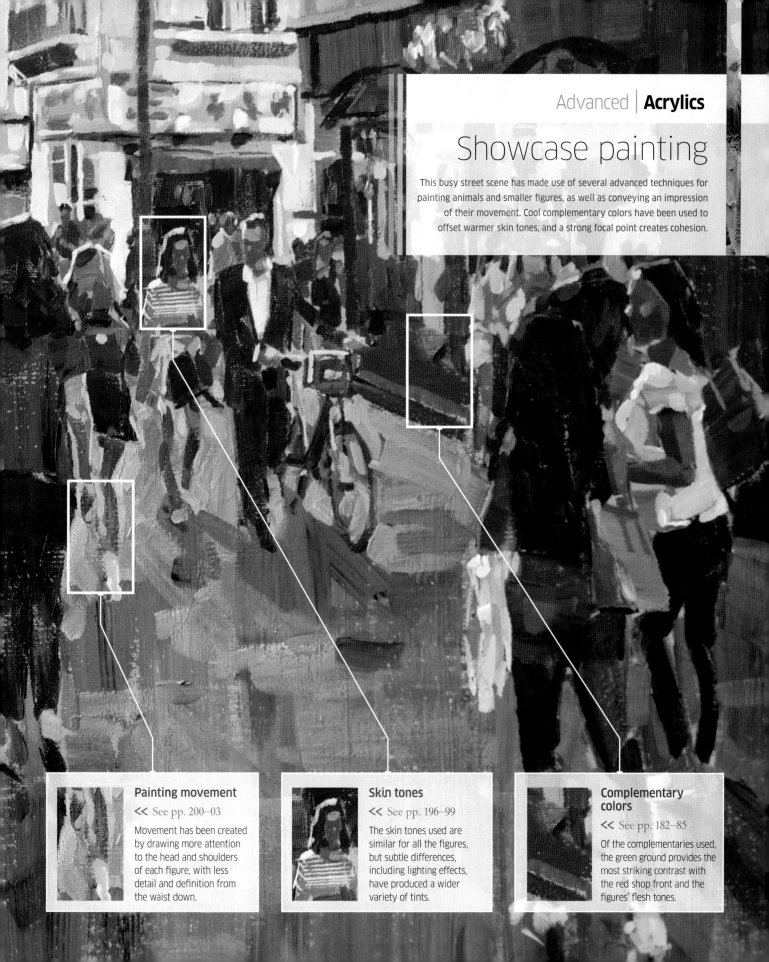

Showcase painting

This busy street scene has made use of several advanced techniques for painting animals and smaller figures, as well as conveying an impression of their movement. Cool complementary colors have been used to offset warmer skin tones, and a strong focal point creates cohesion.

Painting movement

« See pp. 200–03

Movement has been created by drawing more attention to the head and shoulders of each figure, with less detail and definition from the waist down.

Skin tones

« See pp. 196–99

The skin tones used are similar for all the figures, but subtle differences, including lighting effects, have produced a wider variety of tints.

Complementary colors

« See pp. 182–85

Of the complementaries used, the green ground provides the most striking contrast with the red shop front and the figures' flesh tones.

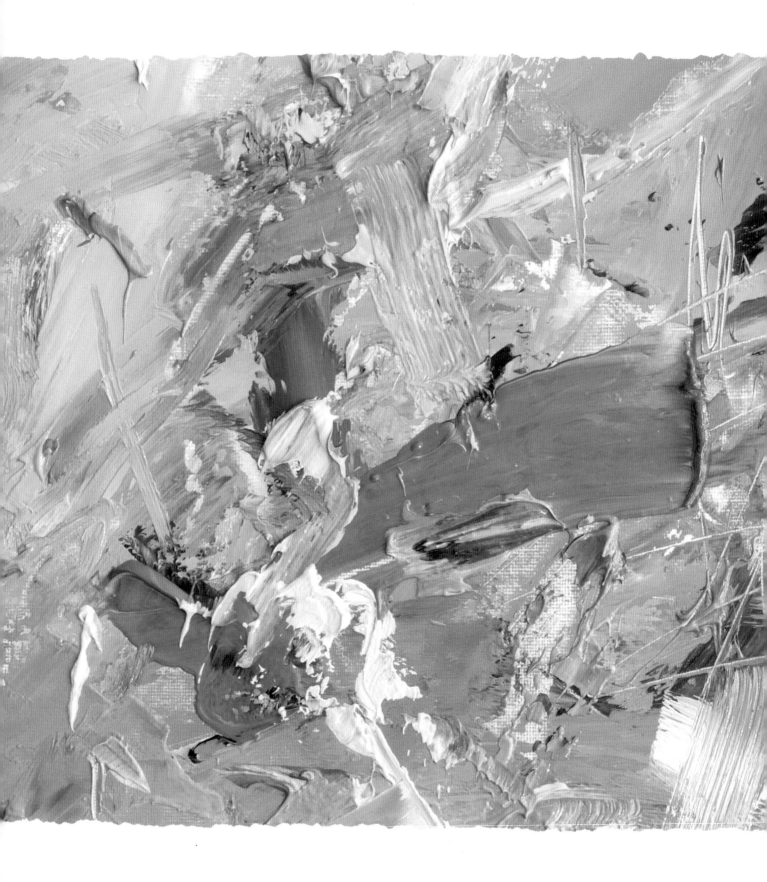

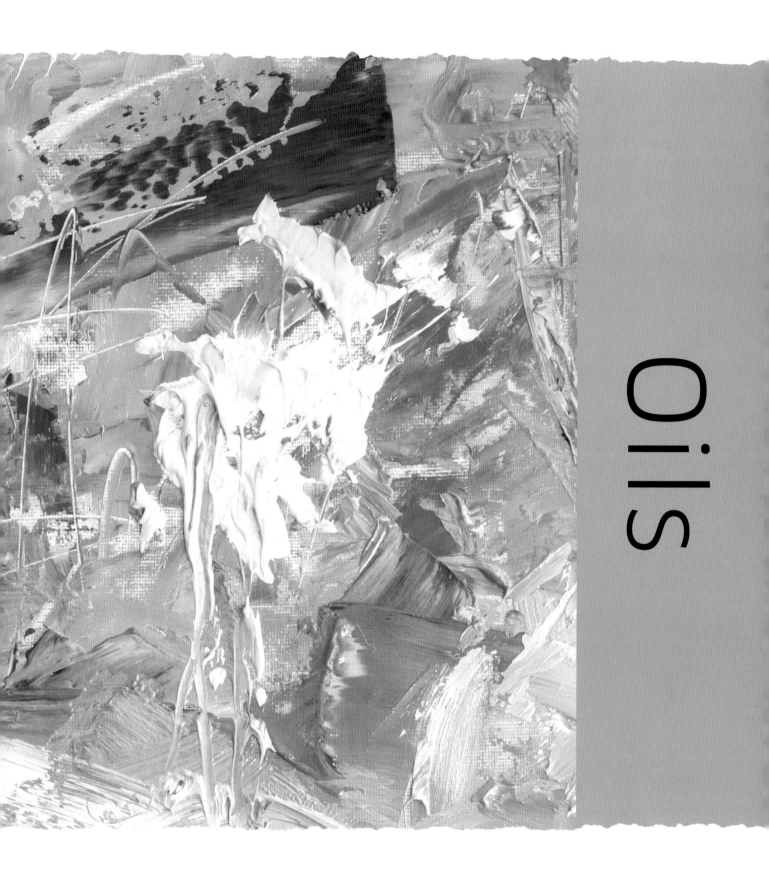

Oils

Painting with **oils**

Oil paints are popular with artists because they are versatile, expressive, and forgiving. Used with a heavy consistency, they can be applied thickly and then sculpted, cut, or scratched back. Alternatively, they can be thinned with solvents or oils to give greater translucency and create thin glazes of color.

On the following pages, you can find out about the paints and materials you are likely to need. Then, three subsections–beginner, intermediate, and advanced–teach you more than 30 step-by-step oil-painting techniques. Each subsection culminates in a showcase painting that demonstrates the techniques you have explored.

1 Beginner techniques

■ See pp. 216-41

In the first section, find out about color mixing, brushwork, using "fat over lean," and layering and blocking your colors. Also look at working in decreasing stages, *alla prima* techniques, and how to create form.

2 Intermediate techniques

■ See pp. 242-65

In this section, find out about aerial perspective, blending, impasto, and how to apply and remove paint from the canvas to create textures and effects, as well as to remove mistakes.

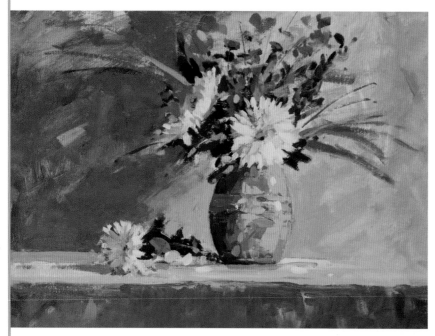

Beginner showcase painting (see pp. 240-41)

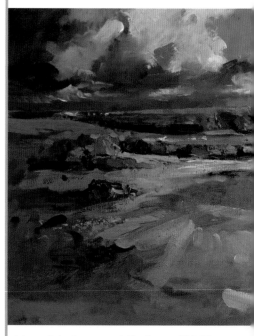

Intermediate showcase painting (see pp. 264-65)

Oil paints have a long, illustrious history, with evidence of their use dating back to the 7th century. The medium was favored by the Old Masters—the great European artists who worked from the 13th to the 17th century.

The introduction of paint tubes in 1841 was an important development for oil paint, making it more accessible and portable. This made it possible to paint outdoors and travel farther afield to capture light and landscape from life. It paved the way for artistic movements such as Impressionism.

Brushes have also played a key role in oil paint's history. The invention of metal ferrules led to flat chiselled brushes, as well as traditional bound, round ones, permitting a greater variety of sculptural marks, and encouraging experimentation and different styles.

Versatile and rich

Oil paint remains a popular choice with artists, mostly due to its versatility. Paints can be opaque, transparent, or translucent, as well as thick or thin, and their luminescence and glossy finish make it possible to create highly realistic paintings. Slow drying times allow for plenty of blending.

Paint can be applied with a brush or palette knife, and there are a great many colors available.

The depth, consistency, and richness of oil paint remain its greatest qualities, and the many techniques available to the oil painter make it the perfect vehicle for artistic expression. Once basic processes are mastered, oils offer a wealth of creative opportunities for both beginners and experienced artists.

3 Advanced techniques

■ See pp. 266-93

The final section looks at skin tones, color harmony, tonal values, and how to use mediums. Also, discover more complex methods of correcting, adjusting, and finishing your painting, and how to find your own style.

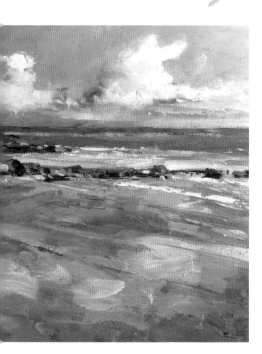

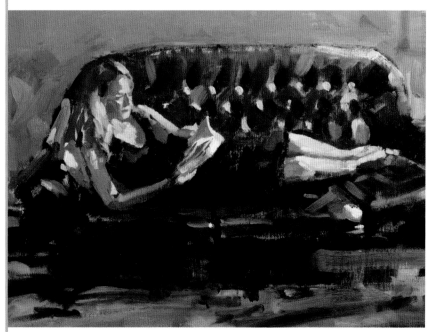

Advanced showcase painting (see pp. 292-93)

Oil paints

THE PROPERTIES OF OILS

Oil paint has a unique quality. Its depth and richness of pigment, together with a thick, buttery consistency, make it a versatile and popular medium. As well as standard oil paints, alkyd oil paints are available. These include an alkyd dryer to speed up the drying process and can dry in as little as a day. If you want to avoid using solvents, oil paints that mix with water are also available.

Oil paint, as the name suggests, is oil-based, with the pigment usually suspended in linseed oil. As oil does not evaporate as water does, oil paints take much longer to dry than water-based paints.

The drying time of paints will vary, depending on the make, and certain colors dry faster than others, depending on the oil content and the materials used to create the pigments. Earth colors, such as burnt sienna or burnt umber, are usually made from iron oxide and dry relatively quickly, making them good, basic colors for underpainting. Transparent colors tend to be used for underpainting and to mix glazes. Most colors applied sparingly will be touch dry within a week, although thick underlying layers can take years to dry.

Choosing oils

There are many different manufacturers of oil paint and most produce two ranges. Artist-quality paints offer the best purity, highest pigment content, and widest range. Student-quality paint is cheaper, because more fillers are used to bulk out the paint and there is less pigment present. A higher pigment content is desirable to achieve purer mixes and more accuracy when color mixing. It will also influence the permanence of your painting's color, increasing its longevity and resistance to fading in sunlight. Both artist- and student-quality paints will produce good results, but artist-quality is recommended.

Within each range, colors are separated into series. Each series has a different price band, which varies according to the cost of the pigment used in manufacture. Some colors are

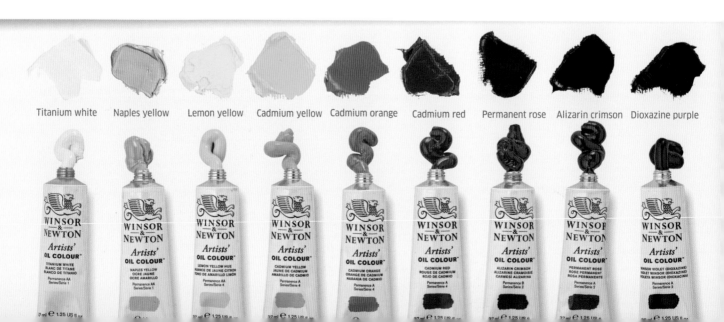

Titanium white   Naples yellow   Lemon yellow   Cadmium yellow   Cadmium orange   Cadmium red   Permanent rose   Alizarin crimson   Dioxazine purple

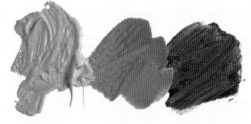

Thick application	Thin application	Transparent pigment	Semi-transparent pigment	Paint thickened with medium	Paint thinned with medium	Paint thinned with solvent

Consistency of oils

A distinguishing feature of oil paints is their thick consistency. You can apply them directly from the tube to capitalize on this quality, or thin them with mediums.

Opacity

Some pigments are more transparent than others. Transparent colors are good for glazing (see pp.284–85) while opaque ones are better for solid coverage.

Adding mediums

Mediums can affect drying times, consistency, and sheen. They can be added to paint on the palette or dipped into like water. Be aware that some may add a yellow tint to colors.

more expensive than others, although alternatives are sometimes offered for costly pigments, such as cadmium colors. Where substitutions have been made, this will be indicated by the word "hue" following the color's name.

Transparency

Colors are also graded from transparent to opaque: transparent, semi-transparent, semi-opaque, and opaque. A color's transparency influences the amount of paint required to give good coverage. However, be mindful of the fat over lean principle (see pp.224–25); for

underpaintings, it is better to mix a transparent color with an opaque color than apply it too thickly. Transparency in a white paint can be useful when mixing colors. Your choices will vary according to your subject matter and style. Note that even colors with the same name may differ from supplier to supplier, even though the same pigment has been used.

Mediums

There are many different oils and prepared mediums available. They can be used to thin or thicken consistency,

hasten or slow drying time, add glazes, or otherwise alter the final appearance of the paint.

Solvents for cleaning brushes and thinning paint include turpentine, mineral spirits, and their low-odor alternatives. There are also more environmentally friendly options based on the zest of citrus fruit, which dilute paint and clean brushes well. Thinners can be reused if carefully decanted into another vessel and left to settle.

Use solvents and oil paints only in well-ventilated areas. Wash your hands well after use, or wear vinyl gloves.

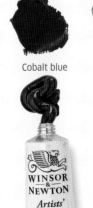
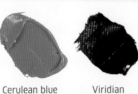

French ultramarine	Cobalt blue	Cerulean blue	Viridian	Burnt sienna

Choosing colors

This selection of oils offers a good range of warm and cool hues. Whichever colors you select, make sure that they are good quality.

Black

There are several to choose from, or you can mix a dark tone with burnt sienna and ultramarine blue to create a warmer (browner) or cooler (bluer) dark.

Brushes and palette knives

HOW TO CHOOSE YOUR BRUSHES

An assortment of brushes is essential for working in oil paint. Some artists have a duplicate brush in each size, one for light paint and one for dark, to keep colors separate and clean during painting. Stiff bristle brushes are the usual choice for oil painting, and palette knives are excellent for mixing paint and creating texture.

Brushes for oil painting need to be stiff enough to move the thick paint and robust enough to withstand cleaning in solvents. Bristle brushes made with hog hair are the traditional favorite, but synthetic fibers also work well and are less expensive. Soft-hair brushes are useful for working into wet paint, but synthetic fibers are more practical than delicate, natural fibers.

Types of brushes

There are various shapes of brushes available, each used for making different marks. Flat brushes have squared tips, which make chiseled marks with the flat side and fine lines with the thin edge. They also have long, springy bristles, which allow you to apply the paint by pressing or sweeping. Short, flat brushes, also known as brights, are similar to flats but the hairs are cut shorter so they are firmer. Filbert brushes have flat ferrules (the metal piece that holds the hairs) and rounded tips, which means they can create broad marks, like a flat brush, but with soft edges, similar to a round brush. Round brushes are bound together in a circle so that the hairs come to a point. They can carry a lot of paint and produce a variety of marks, from wide strokes with the side to delicate dabs with the tip. Fan brushes don't hold much paint, so are useful for dry-brush techniques and gentle blending. Riggers are small brushes with long hairs, and they hold a lot of paint due to their length. They are suited to fine-line work, such as tree branches or rigging on boats.

Palette knives

You can also apply oil paint with palette knives to create bold, direct marks and textures. Palette knives come in a

Brushes

Each shape of brush comes in a range of sizes; the higher the number, the larger the brush. Large and medium-sized brushes are used for covering the canvas in the first stages of painting. Smaller, soft-hair brushes are used for painting details.

Synthetic rigger brush

No. 2 flat hog-bristle brush

No. 4 filbert synthetic brush

No. 8 short flat hog-bristle brush

No. 8 flat hog-bristle brush

Hog-bristle fan brush

No. 6 round synthetic brush

Holding a brush

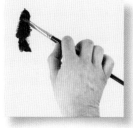

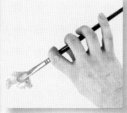

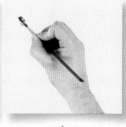

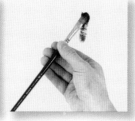

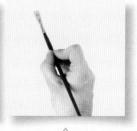

Mid-handle hold
Hold a large flat or filbert brush halfway down the handle to create pressure for broad strokes.

Flat hold
To create expressive marks, place your thumb at the back of the handle for a loose, flat hold.

Shallow angle
Hold the brush close to the ferrule between forefinger and thumb to help you create light, broken lines.

Close pencil hold
For maximum control when you are painting details, hold the brush close to the tip, as you would a pencil.

Flexible pencil hold
Grip the brush like a pencil farther down the handle to give you control and allow you to change pressure.

variety of shapes, widths, and lengths, just as brushes do. Those with flexible handles are best for painting—select larger sizes for laying broad strokes of paint and smaller, narrower shapes for precision work. Use the flat of the blade to apply lots of color, the edge of the blade to scrape into paint and create texture, and the tip to apply small dots and dabs. Flat, straight-edged palette knives are useful tools for mixing and moving paint. Their straight sides make them ideal for removing excess wet paint from the canvas. You can also use them to mix paint on the palette instead of using a brush, which keeps your colors cleaner and prevents your brushes from being contaminated with different colors. Palette knives are easy to clean by wiping with a rag.

Caring for your brushes
Looking after your brushes properly will make them last much longer. After working, wipe the oil paint from your brush with a rag, then rinse it in solvent or mineral spirits to remove any remaining paint. Wash the brush with warm (not hot) water and soap (not detergent), then rinse until the water runs clear. When the brush is clean, wipe it off, gently reshape it, and leave it to dry completely with the bristles facing upward. Do not store the brush until it is completely dry, or it could develop mildew.

Palette knives
Knives with "cranked," or bent, shanks are flexible, and keep your hand away from the canvas as you paint. Grip the handle with your thumb at the front for maximum control. Palette knives that are flatter and straighter are perfect for mixing paint, or scraping it from the canvas.

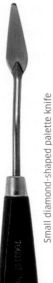

Small diamond-shaped palette knife

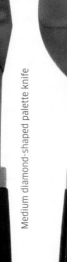

Medium diamond-shaped palette knife

Large trowel-shaped palette knife

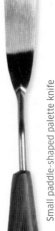

Small paddle-shaped palette knife

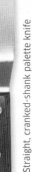

Straight, cranked-shank palette knife

Straight, flat palette knife

Supports and other materials

CHOOSING A SURFACE TO PAINT ON

There are many different supports, or surfaces, that you can paint on using oil paints. They range from canvas to paper and many different types of wood. As long as it is primed well, you can paint on almost any surface. Canvas is the classic oil painting support and is available in cotton or linen, but many artists prefer to paint on board.

All supports need to be primed before use, so that the surface is sealed and the support does not absorb the paint. While many supports are available ready primed, if you are using your own you will need to prime it yourself. Traditionally a gesso mixture made from rabbit-skin glue, chalk, and lead white was used, but ready-mixed acrylic gesso primer is safer and easier to use. Alternatively, a water-based undercoat or primer with a little added chalk and wood glue can work well. Priming with a decorator's brush will leave visible brushstrokes on the surface, creating texture and movement. Use a roller for a more uniform finish, or experiment with imprinting fabrics into the wet gesso to leave texture.

Types of canvas

Canvas is a popular choice and is available in many variations. Linen canvas is the most traditional option, whereas cotton canvas is a more affordable support and has a more regular weave. To create a suitable painting surface, canvas is stretched over a wooden stretcher and secured in place. It is then tightened using wedges around the corners, which push the stretcher bars apart. Canvas is available in a range of textures from fine to coarse. It should be primed before use.

Wooden boards

MDF, hardboard, and plywood are good sheet materials to use for oil painting. The main advantage of these is that they can be cut to any size and primed with a texture of your own choosing. They are also more durable than canvas and easier to store without the risk of

Canvas

MDF

Hardboard

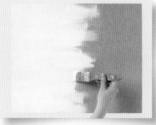
1–apply horizontal brushstrokes

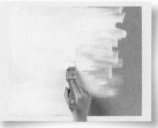
2–apply vertical brushstrokes

3–allow to dry before painting

Papers and boards

Canvas, hardboard, MDF and plywood are all popular supports for oil paints and all have different advantages.

Priming boards

Start by using horizontal brush or roller strokes to cover the support with primer, then allow to dry before applying a second coat using vertical strokes to ensure even coverage. Once this has dried, your support will be ready for paint.

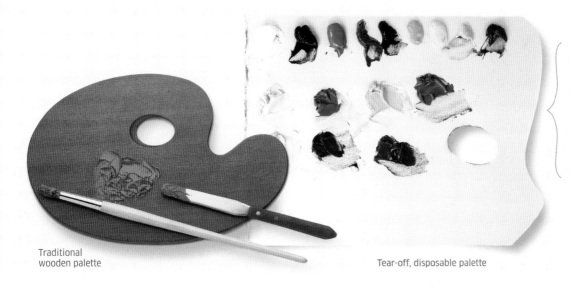

Traditional
wooden palette

Tear-off, disposable palette

Palettes
Traditional wooden palettes are still a popular choice and come in a variety of sizes. Plastic palettes are a cheaper option and are usually white. Tear-off disposable palettes are useful for working outside.

damage. Boards are also useful when painting outside, because you can carry them in a wet panel carrier and they take up less space than canvases. You can also adhere linen or cotton canvas to the surface of the board if you wish.

Using paper

Some artists prefer to work on paper, and oil sketching paper is a canvas-textured paper suitable for oil paints. It is available in blocks, is more affordable than canvas, and can be mounted on a board for rigidity. It is worth having some in the studio to test compositions or color mixes before committing to canvas. Primed heavyweight watercolor paper is also suitable for oil painting.

Easels in the studio

To hold your support you will need an easel of some kind. There are easels designed for every situation, from the dining room table to a large-scale studio. Aluminum easels are lightweight and portable, while wooden easels are strong, long-lasting, and traditional. Wooden easels are heavier, which makes them more difficult to move around, so they are better for studio work. Larger studio models include a crank handle to raise and lower large paintings to make working on different sections easier.

Out and about

Pochade boxes (see also pp. 26–27) store equipment and provide a place to rest a board when working outside. French easels also incorporate a storage box.

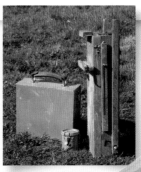

Wet panel carrier and
folded box easel

Wooden standing easel

Mediums and solvents
You can mix mediums with oil paints to make them easier to work with, to thin paint, or to thicken it. Use turpentine or solvent to clean brushes.

Easels
Pochade boxes and box easels fold up into a portable case, so you can use them outdoors. Standing easels are larger, stronger, and heavier. They are ideal for working on paintings in the studio or at home.

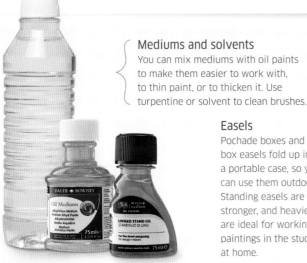

Turpentine   Alkyd drier   Stand oil
or solvent

Color mixing

USING COLOR THEORY TO MIX YOUR OIL PAINTS

You can buy paints in many different hues, but with a few basic colors you will be able to mix numerous variations yourself and so have greater control over your work. Unlike other media, oil paint doesn't change color as it dries, so what you mix is exactly what you'll get.

MIXING METHODS

To create new colors, you will need to mix two or more oil paints together by stirring them into each other. You can do this with a brush or palette knife, either on a palette or directly on the canvas.

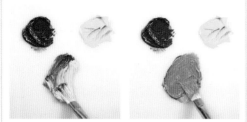

Mixing on a palette
Pick up a little of each color on the same brush. The first mixing stroke will produce different strands of color. Circle the brush a few times to blend the colors.

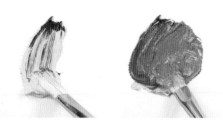

Mixing on the canvas
Pick up a little of each color on the same brush. Mix the colors on the support in one stroke. Circle the brush to blend the colors, first partially and then thoroughly.

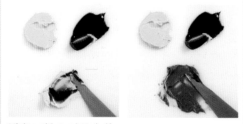

Mixing with a palette knife
Pick up each color on a palette knife and spread them on the palette. After just one movement, the mixed color will be visible. Move the knife back and forth to blend thoroughly.

▉ Color temperature and bias

Reds, oranges, and yellows are considered "warm," while purples, blues, and greens are considered "cool." Your choice of warm or cool colors will affect the balance and mood of your work.

There are also warm and cool variations of every color. For example, a blue with a red bias (purplish-blue) is considered a warm blue, while a blue with a yellow bias (greenish-blue) is considered cool. Because this bias will affect the result when mixing with other colors, you should include a warm and cool version of each primary color on your palette for flexibility.

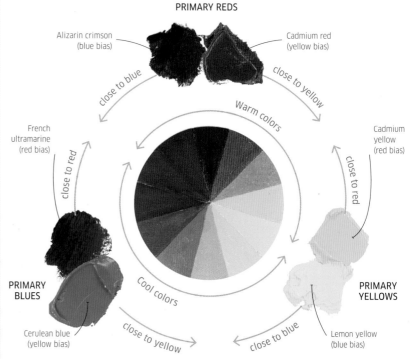

PRIMARY REDS

Alizarin crimson (blue bias)

Cadmium red (yellow bias)

close to blue

close to yellow

Warm colors

French ultramarine (red bias)

Cadmium yellow (red bias)

close to red

close to red

PRIMARY BLUES

Cool colors

PRIMARY YELLOWS

Cerulean blue (yellow bias)

Lemon yellow (blue bias)

close to yellow

close to blue

Color bias wheel
In this version of the color wheel (see also pp. 14–15), the inner circle shows which colors are considered warm and which are cool. The outer circle shows how each color—in this case the primaries—has a warm and cool version.

Mixing vibrant secondary colors

Mixing two primary colors will create a secondary color (see pp. 14–15). If you mix two primaries that are close to the same secondary color on the color wheel, they will create an intense secondary color. For example, French ultramarine and alizarin crimson make a vivid violet because they are both close to purple.

Mixing muted secondary colors

If you mix two primaries that are close to different secondary colors on the color wheel, they will create a muted secondary color. For example, cerulean blue and cadmium red make a subdued violet when mixed together because, on the color wheel, they are close to green and orange, respectively.

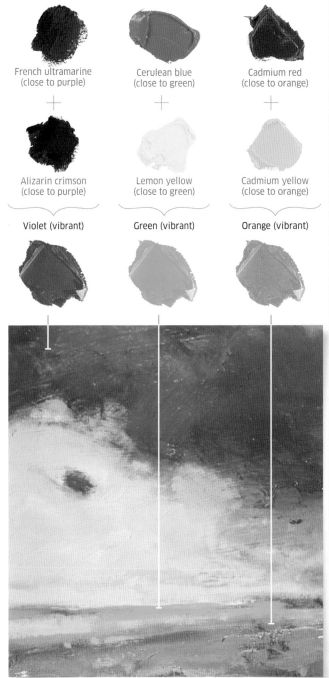

French ultramarine
(close to purple)

+

Cerulean blue
(close to green)

+

Cadmium red
(close to orange)

+

Alizarin crimson
(close to purple)

Lemon yellow
(close to green)

Cadmium yellow
(close to orange)

Violet (vibrant)

Green (vibrant)

Orange (vibrant)

Vibrant landscape

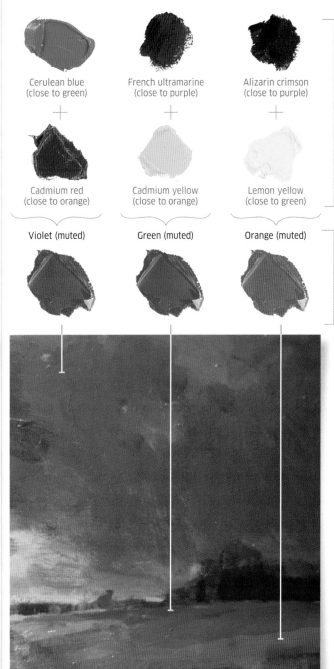

Cerulean blue
(close to green)

+

French ultramarine
(close to purple)

+

Alizarin crimson
(close to purple)

+

Cadmium red
(close to orange)

Cadmium yellow
(close to orange)

Lemon yellow
(close to green)

Violet (muted)

Green (muted)

Orange (muted)

Muted landscape

Primary colors

Secondary colors

■ Mixing all three primary colors to create darks

By mixing all three primary colors together you can create a range of dark, muted colors. Depending on the ratio of each primary in your mix, you can create your own blacks and browns—typically with greater depth and subtlety than bought versions. This can be especially useful for landscape painting.

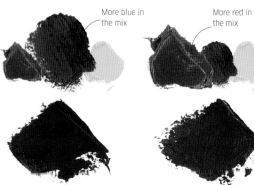

More blue in the mix

More red in the mix

More yellow in the mix

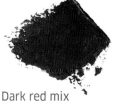

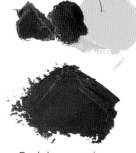

Dark blue mix
Adding more blue will create a dark, cool mix that is almost black.

Dark red mix
Adding more red will create a warm, dark mix with a purple tone.

Dark brown mix
Adding more yellow to the mix will create a lighter brown color.

■ Mixing complementary colors to create grays

Complementary colors are colors that sit opposite each other on the color wheel, for example red and green or yellow and purple (see also pp. 14–15). When placed side by side, complementary colors intensify each other, but when mixed together the effect is reversed and the result is gray.

You can vary the mix to make warm, cool, or colored grays, which will introduce subtlety and depth to your paintings. Adding white will extend the range even further. As you can see in the painting, right, grays can look surprisingly interesting using this method.

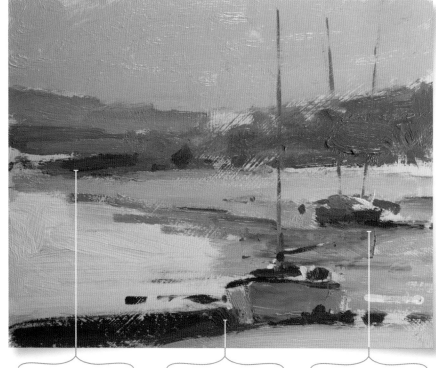

"Mixing your own grays will give your work subtlety and depth."

Alizarin crimson

Viridian green

Cadmium yellow

Dioxazine purple

Cobalt blue

Cadmium orange

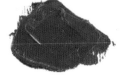

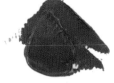

Cool, bluish gray

Warm, reddish gray

Neutral gray

Mixing "light"

Instinctively, we think of adding white to lighten a color, and it often does the job well. However, adding white to a mix desaturates it and gives it a pastel appearance. When light shines on an object, the color is often intensified rather than weakened, so painting light requires judicious use of saturated color and added white.

Pastel colors

Adding white to a color creates a pastel. For example, adding white to red creates a pastel pink.

Cadmium red + white = pastel pink

Using saturated color

In this landscape, a pure saturated color was used to depict a vibrant sunset. No white was used in the mixes.

Warm blue

 French ultramarine + a little cerulean blue + a hint of alizarin crimson

Warm yellow

Cadmium yellow

Warm red

Cadmium red + a hint of cadmium yellow

Warm orange

Cadmium yellow + a hint of Naples yellow + a hint of cadmium red

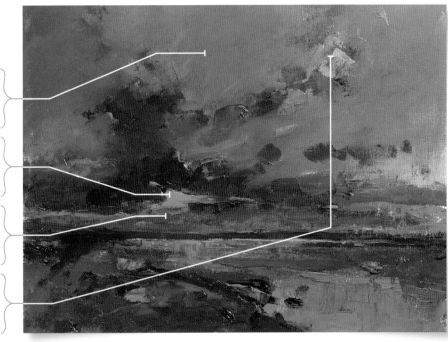

Adding white

Here, white was added to each mix. The resulting pastel colors give the painting a softer, cooler look.

 + white

Warm blue — Pastel blue

 + white

Warm yellow — Pastel yellow

 + white

Warm red — Pastel pink

 + white

Warm orange — Pastel orange

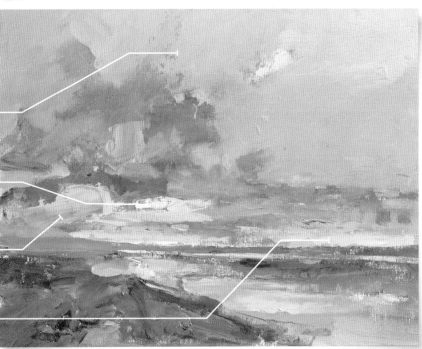

Brushwork

USING BRUSHSTROKES TO CREATE EFFECTS

You can create a variety of effects—from photorealism to abstract expressionism—depending on the brush you choose, the marks it can make, and the way you apply the paint. This will set the mood of your piece, so practicing different ways of making marks will enable you to interpret any subject matter in your own style.

■ Five brushstroke techniques

There are five main brushstroke techniques that will help you to create different textures within a painting. Experiment with all five methods to add depth and interest to your work.

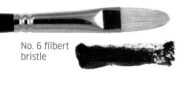

No. 6 filbert bristle

Coarse brush
Use a large-bristle brush to cover a big area quickly. The stroke will retain some of the texture of the bristles.

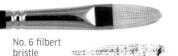

No. 6 filbert bristle

Dry brush
Drag undiluted paint across the canvas to create effects such as shimmering light on water, or to suggest areas of detail.

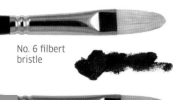

No. 6 filbert bristle

Random expressive marks
Apply multidirectional marks with varying amounts of pressure to create energy and movement.

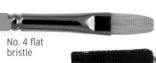

No. 4 flat bristle

Considered line
Use a small-bristle brush for areas that you need to approach carefully, such as working up to a line.

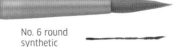

No. 6 round synthetic

Fine brush
Use a small, synthetic brush and diluted paint to make a crisp, detailed mark. For long lines, use a rigger.

PUTTING IT INTO PRACTICE

This sequence shows how to apply the main brushstroke techniques to create a simple yet dynamic study of a family group. Although you are making several different types of marks, it is important to treat the painting as a whole rather than as a series of isolated objects.

1 Coarse brush
Holding a no. 6 filbert-bristle brush flat, paint the darker areas of the figures' coats with bold, coarse strokes. You can cover a large area quickly by applying enough pressure to lay the paint in one pass.

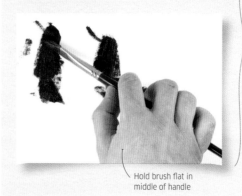

Hold brush flat in middle of handle

2 Dry brush
Use the dry-brush technique to suggest the legs and arms. Hold a no. 6 filbert-bristle brush at a shallow angle to the canvas and gently drag it down the surface using vertical strokes. The broken lines will suggest movement and provide a base for more considered lines later.

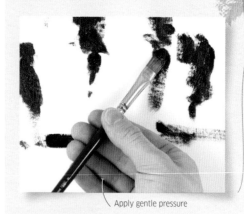

Apply gentle pressure

You will need

Titanium white | Cadmium yellow | Cadmium red | Alizarin crimson | Cerulean blue | French ultramarine | Burnt sienna

- No. 4 flat-bristle, no. 6 filbert-bristle, and no. 6 round synthetic brushes
- 10 x 12in (25 x 30cm) medium-grain canvas board

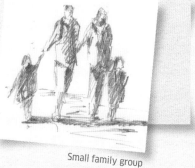

Small family group

4 Considered line

Take your no. 4 flat-bristle brush and hold it halfway along the handle, gripping it as you would a pen or pencil. This will give you the control you need to add detail to the faces, but still allow you to easily change the pressure of each mark to give your work a painterly quality.

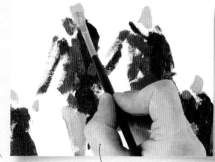

Use a pencil hold to add detail

5 Fine brush

Hold a no. 6 round synthetic brush as if it were a pencil to add final details to the painting. Rest the side of your hand on the canvas for maximum control of the brush. If the area is wet, use your little finger to steady your hand.

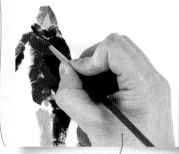

Rest your hand against the canvas

3 Random expressive marks

Use a no. 6 filbert brush to fill in the ground around the figures' legs and feet. Hold the brush flat and loosely for this, as it will enable you to paint freely and create a sense of light and texture on the ground. Vary the color mix as you go along to add interest.

Palette knives

MARK-MAKING WITH KNIVES

Palette knives are great for adding texture and a change of pace to your work. They are available in many different shapes and sizes, and are surprisingly versatile. The straight, durable edge of the blade will give you consistency and control over shapes and hard edges, while the flat surface is ideal for both sweeping strokes of color and more detailed work.

■ Application techniques

There are three main ways of painting with a palette knife: using sweeping, expressive, or fine applications of paint. Combining a range of different brush and palette marks can also produce interesting results.

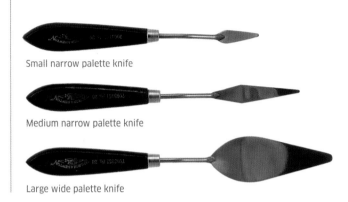

Small narrow palette knife

Medium narrow palette knife

Large wide palette knife

PUTTING IT INTO PRACTICE

This painting of a pretty white stone cottage was created solely with palette knives. The picture features a range of marks made with the three different forms of application.

You will need

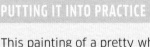

Titanium white

Cadmium yellow

Alizarin crimson

French ultramarine

Burnt sienna

- Large wide, medium narrow, and small narrow palette knives with crank handles
- Rag or kitchen towel for cleaning knives
- 10 x 12in (25 x 30cm) medium-grain canvas board

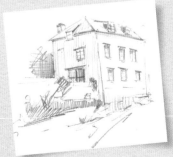

White stone cottage

1 Broad area

Use the largest knife and a sweeping action to cover broad areas of wall quickly. Vary the pressure to control the thickness of the paint.

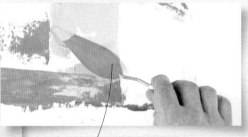

Sweeping action

Edge of palette knife

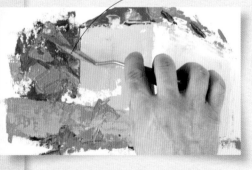

2 Expressive marks

Give the trees texture and a sense of movement by applying expressive marks with the edge of a medium-sized knife. Experiment with hard shapes and marks.

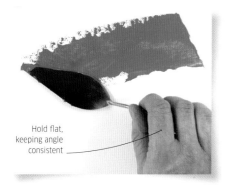

Hold flat, keeping angle consistent

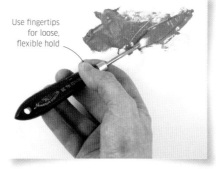

Use fingertips for loose, flexible hold

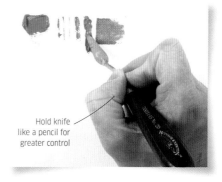

Hold knife like a pencil for greater control

Sweeping application

Block in big areas of color with a large palette knife, holding it as you would a dinner knife. Spread the paint in long sweeps, maintaining a consistent angle.

Expressive application

Scrape the edge of the blade along the surface to create varied shapes and patterns, or work the flat of the blade into areas of wet color.

Fine application

Dip the tip of the knife in paint and apply it to the surface by twisting and turning the knife, changing the angle until you achieve the effect you want.

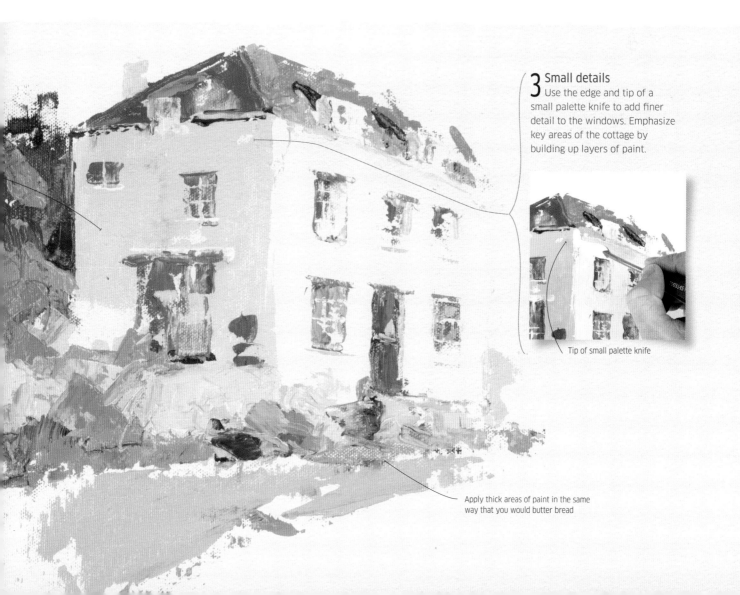

3 Small details

Use the edge and tip of a small palette knife to add finer detail to the windows. Emphasize key areas of the cottage by building up layers of paint.

Tip of small palette knife

Apply thick areas of paint in the same way that you would butter bread

Fat over lean

HOW TO LAYER OIL PAINTS

Undiluted paint has a high oil-to-pigment ratio and is called "fat," while thinned paint has a low oil-to-pigment ratio and is called "lean." Fat paint takes longer to dry than lean and is more flexible, while lean paint dries more quickly and can be brittle. Applying fat paint over lean, therefore, should prevent your work from cracking or discoloring.

■ Preparing each layer

Prepare a lean mix for the initial layers of your painting by thinning paint with turpentine. Build up each layer using progressively fatter paint, either by reducing the amount of turpentine used in each mix, or by adding an oil-based medium.

Very lean paint
Add turpentine to make very lean paint, which you can apply as a wash. The mix will dry quickly as the turpentine evaporates.

Lean paint
Add less turpentine for more dense paint. It will be more workable and some brush marks will be visible.

Visible brush marks

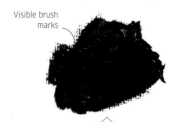

Fat paint
Paint straight from the tube has a high oil content and thick texture. It is easy to sculpt and most brush marks will remain visible.

Added medium

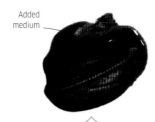

Very fat paint
Adding a medium with a high oil content makes the mix fatter than undiluted paint, even though it may look thinner.

This simple painting of a houseplant on a windowsill was built up in several layers. Following the fat-over-lean principle, the thinnest paint was applied first, with thicker paint added on top.

You will need

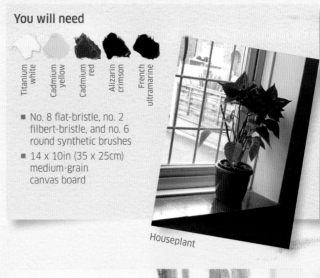

Titanium white · Cadmium yellow · Cadmium red · Alizarin crimson · French ultramarine

- No. 8 flat-bristle, no. 2 filbert-bristle, and no. 6 round synthetic brushes
- 14 x 10in (35 x 25cm) medium-grain canvas board

Houseplant

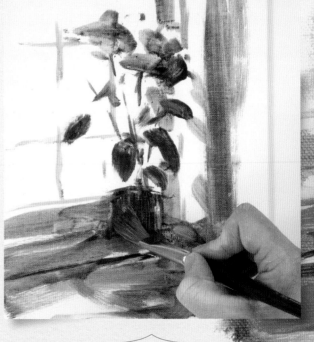

1 Lean paint
Mix French ultramarine, cadmium yellow, and a hint of burnt sienna. Thin the mix with turpentine to create lean paint. Using a large-sbristle brush, paint in the basic shape to establish tonal areas. Allow this initial layer to dry fully.

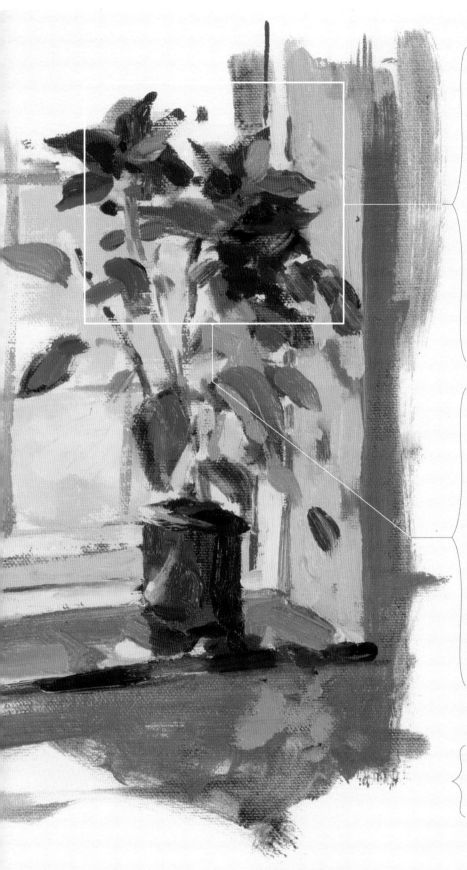

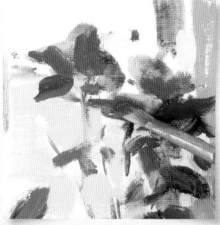

2 Fatter paint
Create the form of the petals by using the same mix of colors, but with the addition of titanium white. Use less turpentine than before to make a fatter, more opaque mix. You will now be able to add texture by using thicker strokes.

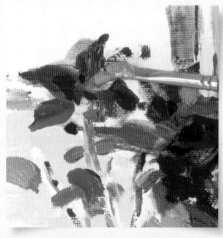

3 Fat paint
Add detail to the petals and leaves that are closest to the viewer using undiluted paint straight from the tube. Use a no. 2 filbert-bristle brush to apply thick strokes.

4 Finishing touches
Switch to a no. 6 round synthetic brush and continue working up the painting, making final adjustments to opacity, tone, and color. Use the fattest paint for these final strokes.

Layering

ADDING DEPTH AND DETAIL

Painting in layers allows you to add depth and detail to your work, with each new layer being slightly more refined than the last. You can also use the technique to create a multilayered finish, in which a part of every layer remains visible in the final piece. Another advantage of working this way is that it gives you time to reflect on your painting as each layer dries.

◼ Loose and refined layering

There is no limit to the number of layers you can add, as long as you follow the fat-over-lean principle (see pp. 224–26). Apply your layers with loose, free strokes to achieve an energetic, painterly style, or use accurate strokes and defined edges to build depth and create more realistic work.

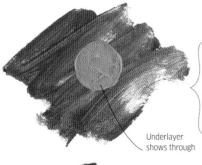

Loose layers
Using loose brushwork for the underlayer and allowing it to show through adds character to your work. The top layer adds depth.

Underlayer shows through

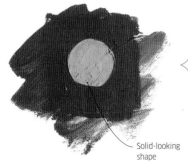

Refined layers
Build a more solid-looking image on the top layer—with crisp outlines and hard edges—by allowing the first layer to dry first.

Solid-looking shape

PUTTING IT INTO PRACTICE

In this painting of a field of cows, the layering technique was used to refine the painting and bring all the elements of the final image together.

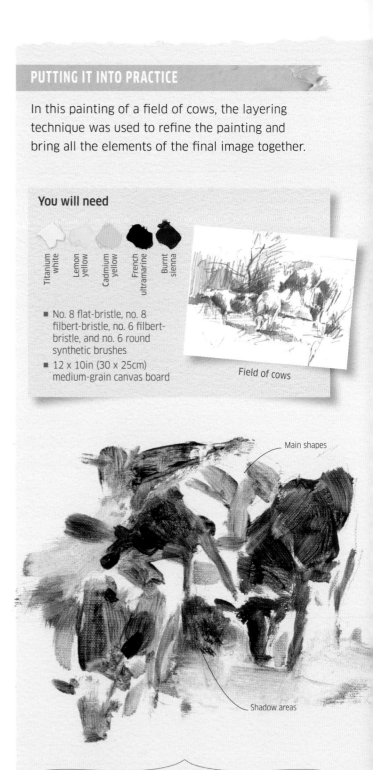

You will need

Titanium white | Lemon yellow | Cadmium yellow | French ultramarine | Burnt sienna

- No. 8 flat-bristle, no. 8 filbert-bristle, no. 6 filbert-bristle, and no. 6 round synthetic brushes
- 12 x 10in (30 x 25cm) medium-grain canvas board

Field of cows

Main shapes

Shadow areas

1 Underpainting layer

Apply an underpainting of thinned paint to block in the shapes and provide a base for the subsequent layers. Use a large, flat brush and a mix of ultramarine and sienna thinned with turpentine. Pay particular attention to the shadows, as they may remain visible in the final painting.

2 Add color
Once the first layer is dry (being thin, this won't take long), add the second one. The aim of this layer is to add color and build up the darker areas. Use a mix of cadmium yellow and ultramarine, applied with a medium-sized bristle brush, to introduce detail.

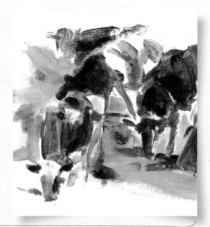

3 Mid tones
For the third layer, use a more opaque mix with a hint of white. Using a medium-sized bristle brush, work up the mid tones. As the paint is thicker, it will create an image with more density. Continue to refine the shapes at each stage, applying more color.

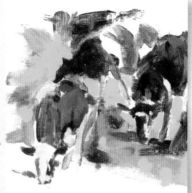

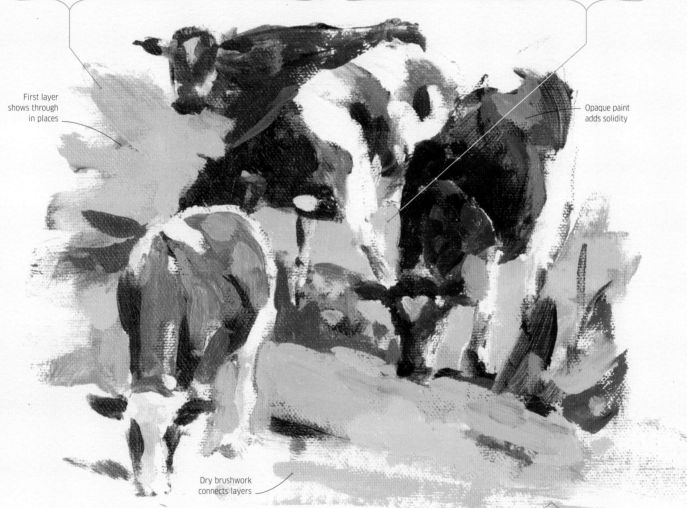

First layer shows through in places

Opaque paint adds solidity

Dry brushwork connects layers

"By working in layers you can **make adjustments** and **refresh areas** that have become muddy."

4 Final details
With most of the mid tones established and the picture taking shape, use smaller-bristle and synthetic brushes to add thick paint in the foreground, to refine details, and to correct any color inconsistencies.

Drawing and underpainting

LAYING A FOUNDATION

The painting process is easier when you work through it in stages. The purpose of drawing and underpainting is to establish the initial structure of your painting and create a starting point from which to work. At this stage, you will draw in basic elements, establish their shape, and block in basic color and tones.

■ Lean paint and simple marks

Thin the paint for your underpainting with a solvent so that it won't compromise subsequent layers, following the fat-over-lean rule (see pp. 224–25). Fine detail isn't needed for an underpainting, so a larger brush will serve most of your needs.

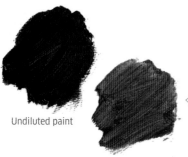

Undiluted paint

Thinned paint

Thinned paint
Thin the paint to a watercolor-like consistency. You can use turpentine, low-odor mineral spirits, or environmentally friendly thinners such as citrus oil paint dilutant. The paint will spread easily and dry quickly.

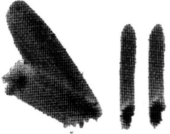

Thick lines made with flat side of brush

Thin lines made with edge of brush

Flat brush
Use a large or medium-sized brush for drawing, to prevent the urge to include too much detail. A flat-bristle brush is versatile enough for you to create a variety of marks.

PUTTING IT INTO PRACTICE

This underpainting is the first stage of a still life with apples. Basic shapes and lines, key tonal differences, and blocks of the main colors were painted in to provide a foundation for later stages.

You will need

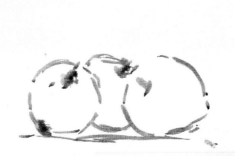

Naples yellow · Cadmium yellow · Alizarin crimson · French ultramarine · Burnt sienna

- No. 8 flat-bristle, no. 2 filbert bristle, and no. 6 round synthetic brushes
- Solvent and a rag
- 8 x 10in (20 x 25cm) medium-grain canvas board

Three apples

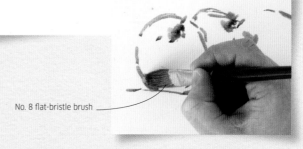

No. 8 flat-bristle brush

1 Drawing in the subject
Use a thinned mix of French ultramarine and burnt sienna to roughly sketch in the subject. You don't need to draw everything in detail at this point—you can reevaluate and redraw as your painting develops.

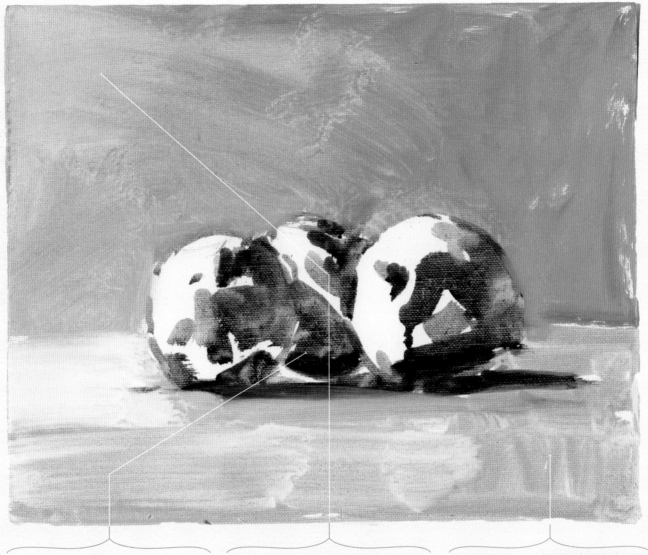

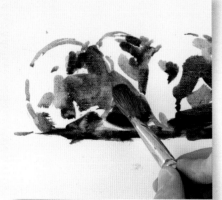

2 Establishing tonal areas
Block in the main shadow areas. Vary your mix of French ultramarine and burnt sienna to create warmer or cooler tones as needed.

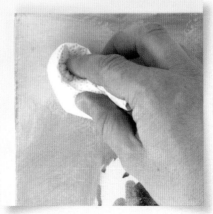

3 Background tones
Apply a wash of paint to the background, adjusting the amount of thinner to vary tone. Wipe the paint if you want to lighten areas.

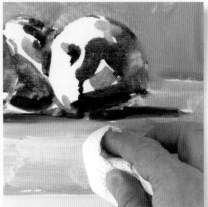

4 Softening shadows
Lighten shadows with a rag, not paint—it is hard to darken oil colors after lightening, so use darker tones for the underpainting.

>

5 Blocking in colors

Apply a thinned mix of cadmium yellow, alizarin crimson, and burnt sienna to block in the main colors of the apples with a no. 2 filbert-bristle brush. Vary your mix to create color changes and suggest the form of the apples. Keep in mind the shadow areas and adjust the tone of your mix accordingly.

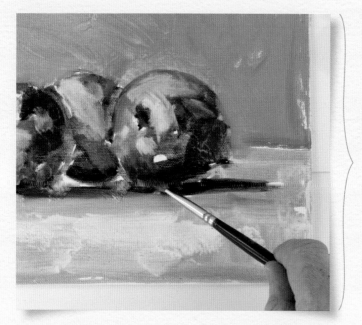

6 Final adjustments

Look for any issues with tone, color, and composition and adjust them if you need to. The underpainting provides an opportunity to tackle problems before you apply thicker paint. Use a small brush to adjust details in the wet paint, such as adding a darker tone for the apple stems.

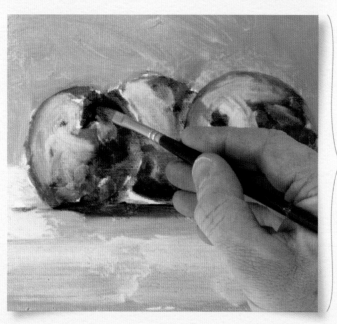

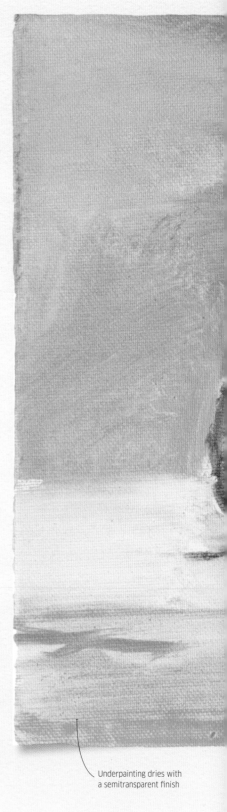

Underpainting dries with a semitransparent finish

"Think of your painting as **an evolution from the drawing stage,** refining it so that it **takes shape as a whole.**"

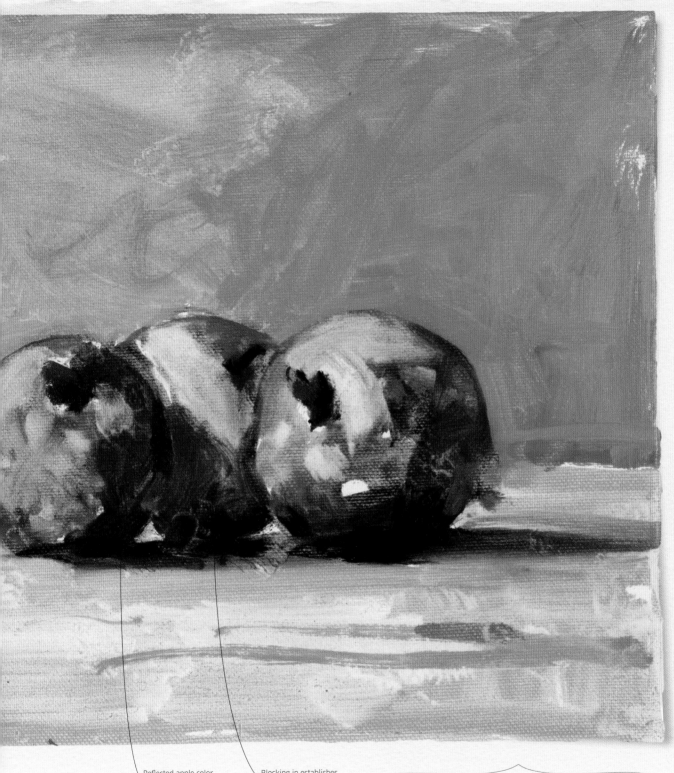

Reflected apple color
in shadows provides
reference for later layers

Blocking in establishes
basic color relationships

7 Reviewing your underpainting
The underpainting will dry quickly due to the thinned paint.
Review the finished result before you apply thicker paint; for
example, you may want to keep some areas semitransparent.

Decreasing stages

PAINTING A SMALLER AREA WITH EACH LAYER

Working in decreasing stages involves refining a smaller portion of your painting with each layer. This helps you to create strong focal points while keeping peripheral areas loose—a visual change of pace that keeps your painting interesting.

▇ Choosing where to add detail

Cover the whole canvas in the first layer, then decrease the area you paint in each subsequent layer by about one-third. This lets you assess your painting as you work. For example, in the next layer, you could make a feature of any accidental marks from the first layer. Let each layer dry fully before adding another, and follow the fat-over-lean principle (see pp. 224–25).

Layer 1
Use large, loose brushstrokes in the first layer

Layer 2
Tighten the structure with more detail and color in the second layer

Layer 3
Use smaller brushes to add more detail

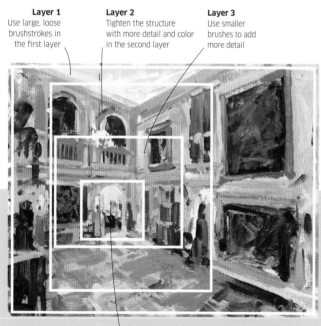

Layer 4
Add the finest details, shadows, and highlights to define the focal point

This complex interior scene was simplified by working in decreasing stages. Only one corner of the room was painted in detail, but the loosely painted surrounding areas create the impression of a large space.

You will need

Titanium white · Naples yellow · Cadmium yellow · Alizarin crimson · French ultramarine · Burnt sienna

The gallery

- No. 8 flat bristle, no. 2 filbert bristle, and no. 6 round synthetic brushes
- 16 x 20in (40 x 50cm) medium-grain canvas board

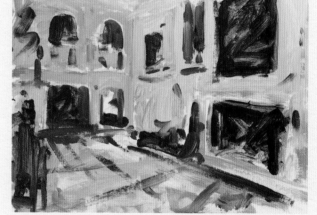

1 The first layer
Block in the whole canvas for the first layer. Using a no. 8 flat brush, apply darker tones at this stage (this will help the highlights you add later to stand out) and keep detail to a minimum.

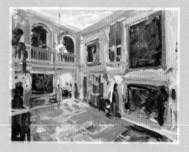

Layer 1

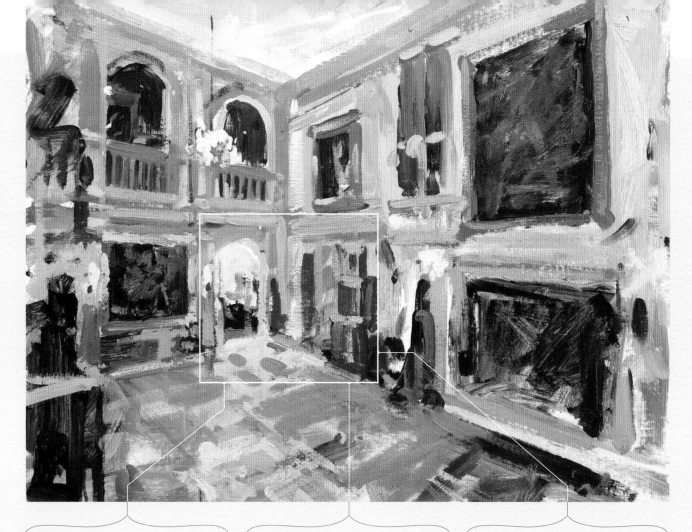

2 Building structure

For the second layer, focus on a smaller section of the painting, leaving the rest as it was painted in the first layer. Add color, tone, and detail in the focal area to give it form.

3 Focusing in

Refine the corner of the hall with a smaller brush. Add brighter colors and a greater contrast of light and dark tones to develop details such as the paintings by the doorway.

4 Final details

Darken shadows and add pale, yellow-and-white highlights around the doorway and the edge of the painting beside it, to help them stand out as the focal points.

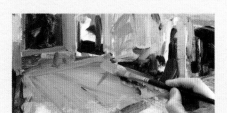

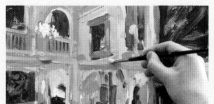

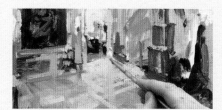

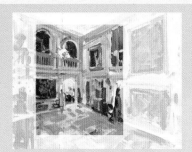

Layer 2

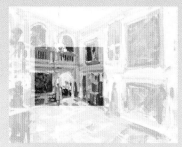

Layer 3

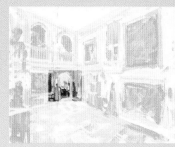

Layer 4

Alla prima

WORKING IN ONE SITTING

Italian for "at first attempt," *alla prima* is a popular method of working, in which a painting is completed in one go. It is a useful technique when working outdoors, as you need to capture the essence of a subject quickly. The technique often results in a fresh "painterly" quality.

■ Working methods

There are three main ways of working *alla prima*: applying a single layer of paint and working around the shapes of objects; working wet-in-wet (see pp. 258–59); and painting over a wiped area. These all involve working into one wet painting and leaving it to dry when it's finished. This creates a fresh, energetic style, as there is less opportunity to overwork the painting. Careful planning before you start is essential.

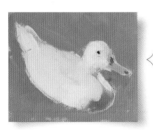

Painting around a shape
"Cutting in" and painting up to the edges of objects keeps your color mixes clean and lines crisp. Plan ahead at the drawing stage to identify which shapes to paint around.

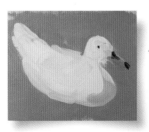

Working wet-in-wet
You can paint layers in wet paint to a certain extent by using a soft brush and applying marks delicately with light pressure.

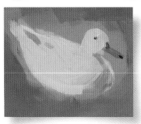

Painting over a wiped area
Use a cloth or rag to wipe out areas of paint. You can then paint back into the area without the risk of interfering with the underlying color. (See also pp. 256–57.)

Working *alla prima* encourages you to look at objects as shapes, work up to edges, and focus on the negative and positive spaces equally. Identify the different planes in the composition during your initial drawing, as shown in the color-coded sketch below, and plan your working methods accordingly.

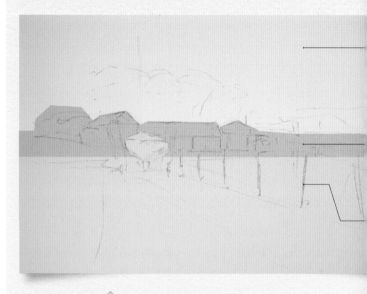

1 Mapping out
Draw the main elements of the scene, paying attention to the different planes (background, middle ground, and foreground) and which objects are in front of others. Begin painting at the horizon; you can work around objects in front of the horizon and revisit them later.

2 Mixing your paints
It's a good idea to spend a little more time than usual mixing your colors in advance—the less you need to adjust color and tone on the canvas, the fresher your painting will look.

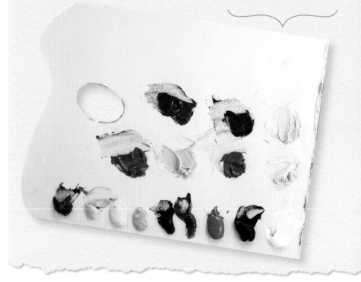

You will need

Titanium white · Naples yellow · Lemon yellow · Cadmium yellow · Cadmium red · Alizarin crimson · French ultramarine · Cerulean blue · Burnt sienna

- No. 8 flat-bristle, no. 4 and no. 2 filbert-bristle, and no. 5 round synthetic brushes
- 14 x 18in (35 x 45cm) medium-grain canvas board

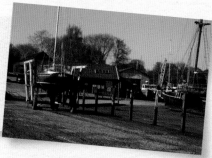

Boatyard

Background: the distant trees provide a backdrop for the buildings and make the sky recede

Middle ground: the buildings cut into the background trees but are behind the foreground objects

Foreground: the posts and red boat sit in front of the middle ground

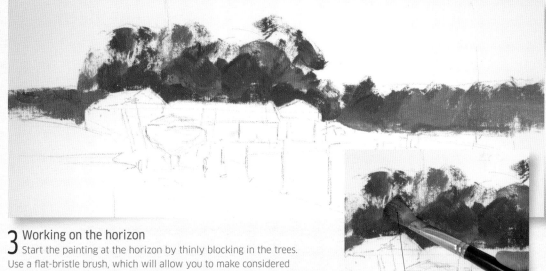

3 Working on the horizon

Start the painting at the horizon by thinly blocking in the trees. Use a flat-bristle brush, which will allow you to make considered brushstrokes as you cut in and around the building. Apply a mix of French ultramarine and Naples yellow to create an opaque green.

A flat brush offers control when "cutting in"

Negative shapes forming in the foreground

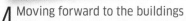

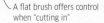

4 Moving forward to the buildings

Apply a mix of sienna and Naples yellow to the buildings using a no. 2 filbert-bristle brush, cutting in around the objects in the foreground. These negative shapes help create the shape of the boat. It is useful to paint simple shapes when working *alla prima*, as it is difficult to paint in detail over a wet area of paint.

5 Painting the sky

Paint the sky by cutting in around the trees and buildings. Use a mix of French ultramarine and titanium white, adding some cerulean blue nearer the horizon. Clean the brush carefully after painting into the darker trees.

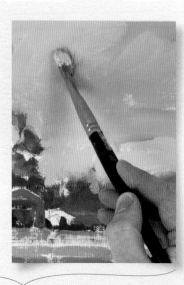

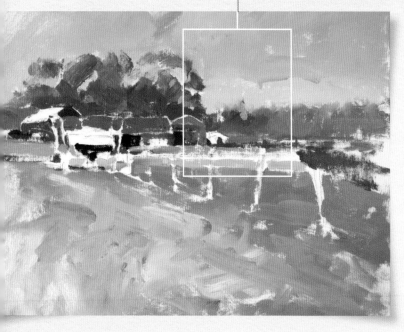

6 Filling the foreground

Paint around the posts using simple brushstrokes to complete the foreground. Mix the colors carefully to try to get them right the first time. This will minimize the amount of reworking you need to do later.

7 Adding the boat

The boat is a good focal point for the composition, so give it a punch of color using a mix of cadmium red and alizarin crimson. Add further detail to the background buildings using a soft brush.

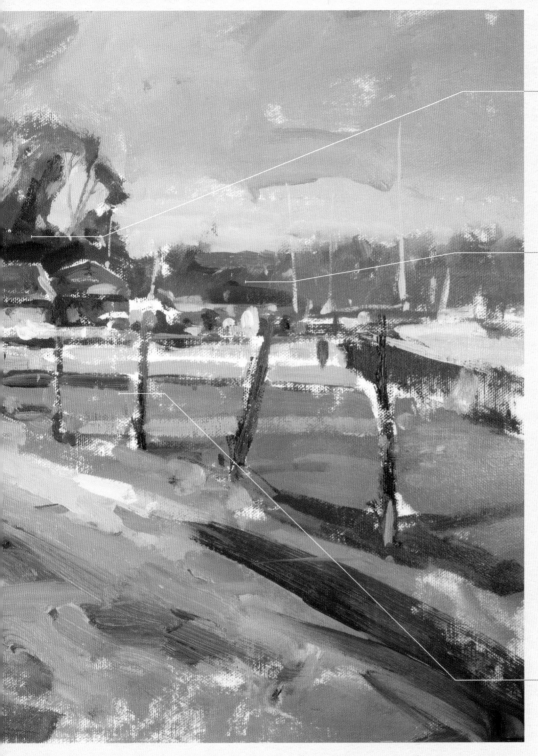

8 Making adjustments
The painting is still wet and everything that has been done so far can be developed further, wiped out, or adjusted. You can make minor alterations to tone and color, such as darkening the base of the trees, by mixing into the existing brushstrokes.

9 Adding structure
Use medium and small soft-hair brushes to add the finer details, such as the boat masts, background objects, and the posts in the foreground.

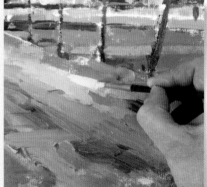

10 Finishing touches
With a soft, synthetic brush, add details to bring the painting together. Use light pressure and resist the urge to go over an area too often.

"Leave an **unpainted gap** between objects to **keep the edges clean.**"

Creating forms

GIVING OBJECTS VOLUME AND SUBSTANCE

Form is the three-dimensional quality of a shape or object. To paint convincingly, you need to create forms with a strong identity. For example, give buildings in the main focal area hard edges and a sense of texture, but use loose, free brushstrokes to paint a moving crowd.

■ Different techniques

You can create form with tone and texture, painting shadows, and adding a background—as shown in the simple cube painting, below. If you want to create a curved surface, gently blend paint from a light to a dark tone. Your use of color, negative space, and brushwork also play a part in creating form.

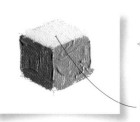

Value and texture
Use three tones of blue to suggest light falling on the cube from the top right. Add texture to the two nearest sides with bold strokes.

Light source from top right

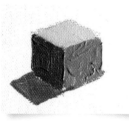

Shadow
Real objects cast a shadow, so paint one in to give the cube weight and presence. This also makes it look as if it is sitting on a surface.

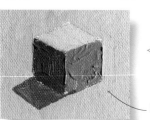

Background
Add a background to give the cube context. Use a different color and texture for the background to create a sense of contrast.

Background adds context

This urban scene includes the solid, hard-edged forms of the buildings as well as the freer, loose-edged forms of the people. It was painted *alla prima* (see pp.234–37), starting with the background.

1 Negative space
Paint in the trees with an initial dark mix of French ultramarine and burnt sienna, with a little cadmium red and Naples yellow. Filling in this negative space starts to create the building's form, and the dark mix emphasizes the light shining on the building.

No. 4 flat-bristle brush

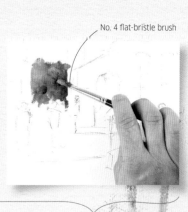

2 Shadows
Add shadows to create a three-dimensional effect. These should all face the same way and vary in length depending on the height of the subject.

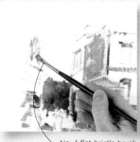

No. 4 flat-bristle brush

3 High contrast
Placing a dark element against a light one creates contrast and separates the forms. This figure is well defined against the bright ground and the sunlit building in the background.

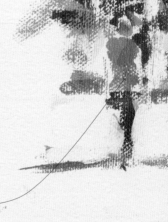

You will need

Titanium white · Naples yellow · Cadmium yellow · Cadmium red · French ultramarine · Burnt sienna

- No. 4 flat-bristle, no. 4 filbert-bristle, no. 6 filbert-bristle, and no. 6 round synthetic brushes
- 12 x 10in (30 x 25cm) medium-texture canvas board

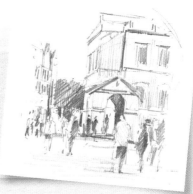

Urban scene

4 Solid shapes
Each solid shape has a shadow and a highlighted side. Use vivid, warm colors for areas of light, and more muted, cool colors to give areas of shadow depth.

Broken lines create the illusion of detail in middle distance

5 Texture
To distinguish between forms of a similar tone, use a range of brushstrokes applied in several different directions. Leaving a sliver of background between these two figures separates them and prevents the forms from looking flat.

6 Movement
Suggest movement and energy with looser strokes and less detail. The dry brushstrokes used here give the marks a light, free touch.

Shadow cast from an object out of view adds authenticity

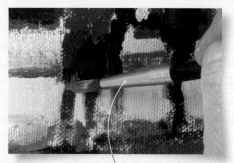

No. 6 round synthetic brush

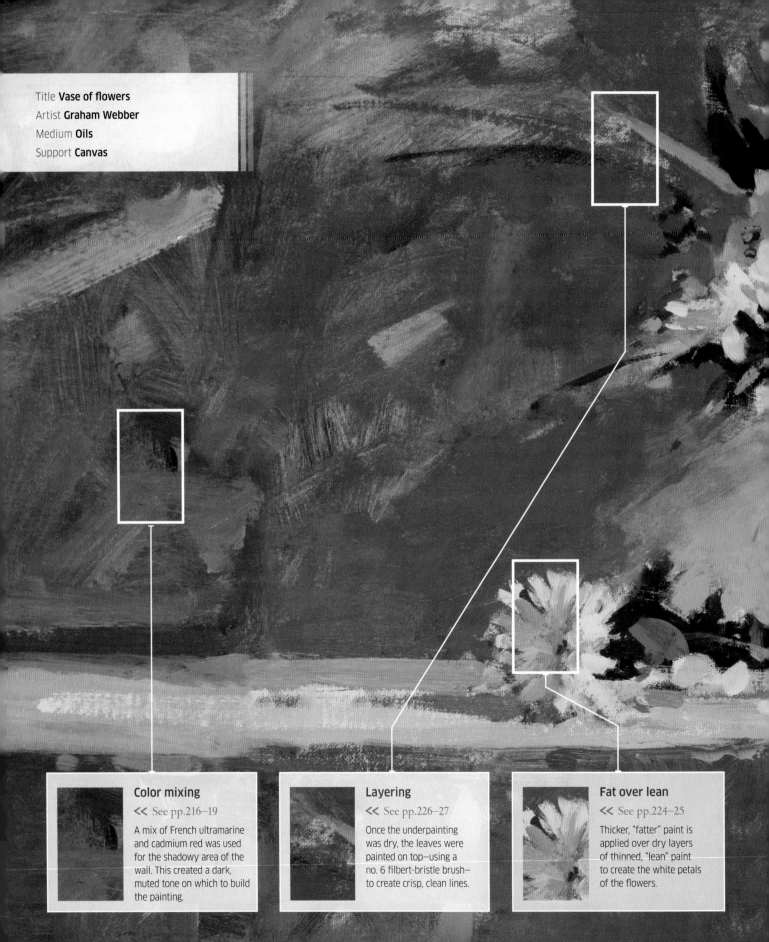

Title **Vase of flowers**
Artist **Graham Webber**
Medium **Oils**
Support **Canvas**

Color mixing
<< See pp.216–19

A mix of French ultramarine and cadmium red was used for the shadowy area of the wall. This created a dark, muted tone on which to build the painting.

Layering
<< See pp.226–27

Once the underpainting was dry, the leaves were painted on top—using a no. 6 filbert-bristle brush—to create crisp, clean lines.

Fat over lean
<< See pp.224–25

Thicker, "fatter" paint is applied over dry layers of thinned, "lean" paint to create the white petals of the flowers.

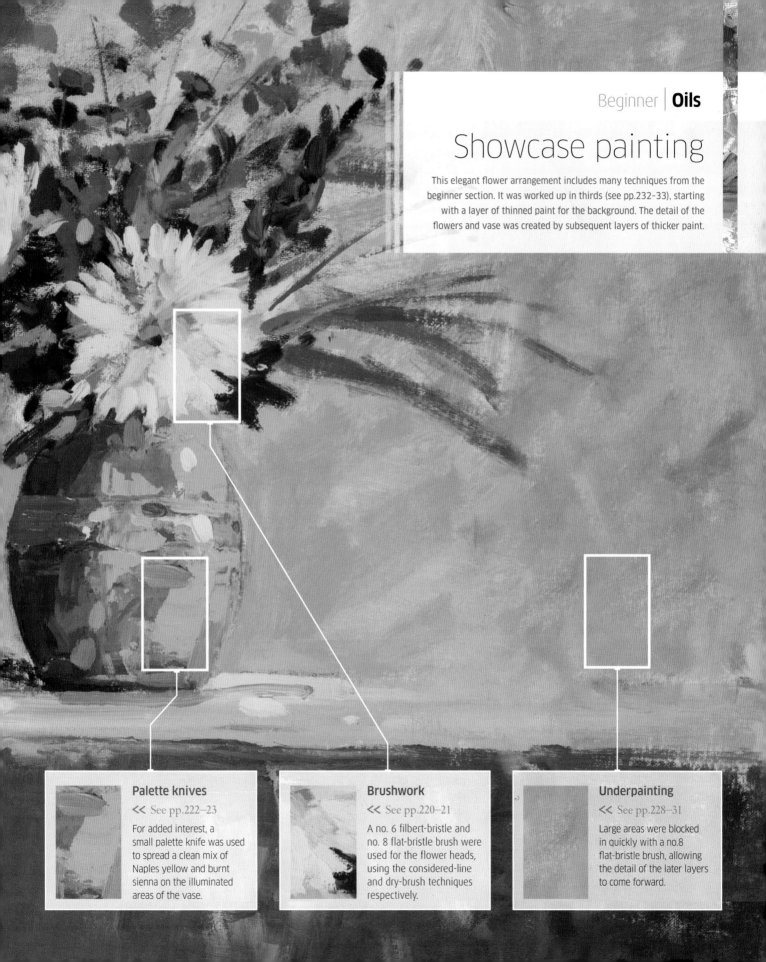

Showcase painting

This elegant flower arrangement includes many techniques from the beginner section. It was worked up in thirds (see pp.232–33), starting with a layer of thinned paint for the background. The detail of the flowers and vase was created by subsequent layers of thicker paint.

Palette knives

« See pp.222–23

For added interest, a small palette knife was used to spread a clean mix of Naples yellow and burnt sienna on the illuminated areas of the vase.

Brushwork

« See pp.220–21

A no. 6 filbert-bristle and no. 8 flat-bristle brush were used for the flower heads, using the considered-line and dry-brush techniques respectively.

Underpainting

« See pp.228–31

Large areas were blocked in quickly with a no.8 flat-bristle brush, allowing the detail of the later layers to come forward.

Aerial perspective

CREATING DISTANCE THROUGH COLOR

The greater the distance between the viewer and an object, the greater the haze of atmosphere between them. This makes colors look gradually cooler and less saturated, the farther away an object is. You can emulate this effect to create an impression of depth in your work.

▇ Color and contrast

Visually, cool colors recede and warm colors come forward. Keeping this in mind, you can vary your color mixes, introducing warm and cool hues to indicate degrees of depth. Contrast also diminishes and softens with distance, so keep high contrast and detail for the foreground.

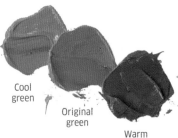

Cool green

Original green

Warm green

Cool and warm
Add white and ultramarine to your mix to create a cooler, lighter green for distant subjects. Add a little cadmium red to make a warmer, deeper color for the foreground.

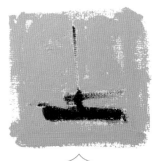

Foreground–high contrast
Use bold colors and areas of high contrast for objects in the foreground.

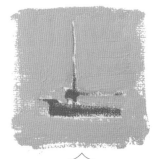

Background–light colors
Use white to desaturate and lighten colors in the background to achieve a sense of depth.

PUTTING IT INTO PRACTICE

Working from the horizon forward, this study of a mountain scene demonstrates aerial perspective, creating a painting with a sense of space and distance.

You will need

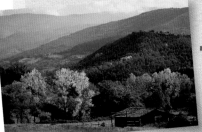

Titanium white — Naples yellow — Cadmium yellow — Cadmium red — French ultramarine — Burnt sienna

- No. 8 flat-bristle, no. 4 flat-bristle, and no. 2 filbert-bristle brushes
- 10 x 12in (25 x 30cm) medium-grain canvas board

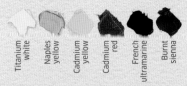

Mountain scene

Less saturated blues help make the distant mountains recede

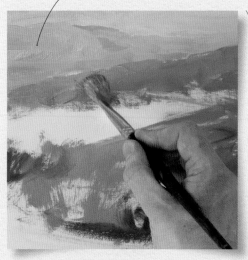

1 Background
Starting at the horizon, paint the most distant mountains with a mix of French ultramarine, Naples yellow, and a little cadmium red using a no. 8 flat brush. Lighten the mix with titanium white for the sky, so that it is paler than the mountains. Keep all detail to a minimum.

2 Middle distance
With a no. 4 flat brush, paint the mountain in the middle distance, adding more cadmium red and using less white in the mix. Use coarse brushwork to suggest more detail.

3 Foreground
Add more warm colors, such as cadmium red and sienna, to bring objects forward. Use a no. 2 filbert to add lighter and darker tones, and create contrasts in the foreground trees.

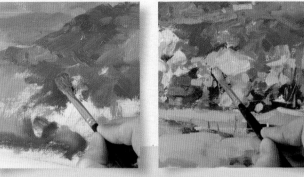

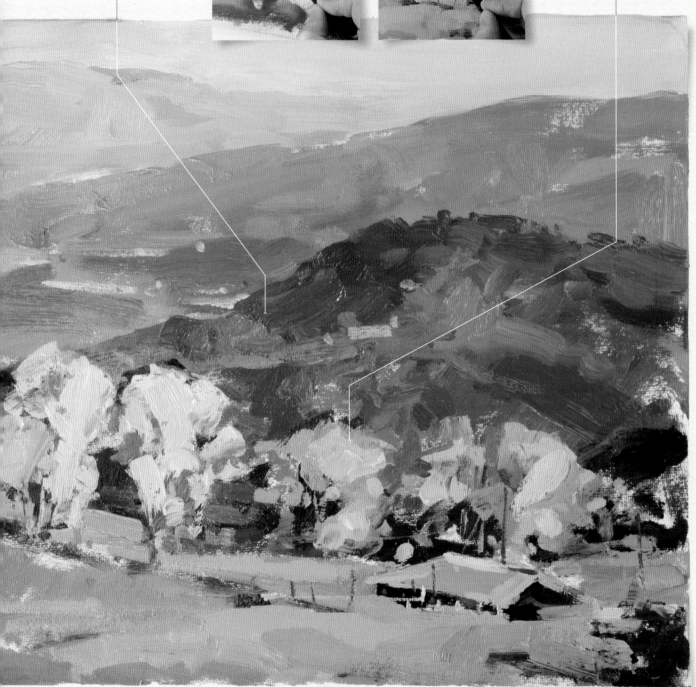

Blending

MIXING COLORS INTO EACH OTHER

Blending allows you to create subtle changes of color, which is great for shading and for giving objects realistic form. You can also bring your point of interest into sharp focus by blending other areas of your painting to soften and blur them. A soft brush is the traditional tool for a delicate effect, but you can also use a palette knife, your fingers, or a rag to blend the colors for a more impressionistic effect.

PUTTING IT INTO PRACTICE

A cloud study is a good subject for practicing blending. Here, different blending techniques were used to depict soft light and clouds on a windy day.

You will need

- Titanium white
- Naples yellow
- Cadmium yellow
- Cadmium red
- French ultramarine
- Cerulean blue
- Burnt sienna

- No. 2 flat-bristle, no. 8 flat-bristle, no. 6 filbert-bristle, and no. 2 filbert-bristle brushes, and a wide, flat synthetic brush
- 10 x 12in (25 x 30cm) medium-grain canvas board

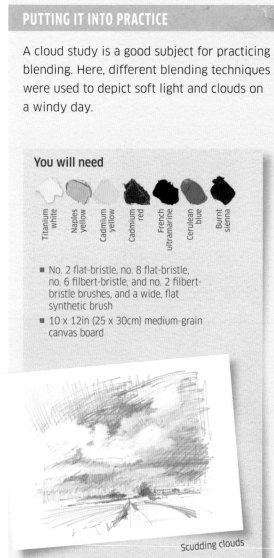

Scudding clouds

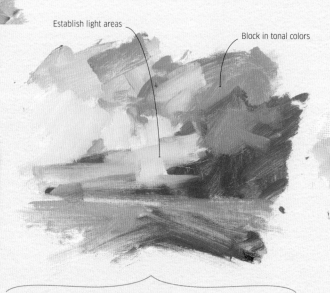

Establish light areas

Block in tonal colors

1 Base layer
Block in the main areas of color without mixing or blending. Establish your light and dark areas at this stage—this will help prevent overmixing or muddying of the colors later. Apply plenty of paint with a no. 6 filbert-bristle brush.

2 Smooth blending
Blend the cloud area with a soft, flat synthetic brush to create a smooth effect. Vary the direction of your strokes to keep a sense of energy in the blended areas.

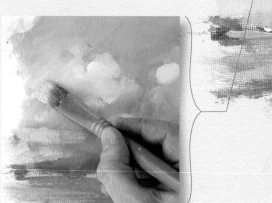

Blending tones

To blend graduated tones, try starting with three basic tones: light, mid, and dark. You can combine these to make intermediate tones, then blend them together to create a smooth transition. Blend from dark to light, because once white is added to wet paint, it is hard to darken it without creating a pastel hue.

From light to dark
Mix a light, mid, and dark tone of a color, and paint them next to each other. French ultramarine is shown here.

Intermediate tones
Combine the light and mid tones to mix an intermediate tone, which you can place in between. Do the same for the mid and dark mixes.

Smoothing the transition
Gently soften the areas in between the tones with a soft brush, your finger, or a rag to create a graduated blend.

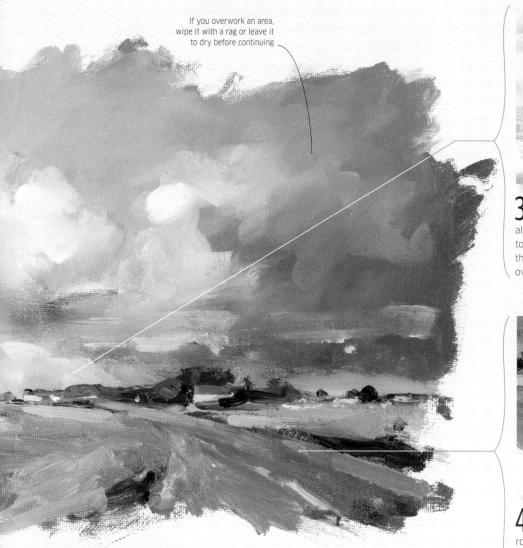

If you overwork an area, wipe it with a rag or leave it to dry before continuing

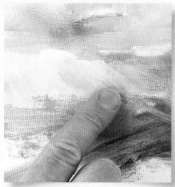

3 Blending with fingers
Create the effect of distant rain along the cloud line. Use your finger to drag the wet paint down to meet the horizon, being careful not to over-blend it.

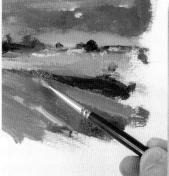

4 Coarse blending
Scrub together the colors in the road area with a no. 2 flat-bristle brush. This coarser blending technique brings details forward and works well in the foreground.

Impasto

ACHIEVING SCULPTURAL EFFECTS

Oil paint has a rich, buttery quality, and the impasto technique—in which you apply thick, undiluted paint to the canvas—makes the most of this trait. While bearing in mind the "fat over lean" rule (see pp. 224–25), you can use impasto to sculpt the surface of your painting and produce highly textured areas. You can also make a feature of the shadows and highlights created by the thick paint.

■ Impasto effects

You can use impasto to create focal points or to emphasize elements in the foreground, achieving contrast by painting thinner layers in the background. Alternatively, you can complete entire works in one thick layer, creating large relief paintings with peaks of paint. Whether applying paint with a palette knife or bristle brush, the aim is to let your method of working show, remembering to apply the thickest paint last. Add paint in one layer to avoid losing its purity and quality.

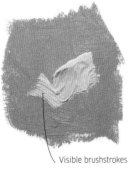

Visible brushstrokes

Brush impasto
Create a thick impasto effect by loading paint onto the brush and rolling it onto the canvas. The paint will retain the brushmarks, adding relief to the surface. Bristle brushes are ideal for this as they are rigid enough to sculpt the paint.

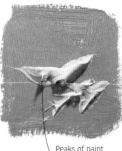

Peaks of paint

Palette knife impasto
A palette knife is a good tool for adding thick, clean mixes to your work. You can also lift peaks of paint like icing on a cake and create great effects by cutting and sculpting the paint on the canvas.

An old artist's table, splattered with dried paint and set with jars of turpentine, makes an ideal subject for the impasto technique. Remember to let layers of paint dry fully and to follow the "fat over lean" rule.

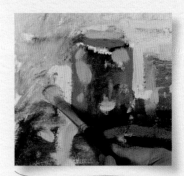

1 Adding texture
Using a no. 6 filbert, roll a loaded brush across the canvas, leaving thick brushstrokes and a buttery texture. You can modify the color at a later stage, but the texture will remain, giving the painting a tactile, sculpted finish.

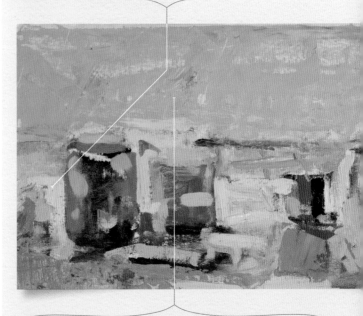

2 Creating a smooth background
Using a long, narrow palette knife, plaster the canvas with a well-mixed layer of gray-blue paint. Keep the paint thick but with a smooth texture, to create a solid background that won't compete with elements in the foreground.

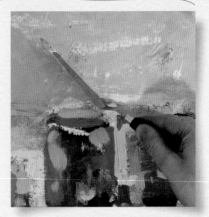

You will need

Titanium white · Naples yellow · Cadmium yellow · Cadmium red · Alizarin crimson · French ultramarine · Cerulean blue · Burnt sienna

- No. 4 flat-bristle, no. 8 flat-bristle, no. 2 filbert-bristle, and no. 6 filbert-bristle brushes
- Long, narrow palette knife
- 12 x 20in (30 x 50cm) medium-grain canvas board

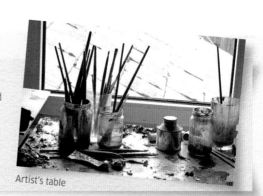

Artist's table

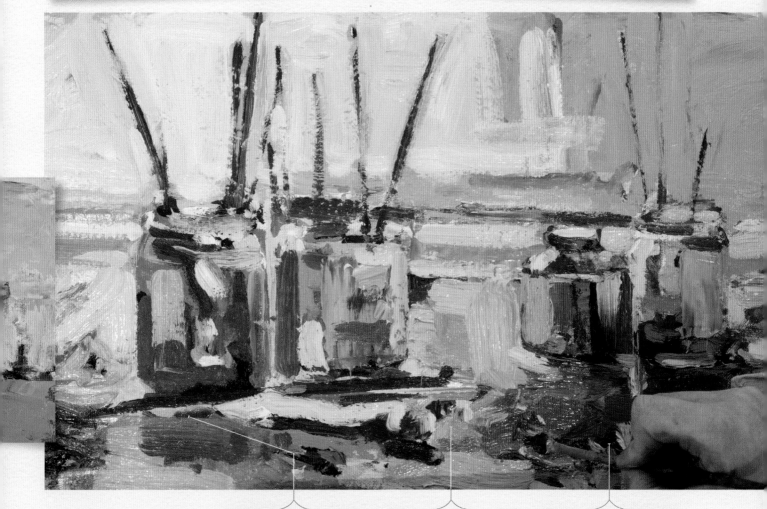

3 Stippling for softer edges

To add a different texture, use a no. 8 flat brush for some stippling, adding small dots of burnt sienna mixed with French ultramarine into the shadow areas. The effect will provide a varied color base for subsequent layers, as well as a softer edge for the shadows.

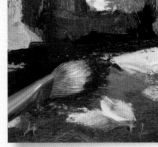

Soften shadows

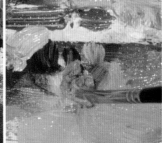

Vary the base colors

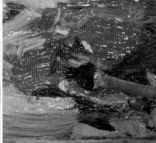

Add texture

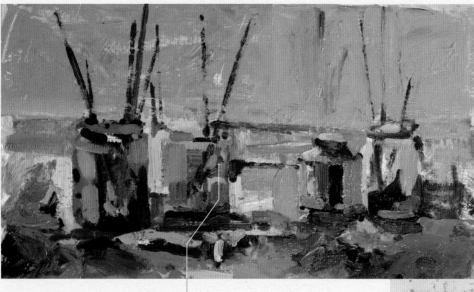

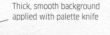

Thick, smooth background applied with palette knife

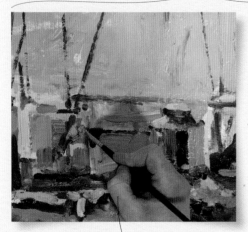

Use thick applications of paint in the foreground

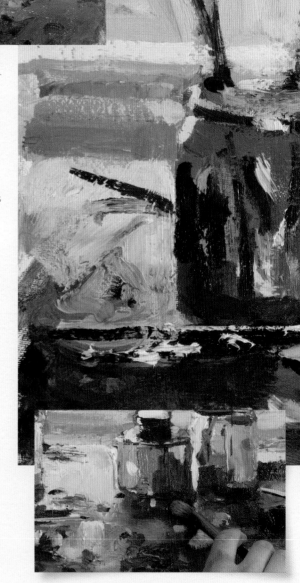

4 Foreground detail
Use a smaller no. 2 filbert brush to add color to the tubes of paint in the foreground. The thicker your applications of paint, the closer objects will seem to the viewer. Apply the same colors used here in other areas of the painting to help unify the separate elements and prevent them from looking "cut out."

"Impasto is the perfect technique for **creating bold artworks** that allow your **method of working** to show through."

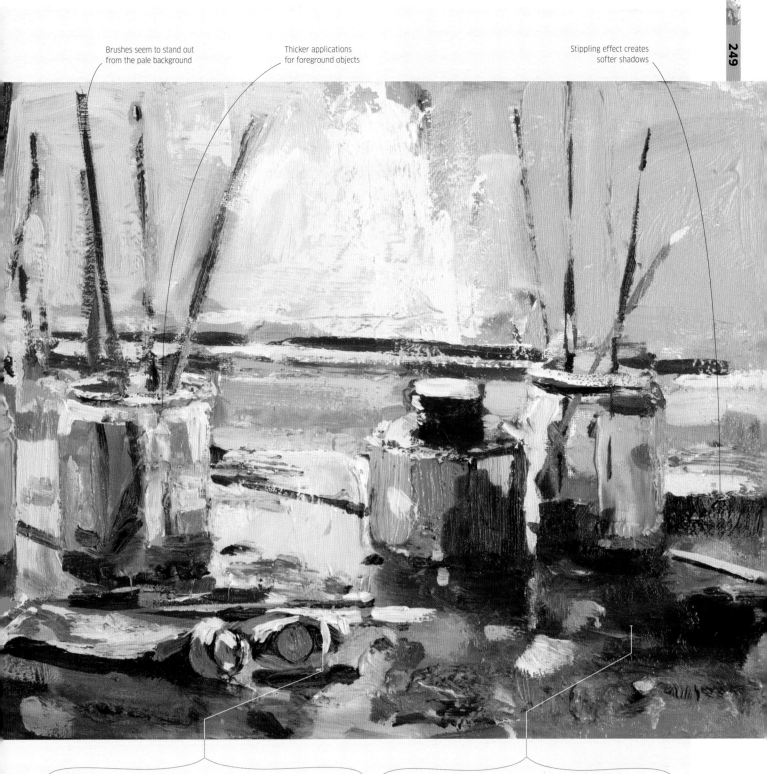

Brushes seem to stand out
from the pale background

Thicker applications
for foreground objects

Stippling effect creates
softer shadows

5 Detail and variation
Once the previous layers have dried, you can add further details
and repaint lines. Use "fatter" paint to prevent any cracking. If you are
using the same unwashed brush from the previous step, you can roll
paint from the top of the bristles to vary the color.

6 Adding shadows
Using the dry-brush technique (see pp. 220–21) and a large
brush, drag light and dark paint over the thick underlayer to
emphasize its texture. Finally, add shadows to peaks of paint
to enhance their three-dimensional quality.

Sgraffito

SCRATCHING THE SURFACE

Sgraffito means "to scratch" in Italian, and you can use this technique to great effect in all kinds of painting. By scratching off areas of a layer of wet paint, you can reveal underlying paint below. Tools for removing paint can range from the end of a brush handle for fine lines to a putty knife for scratching off large areas of paint.

Creating movement and texture

Use crosshatching or scribbling to accent an area of fine detail, to sharpen up lines, or to create texture and movement. You can also use sgraffito on layers of dried paint, which will result in stronger lines. Use this method freely on primed board, but be wary of damage if using canvas.

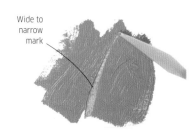

Wide to narrow mark

Vary markings
Manipulate the palette knife to create markings of varying width. Also, use the layer beneath to dictate the color, tone, and energy of the scratches you are making.

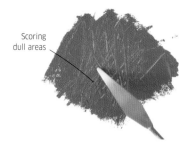

Scoring dull areas

Add movement
If you have made an area too dark or opaque, you can scratch the surface to add interest and movement to the painting.

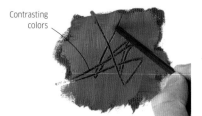

Contrasting colors

Reveal contrasts
Try painting over a layer with a complementary color, then scratching into the top layer to reveal the vibrant complementary color beneath.

The sgraffito technique is perfect for portraying this grassy scene, in which scratches and scrapes through layers of paint help to evoke the textures of grass and scrub.

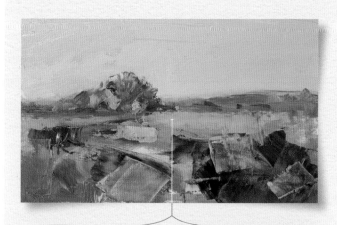

1 A bold base
You can treat sgraffito as you would brushwork with a brush or palette knife (see pp. 220–23). Use a household putty knife to apply paint to areas of broad, bold working, such as the base color of the foreground grass.

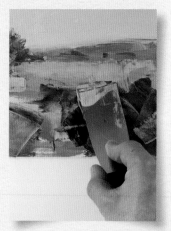

"Use sgraffito to accent an area of **fine detail,** to sharpen up lines, or to create **texture and movement.**"

You will need

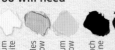

Titanium white | Naples yellow | Cadmium yellow | French ultramarine | Burnt sienna

- No. 4 filbert-bristle, no. 4 synthetic round brush
- Medium-narrow palette knife
- Household putty knife
- 8 x12in (20 x 30cm) medium-grain canvas board

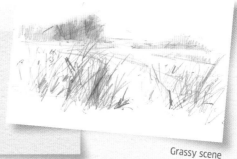

Grassy scene

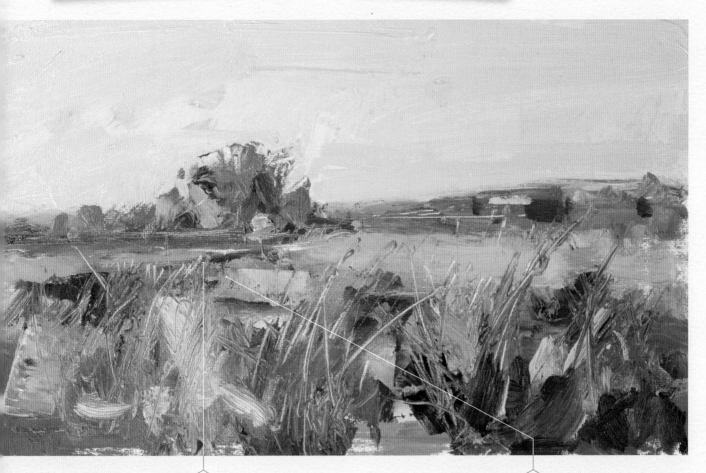

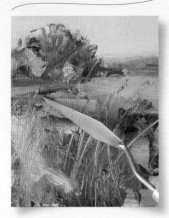

2 Multiple markings

Apply more paint with a no. 4 filbert-bristle brush. Partly cover the initial putty knife markings, then use a medium-sized palette knife to create a variety of scratch marks in all directions. You can rub over areas with a rag or your finger to reduce the severity of a mark.

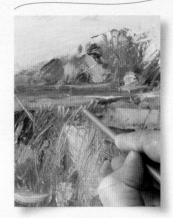

3 Final details

Lastly, with the handle of a small paint brush, refine the details and create a sense of depth and scale with finer marks in the background. Paint over dry marks with a dry brush for added texture, or apply glaze to help them blend in while retaining their texture.

Scumbling

ADDING A LAYER OF BROKEN COLOR

Scumbling is a technique used to create depth and texture by randomly scrubbing thin paint over an existing layer. The original paint shows through and, In the eye of the viewer, mixes with the scumbled layer. The technique can be used to suggest movement, give life to bland areas of solid color, and create subtle changes in atmosphere.

▨ Applying a layer of scumbling

Before scumbling, always make sure the initial layer of paint is dry. That way, you can push and scrub paint over the top without disturbing the underlayer. The less paint you have on your brush, the easier it is to achieve the broken pattern indicative of scumbling. Remove any excess paint with a rag to achieve the level of cover you want. Use larger-bristle brushes to cover bigger areas quickly, and because they are more durable. You can also scumble with a sponge or rag, or using your finger.

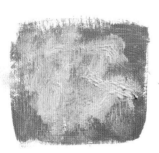

Scumbling with an impasto medium
Adding an impasto medium to your mix before starting will stiffen the paint and give a more textured finish. Roll the brush loosely across the canvas to prevent too much paint from being applied.

Scumbling with a dry brush
If using paint without an added medium, dry the brush on a rag first. Apply paint to the canvas by working quickly across the area with random scrubbing movements, leaving behind small amounts of paint.

In these three paintings, scumbling was used to create a variety of effects. Three different tools were used to change the intensity of colors, introduce texture, and emphasize depth.

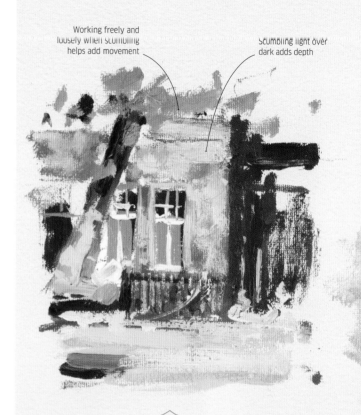

Working freely and loosely when scumbling helps add movement

Scumbling light over dark adds depth

Adding texture
A layer of scumbling was used on the shadows and darker areas of the building to give it a sense of texture. For the highlights on the rough surface of the brick, a dry opaque color was added. A rag was used to apply and move the paint around broad areas, while a brush was used for the finer details.

Emphasizing color
Scumbling was used here to emphasize the bright color of the poppy fields. A little cadmium red was scumbled over darker areas in the background with a rag, to highlight distant poppies and create a sense of depth. In the foreground, thicker red was scumbled with a brush to bring the area forward.

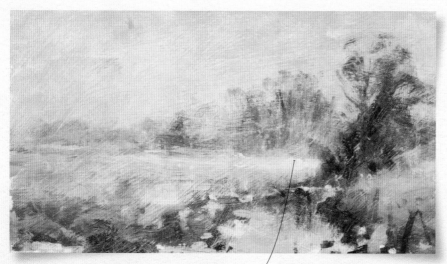

Subduing colors

In this misty river scene, scumbling was used to subdue the colors and create a sense of swirling mist on an autumn day. If a painting has only slight variations in tone and color, as is the case here, scumbling can introduce energy and provide an atmospheric effect that finishes the piece well.

Scumbling with a bristle brush and multi-directional strokes adds movement and energy

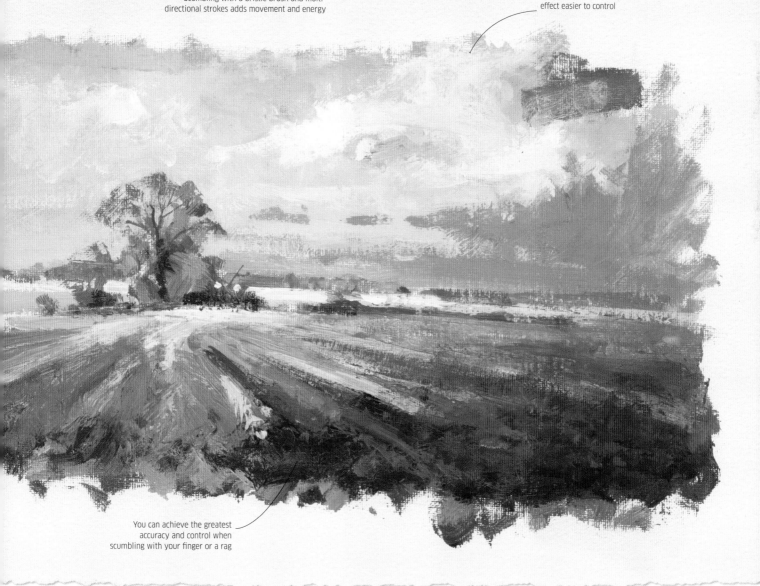

Use less paint than normal when scumbling, to make the effect easier to control

You can achieve the greatest accuracy and control when scumbling with your finger or a rag

Broken color

USING MARBLING EFFECTS

Paint applied to the canvas before it
is mixed into its final color is known
as "broken." This creates a marbling effect
with streaks of color visible in the final
brushstroke. It is particularly effective in
areas with several different colors, or where
you want to suggest movement.
The technique is similar to scumbling
(see pp.252-53), although broken
color uses wet paint rather than
several layers of dried paint.

▮ Degrees of mixing

Broken color is a form of optical color mixing in which
your brain produces the illusion of a mixed color. Once
you apply a brushstroke, you can continue to mix on the
canvas to modify the degree to which the color is
"broken," as shown in the examples below.

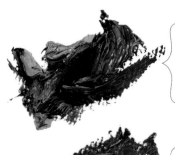

Highly broken
Fench ultramarine and cadmium
yellow have been loaded onto
opposite sides of a no. 5 round
synthetic brush and applied
directly to the canvas.

Moderately broken
The same colors have been
mixed loosely on the palette
first, and then mixed again on
the canvas. This creates a finer
degree of broken color.

Slightly broken
Finally, the colors have been
mixed more thoroughly on the
canvas. A hint of yellow is still
visible, but the final mixed
color is more dominant.

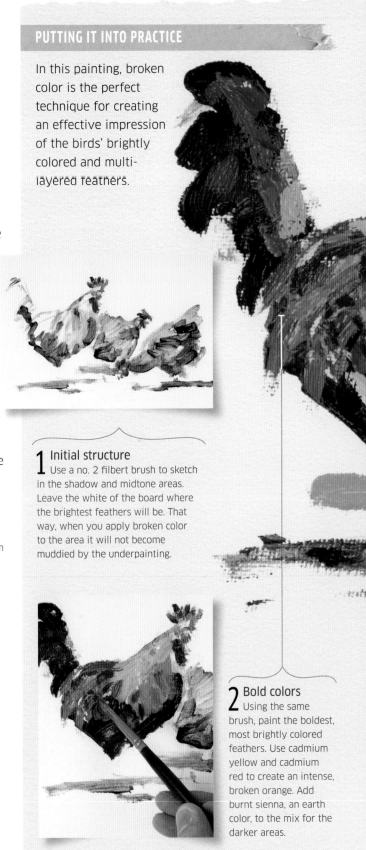

PUTTING IT INTO PRACTICE

In this painting, broken
color is the perfect
technique for creating
an effective impression
of the birds' brightly
colored and multi-
layered feathers.

1 Initial structure
Use a no. 2 filbert brush to sketch
in the shadow and midtone areas.
Leave the white of the board where
the brightest feathers will be. That
way, when you apply broken color
to the area it will not become
muddied by the underpainting.

2 Bold colors
Using the same
brush, paint the boldest,
most brightly colored
feathers. Use cadmium
yellow and cadmium
red to create an intense,
broken orange. Add
burnt sienna, an earth
color, to the mix for the
darker areas.

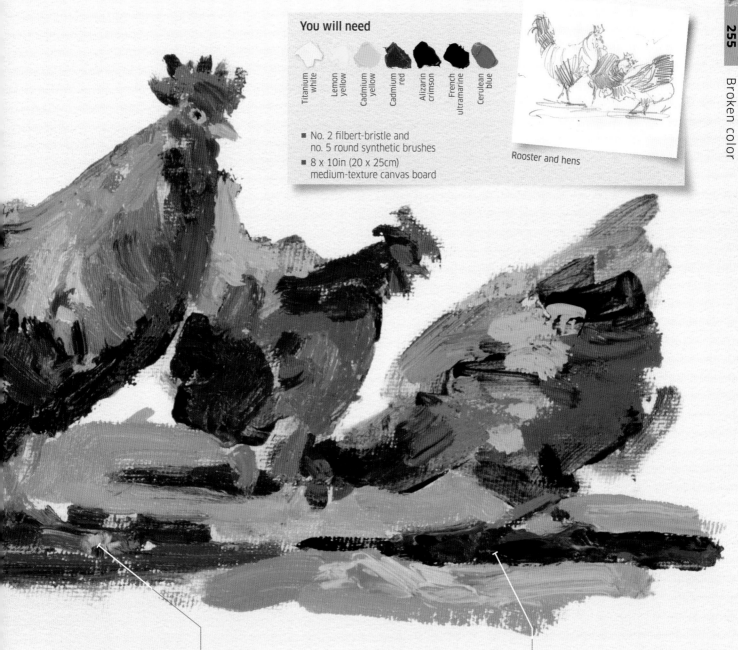

You will need

- Titanium white
- Lemon yellow
- Cadmium yellow
- Cadmium red
- Alizarin crimson
- French ultramarine
- Cerulean blue

- No. 2 filbert-bristle and no. 5 round synthetic brushes
- 8 x 10in (20 x 25cm) medium-texture canvas board

Rooster and hens

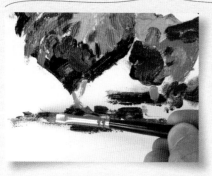

3 Shadow areas
Use the technique more subtly in the shadow areas. This will prevent them from looking too dull and ensure that the full palette of colors is used across the painting, creating harmony and balance.

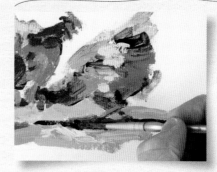

4 Adding color
Use a no. 5 round synthetic brush and a mix of blue and purple to intensify the shadows. A mix of French ultramarine and alizarin crimson will create a vibrant, intense purple.

Wiping and scraping back

REWORKING WET PAINT

Wiping and scraping involves spreading and removing wet paint from the canvas. This technique creates a range of textures that are useful for the initial layers of your painting. You can also use it to block in large areas, mix color on the canvas, and make corrections or additions.

▇ Tools for wiping and scraping

You can remove paint with different tools to create a range of textures. If you use a palette knife to scrape off wet paint, you can also spread and mix the excess paint over other parts of the canvas.

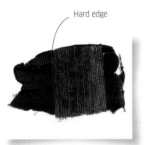

Hard edge

Large palette knife
Scrape with the side edge of a large palette knife or decorator's filling knife to create a smooth, flattened area. Use a single action, applying light pressure and holding the knife at a consistent angle.

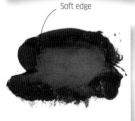

Soft edge

Rag
Wipe with a rag to create a softer effect. Change strokes to create different finishes, from broad sweeps with the flat of your hand to finer details with the tip of your finger.

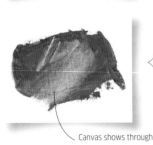

Small palette knife
Scrape vigorously with a small palette knife to reveal the color or texture of the canvas. The harder you press on the blade, the more paint you will remove.

Canvas shows through

This painting is completed *alla prima* (see pp. 234–37), or in one sitting, which means the paint remains wet enough throughout to rework.

You will need

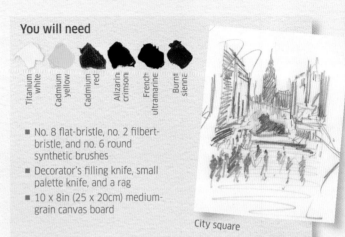

Titanium white | Cadmium yellow | Cadmium red | Alizarin crimson | French ultramarine | Burnt sienne

- No. 8 flat-bristle, no. 2 filbert-bristle, and no. 6 round synthetic brushes
- Decorator's filling knife, small palette knife, and a rag
- 10 x 8in (25 x 20cm) medium-grain canvas board

City square

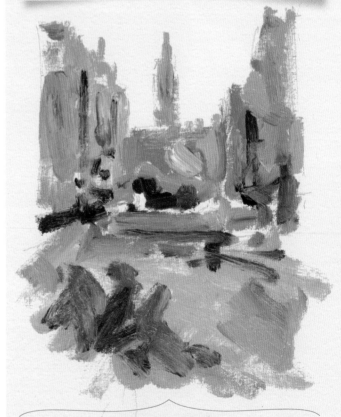

1 Apply the background
Start with fairly thick paint, so that it can be manipulated later. Apply grays mixed from French ultramarine, cadmium red, and white to the buildings, and a dark mix of ultramarine and sienna to the main areas of shadow.

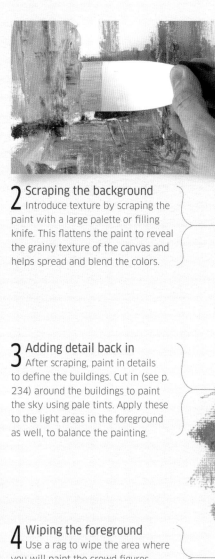

2 **Scraping the background**
Introduce texture by scraping the paint with a large palette or filling knife. This flattens the paint to reveal the grainy texture of the canvas and helps spread and blend the colors.

3 **Adding detail back in**
After scraping, paint in details to define the buildings. Cut in (see p. 234) around the buildings to paint the sky using pale tints. Apply these to the light areas in the foreground as well, to balance the painting.

4 **Wiping the foreground**
Use a rag to wipe the area where you will paint the crowd figures. This creates a dry area that you can paint over.

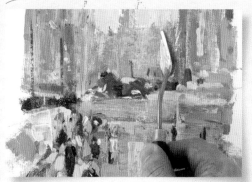

5 **Finishing touches**
Create focal points by introducing touches of strong color to figures in the crowd. Finish by scraping areas at the back of the painting with a small palette knife. This blurred effect creates a sense of distance.

Wet-in-wet

APPLYING LAYERS OF WET PAINT

Wet-in-wet is a technique in which fresh paint is applied on top of an area that is still wet. It can be used to create a single-layered painting, when you want to change a color midway through a painting, or when you want to create soft, subtle changes in color and tone. Wet-in-wet is especially good for painting water and skies, which often include soft shapes, movement, and blending.

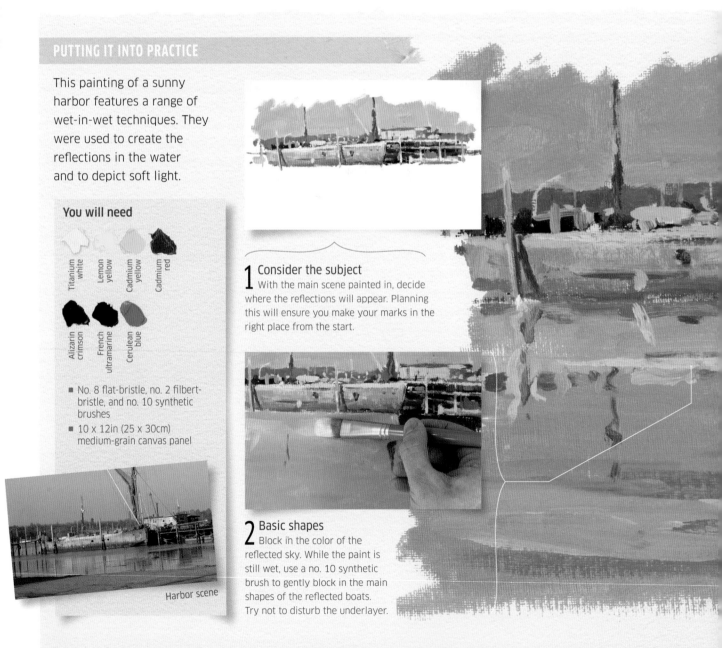

PUTTING IT INTO PRACTICE

This painting of a sunny harbor features a range of wet-in-wet techniques. They were used to create the reflections in the water and to depict soft light.

You will need

Titanium white
Lemon yellow
Cadmium yellow
Cadmium red

Alizarin crimson
French ultramarine
Cerulean blue

- No. 8 flat-bristle, no. 2 filbert-bristle, and no. 10 synthetic brushes
- 10 x 12in (25 x 30cm) medium-grain canvas panel

Harbor scene

1 Consider the subject
With the main scene painted in, decide where the reflections will appear. Planning this will ensure you make your marks in the right place from the start.

2 Basic shapes
Block in the color of the reflected sky. While the paint is still wet, use a no. 10 synthetic brush to gently block in the main shapes of the reflected boats. Try not to disturb the underlayer.

Wet-in-wet effects

One of the challenges of painting wet-in-wet is controlling how much the colors blend. If you use a soft-hair brush and apply only light pressure, you can lay "pure" color without disturbing the underlying paint. If you use a firm-bristle brush, on the other hand, you will stir up the underlying paint and mix the two colors. Both techniques can be used to great effect.

Soft-hair brush
The top layer of blue paint was applied with a soft-hair synthetic brush using light pressure. The colors remain distinct and pure, and the edges are well defined.

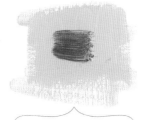

Bristle brush
The top layer of green paint was applied with a bristle brush using firm pressure. Some of the yellow paint has been dragged into the top mix. The edges are soft.

Overworked paint
Try not to overwork an area of wet-in-wet. This can disturb the underlayer, cause the layers to fully combine, and lead to unwanted color mixes.

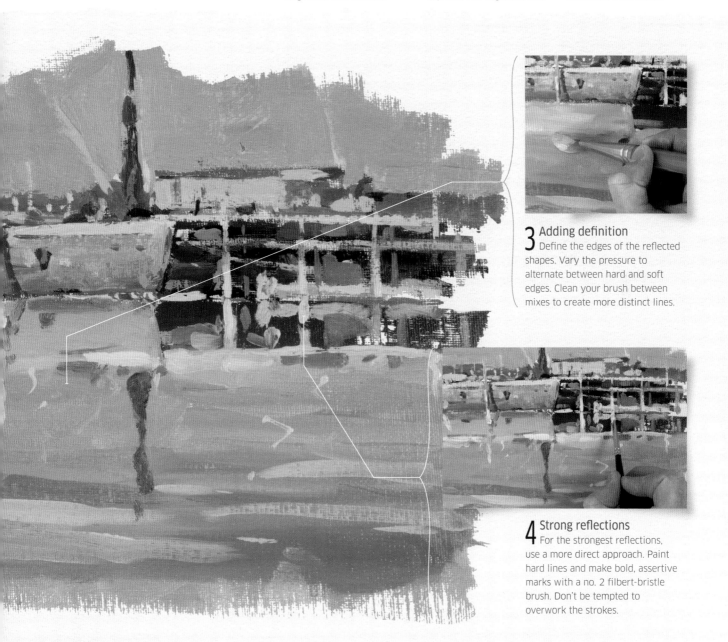

3 Adding definition
Define the edges of the reflected shapes. Vary the pressure to alternate between hard and soft edges. Clean your brush between mixes to create more distinct lines.

4 Strong reflections
For the strongest reflections, use a more direct approach. Paint hard lines and make bold, assertive marks with a no. 2 filbert-bristle brush. Don't be tempted to overwork the strokes.

Texture

MAKING ADDITIONS TO MIXES

Adding texture to your work can introduce unusual and striking effects. Try mixing additional material into the paint, such as sand, sawdust, or chalk. Alternatively, press coarse fabric onto the canvas to leave textured imprints. You can then paint on top of the resulting textures to incorporate them into your finished painting.

Materials and effects

Additions can create texture or alter the quality of the paint. Whenever you add a substance to oil paint, the balance of pigment to binder and filler will change, so add sparingly to ensure the longevity of the painting.

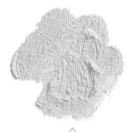

Sand
Adding sand not only gives a great textural effect, but also, once dry, provides a good base for dry brushwork.

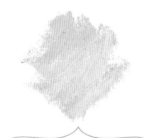

Chalk
The addition of chalk will dry the paint, giving it a matte finish. It will also tend to absorb oil from subsequent layers of paint.

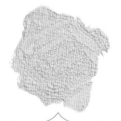

Coarse fabric
Oil paint's thick consistency is ideal for showing imprints of patterns and textures. Thick paint has more oil and will dry slowly.

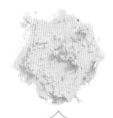

Sawdust
Sawdust, when overpainted, can enhance the effect of dry-brushwork and is great for stony foregrounds or beaches.

PUTTING IT INTO PRACTICE

The sand, shells, seaweed, and stones in this beach scene were ideal for exploring texture. Adding sand and sawdust to the paint mix, and applying it thickly with a palette knife, created a three-dimensional effect.

1 Initial scene
Paint the basic scene with thick strokes using a no. 4 flat-bristle brush. Use Naples yellow, burnt sienna, and titanium white for the sand, French ultramarine and white for the sea, and ultramarine, cerulean, and white for the sky.

"Include additional **textures in your work**, and then paint into and on top of them to create a **rich, multilayered painting**."

You will need

Titanium white · Naples yellow · Cadmium yellow · French ultramarine · Cerulean blue · Burnt sienna

- No. 4 flat-bristle and no. 5 round synthetic brushes
- Coarse sawdust, sand, palette knife
- 8 x 10in (20 x 25cm) medium-grain canvas board

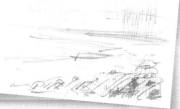

Rocky beach

Mix of cadmium yellow and burnt sienna, with a hint of French ultramarine and titanium white

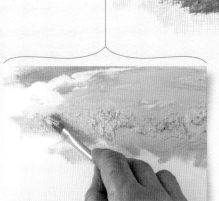

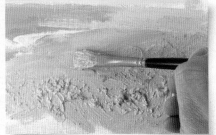

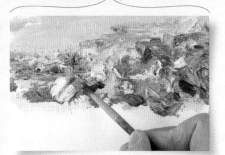

2 Sawdust mix

Build up the foreground, using a no. 4 flat-bristle brush, by adding sawdust to a mix of burnt sienna and titanium white with a little cadmium yellow.

3 Sand mix

Create texture in the middle-distance beach area by adding sand to the mix. Add the sand on the palette and, once mixed with the paint, apply with a no. 4 brush.

4 Palette knife

Use a palette knife to suggest rocks in the foreground, then paint darker shadows around the raised areas with a no. 5 brush, to exaggerate the three-dimensional effect.

Blotting

REMOVING EXCESS PAINT

A buildup of paint can make your work unmanageable. If this happens, you can either wait for the paint to dry or use a blotting technique (called *tonking* in the UK). This involves pressing a sheet of absorbent paper, such as newspaper, onto the surface and then slowly peeling it off to remove some of the paint. The texture left behind can be a feature in itself, providing a contrast and a new surface into which to work.

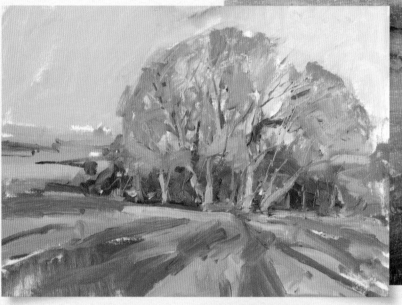

PUTTING IT INTO PRACTICE

Excess paint has been removed from this study of a tree by blotting. This allows an area to be reworked to increase contrast and clarity.

You will need

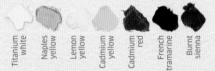

Titanium white · Naples yellow · Lemon yellow · Cadmium yellow · Cadmium red · French ultramarine · Burnt sienna

- No. 4 flat-bristle, no. 8 flatbristle, no. 6 filbert brushes
- Sheet of newspaper
- 16 x 20in (40 x 50cm) medium-grain canvas panel

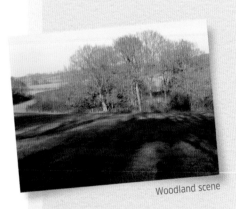

Woodland scene

1 Overworked wet paint
Too much paint has been applied around the base of the trees, leading to a loss of contrast, depth, and definition. Colors have mixed and blended together.

2 Apply newspaper
Place a sheet of newspaper onto the surface, smoothing or pressing down over the problem area. Take care not to manipulate the paint beneath too much.

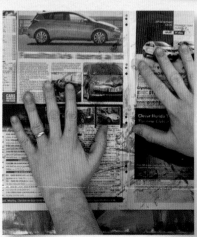

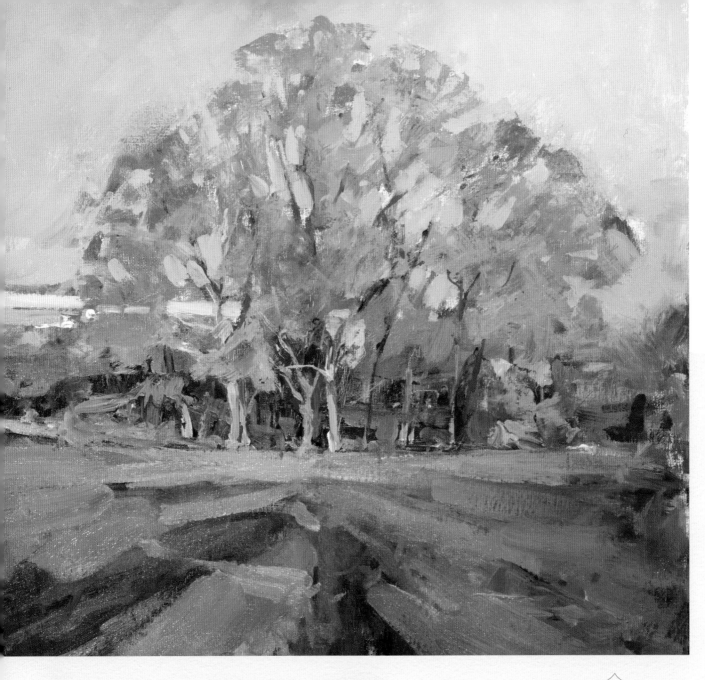

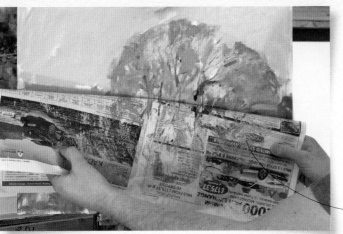

Excess paint adheres
to newspaper

3 Remove paper
Carefully peel back the newspaper to reveal the painting underneath. Different types of paper will have different effects. Impermeable paper will remove less paint from the surface of the painting than absorbent paper.

4 Final painting
Now you can apply fresh color without the paints mixing on the canvas. Here, more detail and contrast have been added to the distant treeline, fresh color has been introduced to the grass, and a pure mix of French ultramarine and white has been painted into the tops of the trees.

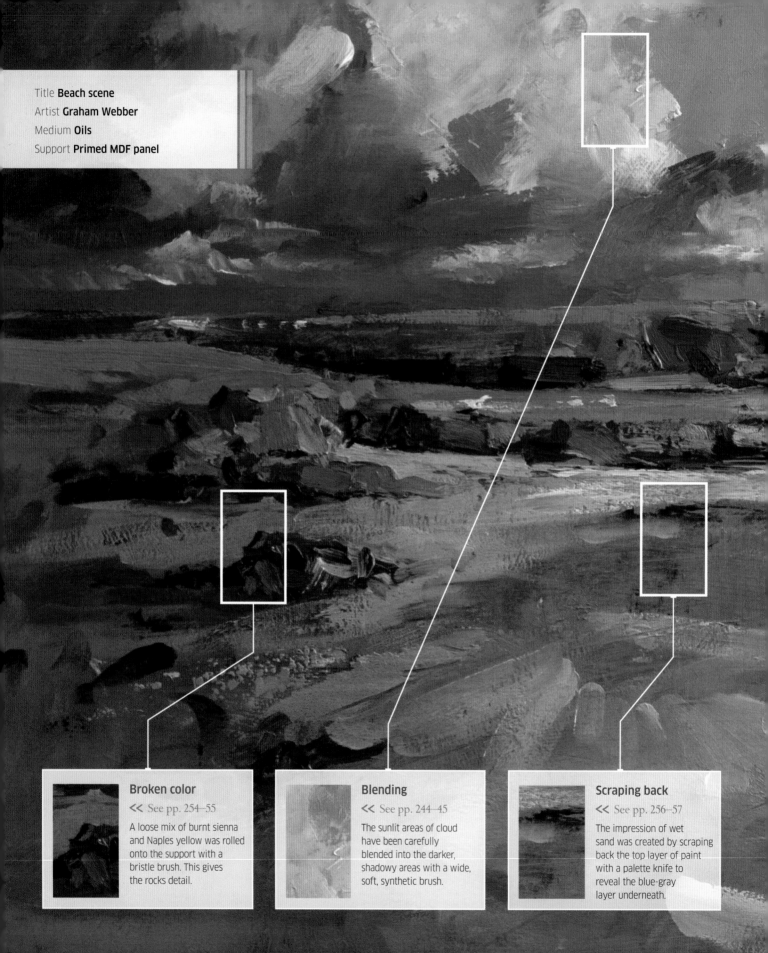

Title **Beach scene**
Artist **Graham Webber**
Medium **Oils**
Support **Primed MDF panel**

Broken color
« See pp. 254–55

A loose mix of burnt sienna and Naples yellow was rolled onto the support with a bristle brush. This gives the rocks detail.

Blending
« See pp. 244–45

The sunlit areas of cloud have been carefully blended into the darker, shadowy areas with a wide, soft, synthetic brush.

Scraping back
« See pp. 256–57

The impression of wet sand was created by scraping back the top layer of paint with a palette knife to reveal the blue-gray layer underneath.

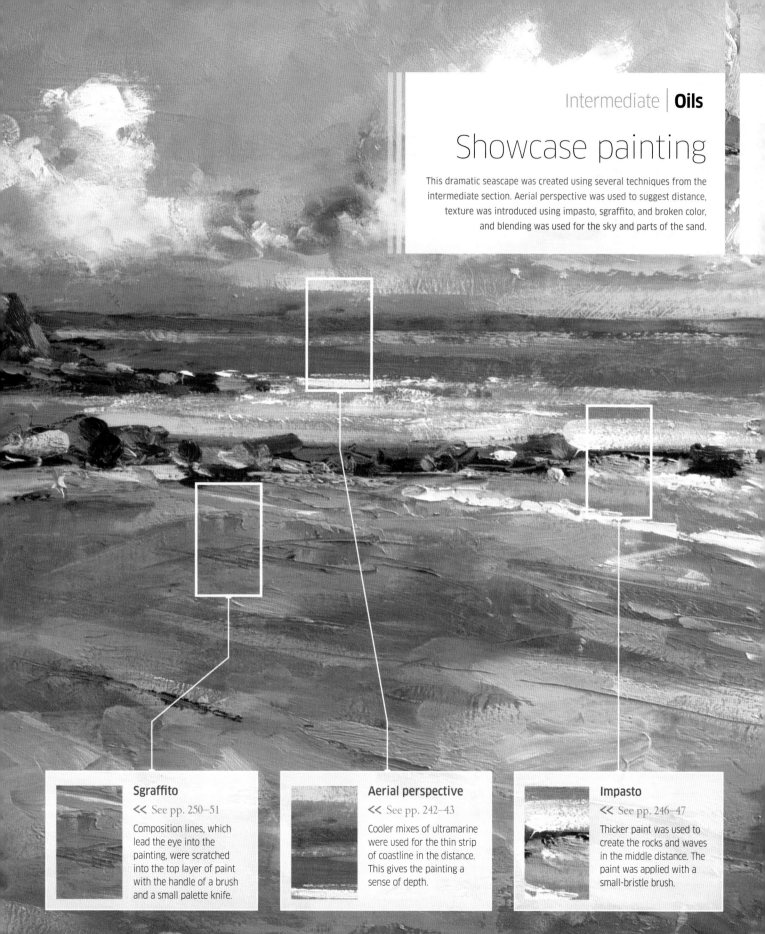

Showcase painting

This dramatic seascape was created using several techniques from the intermediate section. Aerial perspective was used to suggest distance, texture was introduced using impasto, sgraffito, and broken color, and blending was used for the sky and parts of the sand.

Sgraffito

« See pp. 250–51

Composition lines, which lead the eye into the painting, were scratched into the top layer of paint with the handle of a brush and a small palette knife.

Aerial perspective

« See pp. 242–43

Cooler mixes of ultramarine were used for the thin strip of coastline in the distance. This gives the painting a sense of depth.

Impasto

« See pp. 246–47

Thicker paint was used to create the rocks and waves in the middle distance. The paint was applied with a small-bristle brush.

Ground color

PAINTING BACKDROPS

The ground is a layer of paint applied on top of a primed surface before painting begins. If you paint directly onto canvas primed with white paint, you risk creating a painting in too high a tonal key; using a midtone ground will allow you to control the tonal range better. A colored ground—especially when allowed to show through in places—will also help unify a painting.

■ Grounds and effects

Different colored grounds will influence the colors you subsequently apply, while textured applications can add interest. Allowing ground colors to show through in areas will help bring elements together.

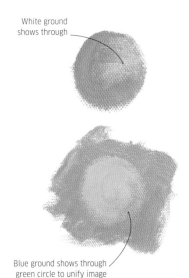

White ground shows through

White ground
On a white ground, areas of thin paint will seem to "glow" where the white shows through. However, the high contrast can make it difficult to control the painting's overall tone.

Dark ground
The dark ground wash was applied generously to provide an opaque layer, leaving visible brushstrokes and variations in tones. The blue ground influences the green color of the circle.

Blue ground shows through green circle to unify image

Complementary ground
The red ground is complementary to the green and highlights the image, making the circle vibrant and intense. Using a colored ground in this way can help shift the eye to the point of interest.

A midtoned ochre background was used in this still life. Allowing the ground to show through gives the piece a natural warmth and helps link the elements.

You will need

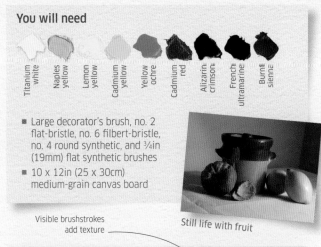

Titanium white · Naples yellow · Lemon yellow · Cadmium yellow · Yellow ochre · Cadmium red · Alizarin crimson · French ultramarine · Burnt sienna

- Large decorator's brush, no. 2 flat-bristle, no. 6 filbert-bristle, no. 4 round synthetic, and ¾in (19mm) flat synthetic brushes
- 10 x 12in (25 x 30cm) medium-grain canvas board

Still life with fruit

Visible brushstrokes add texture

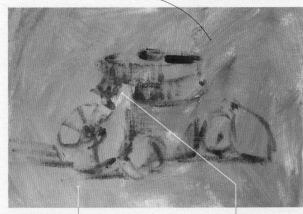

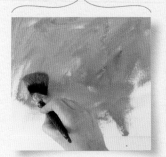

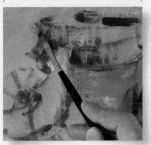

1 Apply the ground
Use a decorator's brush to apply a ground of yellow ochre, French ultramarine, and titanium white, varying the color and tone slightly as you work across the canvas.

2 Sketch shapes
Use a no. 2 flat-bristle brush to draw the subject with a French ultramarine and burnt sienna mix. An accurate sketch will help you plan where to let the ground show through.

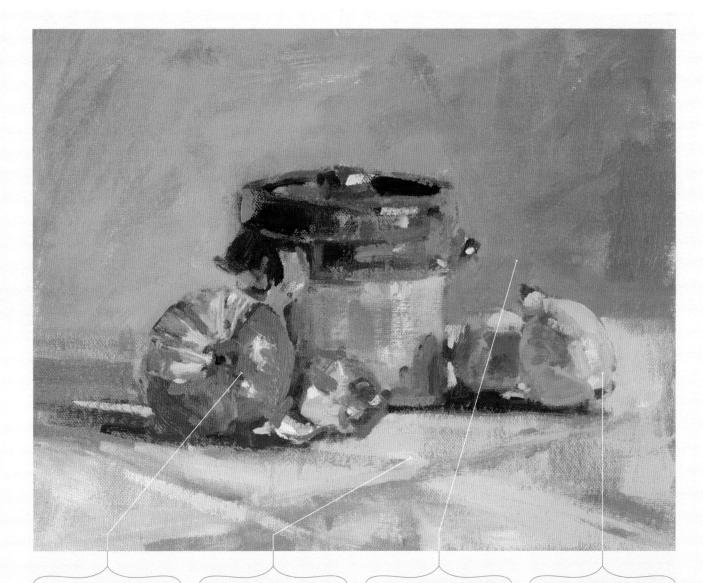

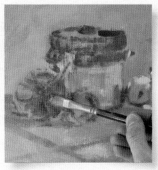

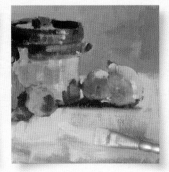

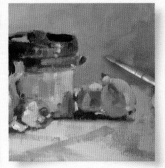

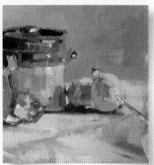

3 Block in main shapes
Add a background of French ultramarine and Naples yellow. Make light brushstrokes with a no. 6 filbert to limit the amount of paint on the surface and allow the ground to show through.

4 Develop tones
With a ¾in (19mm) synthetic brush, use a dry-brush technique to apply a mix of titanium white and burnt sienna to the tablecloth. Make sure the ground is showing through to unite colors.

5 Add detail
With the same brush, add detail to the fruit and pot. Apply dry-brush marks of yellow ochre and French ultramarine around the painting where the ground has been covered too much.

6 Finishing touches
With a no. 4 round synthetic brush, place final highlights on the pot and add detail across the painting, refining it and darkening areas of shadow.

Skin tones

PAINTING FLESH COLORS

The color of our skin constantly changes, becoming paler or more flushed as it adapts to the environment. It is hard to paint skin with a single color, so it makes sense to use a variety of colors and tones. Oil paint is an ideal medium for painting portraits, as the slow drying speed allows greater time to reassess and adjust colors as the portrait progresses.

■ Light source

Skin can appear paler, yellower, and cooler the nearer it is to a light source, while areas of shadow will seem to have greater depth and warmth. Therefore, to prevent the shadows from dominating, paint them using cooler greens and violets. These cool colors will seem to recede slightly, and will complement the reds, yellows, and oranges in the lit areas of skin, giving the portrait a sense of energy and life.

■ Subdued palette

Use duller colors than you might think when starting a portrait: it is easier to add richer colors later than it is to knock back areas of bold color. Assess the high- and midtone areas, and consider the shadow colors. Try painting your own hand, applying basic tones and colors before adding detail, and then apply what you have learned about skin tones to painting a portrait.

■ Flesh tones palette

A good basic palette for portrait painting, regardless of the subject's complexion, should include:

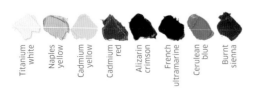

Titanium white · Naples yellow · Cadmium yellow · Cadmium red · Alizarin crimson · French ultramarine · Cerulean blue · Burnt sienna

Olive skin tones

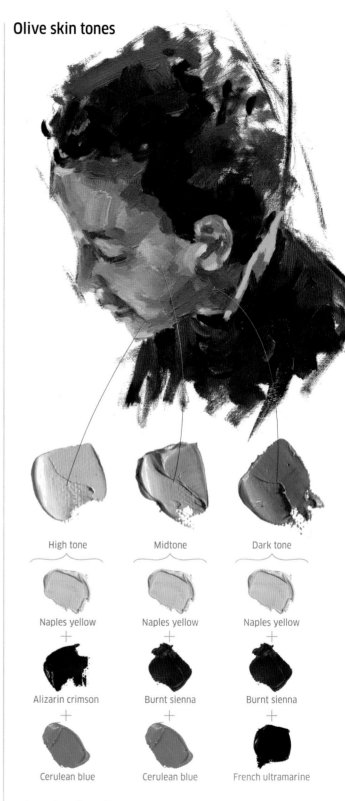

High tone	Midtone	Dark tone
Naples yellow	Naples yellow	Naples yellow
+	+	+
Alizarin crimson	Burnt sienna	Burnt sienna
+	+	+
Cerulean blue	Cerulean blue	French ultramarine

Palette for olive skin

You can create a good range of tones for olive skin using just five colors. Use alizarin crimson instead of burnt sienna for highlights, and French ultramarine instead of cerulean blue for shadow areas.

Dark skin tones

Light skin tones

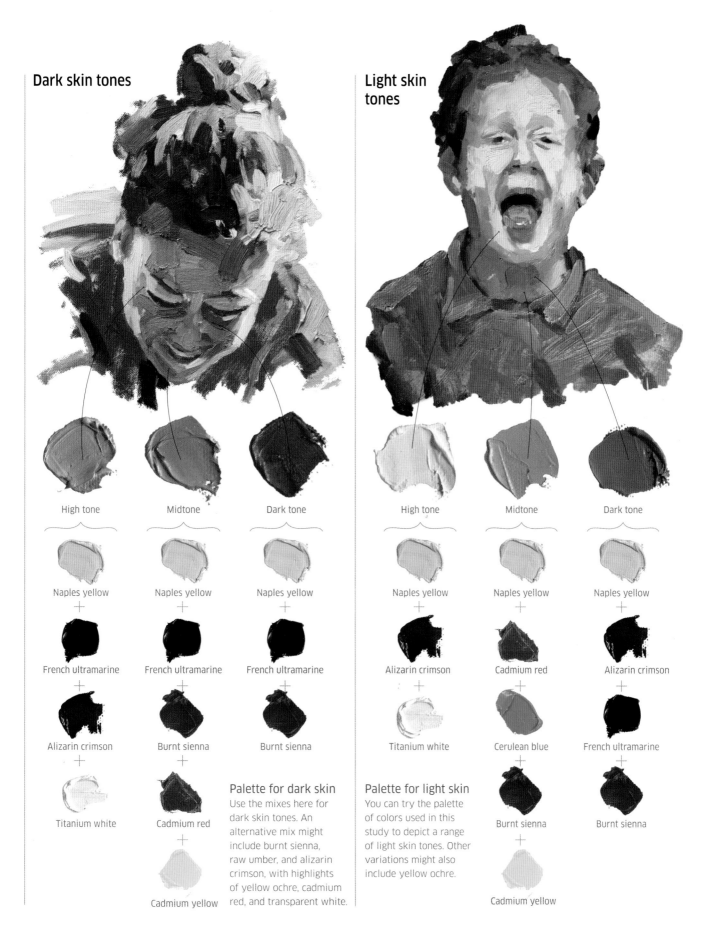

High tone	Midtone	Dark tone
Naples yellow +	Naples yellow +	Naples yellow +
French ultramarine +	French ultramarine +	French ultramarine +
Alizarin crimson +	Burnt sienna +	Burnt sienna
Titanium white	Cadmium red +	
	Cadmium yellow	

Palette for dark skin
Use the mixes here for dark skin tones. An alternative mix might include burnt sienna, raw umber, and alizarin crimson, with highlights of yellow ochre, cadmium red, and transparent white.

High tone	Midtone	Dark tone
Naples yellow +	Naples yellow +	Naples yellow +
Alizarin crimson +	Cadmium red +	Alizarin crimson +
Titanium white	Cerulean blue +	French ultramarine +
	Burnt sienna +	Burnt sienna
	Cadmium yellow	

Palette for light skin
You can try the palette of colors used in this study to depict a range of light skin tones. Other variations might also include yellow ochre.

PUTTING IT INTO PRACTICE

This self-portrait uses a range of colors and tones to convey the contrast between strongly lit parts of the face and those in shadow. Darker tones are established first, followed by mid and light tones. Blocks of color describe facial contours.

You will need

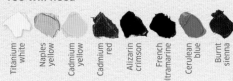

Titanium white • Naples yellow • Cadmium yellow • Cadmium red • Alizarin crimson • French ultramarine • Cerulean blue • Burnt sienna

- No. 6 filbert bristle brush
- 12 x 16in (30 x 40cm) medium-grain canvas

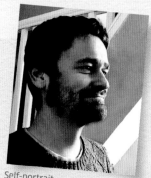

Self-portrait

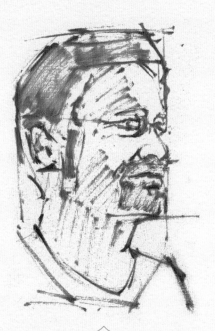

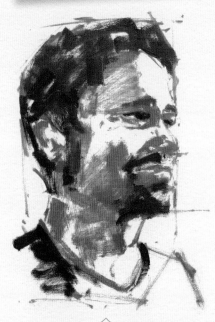

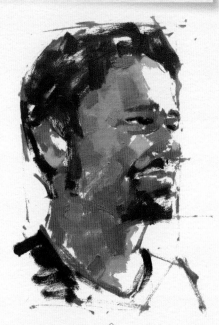

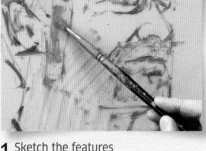

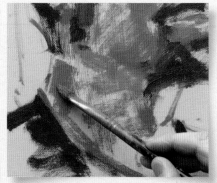

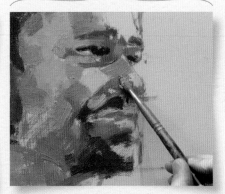

1 Sketch the features

Draw the face with a pencil, ensuring all proportions are correct. Then use a no. 6 filbert to sketch in the basic contours of the face using a thinned mix of burnt sienna and French ultramarine.

2 Shadows

Work from dark to light. With the same brush, paint the skin in shadow with a mix of burnt sienna, French ultramarine, alizarin crimson, and a little Naples yellow. Vary the mix with more alizarin nearer the cheeks, eyes, and nose. Add hair and eyes at this stage, too.

3 Midtones

Mix burnt sienna and Naples yellow, adding a little cadmium red and cadmium yellow to achieve the correct color. Reduce the intensity by adding small amounts of cerulean blue and block in the midtones. Add more blue to shadows and more Naples yellow to highlights.

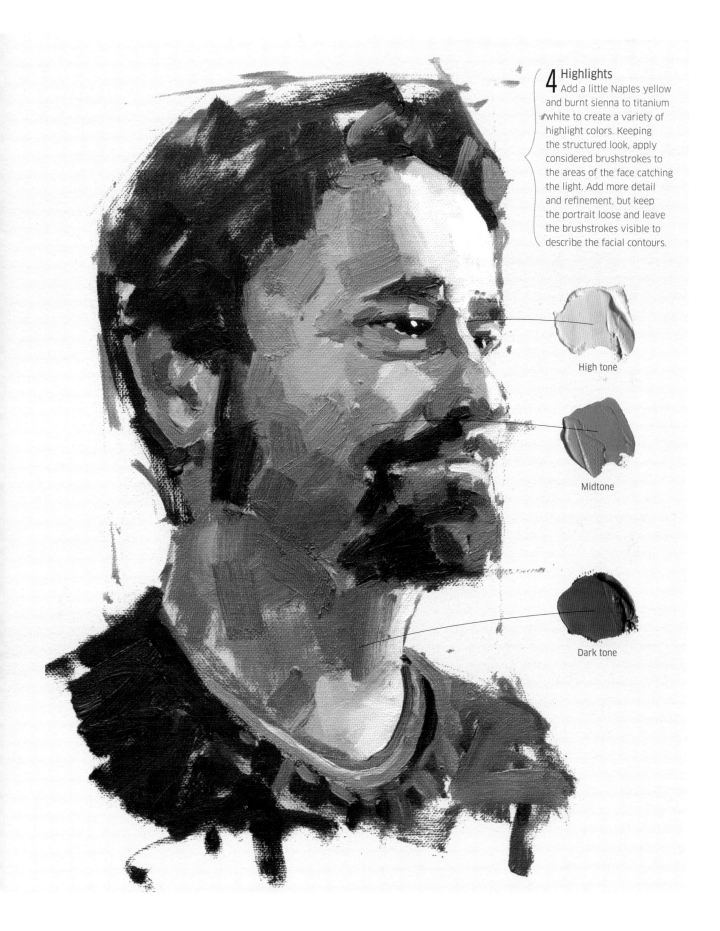

4 Highlights
Add a little Naples yellow and burnt sienna to titanium white to create a variety of highlight colors. Keeping the structured look, apply considered brushstrokes to the areas of the face catching the light. Add more detail and refinement, but keep the portrait loose and leave the brushstrokes visible to describe the facial contours.

High tone

Midtone

Dark tone

Color harmony

CREATING BALANCED PAINTINGS

Color harmony will help you create pleasing, well-balanced paintings. There are several ways to achieve color harmony, and every method requires a considered, unified palette in which each element supports the next. It is important not only to consider the color of your subject, but any additional colors that you may wish to introduce as part of your artistic interpretation of a scene.

◾ Four ways to harmonize color

There are different ways to harmonize color, most of which involve working with a limited palette. Using complementary colors is an effective way to achieve color harmony for vibrant subjects, while a narrow range of analogous natural hues is ideal for landscapes.

Color harmony is as important as drawing in balancing a composition. However, it is important to know when to apply the rules and when to break them—following any one rule too closely can lead to a lack of spontaneity. Look for color harmony in your subject matter, but incorporate colors of your own choosing, too.

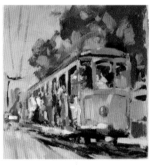

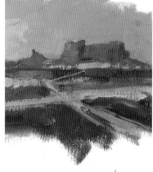

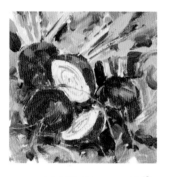

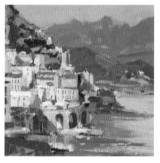

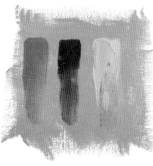

Violet-blue   Violet   Violet-red

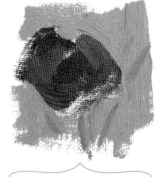

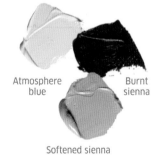

Atmosphere blue · Burnt sienna

Softened sienna

Anchoring the primaries

Vibrant mixes of primary colors can be discordant in a painting. To counter this, introduce an earth color—in this case yellow ochre. The ochre helps link the bold colors and creates a sense of harmony.

Analogous colors

Use a sequence of up to five colors that sit next to each other on the color wheel. For example, a yellow, yellow-orange, and yellow-green will give a harmonious range on which to base your painting.

Complementary colors

Colors that sit opposite each other on the color wheel, such as red and green, have a vibrant color relationship. They won't clash with each other and you can use them with varying intensity for a range of effects.

Atmosphere color

Mixing a central atmosphere color and adding it to subsequent color mixes will link your colors. Here, a central blue mixed into burnt sienna softens the color and brings it into harmony.

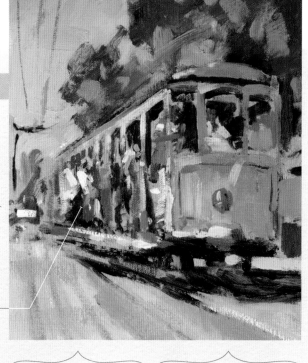

ANCHORING THE PRIMARIES

Using an earth color to anchor the bright colors in this scene links the separate elements and creates a well-balanced painting.

You will need

Titanium white · Cadmium yellow · Yellow ochre · Cadmium red

Alizarin crimson · French ultramarine · Cerulean blue · Burnt sienna

- No. 4 filbert-bristle, no. 6 round synthetic, and no. 6 flat synthetic brushes
- 10 x 8in (25 x 20cm) medium-grain canvas board

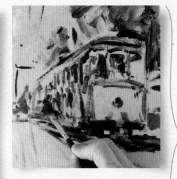

1 Colored ground
Starting on a colored ground of yellow ochre, sketch in the tram and dark areas with a mix of burnt sienna and French ultramarine using a no. 4 filbert.

2 Leaving gaps
Paint the trees and tram, leaving gaps for the ground to show through, and link the yellows, greens, and blues.

3 Adding back
Add a mix of yellow ochre back into areas of the tram, tree, and road. This reduces the intensity of large areas of color.

ANALOGOUS SCHEME

A range of three analogous colors was used to create this desert landscape. Violet, violet-blue, and violet-red all sit next to each other on the color wheel and were used here in varying tones.

Lighter tone used for the sky

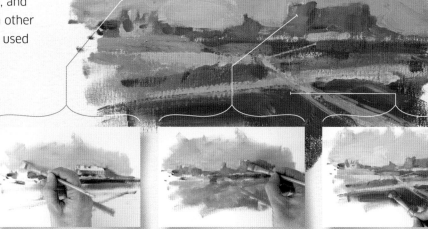

You will need

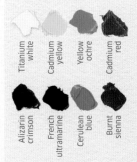

Titanium white · Alizarin crimson · French ultramarine · Burnt sienna

- Small, flat synthetic brush
- 8 x 10in (20 x 25cm) medium-grain canvas board

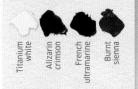

1 Using violet-blue
Apply a light mix of violet-blue to block in the sky with a small, flat synthetic brush. Carefully work up to the rock formations.

2 Adding violet
Add alizarin crimson to the mix and paint the rocks with a warmer mix, slightly darker in tone than the sky. Add cooler blue for the shadows.

3 Warm and dark color
More alizarin crimson makes the mix warmer still, and adding French ultramarine darkens it enough to use in the foreground.

COMPLEMENTARY COLORS

Complementary colors can often be found together in nature. In this painting of radishes, the intensity of the red and green was reduced to create a vibrant yet natural-looking image.

You will need

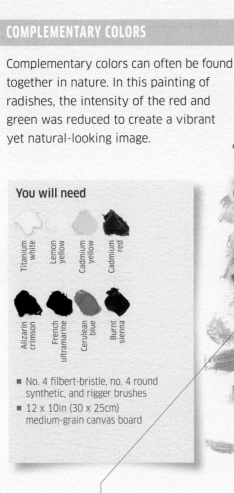

Titanium white
Lemon yellow
Cadmium yellow
Cadmium red

Alizarin crimson
French ultramarine
Cerulean blue
Burnt sienna

- No. 4 filbert-bristle, no. 4 round synthetic, and rigger brushes
- 12 x 10in (30 x 25cm) medium-grain canvas board

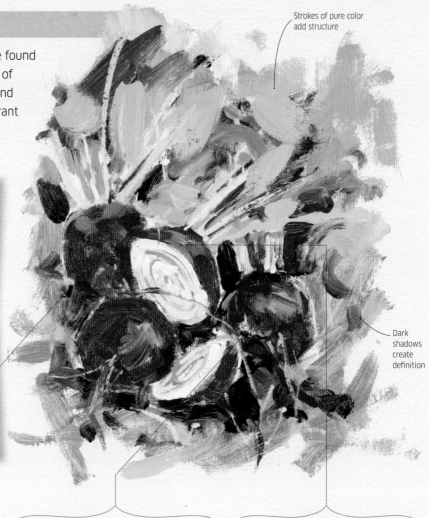

Strokes of pure color add structure

Dark shadows create definition

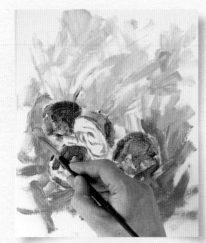

1 Block in main areas
Establish the main areas of color first to ensure that colors don't become muddied later on in the painting.

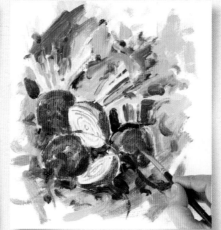

2 Creating definition
Add darker shadows and deeper greens and reds using a no. 4 filbert. This helps create more definition.

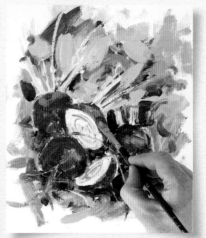

3 Emphasize color
Apply purer reds and greens last to emphasize the color relationship and give structure.

ATMOSPHERE COLOR

The warm haze of this scene is ideal for using atmosphere color. Blues bring the shadows to life and unite the buildings and mountains, bathed in soft light.

You will need

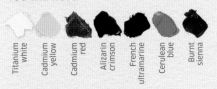

Titanium white | Cadmium yellow | Cadmium red | Alizarin crimson | French ultramarine | Cerulean blue | Burnt sienna

- No. 6 and no. 4 filbert-bristle, and no. 6 round synthetic brushes
- 10 x 12in (25 x 30cm) medium-grain canvas board

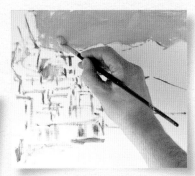

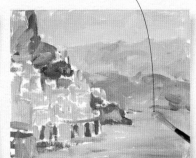

No. 4 filbert brush

1 Atmosphere base color
Paint the sky using an atmosphere mix of French ultramarine, titanium white, and cadmium red.

2 Lighter tone
After painting the background, use a lighter tone of the atmosphere color to add the reflection of the sky in the water.

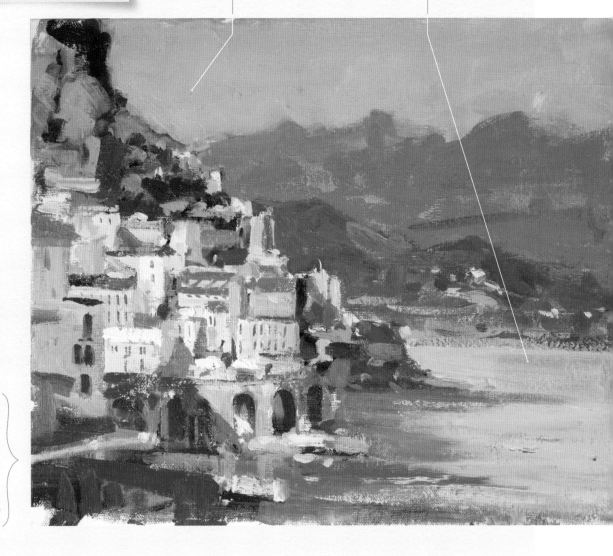

3 Use base mix throughout
Continuing to use the atmosphere blue as a base, mix a variety of colors and tones. Use darker tones in the foreground to create a sense of depth.

Tonal values

PAINTING LIGHT AND SHADE

The tonal value, or key, of a painting is how light or dark it looks. In this regard, you can view a painting in the same way as a photograph. an overexposed photo looks washed out, while an underexposed one lacks clarity and detail. It is best to begin a painting in a lower, or darker, key than you would expect, as it is easier to scale from dark to light. A good tonal range helps create a dynamic finished piece.

Comparing tones in color

Color can be distracting when trying to identify tones. You may assume yellow is lighter than blue, for example, but each color has its own tonal range. Squinting slightly can help you compare different colors tonally. In the examples below, a black and white image of each pair of color mixes makes it easier to assess their tone.

White in both mixes   Less white in yellow   No white added to blue

Tones look similar   Yellow looks darker   Blue looks darker

Similar tones
A mix of cadmium yellow and titanium white (top left) and French ultramarine and titanium white (top right) are similar in tone.

Dark and light
Adding less white to the cadmium yellow mix changes its tone slightly. This time, the blue is lighter in tone than the yellow.

Light and dark
Finally, when placed next to pure French ultramarine, the yellow and white mix is much lighter in tone than the blue.

It is important to consider tone as well as color to create a balanced painting. In this cityscape, low contrast was used to subtly differentiate certain areas, high contrast was used for a bolder statement and, where two objects share the same tonal value, the color was adjusted to distinguish them.

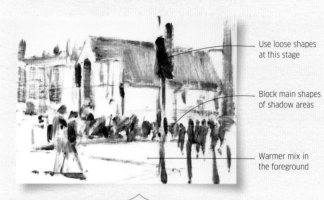

Use loose shapes at this stage

Block main shapes of shadow areas

Warmer mix in the foreground

1 Block shadows
First, assess the tonal values and identify areas of shadow. Then, using a no. 8 flat-bristle brush, apply a mix of French ultramarine and burnt sienna to block in the main shapes of the shadow tones. Subtly change the color from warm to cool as you work.

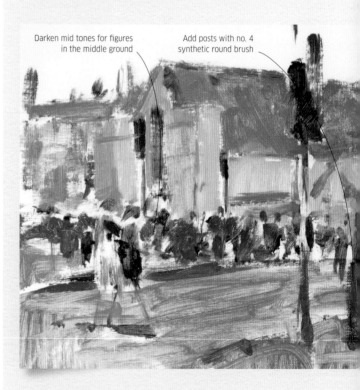

Darken mid tones for figures in the middle ground

Add posts with no. 4 synthetic round brush

You will need

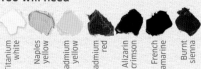

Titanium white | Naples yellow | Cadmium yellow | Cadmium red | Alizarin crimson | French ultramarine | Burnt sienna

- No. 8 flat-bristle, no. 6 filbert-bristle, no. 4 filbert-bristle, no. 4 flat-bristle, and no. 4 round synthetic brushes; synthetic rigger
- 10 x 12in (25 x 30cm) medium-grain canvas board

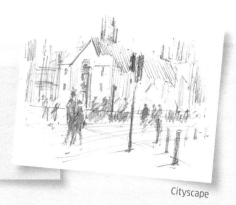

Cityscape

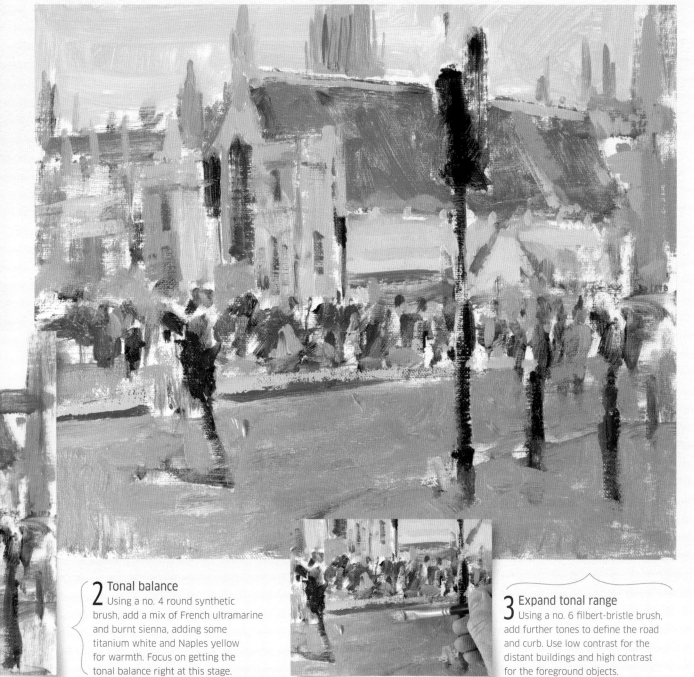

2 Tonal balance
Using a no. 4 round synthetic brush, add a mix of French ultramarine and burnt sienna, adding some titanium white and Naples yellow for warmth. Focus on getting the tonal balance right at this stage.

3 Expand tonal range
Using a no. 6 filbert-bristle brush, add further tones to define the road and curb. Use low contrast for the distant buildings and high contrast for the foreground objects.

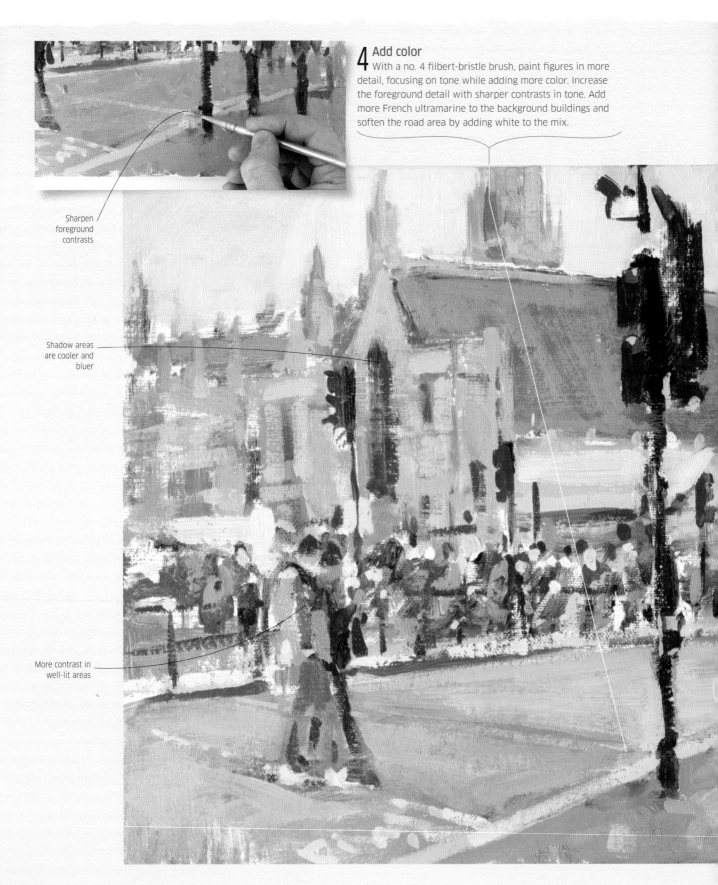

4 Add color
With a no. 4 filbert-bristle brush, paint figures in more detail, focusing on tone while adding more color. Increase the foreground detail with sharper contrasts in tone. Add more French ultramarine to the background buildings and soften the road area by adding white to the mix.

Sharpen foreground contrasts

Shadow areas are cooler and bluer

More contrast in well-lit areas

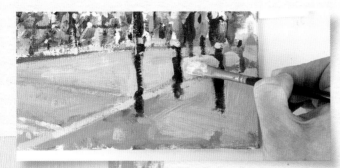

> "Generally, the **darkest darks are found** in the foreground. There is **more contrast in well-lit areas** and less contrast in shadow areas."

5 Check the balance
Finally, check that the painting balances in terms of tone, color, contrast, and detail. Add more color to the foreground figures and paint highlights with a rigger brush for fine detail.

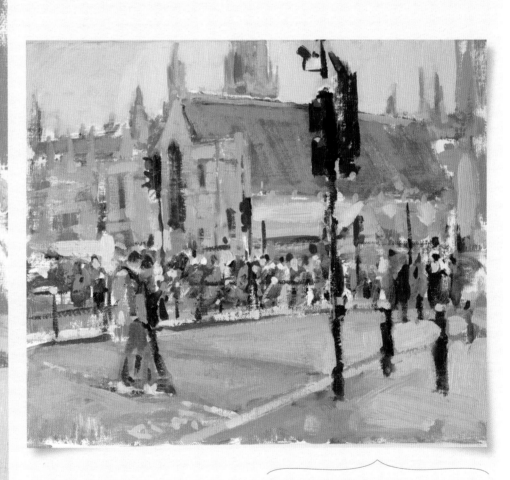

6 Light and balance
Having established a full range of tones at the beginning, the final painting now has a good balance of light and dark areas.

7 Black and white image
A black and white image of the completed painting confirms that the tonal range has been covered from the darkest dark to the lightest light.

Using mediums

TAKING CONTROL OF OIL PAINT

A medium is a liquid or gel that changes the consistency of your paint. Mediums can alter the paint's drying time, texture, thickness, or opacity. This changes the way the paint behaves and makes it easier to achieve certain effects, such as impasto (see pp. 246–49). Always keep in mind the "fat over lean" rule (see pp. 224–25) when using mediums.

▨ Mediums and their uses

Turpentine thins paint and makes it dry faster. You usually mix it with a stand oil, such as linseed. The more oil you add, the glossier and more transparent your paint will become. Alkyd liquids increase the gloss of the paint and, unlike linseed oil, will not yellow over time. Use alkyd impastos to thicken your paint.

Thin mixes

For a smooth finish with less visible brushwork, add an equal mix of turpentine and a stand oil such as linseed.

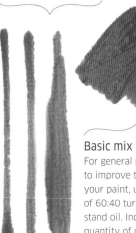

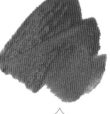

Basic mix

For general painting and to improve the flow of your paint, use a ratio of 60:40 turpentine and stand oil. Increase the quantity of oil as the painting progresses.

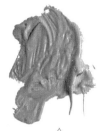

Impasto mix

Adding an alkyd impasto medium helps give body to colors without changing the color consistency. Used sparingly, it can halve drying times.

Several different mediums were used in this pet portrait, to give the paint a range of different properties. This made it easier to create the wide variety of textures needed to portray the dog.

You will need

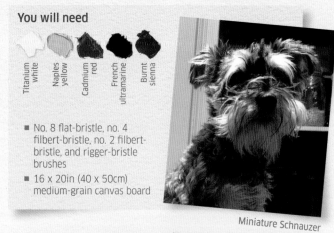

Titanium white · Naples yellow · Cadmium red · French ultramarine · Burnt sienna

- No. 8 flat-bristle, no. 4 filbert-bristle, no. 2 filbert-bristle, and rigger-bristle brushes
- 16 x 20in (40 x 50cm) medium-grain canvas board

Miniature Schnauzer

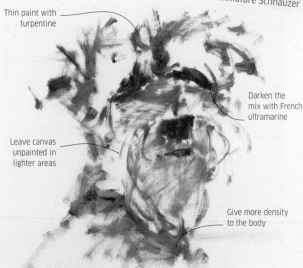

Thin paint with turpentine

Darken the mix with French ultramarine

Leave canvas unpainted in lighter areas

Give more density to the body

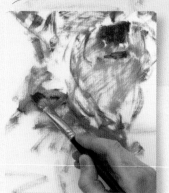

1 Thinning paint
With a no. 8 flat-bristle brush, use a mix of burnt sienna and French ultramarine thinned with turpentine to roughly suggest the main areas. Add more ultramarine for the darker tones. The paint will dry quickly and, after an hour or two, you can start the next stage.

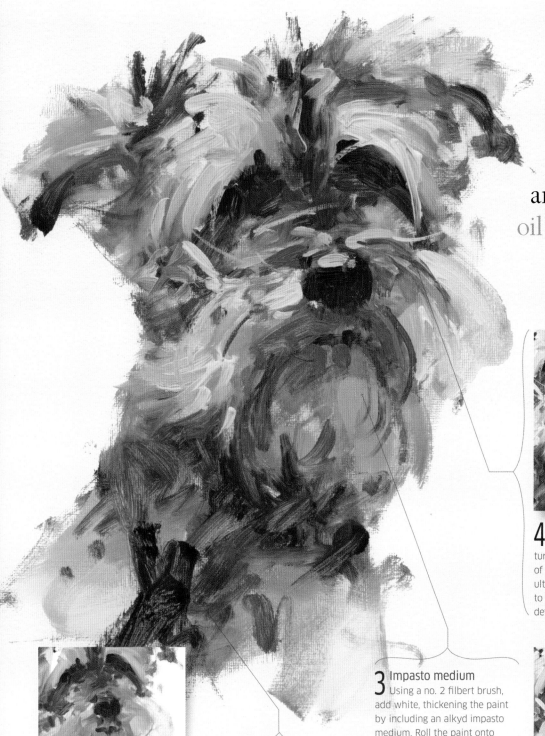

"Mediums alter the **drying time, consistency, and opacity** of oil paint, giving you **greater control.**"

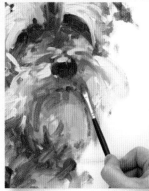

4 Flow medium
Add an equal mix of turpentine and stand oil to a mix of titanium white and French ultramarine. This helps the paint to flow easily when painting fine details with your rigger brush.

3 Impasto medium
Using a no. 2 filbert brush, add white, thickening the paint by including an alkyd impasto medium. Roll the paint onto the canvas board to allow the brushmarks to remain visible. This gives the fur texture and forms a contrast with the thinner, dark paint.

2 Blending and glazing
Use a premixed blending and glazing medium, such as an alkyd liquid, to block in the main colors. This creates softer edges and subtle transitions.

Oiling out

REVIVING AREAS OF DULLNESS

Applying additional oil–such as stand or linseed oil–to "sunken," matte-looking areas of paint can lift the color and restore luster. Sunken paint is caused by some of the oil content of the paint being absorbed into the layer beneath. As sunken areas will draw out oil from subsequent layers of paint, and so exacerbate the problem, it is important to restore the area with oil before applying more paint.

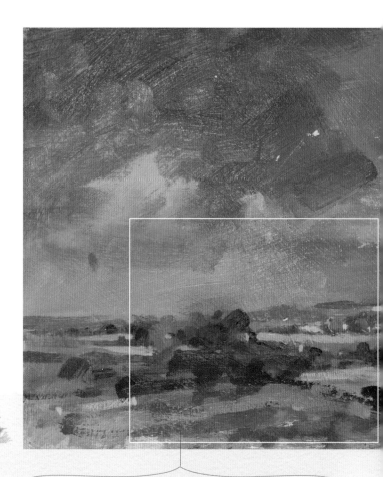

PUTTING IT INTO PRACTICE

You can use pure oil to even out the surface of the painting, but it can take up to a week to dry. Mixing the oil with a thinner, such as turpentine, will speed up the drying time. Aim for a ratio of about 4:1 stand oil to turpentine. You only need a thin layer, so it is important to wipe off any excess oil. The aim is to replace only the oil that has sunk, and it is better to apply it sparingly several times.

You will need

- Stand oil
- Turpentine
- Medium-sized, flat, wide synthetic brush
- Lint-free cloth

"Restore 'sunken' areas of paint with oil **before** applying more paint."

1 Apply oil
Once the painting is touch dry, hold it up to the light and look for any matte areas. Once you have identified any sunken paint, make sure the painting is clean and then apply the oiling-out mix with a flat, synthetic brush.

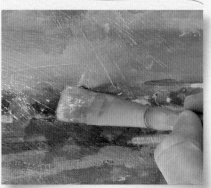

2 Wipe off excess
Wait for a couple of minutes to allow the oil to be absorbed into the paint, and then wipe off the excess with a cloth (use a lint-free cloth to prevent fibers from being introduced to the wet surface).

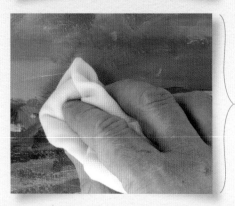

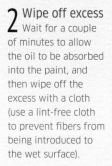

Before
Areas of sunken paint can affect the finish of the painting. A section around the trees in this landscape has a matte finish and is inconsistent with the rest of the work. Make sure the painting is free of dust before oiling out.

> "Areas of **oil paint can 'sink'** over time, which **reduces vibrancy, depth, and sheen. Oiling out will revive your painting.**"

After
Once the oil mix has dried, the inconsistencies in the finish have been corrected and the colors have more depth—in line with the rest of the painting.

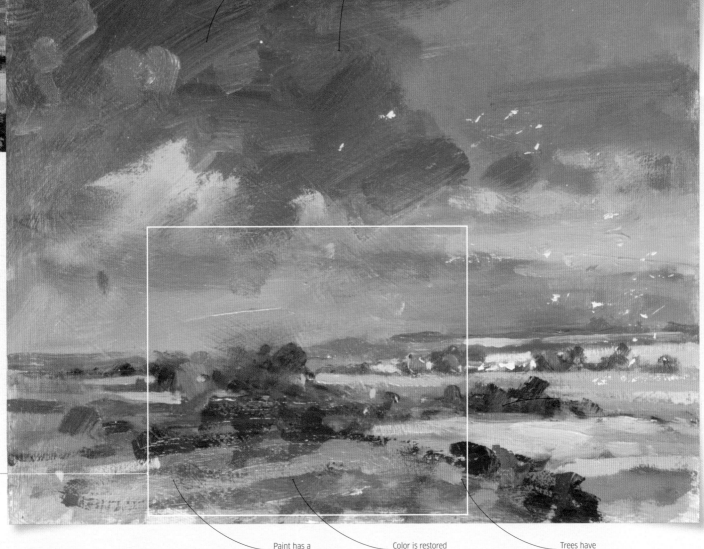

Glossy finish in parts

Color is restored

Painting has a more consistent, glossy finish

Paint has a glossier finish

Color is restored

Trees have more depth

Glazing

USING TRANSPARENT PAINT

You can use glazes of transparent paint to adjust tone, color, definition, and mood. Glazing can create a sense of depth as light passes through the transparent layers for a glowing effect. Whether you apply glazes during your painting or on your finished work, follow the fat-over-lean rule (see pp. 224–25) due to their high oil content.

■ Making glazes

There are two main types of glaze in oil painting: undiluted, semitransparent paints (thick glazes) and paints thinned with a medium to become transparent (thin glazes). Thin glazes must be mixed with an oil-based medium, to prevent cracking. You can buy prepared glazing medium or mix your own using 5 parts turpentine, 1 part stand oil, and 1 part dammar varnish. Layers applied over a glaze must be "fatter" than the glaze.

PUTTING IT INTO PRACTICE

The original painting of this sunset looked disjointed and lifeless. Several types of glazes were applied to transform it into a scene with vibrancy, light, and warmth.

You will need

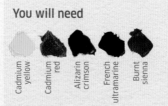

Cadmium yellow | Cadmium red | Alizarin crimson | French ultramarine | Burnt sienna

- No. 4 flat-bristle brush and wide, synthetic soft-hair brush
- Glazing medium
- 10 x 12in (25 x 30cm) medium-grain canvas board

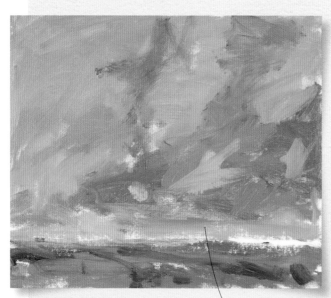

Original painting
This painting lacks drama and depth because the colors don't have enough tonal variation and are too light overall.

Sunset colors look too pastel

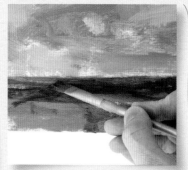

1 Glazing the middle ground
Use a thick glaze of French ultramarine and alizarin crimson to deepen the shadows in the middle ground. Apply a warm-toned thin glaze of cadmium red, alizarin crimson, and French ultramarine at the horizon, to imply the influence of the sun.

Thin glazing
Mix your color first, then add it to a glazing medium to make it transparent. Apply thin glazes with a soft, synthetic brush for smooth brushmarks.

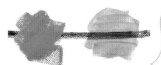
Undiluted paint

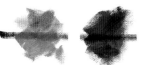
Thin glaze

Thick glazing
Semitransparent pigments, such as those shown here, don't need to be diluted. You can apply them undiluted as denser glazes that show brushmarks.

Indian yellow

French ultramarine

Alizarin crimson

Burnt sienna

Adjusting tone
You can use glazes to adjust tone in an area or in a whole painting. In this example, the underpainting is visible but has been darkened by a glaze.

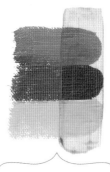

Adjusting color
Colored glazes affect the existing color as if they have been mixed. Here, a yellow glaze makes blue look green, red look orange, and yellow look intense.

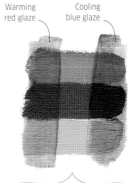

Warming red glaze   Cooling blue glaze

Warm and cool colors
You can alter the visual temperature of a painting with glazes of warm or cool colors. For example, a blue glaze can make a snowy scene feel cooler.

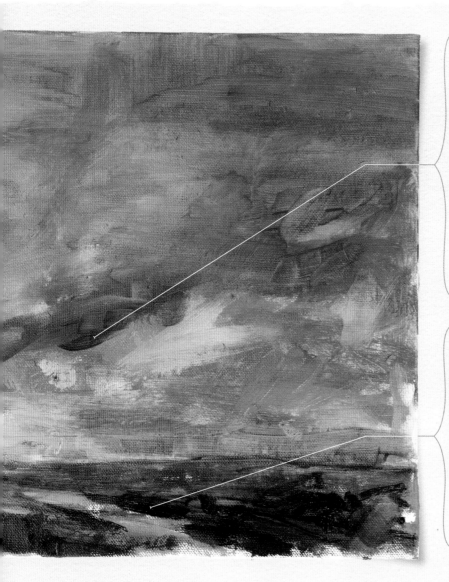

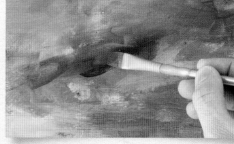

2 Glazing the sky
Apply a thin glaze of cadmium yellow and alizarin crimson to boost the sunset colors. Pastel colors will reflect and glow beneath the light, warm glaze. Harmonize the blue sky by applying the same glaze over it. Darken the top of the sky with a cooler, thin glaze of French ultramarine and burnt sienna.

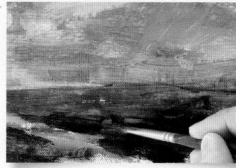

3 Glazing the foreground
Increase the contrast in the foreground area by applying a thick glaze of burnt sienna and French ultramarine with lively brushstrokes.

Reevaluating and correcting

REWORKING AREAS OF PAINT

When reevaluating a painting, you may notice some inconsistencies that need correcting. There are several techniques you can use to amend your work, whether it is still wet or has fully dried.

Manipulating wet and dry paint

You can wipe off areas of wet paint with a rag or your finger, or scrape off thicker paint with a palette knife. Use a firm palette knife or razor blade to shave off dried paint, or sand it back with sandpaper. You can also correct color or tone by adding a glaze.

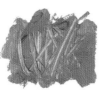
1–wet sgraffito

1–dry paint

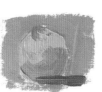
1–wet paint

1–wet paint

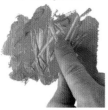
2–rubbing out

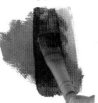
2–applying glaze

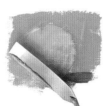
2–scraping off

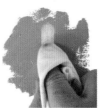
2–wiping off

3–amended area

3–amended area

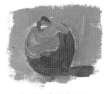
3–repainted area

3–repainted area

Adjusting sgraffito
You can adjust areas of sgraffito or impasto with your finger or the handle of a brush several days after painting.

Adjusting color
You can adjust the color or tone of dried paint with a glaze. This lets the original brushwork show through.

Scraping off
Scrape off thick, wet paint with a palette knife, leaving the area free of brushstrokes and ready to repaint.

Wiping off
You can also wipe off wet paint with your finger or a rag. This gives you more control and creates softer edges.

Several amendments were made to this completed painting of boats at a river's edge. Areas of wet paint were manipulated and remolded, while sections of dry paint were removed and repainted.

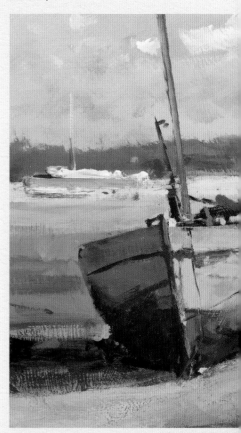

"Reevaluating is **part of the painting process;** correcting mistakes will **improve your work.**"

Amending sgraffito edges

While an area of thick paint is still wet, you can erase sgraffito marks by gently smoothing the furrows with your fingertip. You can then make a new mark (in this case, one at a better angle) with the tip of a palette knife.

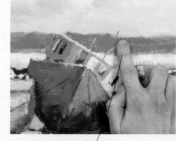
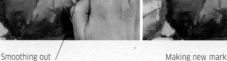

Smoothing out   Making new mark

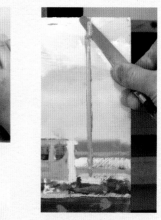

Scraping off

Remove a mast painted in thick impasto by scraping off the paint with a palette knife. The area is now smooth and you can easily repaint the sky.

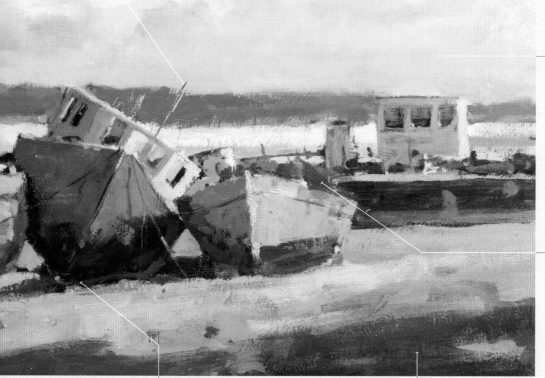

Sanding back

Sand back the dry red paint on the boat to reduce its saturation and intensity. This softens the brushstrokes in the area and prevents it from being too dominant.

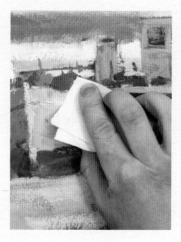

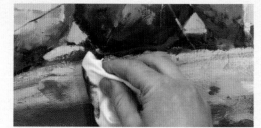

Wiping off

With a wet cloth, wipe off areas of the wet shadow layer where it has been painted too close to the boat. This will improve the composition.

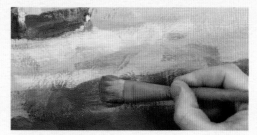

Applying a glaze

Using a medium flat synthetic brush, apply a glaze of sienna over the dry paint in the foreground. This gives the area warmth and helps bring it forward.

Finding your style

CREATING A SERIES AND EXPERIMENTING WITH TECHNIQUES

If you want to take your painting further, it is important to be able to express what you see in your own way. Finding a subject that inspires you is a great starting point—if you are excited about something, you are more likely to want to express yourself and share your feelings with others. Oil paint is an ideal medium for experimentation, as you can create a wide range of effects, and the long drying times involved allow you to develop your work over time.

CREATING A SERIES

Producing a series of similar paintings enables you to develop your own style across multiple pieces of work. Once you have decided on the color and tone, you are free to explore the subject.

You will need

Titanium white · Cadmium yellow · Alizarin crimson · French ultramarine · Cerulean blue · Burnt sienna

- No. 4 flat-bristle, no. 2 filbert-bristle, and no. 6 round synthetic brushes
- 10 x 12in (25 x 30cm) medium-grain canvas board

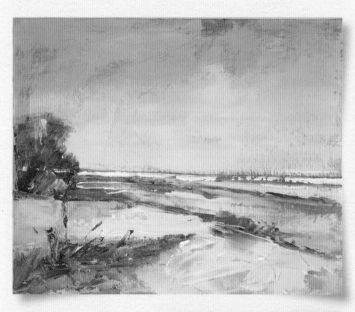

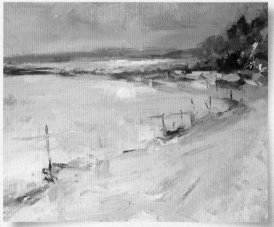

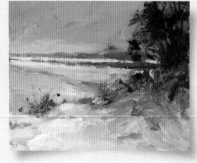

Painting 1
Inspired by a snowy landscape, the first painting in the series focuses on color and tone. Confirm the palette and choose a colored ground—in this case, sienna.

Painting 2
Now that you have set the colors, you can create another painting. This one, focusing on the trees, introduces a distant light that was missing from the first painting.

Painting 3
Heavier clouds and a higher horizon line give the third painting in the series a different dynamic, while staying true to the palette and tone used in the first two.

STYLISTIC APPROACHES

Approach the same subject in different ways, experimenting with brushwork, tone, glazes, and colored grounds. Create individual works until you find a way of painting that suits you, and which you want to develop.

You will need

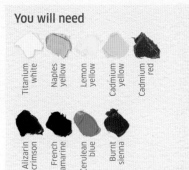

Titanium white · Naples yellow · Lemon yellow · Cadmium yellow · Cadmium red

Alizarin crimson · French ultramarine · Cerulean blue · Burnt sienna

- No. 4 flat-bristle, no. 6 filbert-bristle, and no. 6 round synthetic brushes
- 8 x 10in (20 x 25cm) medium-grain canvas board

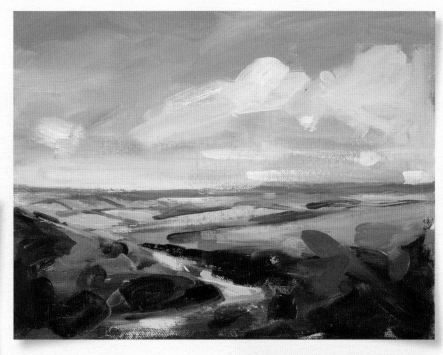

Mood and atmosphere

Here, mood and atmosphere have been created with blending and glazing. Brushstrokes were blended out and a glaze applied to create a painting with a great sense of light.

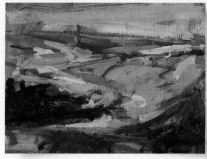

Light and warmth

This painting focuses on the light in the scene, making use of a colored ground and exaggerating the warm colors to create a painting with a strong identity.

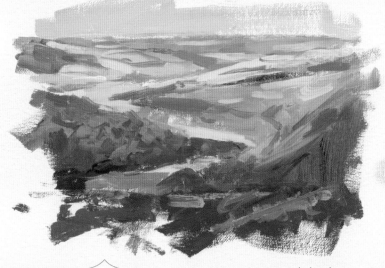

Opaque and softly blended

This painting was created using wet-in-wet techniques to softly blend each area of the scene in a single layer. This helps create an opaque effect.

Loose and simple

Here, a loose and simplified approach was taken. The emphasis is on brushwork and a simple yet bold composition.

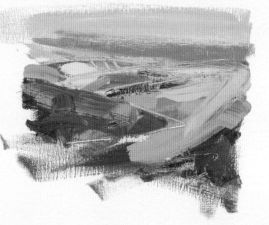

Varnishing

PROTECTING AND ENHANCING

Once you have finished your painting, you will need to leave it to dry thoroughly before applying a varnish. Varnishing has several advantages: It protects the surface of the paint from light damage and atmospheric conditions, deepens rich colors, and enhances the overall appearance. Varnishes are available in matte or gloss finishes, and you can create a satin finish by mixing the two.

■ When to start varnishing

Oil paint can take from two to twelve days to dry, but you should wait at least six months before varnishing—and even longer for very thick paint. Paint dries from the outside in, so although it may feel dry to the touch, it could still be wet underneath. Use mineral spirits to test that it is completely dry first.

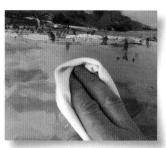

Applying mineral spirits
Dip a lint-free cloth in a little mineral spirits and gently rub it over the surface. If the painting is still wet, some color will come off on the cloth. If the cloth remains clean, the painting is fully dry and ready to varnish.

Testing painting

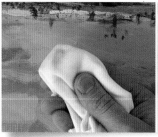

Painting still wet

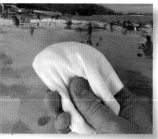

Painting fully dry

Applying varnish to this beach scene has enhanced the colors and made the surface finish more consistent. Always varnish in a well-ventilated, dust-free area, using a clean, dry brush.

You will need:

- Mineral spirits and lint-free cloth
- Gloss varnish
- Large, soft, synthetic brush

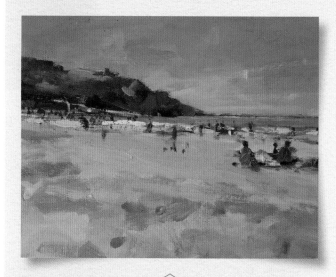

1 Finished dry painting
After several months, when the painting seems dry, test a small area with a lint-free cloth and a little mineral spirits (see left). If it is completely dry, rest the painting flat on a table.

2 Applying varnish
Dip a large brush into the varnish and drain the excess against the side of the vessel. Apply one thin coat in a long, continuous stroke across the canvas. Continue with the second stroke, overlapping slightly, and work down the painting. Once the varnish is dry, apply a second coat.

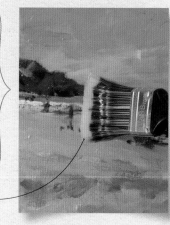

One continuous stroke

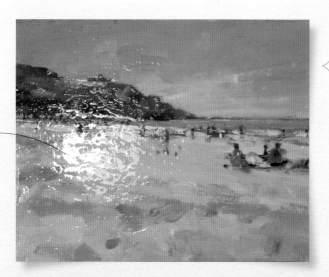

Protect the wet surface from dust

3 Wet varnish
The varnish will take about 24 hours to fully dry. Keep the painting free from dust while it dries. If possible, shield it with a piece of rigid board, such as foam board. Rest the board on household tile spacers so it doesn't come into contact with the varnished surface.

4 Dried varnished painting
After the varnish has dried, the surface should have a consistent finish. Darks will also appear richer.

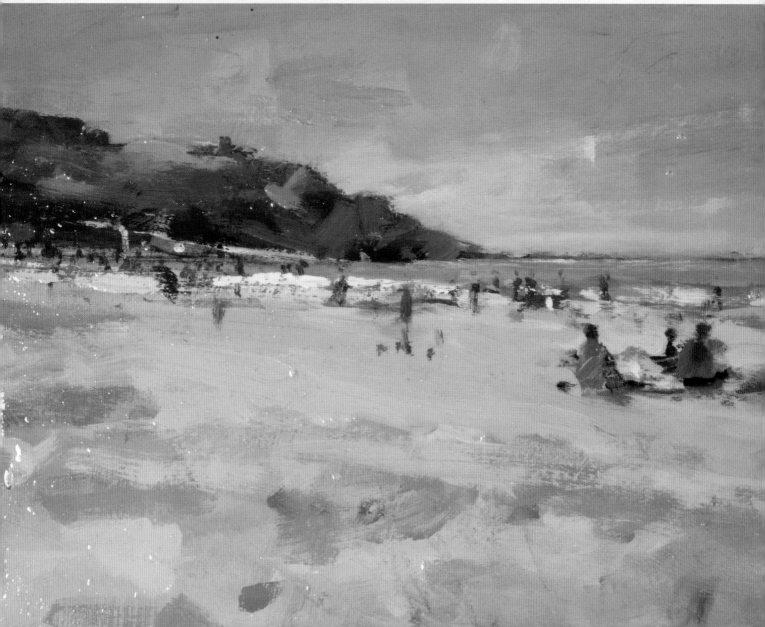

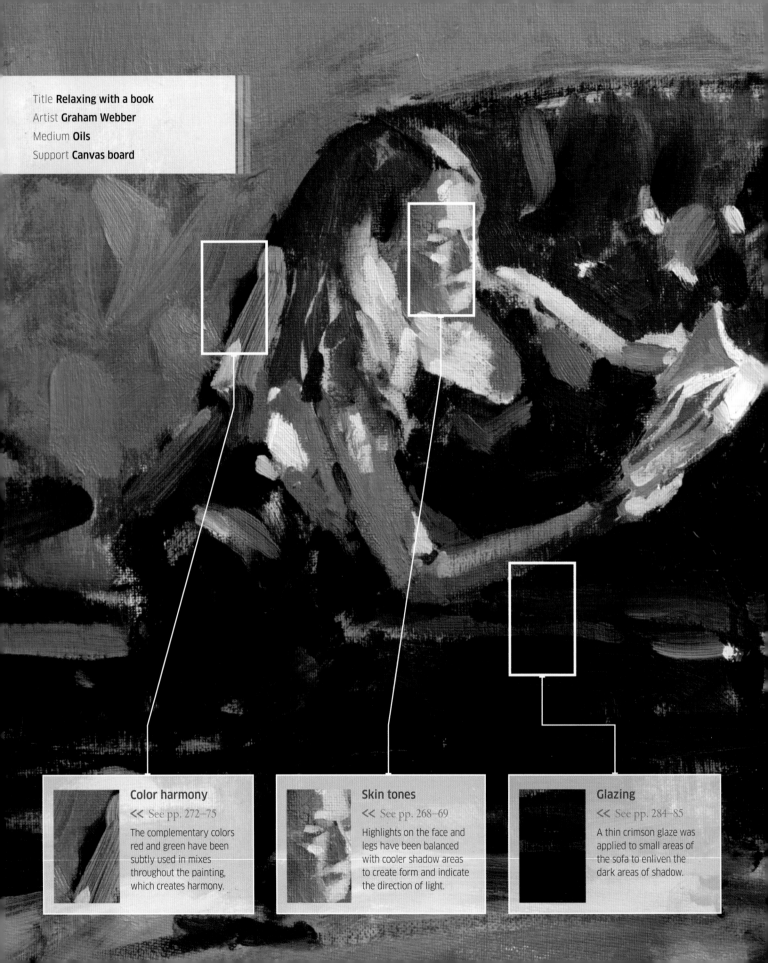

Title **Relaxing with a book**
Artist **Graham Webber**
Medium **Oils**
Support **Canvas board**

Color harmony

≪ See pp. 272–75

The complementary colors red and green have been subtly used in mixes throughout the painting, which creates harmony.

Skin tones

≪ See pp. 268–69

Highlights on the face and legs have been balanced with cooler shadow areas to create form and indicate the direction of light.

Glazing

≪ See pp. 284–85

A thin crimson glaze was applied to small areas of the sofa to enliven the dark areas of shadow.

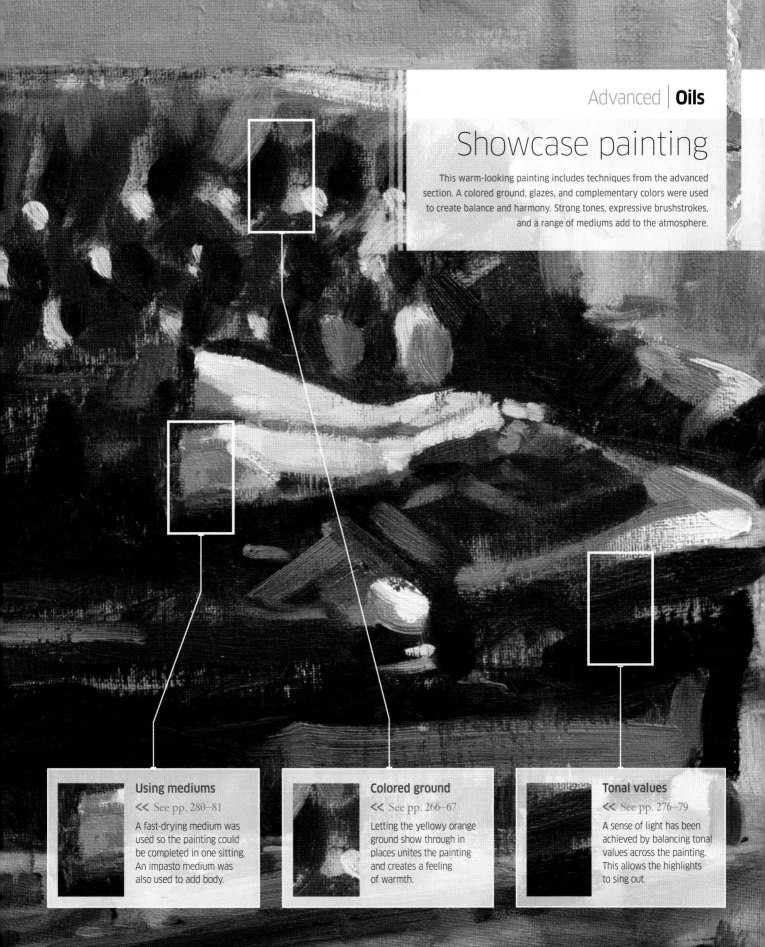

Showcase painting

This warm-looking painting includes techniques from the advanced section. A colored ground, glazes, and complementary colors were used to create balance and harmony. Strong tones, expressive brushstrokes, and a range of mediums add to the atmosphere.

Using mediums

≪ See pp. 280–81

A fast-drying medium was used so the painting could be completed in one sitting. An impasto medium was also used to add body.

Colored ground

≪ See pp. 266–67

Letting the yellowy orange ground show through in places unites the painting and creates a feeling of warmth.

Tonal values

≪ See pp. 276–79

A sense of light has been achieved by balancing tonal values across the painting. This allows the highlights to sing out.

Glossary

Aerial perspective
Where objects in the foreground appear warmer, more detailed, and more focused than those in the background, creating an illusion of depth. Also called atmospheric perspective.

Alla prima
Italian for "at first attempt," this term describes a painting finished in one sitting.

Analogous colors
Colors that are closely related and are next to each other on the **color wheel**—such as yellow and orange.

Blending
A way of letting two colors merge gradually with each other in a painting.

Blooms
Irregular shapes, sometimes called runbacks or cauliflowers, caused when watercolor paint in one color flows into a different one that hasn't fully dried.

Body color
Opaque paint, such as gouache, which will obscure underlying areas of paint.

Buckling
Wrinkling in paper supports, caused by applying washes onto an improperly stretched surface.

Cold-pressed paper
Paper with a slightly textured surface that has been pressed by cold rollers during its manufacture.

Color wheel
A visual device for showing the relationship between **primary**, **secondary**, **tertiary**, and **complementary colors**.

Complementary colors
Colors that are located directly opposite each other on the **color wheel**: yellow and purple, red and green, blue and orange. Complementary colors used next to each other make each other look brighter.

Composition
The way in which the various components of a painting, including the main area of focus, are arranged to create a harmonious whole.

Cool colors
Colors with a bluish tone. They tend to appear to recede in a picture, so can be used to create **aerial perspective**.

Crosshatching
Crisscrossing parallel lines to create tone. The closer the lines, the denser the tone.

Dry brushwork
Virtually dry paint dragged across the paper or canvas to produce textured marks.

Fat over lean
An important rule of oil painting whereby thick paint, which has more oil in it, should be painted over thinned paint, to avoid the surface layer cracking.

Flat wash
A wash produced in watercolor by painting overlapping bands of the same color to create a smooth layer of uniform color.

Focal points
Points of interest that the eye is drawn to immediately, whether because of the **perspective**, the color, or an intricate shape.

Form
The solid, three-dimensional shape of an object.

Glazing
The application of a transparent layer of paint over a layer of paint that has completely dried.

Gradated wash
A wash laid down in bands that are progressively diluted so that the wash is graded smoothly from dark to light.

Granulated wash
A wash in which watercolor pigments separate from the binder and water, creating a grainy texture when dry.

Highlight
The lightest tone in a composition, occurring on the most brightly lit parts of a subject.

Hot-pressed paper
Paper with a very smooth surface that has been pressed between hot rollers.

Hue
Another word for color, generally used to mean the strength or lightness of a particular color.

Impasto
A technique in which paint is applied thickly to create a textured surface.

Key
The overall tone of a painting: a predominantly light painting is said to have a high key.

Layering
Painting one color over another that has been allowed to dry.

Lifting out
Removing paint from the surface of the paper after it has dried, often to create soft highlights.

Linear perspective
A way of portraying three dimensions by showing how parallel lines appear to converge in the distance.

Masking fluid
A latex fluid that is painted onto paper and resists any watercolor paint put over it.

Medium
A substance used to modify the fluidity or thickness of oil or acrylic paints. Also describes the painting materials used, such as oil, acrylic, or watercolor.

Mid tones
All the variations of tone between the darkest and the lightest.

Modeling
Using light and dark tone to create a three-dimensional impression of an object.

Monochrome
Working in any single color.

Negative space
The gaps between objects. Negative space is as important as positive **form** in creating a satisfying composition.

Opaque color
Color that is impervious to light and which obscures anything underneath; the opposite of transparent.

Palette
Any suitable mixing surface for paint. The word is also used to describe colors used by a particular painter or on a particular occasion.

Pan
A small block of solid watercolor paint that can be slotted into a paint box.

Perspective
The method of creating a sense of depth on a flat surface through

the use of **modeling**, **linear**, and **aerial** **perspective**.

Pigment
Particles with inherent color that can be used in paints.

Plein air
Meaning "open air" in French. Describes a painting created outdoors.

Positive shape
The outline shape of an object.

Primary colors
There are three primary colors—yellow, red, and blue—that cannot be made by mixing any other colors. Any two primaries can be mixed together to make a **secondary color**.

Recession
Moving from the near distance to the far distance. Color recession is the use of **warm** and **cool** colors to create a sense of depth.

Resist
A method of preserving highlights by applying a material that repels paint, such as **masking fluid**.

Rigger
A long, fine brush used for detailed work.

Rough paper
Paper with a highly textured surface that has been left to dry naturally, without pressing.

Rule of thirds
An aid to composition that divides a picture into thirds horizontally and vertically to make a grid of nine squares. Points of interest are placed on the "thirds" lines, and focal points on the intersections, for visual effect.

Sable
Sable fur is used in the finest-quality paintbrushes. The long, dark brown hairs have a great capacity for holding paint and create a fine point.

Scraping back
Using a sharp blade to remove layers of dry watercolor paint in order to reveal the white paper below and create highlights.

Scratching in
Any action whereby marks are scratched into applied paint to give added texture.

Scumbling
Applying a thin, irregular layer of paint over a previously painted surface, allowing patches of the color underneath to show through.

Secondary colors
Colors made by mixing two **primary** colors together. They are: green (mixed from blue and yellow), orange (mixed from red and yellow), and purple (mixed from blue and red).

Sgraffito
A technique in which the surface layer is scratched away to reveal a contrasting color underneath.

Shade
A color darkened with black.

Shadow
The darkness cast when light is obscured, either on an object or by it.

Softening
In watercolor, blending the edges of a paint stroke with a brush loaded with clean water to prevent the paint from drying with a hard edge.

Spattering
Flicking paint from a loaded paintbrush or toothbrush to produce texture.

Stand oil
A medium added to oil paint, usually consisting of linseed oil, which thickens it and makes it easier to apply to the surface.

Stay-wet palette
A manufactured palette designed specifically for use with acrylic paints. It has a damp layer under the main mixing surface to keep paints moist while being used.

Stippling
The application of relatively neat dots to form a color field, or to create shading.

Stretching
A method of taping paper down, wetting it with a damp sponge, and letting it dry flat. Stretching paper helps to prevent it from **buckling**.

Structure gel
A painting medium added to thicken acrylic paint in order to build up heavy **impasto** textures.

Support
Any surface onto which paint is laid, such as paper or canvas.

Tertiary colors
The colors between the **primary** and **secondary** colors on a **color wheel**. They are created by mixing a greater proportion of the primary color into the secondary color.

Tint
A color lightened with white.

Turpentine (or turps)
A flammable solvent with a strong smell used as a painting medium to thin oil paints. Also used to clean brushes and hands.

Underpainting
An initial layer of (often monochrome) paint that serves as a base for composition.

Value
The relative lightness or darkness of a color. The value of a paint can be altered by diluting it with water (in watercolor), mixing it with white paint or with a darker pigment, or surrounding it with other colors.

Varnish
A protective resin that is applied to a painting which has thoroughly dried.

Warm colors
Colors with a reddish or orange tone. Warm colors appear to come forward in a picture and can be used to create **aerial perspective**.

Wax resist
A method of using candle wax to prevent the surface of the paper from accepting paint. Once applied, the wax cannot be removed.

Wet-in-wet
In watercolor, adding layers of paint onto wet paper or paint that is still wet.

Wet-on-dry
Adding layers of paint on top of color that has already dried. Painting in this way produces vivid colors with strong edges.

Index

About the artists

Hashim Akib worked as an illustrator for over 15 years before switching to fine arts full time. His paintings have earned him numerous awards, including the Society for All Artists Artist of the Year (2009). He is the author of *Vibrant Acrylics* (2012) and is a regular feature writer for *Artists & Illustrators* magazine. He is represented by multiple galleries in the UK and features in society shows at the Mall Galleries in London, including the Royal Institute of Oil Painters Annual exhibition.

Hashim developed the content for the "Acrylics" chapter, wrote the introductory topics, and contributed the three showcase paintings in that chapter. He also created artworks for, and wrote, the Acrylics techniques on pages 132-33, 138-39, 140-41, 142-43, 144-45, 152-55, 158-61, 162-63, 168-71, 172-15, 182-85, 186-89, and 196-99.

Colin Allbrook, RI RSMA HSEA, has worked as a painter and illustrator since leaving school. He has won several prizes, among them the Turner Watercolor Prize at the Royal Institute of Painters in Watercolors. He exhibits regularly at the Mall Galleries, London, and widely throughout the UK. His work is held in several private and public collections. Colin is an elected member of several national societies, including the Royal Institute of Painters in Watercolors and the Royal Society of Marine Artists.

Colin contributed the intermediate showcase painting in the "Watercolors" chapter, and created artworks for, and wrote, the Watercolors techniques on pages 50-51, 52-53, 56-57, 72-73, 76-77, 82-83, 86-87, 106-07, and 112-13.

Marie Antoniou is an artist and tutor who works primarily in acrylics, a medium that allows her to explore traditional subject matter with a contemporary approach. She is well known for her unique depiction of wildlife, which has earned her numerous awards and accolades. She is represented by several galleries and her paintings are part of many private collections. Her work features in *Complete Guide to Painting in Acrylics* (2014).

Marie created artworks for, and wrote, the Acrylics techniques on pages 128-31, 134-37, 146-47, 148-49, 156-57, 164-65, 166-67, 173, 190-91, and 200-03.

Grahame Booth is a watercolor painter and tutor. A former president of the Ulster Watercolour Society, he exhibits widely and has won numerous major exhibition awards. He holds workshops throughout Europe and provides tutorials online via his website and YouTube channel. He has produced two DVDs and has been a regular contributor to *Artists & Illustrators* magazine since 2013.

Grahame contributed the beginner showcase painting in the "Watercolors" chapter, and created artworks for, and wrote, the Watercolor techniques on pages 40-43, 54-55, 58-59, 66-67, 68-69, 70-71, 94-97, 102-03, 104-05, and 110-11.

John Chisnall is a watercolor artist who enjoys traveling and painting subjects around the world; his main interests are landscapes, architecture, and portraiture. He has exhibited at galleries in the UK and USA, including one-man shows, and his paintings are found in collections internationally. He teaches painting and drawing to groups and on a one-on-one basis.

John developed the content for the "Watercolors" chapter, wrote the introductory topics, and contributed the advanced showcase painting in that chapter. He also created artworks for, and wrote, the techniques on pages 44-45, 46-47, 48-49, 62-63, 64-65, 74-75, 78-81, 84-85, 90-93, 98-99, 100-01, 108-09, and 114-15.

Graham Webber, ROI IEA EAGMA, has won numerous awards for oil painting and exhibits with the Royal Society of Marine Artists and the Royal Society of British Artists in London, as well as galleries around the UK. He shares his passion for oil painting at workshops and demonstrations for art groups and societies.

Graham developed the content for, wrote, and created all the artworks in the "Oils" chapter. He also wrote "The basics" chapter, and contributed the artworks and text for the acrylics techniques on pages 176-77, 180-81, 192-93, and 194-95.

Acknowledgments

The publisher would like to thank Mr. and Mrs. K. Francis for their kind permission to reproduce the painting on pages 92-93, and to Mr. and Mrs. R. Lankester for their kind permission to reproduce the portrait on page 115 (top right).

We are also grateful to Louise Diggle and Debra Huse for their help and advice during the planning stages of this book; Gary Ombler for additional photography; Alice Horne at the DK Picture Library; Tom Morse for creative technical support; Corinne Masciocchi for proofreading; and Vanessa Bird for indexing.

Thanks to US Consultant **Lisa Egeli,** a Fellow of the American Society of Marine Artists, a Signature Member of Oil Painters of America and the Society of Animal Artists, a member of the Salmagundi Club in New York and the Washington Society of Landscape Painters, as well as a Signature Member of the Mid-Atlantic Plein Air Painters Association (lisaegeli.com).